Subject Guide to
U.S. Government Reference Sources

Subject Guide to
U.S. Government Reference
Sources

Judith Schiek Robinson
Associate Professor
School of Information and Library Studies
State University of New York at Buffalo

1985

Libraries Unlimited, Inc.   Littleton, Colorado

The first edition was published under the title *Subject Guide to Government Reference Books*, by Sally Wynkoop (1972).

LIBRARIES UNLIMITED, INC.
P.O. Box 263
Littleton, Colorado 80160-0263

Library of Congress Cataloging in Publication Data

Robinson, Judith Schiek, 1947-
    Subject guide to U.S. government reference sources.

    Rev. ed. of: Subject guide to government reference
books, by Sally Wynkoop, 1972.
    Includes index.
    1. Reference books--Government publications--
Bibliography. 2. United States--Government publications
--Bibliography. 3. Bibliography--Bibliography--
Government publications. I. Wynkoop, Sally. Subject
guide to government reference books. II. Title.
Z1223.Z7R63 1985   [J83]   015.73   85-10120
ISBN 0-87287-496-6

To

Pat Courtade,
whose bibliographic searching is reflected
on every page of this book,

and to

Bruce Robinson

Table of Contents

Part One
General Reference Sources

Part Two
Social Sciences

ECONOMICS AND BUSINESS (cont'd)

Part Three
Science and Technology

Part Four
Humanities

Introduction

Every effort has been extended to make this reference book as complete, accurate, and current as possible. In it, the reader will find descriptions of hundreds of reference materials in the social sciences, sciences, and humanities, which differ from other reference materials in only one key respect: they were published by the U.S. government.

Except for government authorship and publication, these materials are in familiar reference formats: almanacs, atlases, bibliographies, biographical directories, catalogs, data bases, dictionaries, directories, guides, handbooks, indexes and abstracts, and statistical works. These reference sources provide a wealth of ready-reference and in-depth information on a wide range of subjects, and, for the most part, are meant to be consulted for definite items of information rather than read from cover to cover.

This is the first revision of *Subject Guide to Government Reference Books*, which appeared in 1972 and was written by Sally Wynkoop. The new title, *Subject Guide to U.S. Government Reference Sources*, reflects a broadening of scope to include government-produced materials such as machine readable data bases. The new title and coverage reflect a broader definition of "government document," which goes beyond books and print formats to other government information sources. These nonprint resources represent a growing portion of government-produced information which cannot be ignored.

Like its predecessor, this edition offers selective rather than comprehensive coverage. It is intended to serve as a handy one-volume guide to significant government resources on specific subjects. Included are seminal works, unique historical works, comprehensive titles, and sources of first resort for reference searches.

Emphasis is on materials that are accessible through purchase, loan, depository library collections, requests for single free copies, or data base searches. For the most part, publications with fewer than ninety pages have been omitted.

Used as a buying guide for identifying key titles, this book can aid in the development of a well-balanced reference collection. It also serves as a quick, concise orientation guide to key government reference sources. It can be used as a compact companion to *Government Reference Books*, a comprehensive guide to government reference materials (excluding nonprint resources) published biennially by Libraries Unlimited.

Prior knowledge of government documents is not required to use this book. Although it will be especially useful to reference and documents librarians, many other information seekers, including students, researchers, teachers, government officials, and members of the general public, will find it helpful for identifying government information. The reference sources cited contain information that pertains to hundreds of subject areas and that is often original source material, current, and relevant to scholarship, decision making, and public interest questions.

Additions and Changes

OVERLAP WITH FIRST EDITION

Slightly over half of the entries in this edition are new. These include original items making their debut, as well as new titles that supersede earlier ones.

Because the first edition is out of print, some titles from it have been duplicated in this update. Other entries that overlap with the first edition represent new editions of the same titles. All bibliographic citations have been freshly verified, including those for material repeated from the first edition. (In the case of a few historical titles, the original *Monthly Catalog* citation was the most recent verification that could be located.)

SUBJECT ARRANGEMENT

The subject arrangement conforms to that of the first edition, with some additions and deletions. Entries continue to be arranged under four broad categories (General Reference Sources, Social Sciences, Science and Technology, and Humanities), with further subdivision of subject headings under each.

Three major headings have been added: Architecture, under Humanities; Energy, under Science and Technology; and Museums, under General Reference Sources. In addition, sixty-eight new subheadings appear throughout the book. One new subheading, Machine Readable Data, appears under a dozen topics and leads the reader to bibliographic and numeric data bases, computer programs, and related software.

BIBLIOGRAPHIC INFORMATION

Expanded bibliographic details have been included when available. These data include Government Printing Office (GPO) stock number, Dewey Decimal classification number, Library of Congress classification number,

OCLC number, and other "access" information (where to obtain single free copies, addresses, telephone numbers). As in the first edition, Library of Congress (LC) card numbers and Superintendent of Documents classification numbers (SuDocs numbers) are also provided.

ANNOTATIONS

Three-quarters of the annotations have been expanded or fully rewritten.

FORMATS

Both print and nonprint formats have been listed under the topics to which they relate. Nonprint sources added to this edition include data bases and information analysis centers. Print formats continue to predominate, however, including books, serials, and microforms.

SUBJECT BIBLIOGRAPHIES

A complete list of these helpful bibliographies of government publications is given under entry number 129. Individual subject bibliography (SB) numbers are also listed at the end of the subject sections to which they pertain.

How to Use This Book

Entries include the following items (when appropriate) in the order shown below.

1. Entry number.

2. Issuing agency (author, in the case of nongovernmental titles).

3. Title.

4. Personal author, editors, etc.

5. Volume statement.

6. Imprint (publisher and date of publication). Three abbreviations are used for publisher: GPO (Government Printing Office), NTIS (National Technical Information Service), and IA (issuing agency).

7. Frequency.

8. Edition.

9. Pagination.

10. Illustration.

11. Binding information.

12. Series.

13. LC card number.

14. LC classification number.

15. Dewey classification number.

16. OCLC number.

17. Reprint or other availability information.

18. Serial latest edition.

19. Government Printing Office (GPO) stock number (S/N). (Used when ordering the document from GPO. Stock numbers change with new editions. Check the *GPO Sales Publications Reference File* for current S/N.)

20. GPO sales price. (Prices are subject to change. To verify current price for GPO documents, consult the *GPO Sales Publications Reference File.*)

21. SuDocs number (Superintendent of Documents classification number) in boldface.

SAMPLE ENTRY
(showing most frequent bibliographic elements)

1.

2.

348. National Institute of Education.

6.

3.——**Resources in Education**. GPO, 1975-

7.——Monthly. LC 75-644211. Z5813.R4. ——14.

15.——016.370/78. OCLC 02241688.—— 16.

S/N 065-000-80003-9. $95/yr.

19. **ED1.310:vol./nos.**

20.

13.

21.

Access to Materials

In selecting new titles to add to this edition, emphasis has been placed on materials that are available through purchase, loan, depository library collections, requests for single free copies, or data base searches. Details for acquiring materials are given in the pages that follow.

PURCHASE

Government Printing Office

Items available for sale at the time of publication of this book will show publisher, price, and other ordering information. Orders for materials for sale from the Government Printing Office should be mailed to: Superintendent of Documents, U.S. Government Printing Office, Washington, D.C. 20402. GPO orders should include stock number (S/N) and prepayment. It is best to check for current price and stock number in the *GPO Sales Publications Reference File* (described in entry 118 in this book), since these may have changed after this book's publication. Checks or money orders should be payable to the Superintendent of Documents. Orders may also be charged to MasterCard, VISA, or a prepaid Superintendent of Documents deposit account.

National Technical Information Service

The National Technical Information Service (NTIS) also accepts MasterCard and VISA, as well as American Express, and offers a deposit account service. Otherwise, a prepayment by check or money order must be enclosed with the order. Price codes and informational brochures are available from the U.S. Department of Commerce, National Technical Information Service, 5285 Port Royal Road, Springfield, VA 22161; (703) 487-4600 or (202) 377-0365.

Issuing Agency

When the issuing agency is the source of sale, you must purchase the document directly from the agency. Each agency will have its own system of payment and billing, and in some cases the price should be verified before ordering. Occasionally, an issuing agency may send a single copy of a document free of charge to a requestor.

The *United States Government Manual* (entry 563 in this book) provides agency telephone numbers and addresses. The manual also lists regional agency offices, with local addresses and telephone numbers. The regional offices, which some government agencies maintain in larger cities, can often supply copies of agency publications, sometimes free of charge for single copies.

LIBRARY COLLECTIONS

Depository Materials

Federal depository libraries have been established to make government publications accessible to the public without charge; they are located in university, public, state, and other types of libraries. These depository libraries are charged with service not only to individuals in their specific educational or local communities, but also to any member of the public with a need for government documents.

There are approximately 1,400 federal depository libraries dispersed geographically throughout the United States. These depository libraries do not all have the same collection of documents, since each selects publications based on the needs of its clientele. Interlibrary loan from other depositories is available for documents that your depository may not have in its own collection. To locate the depository library closest to you, send for the free list of depositories available from the Superintendent of Documents (entry 21 in this book), check the October issue of the *Monthly Catalog* for a current list, or call the reference desk at your local library and ask them about local depository locations.

Superintendent of Documents
Classification Numbers

Many depository libraries use the Superintendent of Documents classification number (SuDocs number) as a system for shelving federal documents. Do not assume that the library does not own a document if it is not on the shelves under the SuDocs number, however. It may be out on loan or shelved with the general book collection, with reference materials, in microform, or in another special location. It is always best to ask the documents librarian for assistance when you cannot locate a document.

Nondepository Materials

Since depository library collections are not limited to depository titles, a depository library may also own nondepository items listed in this book, including those that are available from the issuing agency or from NTIS. Conferring with a reference or documents librarian will help you determine whether these titles are in the collection.

DATA BASE SEARCHES

Federal production of machine readable data bases has burgeoned in the past decade. These data bases often contain the most up-to-date data available, sometimes with no companion resources available in print format. The Bureau of the Census, for example, has announced that for the 1980 census more data than ever before will be available to the public in machine readable form only.

Data bases are listed in italics in this book within the subject categories to which they pertain, with information on how to gain access to them. Access may be through the agency that produces the data base, through other government agencies that lease the data base, or through commercial vendors. Commercial data base vendors referred to in the text may be accessed at many local libraries, or contacted directly at the following addresses:

ORBIT Information Retrieval System (SDS)
2500 Colorado Avenue
Santa Monica, CA 90406

Bibliographic Retrieval Services, Inc. (BRS)
1200 Route 7
Latham, NY 12110

DIALOG Information Retrieval Services
3460 Hillview Avenue
Palo Alto, CA 94304

INFORMATION ANALYSIS CENTERS

Also listed in this book are information analysis centers, such as the National Center for Health Statistics. These agencies provide a variety of products and services, which may include searches of in-house data files, reference services, and subject-oriented publications.

Acknowledgment

The author welcomes this opportunity to thank the students who assisted in bibliographic searching in support of this book: Mary Bourg, Donna Chan, Nancy Ciliberti, Patricia Courtade, Wendy Newell, Joseph Rosenfeld, and Scott Wicks. I also wish to thank Edward Herman, of the Documents Department, Lockwood Library, State University of New York at Buffalo, and Michael Lavin, of the Buffalo and Erie County Public Library, for their encouragement and assistance. And I express my gratitude to Rita Maedl and Sharon Adamczak, whose support in our department's main office was invaluable.

Part One

General Reference Sources

Bibliographic Aids

GENERAL

1. American Library Association. Government Documents Round Table. **The Complete Guide to Citing Government Documents: A Manual for Writers and Librarians**. By Diane L. Garner and Diane H. Smith. Bethesda, MD: Congressional Information Service, 1984. 142 pp. ISBN 0-88692-023-X. $12.95 (paper).
This style manual describes methods of citing major types of government documents. Chapters on citing federal, state, local, regional, and international documents are included, along with a detailed index and a glossary.

2. Andriot, John L. **Guide to U.S. Government Publications**. McLean, VA: Documents Index, Inc. 2 vols. Vol. 1, 1984. Vol. 2, 1980.
This source provides an annotated guide to important series and periodicals currently issued by federal agencies and to important reference publications issued within series. It also provides a complete listing of Superintendent of Documents (SuDocs) classification numbers issued since the turn of the century.

Volume 1 lists publication series of agencies in existence on January 1, 1980, plus publication series of agencies abolished between 1975 and 1979 and of agencies created since 1980. Arrangement is by SuDocs classification numbers. Volume 2 lists publication series of agencies abolished before 1975, also in SuDocs classification number order. The next edition of volume 2, now out of print in hardcover, is expected in 1985 and would include SuDocs classes for agencies abolished between 1975 and 1980 (transferred from volume 1). This system keeps one main volume for current agencies and a small volume for discontinued agencies. A title and agency index is included.

3. Body, Alexander C. **Annotated Bibliography of Bibliographies of Government Publications and Supplementary Guides to the Superintendent of Documents Classification System**. Kalamazoo, MI: The Author, 1967. 181 pp.

    _____. **Supplement 1**. 1968.

    _____. **Supplement 2**. 1970.

    _____. **Supplement 3**. 1972.

    _____. **Supplement 4**. 1974.

_____. **Supplement 5**. 1977. Comp. by Gabor Kovacs.

_____. **Supplement 6**. 1980. Comp. by Gabor Kovacs.

_____. **Supplement 7**. 1982. Comp. by Gabor Kovacs.

The basic volume lists bibliographies published by the Government Printing Office (GPO) from 1958 through 1969. Entries are arranged by SuDocs classification numbers and contain detailed annotations. They are indexed by government authors, titles, and subjects. Supplements are issued every two to three years to include new and revised bibliographies. Supplements 5 through 7 were compiled and published by Gabor Kovacs, Greeley, Colorado.

4. Boyd, Anne M. **United States Government Publications**. 3d ed. Rev. by Rae E. Ripps. New York: H. W. Wilson, 1949 (repr. 1952). 627 pp. ISBN 0-8242-0051-9.

This guide provides information on the history, organization, and functions of government agencies as they pertain to printing, publishing, and distribution of documents. It is still useful for historical purposes. Indexing is by subject and title.

5. Congressional Information Service. **For the People**. 16-mm film or ¾-in. videocassette. Color, 15 min.

This film describes the variety and scope of government documents and shows how documents are used in their work by an architect, a law student, the director of a ballet company, and a representative of a private sector interest group. It is an excellent film for introducing government documents and their uses. The film is available for sale and preview from: Director of Education Services, Congressional Information Service, Inc., 4520 East-West Highway, Suite 800-DM, Bethesda, MD 20814; (301) 654-1550.

6. **Government Reference Books: A Biennial Guide to U.S. Government Publications**. Littleton, CO: Libraries Unlimited, 1970- . Biennial. LC 76-146307. 1982/83 ed. ISBN 0-87287-467-2. $47.50.

This is a subject guide to government-issued atlases, bibliographies, compendia, dictionaries, directories, guides, handbooks, indexes, and manuals, with complete bibliographic citations and long annotations. It includes GPO and non-GPO materials. The arrangement is by subject categories, with indexes for authors, titles, and subjects.

7. **Index to U.S. Government Periodicals**. Chicago: Infordata International, 1974- . Quarterly, with annual cumulation.

The most comprehensive commercially published index to a wide range of government periodicals, this quarterly publication indexes over 160 government periodicals that include material of lasting research and reference value.

8. Leidy, W. Philip. **A Popular Guide to Government Publications**. New York: Columbia University Press, 1976. 4th ed. 440 pp. LC 76-17803. ISBN 0-231-04019-9. $32.50.

Titles published between 1967 and 1975 are listed with annotations. The arrangement is by broad subjects, with title and agency indexes.

9. Mechanic, Sylvia. **Annotated List of Selected United States Government Publications Available to Depository Libraries**. Comp. for the New York State Library. New York: H. W. Wilson, 1971. 424 pp. LC 78-99430. ISBN 0-8242-0405-0. $19.

This annotated bibliography of nearly five hundred series is arranged by item number (that is, the number given to each series or group of government publications available to depository libraries). Appended information includes "Bibliographies and Lists of

United States Government Publications"; an explanation of the Superintendent of Documents classification system; and lists of SuDocs classes, of depository libraries, and of catalogs, indexes, and guides to government publications. The index is by series or titles.

10. Morehead, Joe. **Introduction to United States Public Documents**. Littleton, CO: Libraries Unlimited, 1983. 3d ed. 309 pp. LC 82-22866. ISBN 0-87287-359-5. $28.50. ISBN 0-87287-362-5 (paper). $19.50.

This text offers an excellent overview of government publishing and description of key titles. It explains the activities of the Government Printing Office, the Superintendent of Documents, and depository libraries. It also describes sources of information about technical reports; congressional, executive, and judicial materials; data bases; statistical information; audiovisual materials; and more. An excellent introduction to federal documents, it is useful for the person who knows nothing about documents as well as the experienced documents user.

11. Nakata, Yuri. **From Press to People: Collecting and Using U.S. Government Publications**. Chicago: American Library Association, 1979. 212 pp. LC 78-26306. ISBN 0-8389-0264-2. $15.

This is another source that provides information on specific titles, as well as an overview of federal government documents. A very readable text, it is designed as a handbook for the beginning documents librarian, but is also helpful for others who need information about the *Monthly Catalog of U.S. Government Publications*, technical reports, data bases, and reference sources for government documents.

12. Newsome, Walter L. **New Guide to Popular Government Publications: For Libraries and Home Reference**. Littleton, CO: Libraries Unlimited, 1978. 370 pp. LC 78-12412. ISBN 0-87287-174-6. $27.50.

This expanded and more recent version of Linda Pohle's *A Guide to Popular Government Publications* (1972) provides annotations and bibliographic information for over twenty-five hundred popular government titles. Publications considered to be interesting and/or useful are included, arranged by subject categories.

13. Schmeckebier, Laurence F. and Roy B. Eastin. **Government Publications and Their Use**. Washington, DC: Brookings Institution, 1969. 2d rev. ed. 502 pp. LC 69-19694. ISBN 0-8157-7736-1.

"The purpose of this volume is to describe the basic guides to government publications, to indicate the uses and limitations of available indexes, catalogs and bibliographies, to explain the system of numbering and methods of titling, to call attention to certain outstanding compilations or series of publications, and to indicate how the publications may be obtained. It is thus a guide to the acquisition and use of government publications and not — even though it cites many publications by title — a catalog, a bibliography, or a checklist" (Foreword). This book, a standard source since the first edition in 1936, is indispensable for those seeking to understand the form and style of U.S. government publishing practices. It is especially helpful for tracing historical materials.

14. Van Zant, Nancy Patton. **Selected U.S. Government Series: A Guide for Public and Academic Libraries**. Chicago: American Library Association, 1978. 172 pp. LC 77-10337. ISBN 0-8389-0252-9. $15.

Designed as a selection aid for public and academic libraries, this source lists and describes federal agency series under broad subject categories.

SPECIALIZED

15. Aluri, Rao and Judith Schiek Robinson. **A Guide to U.S. Government Scientific and Technical Resources**. Littleton, CO: Libraries Unlimited, 1983. 259 pp. LC 83-14991. ISBN 0-87287-377-3. $23.50.

This book provides an overview of government resources for science and technology, along with descriptions of specific titles for accessing technical reports, patents, data bases, audiovisual materials, reference sources, periodicals, and other materials.

16. Lu, Joseph K. **U.S. Government Publications Relating to the Social Sciences: A Selected Annotated Guide**. Beverly Hills, CA: Sage Publications, 1975. 288 pp. LC 74-77288. ISBN 0-8039-0402-9. $29.95.

This is an annotated guide to U.S. government publications in the social sciences. Listings of documents published through mid-1973 are arranged under social science subject areas. Bibliographic data and SuDocs classification numbers are given. This guide also provides definitions of terminology and describes finding aids.

17. O'Hara, Frederic J. **A Guide to Publications of the Executive Branch**. Englewood Cliffs, NJ: Prentice-Hall, 1979. 287 pp. LC 78-66368. ISBN 0-87650-072-6. $37.50. ISBN 0-87650-088-2 (paper). $19.95.

This guide to valuable materials available from the executive branch of the federal government provides descriptions of executive agency missions and a directory of addresses. Titles are annotated, and nonprint materials are included. No attempt is made to cover popular items.

18. Scull, Roberta A. **A Bibliography of United States Government Bibliographies, 1968-1973**. Ann Arbor, MI: Pierian Press, 1975. LC 75-4281. ISBN 0-87650-055-6. $25.

_____. **Bibliography of United States Government Bibliographies, 1974-1976**. Ann Arbor, MI: Pierian Press, 1979. LC 75-4281. ISBN 0-87650-111-0. $29.50.

The basic volume lists about 1,250 bibliographies on a wide range of topics issued by federal government agencies between 1968 and 1973. It provides bibliographic information, including SuDocs classification numbers and annotations. Arrangement is by subject areas. The supplement lists bibliographies published from 1974 through 1976.

19. Yannarella, Philip A. and Rao Aluri. **U.S. Government Scientific and Technical Periodicals**. Metuchen, NJ: Scarecrow Press, 1976. 263 pp. LC 75-38740. ISBN 0-8108-0888-9. $13.

Journals, review serials, indexes, abstracts, and newsletters in the sciences are listed and described. Title/subject and agency indexes are provided.

DIRECTORIES

20. American Library Association. Government Documents Round Table. **Directory of Government Documents Collections and Librarians**. Ed. by Barbara Kile and Audrey Taylor. Bethesda, MD: Congressional Information Service, 1984. 4th ed. 690 pp. LC 78-5459. ISBN 0-88692-011-6. $40.

This state and city listing of documents libraries gives addresses, telephone numbers, and information about collections, depository status, subject specialties, and names of staff members. Other sections list names and locations of library school faculty teaching documents, state document authorities, names to know, subject terms, agency names, and acronyms. This source includes indexes of libraries, documents collections, special collections, and library staff members.

21. Congress. Joint Committee on Printing. **Government Depository Libraries: The Present Law Governing Designated Depository Libraries**. GPO, 1962-Annual. **Y4.P93/1:D44/yr.**
This source serves as a directory of federal depository libraries and provides an overview of the depository library system. Depository libraries, with addresses and telephone numbers, are listed by states and cities and by states and congressional districts. A description of depository regulations and the text of depository laws are given. For a free copy, write to the Government Printing Office, Washington, DC 20402.

22. Gray, Constance Staten. **U.S. Government Directories, 1970-1981: A Selected Annotated Bibliography**. Littleton, CO: Libraries Unlimited, 1984. 260 pp. ISBN 0-87287-414-1. $35.
This selected annotated bibliography lists directories that have been published by U.S. government agencies between 1970 and 1981, all of which have been distributed to depository libraries. Its 575 titles are grouped under 12 categories. Within each category, entries are arranged by SuDocs classification number. Entries include title, subtitle, edition, personal author, issuing agency, date of publication, pagination, series, and format. In case of serials, date of latest depository edition is shown, along with inclusive years of publication and frequency. Appendices include a description of the *GPO Sales Publications Reference File* (PRF) and lists of regional depository libraries and GPO bookstores.

23. Larson, Donna Rae. **Guide to U.S. Government Directories, 1970-1980**. Phoenix, AZ: Oryx Press, 1981. 160 pp. LC 81-9642. ISBN 0-912700-63-7. $47.50.
This is a comprehensive list of government-issued directories. Information is given concerning availability, coverage, arrangement, issuing agency, SuDocs classification number, and frequency. For directories prior to 1970, consult *Directories of Government Agencies* by Sally Wynkoop and David Parish (Libraries Unlimited, 1969).

24. National Audiovisual Center. **Directory of U.S. Government Audiovisual Personnel**. IA, 1980. 7th ed. LC 72-185779. JK849.A24. 353.008/1. OCLC 2239306. **GS4.24:980**.
This source lists federal agencies and personnel involved in radio, television, motion pictures, photography, and sound recording along with addresses and telephone numbers.

General Works

LIBRARY OF CONGRESS
CATALOGS AND UNION LISTS

Copyright Entries

25. Copyright Office. **Catalog of Copyright Entries, 1891-1946**. GPO, 1891-1947. **LC3.6/1-4:vol./nos.**
Part 1 covered *Books* (which included pamphlets, maps, dramatic compositions, and motion pictures); Part 2, *Periodicals and Newspapers*; Part 3, *Musical Compositions*; and Part 4, *Works of Art*. The parts were issued separately and at different intervals of time.

26. Copyright Office. **Catalog of Copyright Entries. 3rd Series**. GPO, 1947-1977. Semiannual. LC 6-35347. Z1219.U58C. **LC3.6/5:vol./nos.**
> Part 1. **Books and Pamphlets, Including Serials and Contributions to Periodicals.**
>
> Part 2. **Periodicals.**
>
> Parts 3-4. **Dramas and Works Prepared for Oral Delivery.**
>
> Part 5. **Music.**
>
> Part 6. **Maps and Atlases.**
>
> Parts 7-11A. **Works of Art, Reproductions of Works of Art, Scientific and Technical Drawings, Photographic Works, Prints, and Pictorial Illustrations.**
>
> Part 11B. **Commercial Prints and Labels.**
>
> Parts 12-13. **Motion Pictures and Filmstrips.**
>
> Part 14. **Sound Recordings.**

27. Copyright Office. **Catalog of Copyright Entries. 4th Series**. GPO, 1978- . LC 79-640899. 019/.1. OCLC 05434808. **LC3.6/6:vol./nos.**
> Part 1. **Nondramatic Literary Works**. Quarterly. S/N 030-002-80019-5 (microfiche). $30/yr.

Part 2. **Serials and Periodicals**. Semiannual. S/N 030-002-80020-9 (microfiche). $6.50/yr.

Part 3. **Performing Arts**. Quarterly. S/N 030-002-80021-7 (microfiche). $27/yr.

Part 4. **Motion Pictures**. Semiannual. S/N 030-002-80022-5 (microfiche). $7/yr.

Part 5. **Visual Arts**. Semiannual. S/N 030-002-80023-3 (microfiche). $10/yr.

Part 6. **Maps**. Semiannual. S/N 030-002-80024-1 (microfiche). $4.75/yr.

Part 7. **Sound Recordings**. Semiannual. S/N 030-002-80025-0 (microfiche). $14/yr.

Part 8. **Renewals**. Semiannual. S/N 030-002-80026-8 (microfiche). $8.50/yr.

The fourth series, which covers the period since January 1978, is published in eight parts and is sold by the GPO in microfiche only.

28. Copyright Office. **Concordance: Title 17, Copyright Law Keyword-in-Context Index**. GPO, 1979. 344 pp. LC 79-65087. S/N 030-002-00144-6. $9. **LC3.2:C74**.

29. Copyright Office. **Decisions of the United States Courts Involving Copyright and Literary Property, 1789-1909, with an Analytical Index**. 4 vols. GPO, 1980. LC 78-57569. KF2990.D37 1980. S/N 030-002-00142-0. $55. **LC3.3/3:13-16**.
This is an index to Copyright Office *Bulletins* 13-16 for copyright decisions.

30. Copyright Office. **Decisions of the United States Courts Involving Copyright, Cumulative Index, 1909-1970**. GPO, 1973. 540 pp. LC 15-26124. S/N 030-002-00137-3. $14. **LC3.3:17-37/ind**.
This is an index to Copyright Office *Bulletins* 17-37 for copyright decisions.

31. Copyright Office. **General Guide to the Copyright Act of 1976**. IA, 1977. 144 pp. LC 77-604835. KF2994.A334. **LC3.7/2:C79**.
The Copyright Act of 1976 was the first extensive revision of copyright law since 1909. This source is a general guide to the new law, and not an official summary of the law. It provides a general overview of the new law and is based on a Copyright Office "minicourse."

See also SB 126.

Library of Congress Catalogs

32. Library of Congress. **A Catalog of Books Represented by Library of Congress Printed Cards [Issued from August 1898 through July 1942]**. 167 vols. LC 43-3338. Z881.A1C3. (Repr.: Rowman & Littlefield, $1,950.)

＿＿＿. **Supplement: Cards Issued August 1, 1942-December 31, 1947**. 42 vols. LC 43-3338. Z881.A1C312. (Repr.: Rowman & Littlefield, $495.)

33. Library of Congress. **The Library of Congress Author Catalog: A Cumulative List of Works Represented by Library of Congress Cards, 1948-52**. 24 vols. LC 47-32682. Z881.U49A2. (Repr.: Rowman & Littlefield, $350.)

34. Library of Congress. **National Union Catalog, Pre-1956 Imprints**. 755 vols., including supplement. Being published by Mansell. Vols. 1-705 in print. Prices available from Mansell. LC 67-30001. Z881.A1U518.

This set, comprising over seven hundred volumes, is a cumulative National Union Catalog (NUC) covering up to 1956. These volumes list the NUC holdings before 1956 and replace the several separate sets published earlier (entries 32 and 33).

35. Library of Congress. Processing Department. **The National Union Catalog: A Cumulative Author List Representing Library of Congress Printed Cards and Titles Reported by Other American Libraries**. IA, 1956-82. Nine monthly issues, three quarterly cumulations, annual cumulations for four years, and a quinquennial cumulation in the fifth year. LC 56-060041. Z881.A1U372. **LC30.8:date**.

Cumulation for 1953-57. 28 vols. (Repr.: Rowman & Littlefield, $395.)

Cumulation for 1958-62. 54 vols. (Repr.: Rowman & Littlefield, $40/vol.)

Cumulation for 1942-62. 152 vols. (Repr.: Gale, $3,250.)

Cumulation for 1963-67. 72 vols. Out of print.

Cumulation for 1956-67. 125 vols. (Repr.: Rowman & Littlefield, $2,750.)

Cumulation for 1968-72. 128 vols. (Repr.: J. W. Edwards, $1,950.)

Quinquennial cumulations through 1972 include *Register of Additional Locations*, *Motion Pictures and Filmstrips*, and *Music and Phono-Records*.

Cumulation for 1973-77. 150 vols. (Repr.: Rowman & Littlefield, $1,687 plus $155 transportation.)

Includes *Films and Other Materials for Projection* and *Music, Books on Music, and Sound Recordings*.

Cumulation for 1978. 16 vols. (LC, $1,100.)

Cumulation for 1979. 16 vols. (LC, $1,150.)

Cumulation for 1980. 18 vols. (LC, $1,275.)

Cumulation for 1981. 18 vols. (LC, $1,375.)

Cumulation for 1982. 18 vols. (LC, $1,450.)

For those volumes available from the LC, write to the Cataloging Distribution Service, Library of Congress, Washington, DC 20541.

The cumulative list of books, pamphlets, periodicals, and other serials cataloged by the Library of Congress or one of over eleven hundred libraries in the United States and Canada is arranged by authors; entries are photographic reproductions of printed catalog cards.

Since January 1983, the *National Union Catalog* has been available only on 48x computer-output microfiche (COM). The 1982 annual cumulation was the last to be published in book format. In addition to cost and space economies, the new register-index offers multiple access points to records. The *National Union Catalog* now appears in four segments, each with its own author, title, subject, and series indexes. These are: *NUC Books* (entry 43), *NUC U.S. Books* (entry 44), *NUC Audiovisual Materials* (entry 45), and *NUC Cartographic Materials* (entry 46). These four microfiche publications supersede the following: *Subject Catalog* (entry 42), *Chinese Cooperative Catalog* (entry 39), *Audiovisual Materials* (entry 38), and *Monographic Series* (entry 40). The *NUC Register of Additional Locations* (cumulative microform edition) continues to supplement the NUC. Each is available for purchase from the Cataloging Distribution Service, Library of Congress, Washington, DC 20541.

36. Library of Congress. **Library of Congress Catalog: Motion Pictures and Film-strips; A Cumulative List of Works Represented by Library of Congress Printed Cards**. IA, 1953-72. LC 53-60011. Z881.U49A25.

> Cumulation for 1953-57. (Repr.: Rowman & Littlefield, $40.)
>
> Cumulation for 1958-62. 2 vols. (Repr.: Rowman & Littlefield, $80.)
>
> Cumulation for 1963-67. 2 vols. (Repr.: J. W. Edwards, $85.)
>
> Cumulation for 1968-72. 4 vols. (Repr.: J. W. Edwards, $140.)

These are separate volumes in the NUC cumulations (entry 35). They are continued by *Films and Other Materials for Projection* (entry 37).

37. Library of Congress. **Films and Other Materials for Projection**. IA, 1973-77. Quarterly. LC 73-64550. Z881.U49A25. 011. OCLC 1788119. **LC30.8/4:date**.

> Cumulation for 1973-77. 7 vols. (Repr.: Rowman & Littlefield, $78.73.)

These are separate volumes in the NUC cumulations (entry 35). They continue *Library of Congress Catalog: Motion Pictures and Filmstrips* (entry 36) and are continued by *Audiovisual Materials* (entry 38).

38. Library of Congress. Cataloging Publication Division. **Audiovisual Materials**. IA, 1979-82. Three quarterly issues with annual and quinquennial cumulations. LC 80-648903. Z881.U49A25. 011/.37. OCLC 04782873. **LC30.8/4:date**.

> Cumulation for 1979. 574 pp. (LC, $70.)
>
> Cumulation for 1980. 1,091 pp. (LC, $75.)

This catalog continues *Films and Other Materials for Projection* (entry 37). It lists the audiovisual holdings of the Library of Congress. Included are motion pictures, film-strips, transparency sets, slide sets, video recordings, and kits. Complete bibliographic data and a summary are provided for each work. Items can be searched by titles. This is no longer available in book form after the 1978-82 quinquennial cumulation. It is continued by *NUC Audiovisual Materials* (entry 45).

39. Library of Congress. Cataloging Publication Division. **Chinese Cooperative Catalog**. IA, 1975-77. Monthly. LC 74-649005. Z881.U49C49. **LC30.18:date**.

> Cumulation for 1975. 3 vols. (LC, $170.)
>
> Cumulation for 1976. 3 vols. (LC, $350.)
>
> Cumulation for 1977. 3 vols. (LC, $350.)

> _____. **Chinese Cooperative Catalog [microfiche]**. IA, 1978-82. Bimonthly. LC 79-641787. Z881.U49. OCLC 04169754. **LC30.18:date**.

> Cumulation for 1978. Out of print.
>
> Cumulation for 1979. (LC, $255.)
>
> Cumulation for 1980. (LC, $295.)
>
> Cumulation for 1981. (LC, $300.)
>
> Cumulation for 1982. (LC, $310.)

Text is in Chinese and English. This is continued in *NUC Books* (entry 43).

40. Library of Congress. Cataloging Publication Division. **Monographic Series**. IA, 1974-82. Three quarterly issues plus an annual cumulation. LC 74-652501. Z881.U49U54a. OCLC 01192456. **LC30.8/9:date**.

> Cumulation for 1974. 4 vols. (LC, $100.)
>
> Cumulation for 1975. 5 vols. (LC, $120.)

Cumulation for 1976. 4 vols. (LC, $150.)

Cumulation for 1977. 4 vols. (LC, $160.)

Cumulation for 1978. 4 vols. (LC, $190.)

Cumulation for 1979. 4 vols. (LC, $200.)

Cumulation for 1980. 4 vols. (LC, $215.)

Cumulation for 1981. 4 vols. (LC, $230.)

Cumulation for 1982. 4 vols. (LC, $250.)

This is a compilation of monograph titles published as parts of series and received by the Library of Congress. The titles are listed under series titles. Personal author series are omitted and are accessible through the National Union Catalog. This is continued by *NUC Books* (entry 43).

43. Library of Congress. Processing Department. **Library of Congress Catalog— Books: Subjects, a Cumulative List of Works Represented by Library of Congress Printed Cards**. IA, 1950-74. Quarterly, with annual and quinquennial cumulations. LC 50-60682. Z881.A1U375. **LC30.8/3:date**.

Cumulation for 1950-54. 20 vols. Out of print.

Cumulation for 1955-59. 22 vols. (Repr.: Rowman & Littlefield, $350.)

Cumulation for 1960-64. 25 vols. Out of print.

Cumulation for 1965-69. 42 vols. (Repr.: J. W. Edwards, $600.)

Cumulation for 1970-74. 100 vols. (Repr.: Rowman & Littlefield, $1,740.)

Continued by *Subject Catalog* (entry 42).

42. Library of Congress. Cataloging Publications Division. **Subject Catalog**. IA, 1975-82. Three quarterly issues, with annual and quinquennial cumulations. LC 75-643000. Z881.A1U375. 017/.5/09753. OCLC 02254684. **LC30.8/3:date**.

Cumulation for 1975. 18 vols. (LC, $800.)

Cumulation for 1976. 17 vols. (LC, $850.)

Cumulation for 1977. 15 vols. (LC, $850.)

Cumulation for 1978. 19 vols. (LC, $890.)

Cumulation for 1979. 21 vols. (LC, $935.)

Cumulation for 1980. (LC, $935.)

Cumulation for 1981. (LC, $1,000.)

Cumulation for 1982. (LC, $1,090.)

The catalog provides a listing by subject of the books, pamphlets, serials, maps, and atlases received by the Library of Congress. Complete bibliographic data are provided for each title, in the language of publication. Belles lettres and imprints are found in the annual and quinquennial cumulations. This is continued by *NUC Books* (entry 43).

43. Library of Congress. **National Union Catalog: Books**. Microfiche edition. IA, 1983- . Monthly. LC 82-6980. $350/yr.

This catalog replaces *The National Union Catalog: A Cumulative Author List* (entry 35), *Monographic Series* (entry 40), *Chinese Cooperative Catalog* (entry 39), and *Subject Catalog* (entry 42). It contains a full record register and four separate cumulative indexes: name, title, subject, and series.

44. Library of Congress. **National Union Catalog: U.S. Books**. Microfiche edition. IA, 1983- . Monthly. LC 82-6947. $195/yr.

Bibliographic records are provided for U.S. imprints in all languages, verified after December 31, 1982. The catalog contains a full record register and four separate cumulative indexes: name, title, subject, and series. Books, pamphlets, and some microforms issued in the United States are included.

45. Library of Congress. **National Union Catalog: Audiovisual Materials.** Microfiche edition. IA, 1983- . Quarterly. LC 82-6948. $23/yr.

This catalog includes motion pictures, video recordings, filmstrips, transparency sets, and slide sets released in the United States or Canada and cataloged by the Library of Congress. It provides a full record register and separate cumulative indexes: name, title, subject, and series. It continues *Audiovisual Materials* (entry 38).

46. Library of Congress. **National Union Catalog: Cartographic Materials.** Microfiche edition. IA, 1983- . Quarterly. LC 82-6945. $105/yr.

This includes the complete Library of Congress maps data base together with entries for currently cataloged maps. There are five separate cumulative indexes: name, title, subject, series, and geographic classification code.

47. Library of Congress. **National Union Catalog of Manuscript Collections.** IA, 1959/61- . Annual. LC 62-17486. Z6620.U5N3. OCLC 01759448. **LC9.8:date.**

This title lists manuscript collections in repositories in the United States. The form, extent, and location of the manuscripts are given.

48. Library of Congress. **The Library of Congress Main Reading Room Reference Collection Subject Catalog.** Comp. by Katherine Ann Gardner. GPO, 1980. 2d ed. 1,236 pp. LC 80-19478. Z1035.1.U526. OCLC 6555179. S/N 030-001-00095-8. $31. **LC1.12/2:R22/980.**

This subject catalog to one of the world's largest general reference collections lists every title in the general reference collections of the Library of Congress main reading room. Entries are arranged alphabetically by subject headings and by main entry. This update of the 1975 edition includes holdings as of August 1980. This is a valuable guide for reference collection evaluation and selection.

49. Library of Congress. **Special Collections in the Library of Congress: A Selective Guide.** Comp. by Annette Melville. GPO, 1980. 464 pp., illus. LC 79-607780. Z733.U58U54 1980. 027.5753. OCLC 05474180. S/N 030-001-00092-3. $17. **LC1.6/4:C68.**

This guide introduces readers to some of the most prized research material in the Library of Congress's special collections. It focuses on 269 thematically related groups of materials maintained as separate units and identified as rare or of potential interest to scholars. Brief essays describe the history, content, scope, subject strengths, and organization of each collection. Included are special collections of books, pamphlets, drawings, films, manuscripts, maps, music, musical instruments, prints, photographs, sound recordings, videotapes, and other nonprint formats.

Serials and Newspapers

50. Library of Congress. **New Serial Titles: A Union List of Serials Commencing Publication after December 31, 1949.** IA, 1953- . Eight monthly issues, three quarterly issues, and annual cumulations that are cumulative through periods of five or ten years. LC 53-060021. Z6945.N44. 016.05. OCLC 01759958. $325/yr. **LC1.23/3:date.**

Cumulation for 1950-70. (R. R. Bowker, microfilm $100.; paper $250.)

Cumulation for 1971-75. 2 vols. (LC, $170.)

Cumulation for 1976-78. 2 vols. (LC, $225.)

Cumulation for 1981. (LC, $235.)

Cumulation for 1982. (LC, $275.)

This is the supplement to *Union List of Serials in Libraries of the United States and Canada* (3d ed., by Edna Brown Titus. H. W. Wilson, 1965. 5 vols. $175). It is arranged alphabetically by title (or issuing body if the title is not distinctive) with place of publication, beginning date, date of cessation (if applicable), International Standard Serial Number (ISSN), and country codes. It includes records of holdings of more than eight hundred U.S. and Canadian libraries. A separate section lists title changes, changes of corporate entry, and similar notes.

51. Library of Congress. General Reference and Bibliography Division. **Union Lists of Serials: A Bibliography**. Comp. by Ruth S. Freitag. GPO, 1964. 150 pp. LC 64-60073. Z6945.U5U53. (Repr.: Gregg Press, $10.75.) **LC2.2:Se6**.

This bibliography brings up to date the "Bibliography of Union Lists of Serials," which was part of Gregory's *Union List of Serials* (2d ed., 1943). It includes union lists of newspapers, periodicals, and annuals that were separately published or were parts of books or journals. It is arranged geographically and indexed by names, subjects, and locations.

52. Library of Congress. Periodical Division. **Check List of American 18th Century Newspapers in the Library of Congress**. GPO, 1936. 401 pp. New ed. rev. and enl. LC 36-26003. Z6951.U47 1936. OCLC 1240308. (Repr.: Greenwood Press, $24.50.) **LC6.2:N42zs/3/936**.

Newspapers are arranged alphabetically within state and city with dates of first publication, variant titles, names of editors, publishers, and printers, and Library of Congress holdings. The listing is indexed by titles, printers, editors, and publishers.

53. Library of Congress. Processing Department. **Newspapers in Microform: Foreign Countries, 1948-1972**. IA, 1973. 269 pp. LC 73-12976. Z6945.U515 1973. For sale by the Cataloging Distribution Service, Library of Congress, Washington, DC 20541. $10. **LC30.2:N47/2/948-72**.

This is supplemented by the annual *Newspapers in Microform* (entry 55).

54. Library of Congress. Processing Department. **Newspapers in Microform: United States, 1948-1972**. IA, 1973. 1,056 pp. LC 73-6936. Z6951.U469. For sale by the Cataloging Distribution Service, Library of Congress, Washington, DC 20541. $30. **LC30.2:N47/948-72**.

This is supplemented by the annual *Newspapers in Microform* (entry 55).

55. Library of Congress. Processing Department. **Newspapers in Microform**. IA, 1973- . Annual. LC 75-644000. Z6945.N754. 016.07. OCLC 1354452. **LC30.2:N47/yr**.

Cumulation for 1973-77. 1,000 pp. (LC, $50.)

1978 ed. 144 pp. Out of print.

1979 ed. 211 pp. (LC, $20.)

1980 ed. 107 pp. (LC, $25.)

1981 ed. 208 pp. (LC, $30.)

This title supplements *Newspapers in Microform: Foreign Countries, 1948-1972* (entry 53) and *Newspapers in Microform: United States, 1948-1972* (entry 54). It lists foreign and U.S. newspapers on microform that are permanently housed in U.S., Canadian, and foreign libraries or in vaults of commercial microform producers. Location codes and brief bibliographic identifications are given.

56. Library of Congress. Serial and Government Publications Division. **Newspapers Received Currently in the Library of Congress.** GPO, 1982. 46 pp. 8th ed. OCLC 07093410. S/N 030-005-00011-2. $4.75. **LC6.7:982.**
This directory lists 349 U.S. and 1,090 foreign newspapers that are received on a permanent basis by the Library of Congress, and an additional 187 U.S. and 49 foreign newspapers that are retained on a current basis. Entries are arranged alphabetically in two sections for U.S. and foreign newspapers. There is a title index.

MATERIALS FOR THE BLIND

57. Library of Congress. Division for the Blind and Physically Handicapped. **Volunteers Who Produce Books: Braille, Tape, Large Type.** IA, 1978. 70 pp. Rev. and enl. ed. LC 78-9942. HV1790.N37 1978. **LC19.2:V88/978.**
This is a list of names of individuals and groups who transcribe books and other reading material for the blind and physically handicapped. It is arranged alphabetically by state with an index of "specialized talents" and is available in braille and large-print editions.

58. National Library Service for the Blind and Physically Handicapped. **Cassette Books.** IA, 1981- . Annual. LC 79-645707. OCLC 5173930. **LC19.10/3:yr.**
This is a listing of adult and young adult books produced on cassette by the National Library Service for the Blind and Physically Handicapped. Arranged by subjects, it lists author, title, number of cassettes, code number, date, and annotation. It is in large-print format. It was issued biennially from 1977/78 to 1979/80; there was also an edition for 1974-76.

59. National Library Service for the Blind and Physically Handicapped. **Library Resources for the Blind and Physically Handicapped.** IA, 1978- . Annual. LC 76-640140. Z675.B6L52. 027.6/63/02573. OCLC 02977219. **LC19.16:yr.**
This is a directory of the network libraries and machine-lending agencies that make up the free national library service providing braille and recorded materials for blind and physically handicapped persons. The network libraries listed circulate materials by postage-free mail, offer reference, readers' advisory, and other services, and may loan playback equipment and accessories. This state-by-state directory gives address, telephone, TTY, WATS, name of librarian, and description of services.

60. National Library Service for the Blind and Physically Handicapped. **Magazines.** IA, 1978- . Biennial. LC 79-643335. Z5346.A2M33. 016.3624/1/05. OCLC 03884827. **LC19.2:M27/yr.**
This is a descriptive list of selected periodicals available in braille, disk, cassette, large type, moon type, and open-reel tape. It is also available in braille and flexible disc.

BIBLIOGRAPHIES BY COUNTRY

General

61. Library of Congress. General Reference and Bibliography Division. **Current National Bibliographies**. Comp. by Helen F. Conover. GPO, 1955. 132 pp. LC 55-60025. Z1002.A2U52. (Repr.: Greenwood Press, $14.50.)

Now somewhat outdated, this annotated bibliography is of historical interest. It lists national and trade bibliographies published in 67 foreign countries, periodical indexes, directories, and government publications, and has a title index. It is updated by the UNESCO publication *Bibliographical Services throughout the World* (1950-59) by R. L. Collison, 1961; (1960-64) by Paul Avicenne, 1967; (1965-69) by Paul Avicenne, 1972; and (1970-74) by Marcelle Beadiquez, 1977.

Africa

62. Library of Congress. General Reference and Bibliography Division. **Sub-Saharan Africa: A Guide to Serials**. IA, 1970. 409 pp. LC 70-607392. Free from the Central Services Division, Library of Congress, Washington, DC 20540. **LC2.8:Af8/2**.

63. Library of Congress. General Reference and Bibliography Division. **The United States and Africa: Guide to U.S. Official Documents and Government-Sponsored Publications on Africa, 1785-1975**. Comp. by Julian W. Witherell. GPO, 1978. 949 pp. LC 78-1051. Z3501.W57. 016.96. OCLC 3627152. S/N 030-000-00098-6. $22. **LC1.2:Af8/2/785-975**.

This selection of unclassified publications on Africa issued by the U.S. government between the late eighteenth century and 1975 is arranged in five chronological sections, subdivided by region or country. Except for publications specifically on Egypt, all of Africa is covered. Many have descriptive notes or scope notes.

64. Library of Congress. Library of Congress Office, Nairobi. **Accessions List, Eastern Africa**. IA, 1972- . Bimonthly. LC 76-607943. 016.9167. OCLC 02403577. **LC1.30/8:vol./nos**.

This accessions list from the Library of Congress Special Foreign Acquisition Program is available from the Field Director, Karachi-LOC, U.S. Department of State, Washington, DC 20520.

Asia and the Middle East

65. Library of Congress. **Guide to Japanese Reference Books: Supplement**. By Nihon No Sanko Tosho Henshu Iinkai. English-language edition. GPO, 1979. 300 pp. LC 77-608084. J3.N5513 Suppl. 011.02. OCLC 3069592. **LC1.12/2:J27/2**.

This title supplements *Guide to Japanese Reference Books*, published in 1966 by the American Library Association. The 1966 guide covered books published up to 1964. This supplement covers works published between 1964 and 1970. It gives Japanese and translated titles, and English annotations for titles that would be helpful to the general user or valuable in building a basic library reference collection.

66. Library of Congress. **Japanese National Government Publications in the Library of Congress: A Bibliography**. By Thaddeus Y. Ohta. GPO, 1981. LC 80-607001. Z3305.U54 1981. S/N 030-001-00097-4. $15. **LC1.12/2:J27/3**.

This is an inventory of official Japanese government publications in the collections of the Library of Congress through 1977. The bulk of the holdings were acquired after an exchange agreement between the Library of Congress and Japan in 1956. It includes publications of Japanese legislative, executive, and judicial agencies and of commercial publishers serving the government or quasi-governmental bodies. Most of the titles are serials.

67. Library of Congress. **Persian and Afghan Newspapers in the Library of Congress, 1871-1978**. Comp. by Ibrahim V. Pourhadi. GPO, 1979. 102 pp. LC 79-12160. Z6958.I65P875. 016.079/55. OCLC 4857473. S/N 030-000-00109-5. $5. **LC1.12/2:P43/871-978**.

This is a valuable guide for researchers of the politics, history, religion, literature, or journalism of Iran and Afghanistan, where newspapers have played a significant role in shaping public opinion. It is an alphabetical inventory of Library of Congress holdings of newspapers from Iran and Afghanistan, with short annotations. An introductory essay describes the thirteen categories of newspapers in the collection and their significance. A chronological index shows the first year of publication and place of publication. There is also an index of editors, publishers, and newspaper owners.

68. Library of Congress. Africa and Middle Eastern Division. **Arab-World Newspapers in the Library of Congress: A List**. By George Simitri Selim. GPO, 1980. 85 pp. OCLC 07297969. S/N 030-000-00120-6. $5.50. **LC41.9:Ar1**.

Newspapers held by the Library of Congress which were published in Arab countries in either Arabic or Latin scripts, and those published in Arabic script outside the Arab countries, are listed.

69. Library of Congress. Asian Division. **Southeast Asia: Western-Language Periodicals in the Library of Congress**. Comp. by A. Kohar Rony. GPO, 1979. 201 pp. LC 79-607777. Z3221.U524 1978. 016.959. S/N 030-000-00113-3. $11. **LC17.2:As4/4**.

This guide to the Library of Congress's extensive collection of periodicals containing information on Southeast Asia lists 2,293 titles published both in and outside Southeast Asia, in alphabetical arrangement. Subject and issuing body indexes are also included.

70. Library of Congress. Asian Division. **Vietnamese Holdings in the Library of Congress: A Bibliography**. Comp. by A. Kohar Rony. GPO, 1982. 236 pp. LC 81-2847. Z3228.V5L52 1981. 016.9597. OCLC 07329336. S/N 030-000-00136-2. $12. **LC17.9:V67**.

This first special bibliographic guide to the Library of Congress's Vietnamese holdings will assist those wishing access to the nonlegal Vietnamese language collections in the Asian Division. It includes monographs, serials, and newspapers with subject and issuing body indexes.

71. Library of Congress. General Reference and Bibliography Division. African Section. **Kenya: A Subject Guide to Official Publications**. Comp. by John Bruce Howell. GPO, 1978. 423 pp. LC 78-1915. Z3587.H68. 015/.676/2. OCLC 3728868. S/N 030-001-00073-7. $11. **LC2.7/2:K42**.

This is an unannotated bibliography of official publications of Kenya between 1886 and 1975. It is arranged by subjects; locations in the Library of Congress and North American libraries are given.

72. Library of Congress. Library of Congress Office, Jakarta. **Accessions List, Southeast Asia**. IA, 1982- . Bimonthly. LC 75-940200. Z3221.U53a. 016.959. OCLC 02088682. **LC1.30/10:vol./nos**.

This accessions list from the Library of Congress Special Foreign Acquisition Program is available to libraries from the Field Director, Karachi-LOC, Department of State, Washington, DC 20520. It supersedes accessions lists for Indonesia, Malaysia, Singapore, and Brunei.

73. Library of Congress. Library of Congress Office, Karachi. **Accessions List, Middle East**. IA, 1982- . Bimonthly. LC 83-643600. OCLC 05918016. **LC1.30/3:vol./nos**.

This accessions list from the Library of Congress Special Foreign Acquisition Program is available to libraries from the Field Director, Karachi-LOC, Department of State, Washington, DC 20520.

74. Library of Congress. Library of Congress Office, New Delhi. **Accessions List, South Asia**. IA, 1981- . Monthly. LC 81-644186. Z3185.L52a. 015.59. OCLC 06674270. **LC1.30/10-3:vol./nos**.

This accessions list from the Library of Congress Special Foreign Acquisition Program is available to libraries from the Field Director, Karachi-LOC, Department of State, Washington, DC 20520. It merges accessions lists for Afghanistan, Bangladesh, India, Nepal, Pakistan, and Sri Lanka.

75. Library of Congress. Orientalia Division. **Chinese-English and English-Chinese Dictionaries in the Library of Congress: An Annotated Bibliography**. GPO, 1977. 148 pp. LC 76-608329. Z3109.U53 1977. S/N 030-000-00093-5. $7. **LC17.2:C43/5**.

76. Library of Congress. Orientalia Division. **Chinese Periodicals in the Library of Congress**. Comp. by Han Chu Huang. GPO, 1978. 521 pp. LC 76-608330. Z6958.C5U53 1978. 016.05. OCLC 2596899. S/N 030-000-00100-1. $12. **LC17.2:C43/6**.

This is a list of over sixty-four hundred serial titles issued between 1868 and 1975, representing the largest serial collection outside China. Serials listed are on all subjects except law. Chinese legal serials are in the collection of the Far Eastern Law Division, Library of Congress Law Library. Titles are given in Chinese, with some also given in English.

77. Library of Congress. Orientalia Division. **Southern Asia Accessions List**. IA, 1952-60. 9 vols. in 6. LC 52-60012. Z3221.U52. (Repr.: Arno, $175.)

This is a bibliography of publications pertaining to Southern Asia that were accessioned by the Library of Congress and cooperating U.S. libraries from 1952 to 1960. "The list includes all monographs in certain languages of South Asia and South-east Asia bearing an imprint of 1947 or later [and] selected articles from periodicals ... published since January 1954" (Preface). The first part of each issue included materials in Western languages by country and then by subject. Part 2 included materials in vernacular languages.

Europe

78. Library of Congress. **The Portuguese Manuscripts Collection of the Library of Congress: A Guide**. Comp. by Christopher C. Lund and Mary Ellis Kahler. GPO, 1980. 187 pp. LC 80-607039. Z6621.U582P68. 091. OCLC 6093542. S/N 030-003-00020-9. $11. **LC1.6/4:P83**.

This guide describes 537 items, many of them originals, held in the Library of Congress Manuscript Division. Of both historic and literary interest, these manuscripts cover a broad range of topics and date from the fifteenth to the twentieth century.

79. Library of Congress. Hispanic Foundation. **Spanish and Portuguese Translations of United States Books, 1955-1962: A Bibliography.** GPO, 1963. 506 pp. (Hispanic Foundation bibliographical series no. 8.) LC 63-60091. Z2685.H5 no.8. Free from the Library of Congress, Central Services Division, Washington, DC 20540. **LC24.7:8.**

This supersedes two earlier works: *A Provisional Bibliography of United States Books Translated into Portuguese* (GPO, 1957) and *A Provisional Bibliography of United States Books Translated into Spanish* (GPO, 1957)

80. Library of Congress. Slavic and Central European Division. **The Federal Republic of Germany: A Selected Bibliography of English-Language Publications.** Comp. by Arnold H. Price. GPO, 1978. 2d rev. ed. 116 pp. LC 77-608128. Z2240.3.P75 1977. 016.943. OCLC 3088710. S/N 030-020-00012-0. $6. **LC35.2:G31/3/978.**

This second edition contains largely new entries, reflecting changes between 1966 and 1976. The bibliography reflects the positions of American scholars on recent developments. Entries are arranged by subject and are not annotated.

81. Library of Congress. Slavic and Central European Division. **Newspapers of East Central and Southeastern Europe in the Library of Congress.** Ed. by Robert G. Carlton. GPO, 1965. 204 pp. LC 65-60088. Z6955.U52. Free from the Central Services Division, Library of Congress, Washington, DC 20540. **LC35.2:Eu7.**

This compilation lists over seven hundred post-World War I newspapers from East Central and Southeastern Europe in the Library of Congress collections (in both microfilm and print form). It is arranged by country and city and indexed by language and place of publication. It indicates the latest place of publication, most recent title, language, frequency, date of establishment, and publisher.

82. Library of Congress. Slavic and Central European Division. **Polish Books in English, 1945-1971.** GPO, 1974. 163 pp. LC 74-6163. Z2528.L5H37. 016.91438/03. OCLC 868066. Free from the Library of Congress, Central Services Division, Washington, DC 20540. **LC35.2:P75/4.**

Latin America

83. Library of Congress. **A Bibliography of Latin American Bibliographies.** Comp. by Cecil Knight Jones and James A. Granier. GPO, 1942. 2d ed. rev. and enl. 311 pp. (Latin American series, no. 2). LC 42-38983. Z1601.A2J7 1942. (Repr.: Greenwood Press, or Negro Universities Press, $21.) **LC1.16:2.**

The first edition of this bibliography was published in 1922 with the title *Hispanic American Bibliographies*. The 3,016 entries cover separately published bibliographies, collective bibliographies, histories of literature, and general reference works. Arrangement is by country and then alphabetically by author, with one chapter for general and miscellaneous publications. An author/subject index and a list of publications related to Latin America issued by the Library of Congress are included. A greatly enlarged and updated version by Arthur E. Gropp is available from Scarecrow Press (1969 and supplement 1971, $35).

84. Library of Congress. Latin American, Portuguese, and Spanish Division. **Latin America, Spain, and Portugal: An Annotated Bibliography of Paperback Books**. GPO, 1976. 2d ed. 323 pp. (Hispanic Foundation bibliographical series, no. 14.) LC 75-619187. Z2685.H5 no.14. 016.98. OCLC 1528846. S/N 030-013-00007-7. $9. **LC24.7:14**.

This second edition of the 1971 bibliography of the same title lists and briefly annotates over twenty-two hundred titles about the Hispano-Luso-American world currently available in paperback. It includes listings for dictionaries, grammars, readers, and textbooks.

85. Library of Congress. Library of Congress Office, Brazil. **Accessions List, Brazil**. IA, 1978- . Bimonthly. LC 75-646453. Z1671.U53a. 015/.81. OCLC 01559825. **LC1.30/11:vol./nos**.

This accessions list is available to libraries from the Field Director, New Delhi-LOC, Department of State, Washington, DC 20520.

Soviet Union

86. Library of Congress. Processing Department. **Monthly Index of Russian Accessions**. 22 vols. GPO, 1948-69. Monthly. LC 48-46562. **LC30.10:vol./nos**.

From 1948 to 1957 the title of this source was *Monthly List of Russian Accessions*. This valuable bibliography is a union list of publications in the Russian language (regardless of country of publication) received by the Library of Congress and a group of cooperating libraries. "Whenever possible, publications printed in other languages spoken in the Soviet Union are also included" (Introduction).

It is published in four main sections: A, monographic works (by broad subjects); B, periodicals (with table of contents translated into English, arranged by broad subjects); C, list of periodicals indexed and abbreviations used; and D, subject index to parts A and B. Titles are given in English with Russian transliteration. Included are two annual indexes – one locating serials, and one to authors of monographs. It also lists Russian periodicals for which English translations are available.

87. Library of Congress. Reference Department. **Russia: A Checklist Preliminary to a Basic Bibliography of Materials in the Russian Language**. 10 pts. IA, 1944-46. LC 44-51007.

> Part 1. **Belles Lettres**. 1944. 99 pp.
>
> Part 2. **Economic Conditions and Social History prior to 1918**. 1944. 74 pp.
>
> Part 3. **Fine Arts**. 1944. 38 pp.
>
> Part 4. **Law and Institutions prior to 1918**. 1944. 62 pp.
>
> Parts 5-6. **Folklore, Linguistics and Literary Forms: Church and Education prior to 1918**. 1944. 54 pp.
>
> Part 7. **History, Including Auxiliary Sciences, prior to 1918**. 1945. 123 pp.
>
> Part 8. **Theatre and Music prior to 1918**. 1945. 23 pp.
>
> Part 9. **Soviet Union**. 1945. 86 pp.
>
> Part 10. **Reference Books**. 1946. 227 pp.

The arrangement in each part is alphabetical. Titles are transliterated. Part 10 contains a section listing reference books in languages other than Russian.

88. Library of Congress. Reference Department. **Half a Century of Soviet Serials, 1917-68: A Bibliography and Union List of Serials Published in the**

USSR. Comp. by Rudolf Smits. 2 vols. GPO, 1968. 1,661 pp. LC 68-62169. Z6956.R9S58. Available to U.S. libraries and institutions from the Central Services Division, Library of Congress, Washington, DC 20540. **LC29.2: So8/3/v.1,2.**

All known serial publications appearing in the Soviet Union at regular or irregular intervals since 1917, in all except oriental languages, are included. Serials published outside the Soviet Union and newspapers are excluded. Symbols of libraries in the Unites States and Canada in which a title is known to be represented have been taken from the 1967 edition of *Union List of Serials*, from *New Serial Titles*, or from catalog cards sent to the Slavic Union Catalog by cooperating libraries. The work contains 29,761 entries arranged alphabetically by title (or issuing body when the title is not distinctive). For each entry it lists the language (when not Russian) in parentheses following the title, place of publication, name of issuing body (for title entries), frequency, miscellaneous remarks concerning title changes, suspensions of publication for periods of time, and so on, and data regarding library holdings in the United States and Canada. Over 28,000 cross references are also provided. Some serials which the Library of Congress has classified separately as monographs are included, with a special note to that effect.

This bibliography supersedes *Serial Publications of the Soviet Union, 1939-57* (LC, 1958, 459 pp.) but it does not include an English-language subject index, which was included in the 1958 edition.

89. Library of Congress. Slavic and Central European Division. **Eighteenth Century Russian Publications in the Library of Congress: A Catalog**. By Tatiana Fessenko. GPO, 1961. 157 pp. LC 61-60095. **LC35.2:R92.**

This bibliography contains about thirteen hundred entries (in the form of reproductions of Library of Congress catalog cards) arranged alphabetically by author or, if the author is unknown, by title. It identifies many foreign authors of Russian translations who were previously listed as anonymous in Russian bibliographies. Asterisks by entries mark "rare" and "very rare" publications. The title index also contains references to variant forms of titles. Appendixes include: (1) a transliteration table of the Russian alphabet; (2) an itemized list of Library of Congress holdings for incomplete sets (serial or monographic); and (3) a tentative list of originals of some Russian translations.

90. Library of Congress. Slavic and East European Division. **Russian, Ukranian and Belorussian Newspapers, 1917-53: A Union List**. Comp. by Paul L. Horecky. IA, 1953. 218 pp. LC 54-60001.

The holdings of 859 newspapers in 39 U.S. libraries are listed, arranged by place of publication.

91. Library of Congress. Slavic and East European Division. **The USSR and East Central and South-Eastern Europe: Periodicals in Western Languages**. Comp. by Janina W. Hoskins. GPO, 1979. 4th ed. 87 pp. LC 78-022038. Z2483.H63 1978. 016.94/005. OCLC 4504699. S/N 030-020-00013-8. $5.50. **LC35.2: P41/979.**

This is a new edition of *The USSR and Eastern Europe: Periodicals in Western Languages*, first published in 1958 and considered to be an essential research tool through each of its previous three editions. A list of periodicals on the Soviet Union and satellite countries is given, along with brief annotations. The journals covered are in the social sciences and humanities, with articles in West European languages on Albania, the Baltic countries, Bulgaria, Romania, Yugoslavia, and the Soviet Union. This edition covers periodicals current through 1977, and includes a list of discontinued titles.

92. Library of Congress. Slavic and East European Division. **Yugoslavia: A Bibliographic Guide**. By Michael B. Petrovich. GPO, 1974. 270 pp. LC 72-11512. Z2956.P48. Free from the Central Services Division, Library of Congress, Washington, DC 20540. **LC35.2:Y9/3**.

Bibliographies of Government Publications

GENERAL

93. Library of Congress. **Government Organization Manuals: A Bibliography**. By Vladimir M. Palic. GPO, 1975. 105 pp. LC 75-26755. Z7164.A2P33. Free from the Central Services Division, Library of Congress, Washington, DC 20540. **LC1.6/4:G74**.

"This bibliography is essentially a list of materials and other publications that outline in more or less detail, the organization of national governments" (Preface). It is arranged alphabetically by countries, with an introductory section of general and regional manuals.

94. Library of Congress. **Government Publications: A Guide to Bibliographic Tools**. By Vladimir M. Palic. GPO, 1974. 4th ed. 441 pp. LC 74-34440. Z7164.G7C5. Available to U.S. libraries and institutions from the Central Services Division, Library of Congress, Washington, DC 20540. (Repr.: Pergamon Press, $40.) **LC1.12/2:G74**.

This supersedes *Government Document Bibliography in the United States and Elsewhere* (GPO, 1942). It is a bibliography of documents and indexes to documents of federal, state, local, and foreign governments. Titles listed are both current and retrospective. It also includes a bibliography of materials describing foreign government organization. The Pergamon Press reprint incorporates *Government Organization Manuals: A Bibliography* (entry 93) in the same volume.

BIBLIOGRAPHIES BY COUNTRY

Africa

95. Library of Congress. **East African Community: Subject Guide to Official Publications.** Comp. by John Bruce Howell. GPO, 1976. 272 pp. LC 76-608001. Z3582.H69. 015/.67. OCLC 2021205. Free from the Central Services Division, Library of Congress, Washington, DC 20540. **LC1.12/2:Af8.**

This is a subject bibliography of official publications of the East African Community and its predecessors, 1926-74, and of the East African region, 1859-1974, issued by Great Britain or one of the three partner states.

96. Library of Congress. General Reference and Bibliography Division. **Botswana, Lesotho, and Swaziland: A Guide to Official Publications, 1868-1968.** Comp. by Mildred Grimes Balima. GPO, 1971. 84 pp. LC 74-171029. Z3559.B3. Free from the Central Services Division, Library of Congress, Washington, DC 20540. **LC2.8:B65/868-968.**

This bibliography contains a list of published official records of Botswana, Lesotho, and Swaziland from 1868 to 1968. Included are citations to documents of the former High Commission Territories during British protection and since independence and a selection of publications issued by the Colony of the Cape of Good Hope, the South African Republic, and Transvaal Colony. Also included is a brief history of the three countries.

97. Library of Congress. General Reference and Bibliography Division. **French-Speaking Central Africa: Guide to Official Publications in American Libraries.** Comp. by Julian W. Witherell. GPO, 1973. 314 pp. LC 72-5766. Z3692.W5. Free from the Central Services Division, Library of Congress, Washington, DC 20540. **LC2.8:Af8/3.**

98. Library of Congress. General Reference and Bibliography Division. **Ghana: A Guide to Official Publications, 1872-1968.** IA, 1969. 110 pp. LC 74-601680. Z3785.W5. OCLC 30009. Free from the Central Services Division, Library of Congress, Washington, DC 20540.

99. Library of Congress. General Reference and Bibliography Division. **Madagascar and Adjacent Islands: A Guide to Official Publications.** GPO, 1965. 58 pp. LC 65-61703. Z3702.U5. Free from the Central Services Division, Library of Congress, Washington, DC 20540. **LC2.8:M26.**

100. Library of Congress. General Reference and Bibliography Division. **Official Publications of British East Africa.** 4 pts. IA, 1960-63. LC 61-60009. Z3582.U5. **LC2.2:Af8/4/pt.1-4.**

> Part 1. **The East Africa High Commission and other Regional Documents.** Comp. by Helen F. Conover. 1960. 67 pp.

This work attempts to list comprehensively the papers and reports of institutions and services of the High Commission. It includes publications of the Conference of Governors and other official bodies concerned with East Africa as a unit prior to 1948, and a selection of British official documents. There is an author/subject index.

> Part 2. **Tanganyika.** Comp. by Audrey A. Walker. 1962. 134 pp.

Part 3. **Kenya and Zanzibar**. Comp. by Audrey A. Walker. 1962. 162 pp. Free from the Central Services Division, Library of Congress, Washington, DC 20540.

Part 4. **Uganda**. Comp. by Audrey A. Walker. 1963. 100 pp.

Bibliographies of official publications of these four countries are given. Numbered entries are arranged by author (personal and governmental) in each chapter. Full bibliographic information is given. Each volume has its own index.

101. Library of Congress. General Reference and Bibliography Division. **Official Publications of Sierra Leone and Gambia**. Comp. by Audrey A. Walker. GPO, 1963. 92 pp. LC 63-60090. Z3553.S5U5. Free from the Central Services Division, Library of Congress, Washington, DC 20540. **LC2.2:Si1/2**.

This covers material dating from the establishment of the central government in both Sierra Leone and Gambia, with some pertinent British government publications. The first part records publications related to Sierra Leone, and the second part to Gambia. Entries are alphabetical by author and title. The bibliography is based primarily on holdings of the Library of Congress, with some entries from holdings of other libraries as reported to the National Union Catalog, and from some other bibliographies. It is indexed by subjects and authors.

102. Library of Congress. General Reference and Bibliography Division. **Portuguese Africa: A Guide to Official Publications**. Comp. by Mary Jane Gibson. GPO, 1967. 217 pp. LC 68-60004. Z3871.G5. **LC2.8:P83**.

This guide covers as comprehensively as possible the documents of Portuguese Africa from 1850 to 1964. It lists publications of the governments of Angola, the Cape Verde Islands, Mozambique, Portuguese Guinea, and the Sao Tome e Principe Islands and also of Portugal pertaining to its African possessions. Entries are numbered and listed by author within breakdowns by countries. Full bibliographic information and U.S. library locations are given. Indexes are to subjects and personal authors.

103. Library of Congress. General Reference and Bibliography Division. **The Rhodesias and Nyasaland: A Guide to Official Publications**. Comp. by Audrey A. Walker. GPO, 1965. 285 pp. LC 65-60089. Z3573.R5U5. Free from the Central Services Division, Library of Congress, Washington, DC 20540. **LC2.8:R34**.

This guide covers, as comprehensively as possible, the published records of administration in the former Federation of Rhodesia and Nyasaland and in the three territorial governments of Northern Rhodesia, Southern Rhodesia, and Nyasaland from 1889 to 1963. Chapters are on the former federation, the three countries, the Central African Interterritorial Agencies prior to the federation, the British South African Company, and Great Britain. Each chapter first lists publications under names of government departments and then cites materials under titles, personal authors, and nongovernmental corporate authors. Nearly two thousand publications are listed. There is an author and subject index.

104. Library of Congress. General Reference and Bibliography Division. **Uganda: Subject Guide to Official Publications**. Comp. by Beverly Ann Gray. GPO, 1977. 271 pp. LC 77-608126. Z3586.G7. 015/.676/1. OCLC 3166676. S/N 030-001-00064-8. $14. **LC2.8:Ug1**.

This list of official Ugandan publications, 1893-1974, is arranged under general subject categories. Location of publications in the Library of Congress and other libraries is noted.

Latin America

105. Library of Congress. **Guide to Official Publications of Other American Republics.** James B. Childs, gen. ed. 19 vols. GPO, 1945-49. (Published as a subseries in the Latin American series.) LC 45-36618. Z1605.U64. (Repr.: Johnson, New York, 2 vols. $75.) **LC1.16:nos. vary.**

    Vol. 1. **Argentina.** 1945. 124 pp. (Latin American series 9.)

    Vol. 2. **Bolivia.** 1945. 66 pp. (Latin American series 10.)

    Vol. 3. **Brazil.** Comp. by John de Noia. 1948. 223 pp. (Latin American series 35.)

    Vol. 4. **Chile.** Comp. by Otto Neuburger. 1947. 94 pp. (Latin American series 17.)

    Vol. 5. **Colombia.** Comp. by James B. Childs. 1948. 89 pp. (Latin American series 33.)

    Vol. 6. **Costa Rica.** Comp. by Henry V. Besso. 1947. 92 pp. (Latin American series 24.)

    Vol. 7. **Cuba.** 1945. 40 pp. (Latin American series 11.)

    Vol. 8. **Dominican Republic.** Comp. by John de Noia. 1947. 40 pp. (Latin American series 25.)

    Vol. 9. **Ecuador.** Comp. by John de Noia. 1947. 56 p. (Latin American series 31.)

    Vol. 10. **El Salvador.** Comp. by John de Noia. 1947. 64 pp. (Latin American series 19.)

    Vol. 11. **Guatemala.** Comp. by Henry V. Besso. 1947. 64 pp. (Latin American series 30.)

    Vol. 12. **Haiti.** 1947. 25 pp. (Latin American series 23.)

    Vol. 13. **Honduras.** 1947. 31 pp. (Latin American series 29.)

    Vol. 14. **Nicaragua.** Comp. by John de Noia. 1947. 33 pp. (Latin American series 27.)

    Vol. 15. **Panama.** Comp. by James B. Childs. 1947. 61 pp. (Latin American series 22.)

    Vol. 16. **Paraguay.** Comp. by James B. Childs. 1947. 61 pp. (Latin American series 15.)

    Vol. 17. **Peru.** Comp. by John de Noia. 1948. 90 pp. (Latin American series 36.)

    Vol. 18. **Uruguay.** Comp. by John de Noia and Glenda Crevenna. 1948. 91 pp. (Latin American series 37.)

    Vol. 19. **Venezuela.** Comp. by Otto Neuburger. 1948. 59 pp. (Latin American series 34.)

United States

General

106. Library of Congress. Exchange and Gift Division. **Non-GPO Imprints Received in the Library of Congress: A Selective Checklist.** IA, 1967-75. Annual. LC 73-600148. Z1223.A1U54a. OCLC 3024625. $1.25 per annual volume from

Cataloging Distribution Service, Library of Congress, Washington, DC 20541. **LC30.2:Im7/yr.**
Non-GPO imprints of research value that were not included in the *Monthly Catalog of United States Government Publications* are listed. The list is indexed, but not annotated. When coverage of the *Monthly Catalog* was greatly expanded in 1976, publication of this title ceased.

107. Library of Congress. Serial Division. **Popular Names of U.S. Government Reports: A Catalog.** Comp. by Bernard A. Bernier, Jr., Katherine F. Gould, and Porter Humphrey. GPO, 1976. 3d ed. 263 pp. LC 75-619301. Z1223.A199U54 1976. 015/.73. OCLC 1735125. S/N 030-005-00007-4. $13. **LC6.2:G74/976.**
This source aids the person who knows the short, popular name of a government report, but does not know the official title or issuing agency. Reports of government agencies are listed in popular name order, with the Library of Congress catalog cards reproduced for each. Both GPO and non-GPO reports are covered and are indexed by subject.

Retrospective

108. Congress. **Descriptive Catalogue of the Government Publications of the United States, September 5, 1774-March 4, 1881.** Comp. by Benjamin Perley Poore. GPO, 1885. 1,392 pp. (Senate miscellaneous document 67, 48th Congress, 2d session.) (Repr.: Johnson, $115.) **Congressional Serial Set 2268.**
This work was the first guide to publications in all branches of the federal government: legislative, judicial, and executive. It is arranged chronologically. Executive and judicial publications are listed at the beginning of the section for each year, followed by congressional publications, which are listed by the date on which Congress ordered the printing. For each entry, Poore gives the full title, author, date, and a brief annotation as well as a reference for locating the publication in the congressional reports and documents series. A general index completes the work. Although it purports to cover documents from all three branches, there is a strong emphasis on congressional materials. Neither the bibliography nor the index is comprehensive. Specific publications are fairly easy to locate through the index. However, all entries for specific subjects are lumped together with no indication of contents. It is, therefore, necessary to check entries on each page referred to by the index.

109. Congress. **Comprehensive Index to the Publications of the United States Government, 1881-1893.** By John Griffith Ames. 2 vols. GPO, 1905. 1,590 pp. (House document 754, 58th Congress, 2d session.) (Repr.: Johnson, $115.) **Congressional Serial Set 4745,4746.**
This index to government publications issued from 1881 to 1893 covers the period between Poore's *Descriptive Catalogue* and the *Document Catalog.* It is arranged by subjects or key words in titles. In the columnar arrangement, the main subject entry is in the center column with a brief description of the contents and the date of publication. Authors are listed in the left column, and citations for locating documents are in the right column. Some issuing agencies are given in the subject entries with their publications, but this is not done consistently. In some instances, the contents of books are listed separately under different subjects. There is an index to personal names of authors at the end of volume 2. Although this is called a comprehensive index, many departmental publications were omitted and the emphasis is on congressional materials.

110. Superintendent of Documents. **Catalog of the Public Documents of Congress and of All Departments of the Government [March 4, 1893-December 31, 1940].** 25 vols. GPO, 1896-1945. **GP3.6:date.**

Also known as the *Document Catalog*, this catalog includes references to publications from the 53d Congress (1893/94) through the 76th Congress (1939/40). It was issued biennially with each volume covering a single Congress, except for volumes 2 and 3, which covered the first and second sessions of the 54th Congress, respectively. This is a dictionary catalog containing entries for subjects, personal authors, departmental authors, and, in some cases, titles. Complete bibliographic citations are provided, including Congressional Serial Set numbers for congressional publications.

111. Superintendent of Documents. **Checklist of United States Public Documents, 1789-1909**. GPO, 1911. 3d ed., rev. and enl. 1,707 pp. (Repr.: Kraus, $54.) **GP3.2:C41/2**.

This source includes both congressional publications through the 60th Congress and departmental publications through 1909 in a shelflist arrangement according to SuDocs classification numbers. Complete citations are given, and note is made of different editions of publications, numbers and/or volumes issued for periodicals, and dates of publication. Under the heading of each agency or department is a brief history of that agency including name changes or departmental transfers. Congressional Serial Set volumes are listed numerically with brief notes on the contents of each. This volume also lists the *American State Papers*, papers of the Revolutionary period, proceedings and miscellaneous congressional publications, and committee reports. Individual titles are not given for serial publications (such as the Geological Survey bulletin series) or for individual items in Congressional Serial Set volumes. For items in Congressional Serial Set volumes, the *Checklist* shows the volume number, part number, and document number(s) in each volume. A second volume was planned to contain an index, but it was never published.

112. **Index to the Reports and Documents of Congress**. 43 vols. GPO, 1895-1933. **GP3.7:1-43**.

This series, known as the *Document Index*, covers House and Senate documents and reports exclusively. It was issued at the end of each session of Congress, and contained numerical lists of the reports and documents of that session and a schedule of Congressional Serial Set volumes showing the reports and documents bound in each volume. It also contained a subject index, which was discontinued in 1933, when this title was superseded by the *Numerical Lists and Schedule of Volumes* (entry 128).

113. Superintendent of Documents. **Tables and Annotated Index to the Congressional Series of United States Public Documents**. GPO, 1902. 769 pp. **GP3.2:P96**.

Part 1 of this guide to congressional publications, "Tables," is a list of the documents and reports of the 15th through 52d Congresses (i.e. 1817-93) arranged by series number. This part was superseded by the 1911 *Checklist* (entry 111). However, part 2, "Index," is still useful for locating congressional materials published before 1893. The Index cites each document and report and its Congressional Serial Set number. However, it does not give the number or session of the Congress. This is not a comprehensive list, but a selected list of congressional publications, and therefore should be used in conjunction with other references for a thorough search on a particular subject.

Current

114. General Services Administration. Consumer Information Center. **Consumer Information Catalog**. GPO, 1977- . Quarterly. OCLC 03458485. Free. **GS11.9: date**.

This is a list of free or inexpensive booklets on popular topics, designed to help federal agencies share useful consumer information and increase public awareness of government publications. Topics covered include automobiles, children, food, health, gardening, and others of general interest. For a free copy write Consumer Catalog, Pueblo, CO 81009.

115. Library of Congress. Exchange and Gift Division. **Monthly Checklist of State Publications**. GPO, 1910- . Monthly. LC 10-8924. Z1223.5.A1U5. OCLC 02553426. S/N 030-017-80001-0. $29/yr. (Repr.: vols. 1-29 [1910-38], Kraus, $1,202.) **LC30.9:yr./nos.**

This is a list of documents and publications issued by any of the fifty states and received by the Library of Congress. An annual index to monographs appears early in the following year. June and December issues contain a periodicals listing. Agencies submitting state publications to the Library of Congress for its collections may receive a free subscription.

116. National Audiovisual Center. **Quarterly Update: A Comprehensive Listing of New Audiovisual Materials and Services Offered by the National Audiovisual Center**. IA, 1980- . Quarterly. OCLC 06597469. **GS4.17/5-3:date.**

117. National Audiovisual Center. **A Reference List of Audiovisual Materials Produced by the United States Government**. IA, 1978. 354 pp. LB1043.Z9N28 1978. 011. OCLC 4055869. **GS4.2:Av2/978.**

_____. **Supplement**. GPO, 1980. 82 pp. OCLC 6535516. S/N 022-002-00069-4. $5. **GS4.2:Av2/980/supp.**

The most comprehensive listing of federally produced audiovisual materials, including films, slide sets, filmstrips, videotapes, videocassettes, and multimedia kits from nearly three hundred federal agencies, this title may be searched by subject or by specific titles of audiovisual productions. Entries include title, format, a short description, and availability. New editions are published irregularly, with supplements occasionally published between editions.

118. Superintendent of Documents. **GPO Sales Publications Reference File**. GPO, 1977- . Bimonthly with monthly supplement. OCLC 06343237. S/N 021-000-80004-0 (microfiche). $125/yr. S/N 021-000-80007-4 (computer tapes). $850/yr. (Subscription includes biweekly magnetic computer tapes.) **GP3.22/3: date.**

The *GPO Sales Publications Reference File* (PRF) is a microfiche catalog of all publications in stock and available for sale from the Superintendent of Documents. It also lists forthcoming and recently out-of-stock titles. It can be used to find specific GPO publications and bibliographic details about them, to determine what the government is publishing on any subject, or to identify publications that may be available at some of the nearly fourteen hundred depository libraries throughout the United States. The PRF can be searched by GPO stock numbers; by SuDocs classification numbers; or by subjects, titles, agency series and report numbers, key words, and personal authors through its alphabetical dictionary arrangement.

A companion resource, *Exhausted GPO Sales Publications Reference File* (EPRF), lists publications that went out of stock from 1972 to 1979. It is updated by annual supplements. A monthly supplement to the PRF, *GPO New Sales Publications*, consists of a single fiche and lists new publications added to the sales program during the previous month. A concise and helpful user's manual is titled *PRF User's Manual: A Guide to Using the GPO Sales Publications Reference File* (GPO, 1981. GP3.22/3:Manual/981).

119. Superintendent of Documents. **Government Periodicals and Subscription Services**. GPO, 1961- . Quarterly. (Price List 36.) OCLC 02946561. Free. **GP3.9:36/nos.**

This is a bibliographic listing of government periodicals and looseleaf subscription services available on subscription from the Superintendent of Documents, with some annotations. It is also called *Price List 36*. A free copy may be requested from the Government Printing Office, Superintendent of Documents, Washington, DC 20402.

120. Superintendent of Documents. **Monthly Catalog of United States Government Publications**. GPO, 1895- . Monthly, with semiannual and annual cumulative indexes and serials supplement. LC 4-18088. OCLC 02264351. S/N 021-000-80002-3 (paper). $215/yr. Semiannual index, $32 (separate). Annual index, $72 (separate). Serials supplement, $11 (separate). S/N 021-000-80008-2 (microfiche). $50/yr. Semiannual index, $7 (separate). Annual index, $12 (separate). Serials supplement, $3.50 (separate). **GP3.8:date**.

_____. **Supplements, 1941-42; 1943-44; 1945-46**. 3 vols. GPO, 1947-48.
As the most comprehensive index available for general U.S. government publications, this source is a starting point for many government literature searches. Published since 1895 under various titles, the *Monthly Catalog* attempts to index all unclassified government publications. While the *Monthly Catalog* falls short of this ambitious goal, it does offer the most inclusive coverage of agency and departmental publications in hundreds of subject areas.

This source does not index individual articles in government periodicals, provide abstracts, or comprehensively index technical reports and certain agency special publications, such as those of NASA or the Department of Defense. The *Serials Supplement*, issued annually as a supplement, lists federal publications issued three or more times a year and selected looseleaf services available on subscription from the Superintendent of Documents. This source also serves as a guide to indexes of government periodicals and indicates which titles are self-indexed.

The format of the *Monthly Catalog* changed drastically in mid-1976. Individual entries, which are numbered consecutively throughout each year, were clarified by adding a two-digit prefix for the year. Library of Congress subject headings were incorporated, along with Anglo-American cataloging rules. In addition to personal and agency author, SuDocs classification number, publisher, price, GPO stock number, pagination, depository status, and Library of Congress card number, entries now include the Library of Congress and Dewey classification numbers, OCLC number, and additional subject headings. Indexes include: author, title, subject, series/report number, keyword, and SuDocs classification number.

The *Monthly Catalog* was issued under various titles until 1951, when the present title was adopted. Previous titles were: *Catalogue of Publications Issued by the Government of the United States* (January-March 1895); *Catalogue of the United States Public Documents* (April 1895-June 1907); *Monthly Catalog, United States Public Documents* (July 1907-December 1939); and *United States Government Publications: A Monthly Catalog* (1940-1950).

The three supplements issued in 1947 and 1948 list those publications issued from 1941 to 1946 which were received too late for inclusion in the current issues as well as some declassified materials from the World War II period.

The decennial and quinquennial cumulative indexes are great time-savers. Each index entry refers to the year and the entry number (or page prior to 1948) of the *Monthly Catalog* listing. These indexes provide subject, title, author, and series entries. Names of personal authors were not indexed in the *Monthly Catalog* from 1947 until 1962.

121. Superintendent of Documents. **Monthly Catalog of United States Government Publications. Decennial Cumulative Index, 1941-50**. GPO, 1953. 1,848 pp. **GP3.8/3:941-50**.

This index includes references to the separate supplements issued for 1941-42, 1943-44, and 1945-46 publications in addition to the monthly issues.

122. Superintendent of Documents. **Monthly Catalog of United States Government Publications. Decennial Cumulative Index, 1951-60; Decennial Index to the Monthly Issues from January 1951-December 1960**. 2 vols. GPO, 1968. 2,639 pp. LC 4-18088. **GP3.8/3:951-60/v.1,2.**

123. Superintendent of Documents. **Monthly Catalog of United States Government Publications Cumulative Index, 1961-1965: Index to the Monthly Issues from January 1961-December 1965**. 2 vols. GPO, 1976. 2,505 pp. LC 4-18088. **GP3.8/3:961-65/v.1,2.**

124. Superintendent of Documents. **Monthly Catalog of United States Government Publications Cumulative Index, 1966-1970: Index to the Monthly Issues from January 1966 to December 1970**. 2 vols. GPO, 1978. 2,752 pp. LC 4-18088. S/N 021-000-00086-8. $37 (set). **GP3.8/3:966-70/v.1,2.**

125. Superintendent of Documents. **Monthly Catalog of United States Government Publications Cumulative Index, 1971-1976: Index to the Monthly Issues from January 1971 to June 1976**. 2 vols. GPO, 1981. 2,760 pp. LC 4-18088. S/N 021-000-00103-1. $36 (set). **GP3.8/3:971-76/v.1,2.**

126. Superintendent of Documents. **Monthly Catalog of United States Government Publications Cumulative Index, July 1976-1980 [microfiche]**. GPO, 1983. LC 4-18088. S/N 021-000-00117-1 (microfiche). $24. **GP3.8/3:976-80.**

127. Superintendent of Documents. **New Books**. GPO, 1982- . Bimonthly. Free. **GP3.17/6:vol./no.**
This unannotated listing of new titles placed on sale by the Superintendent of Documents provides abbreviated bibliographic information including title, issuing agency, SuDocs classification number, stock number, and price. Each issue includes an order form. Libraries will receive copies automatically. Others wishing to be added to the mailing list should write to the Superintendent of Documents, Government Printing Office, Washington, DC 20402.

128. Superintendent of Documents. **Numerical Lists and Schedule of Volumes of the Documents and Reports of Congress**. GPO, 1934- . Annual. LC 34-28260. OCLC 07929780. **GP3.7/2:Cong./sess.**
The material contained in the *Numerical Lists* was previously included as a part of the *Document Index* (entry 112). It is a numerical list of the documents and reports of the House of Representatives and the Senate, and the Congressional Serial Set volume in which each publication may be found. It also includes a list by Congressional Serial Set number with the contents of each volume. There is no subject access to the *Numerical Lists* such as was available in the *Document Index*. The *CIS U.S. Serial Set Index*, published by the Congressional Information Service, provides subject and keyword access to the Congressional Serial Set for 1789-1969. The *CIS/Index* from the same publisher covers the period from 1970 forward.

129. Superintendent of Documents. **Subject Bibliographies**. GPO, 1975- . Irregular. Free. **GP3.22/2:nos.**
These handy bibliographies list government publications available from the Superintendent of Documents and related to particular topics. They provide titles of relevant documents, stock number and price, SuDocs classification number, and, in many cases, a description of the publication. An order form is included in each *Subject*

Bibliography (SB). Over two hundred fifty SBs are available free of charge, including the Index (SB-599), which lists SBs by general subject categories. The *Subject Bibliography* series has replaced the *Price Lists*, which were similar in scope. Price List 36, *Government Periodicals and Subscription Services* (entry 119), is the only Price List still available.

To order SBs or the Index write to the Superintendent of Documents, Government Printing Office, Washington, DC 20402. Subject Bibliographies, regularly revised, generally maintain the same SB numbers. A list of current SBs follows. Many are also cited by SB number in subject sections of this book.

2. Consumer Information.

3. Highway Construction, Safety and Traffic.

4. Business and Business Management.

5. Canning, Freezing and Storage of Foods.

6. Minorities.

7. Soil and Soil Management.

8. Diseases in Humans.

9. Solar Energy.

10. Livestock and Poultry.

11. United States Postage Stamps.

12. Federal Aviation Regulations.

13. Aircraft, Airports and Airways.

14. Airman's Information Manual

15. Smoking.

16. Historical Handbook Series.

17. Recreational and Outdoor Activities.

18. Aviation Information and Training Materials.

19. Nursing and Nursing Care.

21. Patents and Trademarks.

22. Dentistry.

23. Hearing and Hearing Disability.

24. Mathematics.

25. United States Reports.

27. Customs, Immunization and Passport Publications.

28. Care and Disorders of the Eyes.

29. Navigation.

30. Social Welfare and Services.

31. Department of Agriculture Yearbooks.

32. Oceanography.

34. Insects.

35. Children and Youth.

36. Crime and Criminal Justice.

37. The Handicapped.

39. Aging.

40. Shipping and Transportation.

41. The Home.
42. Accounting and Auditing.
43. Publications Relating to the National High School Debate Topic.
44. Employment and Occupations.
46. Air Pollution.
48. Radiation and Radioactivity.
49. Motor Vehicles.
50. Water Pollution and Water Resources.
51. Computers and Data Processing.
52. U.S. Court of Customs and Patent Appeals Reports and U.S. Court of International Trade.
53. Electricity and Electronics.
55. Mass Transit.
57. Posters, Charts, Picture Sets and Decals.
59. Revenue Sharing.
63. Noise Abatement.
64. Labor-Management Relations.
65. Cookbooks and Recipes.
66. Internal Revenue Cumulative Bulletins.
67. Board of Tax Appeals and Tax Court Reports.
68. Secondary Education.
69. Immigration, Naturalization, and Citizenship.
70. Mammals and Reptiles.
72. Photography.
73. Motion Pictures, Films, and Audiovisual Information.
74. Juvenile Delinquency.
75. Foreign Affairs of the United States.
76. Firefighting, Prevention, and Forest Fires.
77. Printing and Graphic Arts.
80. Veterans Affairs and Benefits.
81. Rehabilitation.
82. Foreign Languages.
83. Educational Statistics.
85. Financial Aid for Students.
86. Trees, Forest Products, and Forest Management.
87. Stenography, Typing and Writing.
88. Environmental Education and Protection.
90. Federal Government Forms.
91. Courts and Correctional Institutions.
92. Day Care.
93. Background Notes.
94. Irrigation and Reclamation.
95. Waste Management.

97. National and World Economy.

98. Military History.

99. Minerals Yearbook.

100. Federal Trade Commission Decisions and Publications.

102. Maps and Atlases (United States and Foreign).

104. Heart and Circulatory System.

106. Presidents of the United States.

107. Art and Artists.

108. Workers' Compensation.

109. Weights and Measures.

110. Vocational and Career Education.

111. Women.

114. Directories and Lists of Persons and Organizations.

115. Astronomy and Astrophysics.

116. Wildlife Management.

117. Law Enforcement.

118. Annual Reports.

119. Hospitals.

121. Vital and Health Statistics.

122. Public Health.

123. Foreign Trade and Tariff.

125. Marketing Research.

126. Copyrights.

127. Disarmament and Arms Control.

128. Banks and Banking.

129. Procurement, Supply Cataloging and Classification.

130. Publications en Español (Spanish Publications).

131. Armed Forces.

132. Engineering Other Than Civil.

133. National Bureau of Standards Handbooks and Monographs.

137. Teachers and Teaching Methods.

138. Building Sciences Series.

139. National Standard Reference Data Series.

140. Public Buildings, Landmarks and Historic Sites of the United States.

141. Federal Government.

142. Poetry and Literature.

143. Fossils.

144. American Revolution.

146. Census of Manufactures.

148. National Bureau of Standards Technical Notes.

149. Census of Transportation.

150. Libraries and Library Collections.

151. Minerals and Mining.
152. Census of Business.
153. National Defense and Security.
154. Medicine and Medical Science.
156. Census of Governments.
157. Census of Construction.
158. Army Technical and Field Manuals.
160. Earth Sciences.
161. Farms and Farming.
162. Agricultural Research, Statistics, and Economic Reports.
163. Drug Education.
164. Reading.
165. Social Security.
166. Foreign Area Studies.
167. Mental Health.
168. Rural Electrification Administration (REA) Forms and Bulletins.
169. Postal Service.
170. National Park Service Folders.
171. How to Sell to Government Agencies.
173. Naval Personnel Bureau and Naval Education Training Command Publications.
174. U.S. Court of Claims Reports.
175. Alcoholism.
176. Publications Relating to the College Debate Topic.
177. Birds.
181. Census of Population.
182. United States Air Force Manuals.
183. Surveying and Mapping.
185. Digest of U.S. Practice in International Law and Digest of International Law.
186. Civil Aeronautics Board Reports.
187. Interstate Commerce Commission Decisions and Reports.
190. Federal Maritime Commission Publications.
191. Treaties and Other International Agreements of the United States.
192. Civil War.
195. Taxes and Taxation.
196. Elementary Education.
197. United States Code, 1982.
198. Coins and Medals.
200. Atomic Energy and Nuclear Power.
201. Congress.
202. Personnel Management, Guidance and Counseling.

204. Budget of the United States Government and Economic Report of the President.

205. Anthropology and Archeology.

207. Civil Rights and Equal Opportunity.

209. Fish and Marine Life.

210. Foreign Relations of the United States.

211. Intergovernmental Relations.

213. Occupational Safety and Health Publications.

214. Adult Education.

215. Architecture.

216. Construction Industry.

217. Higher Education.

218. Railroads.

219. Naval Facilities Engineering Command Publications.

220. National Science Foundation Publications.

221. Music.

222. NASA Educational Publications.

223. School Administration, Buildings, and Equipment.

225. Ships, Shipping, and Shipbuilding.

226. Prices, Wages and the Cost of Living.

227. Pesticides, Insecticides, Fungicides, and Rodenticides.

228. Congressional Directory.

229. Accidents and Accident Prevention.

231. Where You Can Obtain Government Specifications, Federal Standards, Drawings, and the Indexes Which List These Specifications.

234. Weather.

235. Foreign Education.

236. United States Naval History.

237. Marine Corps Publications.

238. Conservation.

239. Physical Fitness.

241. Disaster Preparedness and Civil Defense.

243. Science Experiments and Projects.

244. U.S. Government Printing Office Publications.

245. Voting and Elections.

246. Alcohol, Tobacco, and Firearms.

247. General Services Administration Publications.

249. Bureau of Reclamation Publications.

250. General Accounting Office Publications.

252. Smithsonian Institution Popular Publications.

256. Bureau of Land Management Publications.

257. NASA Scientific and Technical Publications.

258. Grants and Awards.

259. Subversive Activities.
260. National Ocean Survey Publications.
261. U.S. Army Corps of Engineers Publications.
262. United States Coast Guard Publications.
267. National Credit Union Administration Publications.
270. Occupational Outlook Handbook.
271. National Bureau of Standards Special Publications.
272. United States Intelligence Activities.
273. Statistical Publications.
275. Foreign Investments.
277. Census of Agriculture.
278. Canada.
279. Soviet Union.
280. Housing, Urban and Rural Development.
281. Federal Communications Commission.
282. Congressional Budget Office Publications.
284. Africa.
285. Retirement.
286. Middle East.
287. Latin America and the Caribbean.
288. Asia and Oceania.
289. Europe (Including the United Kingdom).
291. Food, Diet, and Nutrition.
292. Family Planning.
294. Insurance.
295. Securities and Investments.
296. Telecommunications.
297. Space, Rockets, and Satellites.
298. Public and Private Utilities.
299. China.
300. Office of Personnel Management Publications.
301. Gardening.
302. Travel and Tourism.
303. Energy Management for Consumers and Businesses.
304. Energy Supplies, Prices, and Consumption.
305. Energy Policy: Issues and Programs.
306. Energy Conservation and Research Technology.
307. Small Business.
308. Civil and Structural Engineering.

130. Superintendent of Documents. **United States Government Books**. GPO, 1982- . Quarterly. Free. **GP3.17/5:vol./no.**

This is an annotated listing of about one thousand document "best sellers," including general books, magazines, and posters, organized into subject categories. Citations include bibliographic information, price, and annotations. This quarterly title replaces the now defunct *Selected U.S. Government Publications*, but, unlike the "Selected List," the listings will not change with each issue. "The catalog will be reviewed quarterly but the selection of books will remain essentially static, with only a small percentage of poor sellers being rotated out and an equal number of promising new titles being substituted."

For a free copy write to: New Catalog, Superintendent of Documents, Government Printing Office, Washington, DC 20402. Libraries and people on the mailing list for Price List 36, *Government Periodicals and Subscription Services*, will automatically receive copies of *U.S. Government Books*. Unlike the "Selected List," there will be no permanent mailing list for each quarterly issue, although purchasers from one edition will receive the next edition.

See also SB 244.

Abbreviations

NOTE: When ordering Joint Publications Research Service publications from the National Technical Information Service (NTIS), give the JPRS number in the order. Do not give the SuDocs classification number.

131. Joint Publications Research Service. **Reference Aid: Abbreviations, Acronyms, and Special Terms Used in the Hungarian Press.** NTIS, 1978. 234 pp. (JPRS 70644.) OCLC 3688304. **Y3.J66:13/70644.**

132. Joint Publications Research Service. **Reference Aid: Abbreviations, Acronyms, and Special Terms Used in the Turkish Press.** NTIS, 1976. 100 pp. (JPRS 66849.) OCLC 2044742. **Y3.J66:13/66849.**

133. Joint Publications Research Service. **Reference Aid: Abbreviations and Acronyms Used in Bulgarian Press.** Comp. by Theodore Guerchon. NTIS, 1978. 324 pp. (JPRS 71080.) OCLC 3925472. **Y3.J66:13/71080.**

134. Joint Publications Research Service. **Reference Aid: Abbreviations in Cambodian and Lao Press, Asia.** (English and French.) NTIS, 1974. 59 pp. (JPRS 62295.) **Y3.J66:13/62295.**

135. Joint Publications Research Service. **Reference Aid: Abbreviations in Latin American Press, Latin America.** NTIS, 1975. (JPRS 64152.) **Y3.J66:13/64152.**

136. Joint Publications Research Service. **Reference Aid: Abbreviations in Romanian Press, East Europe.** (English and Romanian.) NTIS, 1974. 72 pp. (JPRS 62348.) **Y3.J66:13/62348.**

137. Joint Publications Research Service. **Reference Aid: Glossary of Abbreviations, Acronyms, and Terms Used in West European Press, West Europe.** NTIS, 1973. 62 pp. (JPRS 58963.) **Y3.J66:13/58963.**

138. Joint Publications Research Service. **Reference Aid: Glossary of Special Terms, Acronyms and Abbreviations As Used in East German and Other German Publications, East Europe.** NTIS, 1975. 166 pp. (JPRS 64561.) **Y3.J66:13/64561.**

139.   Library of Congress. Aerospace Technology Division. **Glossary of Russian Abbreviations and Acronyms**. GPO, 1967. 806 pp. LC 68-60006. PG2963.U47. Free from the Central Services Division, Library of Congress, Washington, DC 20540. **LC38.2:R92.**

Previous editions (1952 and 1957) are titled *Russian Abbreviations: A Selective List*. Over twenty-three thousand abbreviations commonly used by authors, scientists, journalists, librarians, and others in Soviet publications since World War II are included. These entries were selected from the over forty thousand abbreviations in the Aerospace Technology Division, and therefore the emphasis is on scientific and technical terms. Entries contain Russian abbreviations, Russian words in full, transliterated abbreviations, and English translations of words in full. A brief bibliography of sources is included.

140.   Library of Congress. Slavic and Central European Division. **Czech and Slovak Abbreviations: A Selective List**. Ed. by Paul Horecky. IA, 1956. 164 pp. LC 56-60067.

This compilation includes a number of abbreviations that were collected by Ludovit G. Ruhmann in connection with his work as editor of the *East European Accessions List*. Entries for the most part denote governmental, political, economic, cultural, and social bodies and some technical terms. Entries include abbreviation, full name, and English translation.

141.   Library of Congress. Slavic and Central European Division. **Polish Abbreviations: A Selective List**. Comp. by Janina Wojcicka. IA, 1957. 2d ed., rev. and enl. 164 pp. LC 57-60055.

This list contains about twenty-five hundred abbreviations that have been used commonly since World War II, particularly names of corporate bodies. Full Polish and English forms are given.

142.   Library of Congress. Slavic and Central European Division. **Yugoslav Abbreviations: A Selective List**. By Llija P. Plamenatz. GPO, 1962. 2d ed. 198 pp. LC 62-60076. PG1386.P55 1962. **LC35.2:Y9/2/962.**

This includes the more common abbreviations that have come into use since World War II, especially names of government institutions and official bodies, industrial and trade establishments, and the more important newspapers and periodicals. The abbreviation is followed by the full name, the English translation, and, for organizations, the location. Asterisks denote abbreviations other than Serbo-Croat.

Biographical Sources

143. Library of Congress. General Reference and Bibliography Division. **Biographical Sources for Foreign Countries**. 4 pts. GPO, 1944-45. LC 45-35383. Z5301.U5. **LC2.2:F76/6/pt.1-4**.

> Part 1. **General**. Comp. by Helen D. Jones. 1944. 76 pp.
>
> Part 2. **Germany and Austria**. Comp. by Nelson Burr. 1945. 211 pp. Available to U.S. libraries and institutions from the Central Services Division, Library of Congress, Washington, DC 20540.
>
> Part 3. **Philippines**. Comp. by Helen D. Jones. 1945. 60 pp.
>
> Part 4. **Japanese Empire**. Comp. by Nelson Burr. 1945. 114 pp. Available to U.S. libraries and institutions from the Central Services Division, Library of Congress, Washington, DC 20540.

These bibliographies were designed to be a guide to biographical sources for living people in foreign countries and were limited to materials published from about 1925 through 1944. A wide variety of tools are listed and annotated. They are indexed by authors and subjects.

144. Library of Congress. General Reference and Bibliography Division. **Biographical Sources for the United States**. Comp. by Jane Kline. GPO, 1961. 58 pp. LC 61-60065. Z5301.U53. (Repr.: Gregg Press, $8.25.)

This "annotated bibliography is presented as a guide to current biographical information about living Americans, especially those who have made notable contributions to the arts and the professions, to business and corporate enterprise, and to military and civilian affairs." The bibliography lists 163 state, federal, and commercially issued biographical dictionaries and directories from the Library of Congress collection. Most were published between 1945 and 1960. Arrangement is by broad subjects. There are author, keyword title, and subject indexes.

145. Library of Congress. Orientalia Division. **Eminent Chinese of the Ch'ing Period, 1644-1912**. Ed. by Arthur W. Hummel. 2 vols. GPO, 1943-44. LC 43-53640. (Repr.: Chinese Materials Center, 2 vols. in 1, $26.67.) **LC17.2: C43/2/v.1-2**.

This major work of Chinese biography sketches the biographies of about eight hundred people from 1644 to 1912. Entries are detailed and contain bibliographic source notes. Some people living after 1912 were also included.

See also SB 114.

Library Science

GENERAL

146. Library of Congress. **For Congress and the Nation: A Chronological History of the Library of Congress**. By John Y. Cole. GPO, 1977. 196 pp., illus. LC 76-608365. Z733.U6C565. 027.5753. S/N 030-003-00018-7. $12. **LC1.2:C76/6.**
A chronology of events details the origins of the Library of Congress's principal collections, services, and administrative units. Emphasis is on the early development of collections, and how the Library of Congress acquired its many functions. The chronology spans 1774 to 1975.

147. Office of Education. **Library Science Dissertations, 1925-60: An Annotated Bibliography of Doctoral Studies**. Comp. by Nathan M. Cohen et al. GPO, 1963. 120 pp. (Bulletin 1963, no. 38.) **FS5.215:15044.**
This bibliography attempts to provide summaries of all dissertations related to library science completed between 1925 and 1960. It includes dissertations accepted by all accredited U.S. library schools and those from other university departments when library science is a main concern. It is arranged first by broad subjects (administration, readers' services, technical services, etc.) and then chronologically. Entries are numbered, and there are author and subject indexes.

BIBLIOGRAPHIES

148. Library of Congress. General Reference and Bibliography Division. **African Libraries, Book Production, and Archives: A List of References**. Comp. by Helen F. Conover. IA, 1962. 64 pp. LC 62-64603. Z857.U54. **LC2.2:Af8/9.**

CATALOGING AND CLASSIFICATION

149. Library of Congress. **Special Problems in Serials Cataloging**. By Judith Proctor Cannan. IA, 1979. 97 pp. LC 79-013774. Z695.7.C34. 025.3/4/3. **LC1.2:Se6/4.**

150. Library of Congress. Catalog Publication Division. **Name Authorities. Cumulative Microform Edition**. IA, 1977/79- . Quarterly. LC 79-647358. Z695.1.P4. OCLC 05996698. **LC30.21:date.**

This listing contains all name authority records in the computerized master file at the Library of Congress. Each issue completely supersedes its predecessor. The first issue was accompanied by a pamphlet describing its scope and use.

151. Library of Congress. Dewey Classification Office. **Dewey Decimal Classification and Relative Index.** 3 vols. IA, 1979, 19th ed. 3,273 pp. LC 77-27967. Z696.D519 1979. 025.4/3. Available from Forest Press, $150 per set or $35 per vol. plus postage and handling. **LC37.8:date.**

_____. **11th Abridged Edition.** IA, 1979. 618 pp. LC 78-12514. Z696.D5192 1979. Available from Forest Press, $27 plus postage and handling.

152. Library of Congress. Processing Department. **Library of Congress Filing Rules.** IA, 1980. 111 pp. LC 80-607944. Z695.95.R37 1980. OCLC 6627804. Available from the Cataloging Distribution Service, Library of Congress, Washington, DC 20541. **LC30.6:F47/980.**
This title supersedes *Filing Rules for the Dictionary Catalogs of the Library of Congress* (1956). These filing rules are designed to meet the changing cataloging procedures of Anglo-American cataloging rules 2 (AACR2). Interfiling of pre-AACR2 cards is shown. Examples for each rule are included.

153. Library of Congress. Subject Cataloging Division. **Library of Congress Classification, A-Z.** IA, 1917- . All are available from the Cataloging Distribution Service, Library of Congress, Washington, DC 20541, at the price indicated below. **LC26.9:ltrs.**

    A. **General Works.** 1973. 4th ed. 40 pp. LC 73-8530. Z696.U5A 1973. $5.

    B. **Philosophy and Religion.** Part 1. **B-BJ. Philosophy and Psychology.** 1979. 3d ed. 250 pp. LC 79-526. Z696.U5B1 1979. 025.4/6/1. OCLC 4638910. $10.

    B. **Philosophy and Religion.** Part 2. **BL-BX. Religion.** 1962. 2d ed. 639 pp. LC 62-60072. Z696.U5B2 1962. 025.4/6/2. OCLC 2655824. $4.50.

    C. **Auxiliary Sciences of History.** 1975. 3d ed. 126 pp. LC 75-619090. Z696.U5C 1975. 025.4/6/9. OCLC 1323498. $6.75.

    D. **History: General and Old World.** 1959 (repr. with supplementary pages 1966). 2d ed. 802 pp. LC 65-62173. Z696.U5D 1966. $4.25.

    E-F. **History: America.** 1958 (repr. with supplementary pages 1965). 3d ed. 630 pp. LC 65-60055. Z696.U5E 1965. OCLC 2680701. $3.50.

    G. **Geography, Maps, Anthropology, Recreation.** 1976. 4th ed. 435 pp. LC 76-4560. Z696.U5G 1976. 025.4/6. OCLC 2072793. $15.

    H. **Social Sciences. Subclasses H-HJ. Economics.** 1981. 4th ed. 400 pp. LC 80-607827. Z696.U5H-HJ 1981. 025.4/63/2/19. OCLC 6920697. $10.

    H. **Social Sciences. Subclasses HM-HX. Sociology.** 1980. 4th ed. 169 pp. LC 80-607033. Z696.U5HM-HX 1980. 025.4/6301. OCLC 6279373. $10.

    J. **Political Science.** 1924 (repr. with supplementary pages 1966). 595 pp. LC 66-60021. Z696.U51 1966. $4.

    K. **Law. Subclass K. Law (General).** 1977. 92 pp. LC 76-58352. Z696.U5K23 1977. 025.4/6/34. OCLC 2968626. $6.

    K. **Law. Subclass KD. Law of the United Kingdom and Ireland.** 1973. 163 pp. LC 73-8416. Z696.U5K 1973. $5.75.

K. **Law. Subclass KE. Law of Canada.** 1976. 181 pp. LC 76-54307. Z696.U5K4 1976. 025.4/6/34. OCLC 2597374. $10.

K. **Law. Subclass KF. Law of the United States.** 1969. Prelim. ed. 333 pp. LC 69-60005. Z696.U5K 1969. 025.4/6/3400973. $5.

K. **Law. Subclass KK-KKC. Law of Germany.** 1982. 581 pp. LC 82-600185. Z696.U5K7 1982. $20.

L. **Education.** 1951 (repr. with supplementary pages 1966). 3d ed. 269 pp. LC 66-61846. Z696.U5L 1966. 025.4/6/37. $2.

M. **Music and Books on Music.** 1978. 3d ed. 228 pp. LC 78-606179. 025.4/6/78. OCLC 3839020. $7.

N. **Fine Arts.** 1970. 4th ed. 280 leaves. LC 78-606523. Z696.U5N 1970. $3.

P. **Philology and Literature. Subclasses P-PA. Philology, Linguistics, Classical Philology, Classical Literature.** 1928 (repr. with supplementary pages 1968). 510 pp. LC 67-61607. Z696.U5P6 1968. 025.4/6/4. OCLC 582688. $3.25.

P. **Philology and Literature. Subclass PA. Supplement. Byzantine and Modern Greek Literature, Medieval and Modern Latin Literature.** 1942 (repr. with supplementary pages 1968). 25 pp. LC 68-60095. Z696.U5P613 1968. 025.4/6/88. OCLC 452477. 75 cents.

P. **Philology and Literature. Subclasses PB-PH. Modern European Languages.** 1933 (repr. with supplementary pages 1966). 276 pp. LC 65-62403. Z696.U5P63 1966. OCLC 581749. $2.50.

P. **Philology and Literature. Subclasses PJ-PM. Languages and Literatures of Asia, Africa, Oceania, America, Mixed Languages, Artificial Languages.** 1935 (repr. with supplementary pages 1965). 435 pp. LC 65-60071. Z696.U5P64 1965. OCLC 581751. $3.25.

P. **Philology and Literature. Subclasses P-PM. Supplement. Index to Languages and Dialects.** 1957 (repr. with supplementary pages 1965). 2d ed. 76 pp. LC 65-61907. Z696.U5P65 1965. 025.4/6/84. OCLC 581734. 90 cents.

P. **Philology and Literature. Subclass PG (in part). Russian Literature.** 1948 (repr. with supplementary pages 1965). 271 pp. LC 65-60025. Z696.U5P635 1965. $2.

P. **Philology and Literature. Subclasses PN, PR, PS, PZ. General Literature, English and American Literature, Fiction in English, Juvenile Belles Lettres.** 1978. 2d ed. 351 pp. LC 78-2091. Z696.U5P7 1978. 025.4/6/8. OCLC 3706915. $8.

P. **Philology and Literature. Subclass PQ,** Part 1. **French Literature.** 1936 (repr. with supplementary pages 1966). 202 pp. LC 66-61874. Z696.U5P8 1966. 025.4/6/84. $1.75.

P. **Philology and Literature. Subclass PQ,** Part 2. **Italian, Spanish, and Portuguese Literatures.** 1937 (repr. with supplementary pages 1965). 252 pp. LC 65-60056. Z696.U5P82 1965. 025.4. OCLC 2680703. $2.

P. **Philology and Literature. Subclass PT,** Part 1. **German Literature.** 1938 (repr. with supplementary pages 1966). 329 pp. LC 66-60026. Z696.U5P85 1966. 025.4683. OCLC 581743. $2.35.

P. **Philology and Literature. Subclass PT,** Part 2. **Dutch and Scandinavian Literatures.** 1942 (repr. with supplementary pages 1965). 134 pp. LC 65-60061. Z696.U5P87 1965. $1.

P. **Philology and Literature. Subclasses P-PZ. Language and Literature Tables.** 1982. 43 leaves. LC 81-23640. Z696.U5P88 1982. $7.

Q. **Science.** 1973. 6th ed. 415 pp. LC 72-10222. Z696.U5Q 1973. $9.

R. **Medicine.** 1980. 4th ed. 363 pp. LC 79-607135. Z696.U5R 1980. 025.4/6/61. OCLC 5891633. $10.

S. **Agriculture.** 1982. 4th ed. 278 pp. LC 82-600303. Z696.U5S 1982. OCLC 581763. $15.

T. **Technology.** 1971. 5th ed. 370 pp. LC 76-611341. Z696.U5T 1971. $3.50.

U. **Military Science.** 1974. 5th ed. 75 leaves. LC 74-12064. Z696.U5U 1974. $5.

V. **Naval Science.** 1974. 3d ed. 91 pp. LC 74-12087. Z696.U5V 1974. $5.25.

Z. **Bibliography and Library Science.** 1980. 5th ed. 354 pp. LC 80-607921. Z696.U5Z 1980. 025.4/602/2/19. OCLC 6816279. $10.

154. Library of Congress. Subject Cataloging Division. **LC Classification, Additions, and Changes.** IA, quarterly. Z696.U51. OCLC 01768490. Available from the Cataloging Distribution Service, Library of Congress, Washington, DC 20541. $50/yr. **LC26.9/2:date.**

155. Library of Congress. Subject Cataloging Division. **LC Classification Outline.** IA, 1978. 4th ed. 32 pp. LC 77-608191. Z696.U40 1978. OCLC 3538112.

156. Library of Congress. Subject Cataloging Division. **LC Period Subdivisions under Names of Places.** Comp. by Marguerite V. Quattlebaum. IA, 1975. 2d ed. 111 pp. LC 75 619095. Z695.1.G4U5 1975. Available from the Cataloging Distribution Service, Library of Congress, Washington, DC 20541. $2. **LC26.2:P41/975.**

157. Library of Congress. Subject Cataloging Division. **Library of Congress Subject Headings.** 2 vols. IA, 1979. 9th ed. LC 79-22742. Z695.U4749 1980. Available from the Cataloging Distribution Service, Library of Congress, Washington, DC 20541. $75. **LC26.7:8/ed.**

_____. **Supplement to LC Subject Headings.** IA, 1974- . Three quarterly issues and annual cumulation. OCLC 03456919. $60/yr.
This is the standard subject heading authority used in large libraries. It is a dictionary listing of subject headings used in the Library of Congress catalog with cross references to and from related subjects.

158. Library of Congress. Subject Cataloging Division. **Subject Headings in Microform.** IA, 1976- . Quarterly. Available from the Cataloging Distribution Service, Library of Congress, Washington, DC 20541. OCLC 03454199. $60/yr. **LC26.7/2:date.**
The introduction is available separately in book form, and not in microform. Each issue is cumulative.

159. National Library of Medicine. **Medical Subject Headings: Annotated Alphabetic List.** NTIS, annual. Z695.1.M48U52c. 025.3361. OCLC 3198173. 1983 ed. PB83-223 156 **HE20.3612/3-4:yr.**
This is an alphabetic listing of all subject descriptors used for cataloging and indexing at the National Library of Medicine. It includes subject headings, cross references,

geographic headings, non-MESH terms, check tags, tree numbers, and notes for indexers, catalogers, and online searchers.

160. National Library of Medicine. **Medical Subject Headings: Tree Structures.** NTIS, annual. Z695.1.M48U52b. 025.3361. OCLC 1778210. 1984 ed. PB83-223 164. **HE20.3612/3-5:yr.**

161. National Library of Medicine. **National Library of Medicine Classification: A Scheme for the Shelf Arrangement of Books in the Field of Medicine and Its Related Sciences.** GPO, 1981. 4th ed. 441 pp., illus. Z697.M4U5 1981. 025.4/6/61. OCLC 3868842. S/N 017-052-00222-8. $16. **HE20.3602:C56/981.**
First published in 1951, this classification scheme covers medicine and related sciences, using schedules permanently excluded from Library of Congress classification (QS-QZ and W). This volume contains the schedules and index to the classification.

162. National Library of Medicine. **Permuted Medical Subject Headings.** NTIS, 1979- . Annual. LC 80-645349. Z695.1.M48U52d. 025.4/961. OCLC 03467406. 1984 ed. PB83-234 781. **HE20.3612/3-3:yr.**

DIRECTORIES

163. Bureau of Education. **Special Collections in Libraries in the United States.** By William Dawson Johnston and I. G. Mudge. GPO, 1912. 140 pp. (Bulletin 1912, no. 23.) **I16.3:912/23.**
This directory should be consulted as an historical work only. It has a subject arrangement with library names, statistics, descriptions of collections, and references to other sources and is indexed by subject and library names.

164. National Center for Education Statistics. **Directory of Library Networks and Cooperative Library Organizations.** GPO, 1980- . OCLC 07021460. **ED1.102: L61/yr.**
Based on the first national survey of cooperative library organizations, this directory provides otherwise elusive resource materials for researchers, students, and the public. Libraries included are those engaging in cooperative activities beyond the scope of traditional interlibrary loans and reciprocal borrowing. Organizations are listed within each state, with information on address, telephone number, director's name, whether computerized, teletype number, participation, and activities.

PRESERVATION OF MATERIALS

165. Library of Congress. **Bookbinding and the Conservation of Books: A Dictionary of Descriptive Terminology.** By Matt T. Roberts and Don Etherington. GPO, 1982. 296 pp., illus. LC 81-607974. Z266.7.R62. 686.3'03. OCLC 07555465. S/N 030-000-00126-5. $27. **LC1.2:B64/3.**
This is the first comprehensive dictionary of the nomenclature of bookbinding, with definitions drawn from the most authoritative sources available. It provides succinct, up-to-date definitions and explanations, biographical vignettes, and a bibliography. It is enhanced by color plates of endpapers and rare bindings.

166. Library of Congress. **Boxes for the Protection of Rare Books: Their Design and Construction.** By Margaret R. Brown. GPO, 1982. 293 pp., illus. LC 81-607965. Z1029.B76. 676'.32. OCLC 07555459. S/N 030-000-00124-9. $18. **LC1.2:B69.**

Intended to serve as a standard reference in the field of book preservation, this comprehensive guide gives detailed instructions and step-by-step drawings for eight types of boxes for housing and protecting volumes. Each box has special features to solve specific problems in protecting books of value, rarity, aesthetic qualities, or special condition.

167. Library of Congress. Geography and Map Division. **Maps: Their Care, Repair, and Preservation in Libraries.** By Clara Egli LeGear. IA, 1956. Rev. ed. 75 pp. LC 56-60030. Z692.M3U6 1956.

STATISTICS

168. National Center for Education Statistics. **Library Human Resources: A Study of Supply and Demand.** By King Research, Inc. IA, 1983. 229 pp., illus. OCLC 10001160. **ED1.115:L61.**

An update of *Library Manpower: A Study of Demand and Supply* (1975), this report describes projected changes in the employment of librarians through 1990.

169. National Center for Education Statistics. **Library Statistics of Colleges and Universities. Institutional Data.** IA, 1971- . Annual. LC 72-627021. Z675.U5U54. 027.7/0973. OCLC 01779122. **ED1.122:yr.**

Data are provided on college library collections, expenditures, staff, salaries, services, and management, including institutional-level data on control of the library, collections, and expenditures. A companion volume, *Library Statistics of Colleges and Universities: Trends 1968-1977, Summary Data 1977* (PB82-127275), discusses trends in collections, circulation, loans, staffing, and expenditures and relates these data to enrollment and the cost of living.

170. National Center for Education Statistics. **Statistics of Public Libraries.** GPO, 1956- . Quadrennial. OCLC 3366368. **ED1.122/2:yr.**

Basic statistics on library collections, staffing, expenditures, receipts, loans, and facilities are arranged by region, population served, and location in the standard metropolitan statistical areas (SMSAs).

See also SB 150.

Microforms

171. Library of Congress. Processing Department. **British Manuscripts Project: A Checklist of the Microfilms Prepared in England and Wales for the American Council of Learned Societies. 1941-45**. Comp. by Lester K. Born. IA, 1955. 179 pp. LC 55-60041. Z6620.G7U5. (Repr.: Greenwood Press, $18.75.)

The contents of 2,652 reels of microfilm that were the result of a project carried on during World War II are listed. With the cooperation of the Library of Congress and the British Museum, the Carnegie United Kingdom Trust microfilmed manuscripts and rare printed documents housed in libraries in England and Wales.

172. Library of Congress. Processing Department. **National Register of Microform Masters**. IA, 1965- . Annual. LC 65-29419. Z1033.M5N3. 011. OCLC 0936298. Available from the Cataloging Distribution Service, Library of Congress, Washington, DC 20541 at price listed below.

    1965-75. 6 vols. $190.

    1976. 807 pp. $35.

    1977. 1,018 pp. $50.

    1978. 2 vols. $85.

    1979. 1,096 pp. $100.

    1980. 1,213 pp. $110.

    1981. 2 vols. $125.

This is a catalog of library materials which have been filmed and for which master negatives exist from which copies can be made. It covers only master microforms kept for the purpose of making copies, and master preservation microforms stored under optimum conditions by nonprofit institutions. Master microforms for foreign and U.S. books, pamphlets, serials, and foreign doctoral dissertations are listed. Those for technical reports, typescript collections, U.S. dissertations and master's theses, and newspapers are omitted. Newspapers are covered in a separate publication, *Newspapers in Microform*. Archival materials and manuscripts are covered in the *National Union Catalog of Manuscript Collections*. Because most of the entries in the *Register* are duplicated in the National Union Catalog, full bibliographic data are given in the latter. Entries include author, condensed title, imprint, collation, and location code.

Museums

173. Library of Congress. American Folklife Center. **Maritime Folklife Resources: A Directory and Index.** By Peter Bartis. IA, 1980. 129 pp. (Publications of the American Folklife Center, no. 5.) LC 80-602335. GR105.B37. OCLC 6399626. **LC39.9:5.**
The directory lists museums and other institutions with holdings on vessels and water-related activities. The institution name, address, phone number, hours, and a description of holdings and activities are given.

174. National Endowment for the Arts. **Museums USA: A Survey Report.** GPO, 1979. 740 pp. **NF2.2:M97/3.**
This report represents information gleaned from a major survey of museums; it is designed to present a comprehensive snapshot of the state of the nation's museums. Tables and notes cover the formation, character, and distribution of museums; their purposes and functions; programs; collections and exhibitions; accessibility and attendance; personnel; trustees; facilities; and finances.

175. National Park Service. **Manual for Museums.** By Ralph H. Lewis. GPO. 1976 (repr. 1980). 412 pp. LC 75-025982. AM5.L48. 069/.0973. OCLC 1584039. S/N 024-005-00643-5. $8.50. **I29.9/2:M97.**
A standard reference for museum workers, this publication was inspired by *Field Manual for Museums* (1941), which went out of print during World War II but continued to be in demand. This manual emphasizes day-to-day museum operations and curatorial standards, and brings the literature of good museum practice up to date.

176. Smithsonian Institution. Office of Museum Programs. **Museum Studies Programs in the United States and Abroad.** IA, 1979. 96 pp. Includes Addendum, 1978. OCLC 5134203. **SI1.2:M97/4/976/add.**
This nonevaluative listing of museum training opportunities in numerous countries briefly describes the type of program offered and gives the contact person and address for more information.

Style Manuals

177. Government Printing Office. **U.S. Government Printing Office Style Manual.** GPO, 1984. 28th ed. 479 pp. LC 84-600037. Z253.U58 1984. 808'.02. S/N 021-000-00121-0. $15. **GP1.23/4:St9/984.**

This GPO printer's stylebook includes rules for submission of copy to the GPO. The manual is useful for achieving uniform word and type treatment and economy of word use. This edition reflects the newer language of electronic photocomposition, but retains traditional printing terminology to bridge the gap between the old and new printing methods.

178. Government Printing Office. **Word Division: Supplement to Government Printing Office Style Manual.** GPO, 1984. 120 pp. S/N 021-000-00123-6. $2.25. **GP1.23/4:St9/984.**

This pocket-size supplement to the GPO *Style Manual* shows proper line breaks for tens of thousands of words.

179. Library of Congress. General Reference and Bibliography Division. **Bibliographical Procedures and Style: A Manual for Bibliographers in the Library of Congress.** By Blanche F. McCrum and Helen D. Jones. GPO, 1954 (repr. 1966). 133 pp. LC 66-60057. Z1001.U63 1966. Free from the Central Services Division, Library of Congress, Washington, DC 20540. **LC2.8:B47/966.**

Part Two

Social Sciences

General Works

180. Library of Congress. **Directory of Information Resources in the United States: Social Sciences**. GPO, rev. 1973. 700 pp. LC 73-3297. AS25.A46. S/N 030-000-00065-0. $12. **LC1.31:D62/2/973**.

Anthropology and Ethnology

GENERAL WORKS

181. Bureau of American Ethnology. **General Index to Reports of the Bureau of American Ethnology: Volumes 1-48, 1879-1931.** By Biren Bonnerjea. GPO, 1931. (Annual Report, 1931, pp. 25-1,220.) **SI2.1:931.**
This index to annual reports was published in the 48th annual report of the Bureau of American Ethnology.

182. Bureau of American Ethnology. **Index to Bulletins 1-100.** By Biren Bonnerjea. GPO, 1963. (Bulletin 178.) LC 64-60461. **SI2.3:178.**
In addition to indexing Bureau of American Ethnology *Bulletins* numbers 1-100, this publication indexes *Contributions to North American Ethnology* (published by the Department of the Interior as part of the Powell Survey, 1874-79), and miscellaneous Bureau of American Ethnology publications. It includes author, title, subject, and illustrations indexes.

183. Bureau of American Ethnology. **List of Publications with Index to Authors and Titles, Revised to December 31, 1961.** GPO, 1962. 132 pp. **SI2.5:961.**

184. Immigration Commission. **Dictionary of Races or Peoples.** By Daniel Folkmar. GPO, 1911, 150 pp. (Reports of the Immigration Commission, vol. 5.) (Senate document 662, 61st Congress, 3d session.) **Congressional Serial Set 5867.**
"Intended primarily as a discussion of the various races and peoples indigenous to the countries furnishing the present immigration movement to the United States or which may become sources of future immigration" (Preface). The dictionary covers more than six hundred subjects with cross references to related subjects. A five-page correction was issued in *Reports of the Immigration Commission*, volume 7.

AMERICAN INDIANS

North American Indians

General Works

185. Bureau of Indian Affairs. **Information Profiles of Indian Reservations in Arizona, Nevada, and Utah.** IA, 1976. 186 pp. OCLC 2126679. **I20.2:R31/4.**
Profiles based on data collected in 1975 include information on employment, housing, education, income, and health on specific reservations. Bureau of Indian Affairs and tribal officials and offices are also identified.

186. National Archives and Records Service. **Guide to Records in the National Archives of the United States Relating to American Indians.** Comp. by Edward Hill. GPO, 1981. 467 pp., illus. LC 81-022357. Z1209.2.U5H54. 016.3231/97/073. OCLC 08052671. S/N 022-002-00098-8. $13. **GS1.6/6:Am3.**
This is a descriptive list and location guide for materials in the National Archives concerning American Indians and the relations between them and the U.S. government and the American people. It deals primarily with Indians in tribes with which the United States has had a relationship through the Bureau of Indian Affairs or military operations.

187. National Archives and Records Service. **List of Cartographic Records of the Bureau of Indian Affairs.** Comp. by Laura E. Kelsay. IA, Rev. 1977. 187 pp. (Special list no. 13.) LC 77-009434. CD3035.B8 1977. 016.912/73. OCLC 3034532. **GS4.7:13/3.**
The list provides revised descriptions of cartographic records of the Bureau of Indian Affairs (BIA) maintained as central maps files and originally listed in the 1954 edition of this title, along with descriptions from ten BIA divisions, a few Indian agencies, and field offices. All maps listed may be examined or reproduced.

188. Smithsonian Institution. **Material Culture of the Numa: The John Wesley Powell Collection, 1867-1880.** By Don D. Fowler and John F. Matley. IA, 1979. 181 pp., illus. (Smithsonian contributions to anthropology no. 26.) LC 78-022066. GN1.S54 no.26. 301.2/085. OCLC 4504674. **SI1.33:26.**
About half of the total collections in the National Museum of Natural History, gathered by John Wesley Powell between 1867 and 1880, are described. The aboriginal crafts are from Numic-speaking Indians of the western United States and reflect their manner of life in the 1870s.

Bibliographies

189. Bureau of American Ethnology. **Bibliographies of American Indian Languages.** By James Constantine Pilling. 9 vols. GPO, 1887-94. (Bulletin series.) **SI2.3:nos. vary.**
    Bibliography of the Algonquin Languages. 1891. 614 pp. (Bulletin 13.)
    Bibliography of the Athpascan Languages. 1892. 125 pp. (Bulletin 14.)
    Bibliography of the Chinookan Languages. 1893. 81 pp. (Bulletin 15.)
    Bibliography of the Eskimo Languages. 1887. 116 pp. (Bulletin 1.)

Bibliography of the Iroquoian Languages. 1888. 208 pp. (Bulletin 6.)

Bibliography of the Muskhogean Languages. 1889. 114 pp. (Bulletin 9.)

Bibliography of the Salishan Languages. 1893. 86 pp. (Bulletin 16.)

Bibliography of the Siouan Languages. 1887. 87 pp. (Bulletin 5.)

Bibliography of the Wakashan Languages. 1894. 70 pp. (Bulletin 19.)

The aim of this series is to "include in each bibliography everything printed or in manuscript relating to the family of languages to which it is devoted: books, pamphlets, articles in magazines, tracts, serials, etc. and such reviews and announcements of publications as seemed worthy of notice" (Introduction). Each is arranged by author with a chronological index.

190.   Bureau of Indian Affairs. **Economic Development of American Indians and Eskimos, 1930-1967: A Bibliography.** By Marjorie P. Snodgrass. GPO, 1969. 263 pp. LC 79-601798. **I20.48:Ec7/930-67.**

"This bibliography is a unique attempt to bring together in one place as much valuable information as possible on the economic development of the American Indians and Eskimos." It includes materials published in the United States from 1930 through 1967 and many unpublished works. It is arranged alphabetically by author under fourteen subject areas. It is not annotated. A reservation index and an appendix of Bureau field offices are included.

191.   Library of Congress. General Reference and Bibliography Division. **Folklore of the North American Indians: An Annotated Bibliography.** Comp. by Judith C. Ullom. GPO, 1969. 126 pp. LC 70-601462. Z1209.U4. Free from the Central Services Division, Library of Congress, Washington, DC 20540. **LC2.2:In25.**

This selective bibliography of the recorded folklore of North American Indians is arranged by eleven culture areas, including Eskimos. Within each area are listed the source books, followed by editions for children. A section of general background information includes an annotated bibliography of folklore studies, anthologies, children's anthologies, bibliographies, and indexes. The bibliography is indexed by subjects, authors, and titles.

192.   National Institute of Mental Health. **Handbook of Asian American/Pacific Islander Mental Health.** By James K. Morishima et al. GPO, 1979. 135 pp. OCLC 5652085. S/N 017-024-00937-7. $6. **HE20.8108:As4/v.1.**

This is a multidisciplinary bibliography of research on American Indian mental health issues, or variables affecting mental health. It is nonevaluative; all relevant items in English have been included regardless of publication date. The term "American Indians" designates all North American native people, including Indians, Aleuts, Eskimos, and Metis.

Biographies

193.   Bureau of Indian Affairs. **Biographical Sketches and Anecdotes of Ninety-Five of 120 Principal Chiefs from the Indian Tribes of North America.** By Thomas L. McKenney and James Hall. GPO, 1967. 452 pp. LC 68-60299. **I20.2:In2/27.**

An interesting reprint of a work originally published in 1838, this biographical directory will be useful for students of North American Indian history or anyone wanting detailed biographical information on Indian chiefs. Sketches usually give physical descriptions of the subjects.

194. Bureau of Indian Affairs. **Famous Indians: A Collection of Short Biographies.** GPO, 1975. 50 pp. E89.U59 1975. 970/.004/97. OCLC 2819211. **I20.2:In2/26/974.**

Handbooks

195. Bureau of American Ethnology. **Handbook of American Indians North of Mexico.** Ed. by Frederick Webb Hodge. 2 vols. GPO, 1907-10. (Bulletin 30.) (Repr.: Scholarly Publications, $295.) **SI2.3:30.**
"Contains a descriptive list of the stocks, confederacies, tribes, tribal divisions, and settlements north of Mexico, accompanied with the various names by which these have been known, together with biographies of Indians of note, sketches of their history, archaeology, manners, arts, customs, and institutions, and aboriginal words incorporated into English" (letter of transmittal). "Under the tribal descriptions a brief account of the ethnic relations of tribe, its history, its location at various periods, statistics of population, etc. are included ... a reference to the authority is noted, and these references form practically a bibliography of the tribe for those who wish to pursue the subject further" (Preface).

196. Bureau of American Ethnology. **The Indian Tribes of North America.** By John R. Swanton. GPO, 1952. 726 pp. (Bulletin 145.) LC 52-61970. (Repr.: Smithsonian, $35.) **SI2.3:145.**
The purpose of this work is "to inform the general reader what Indian tribes occupied the territory of his state and to add enough data to indicate the place they occupied among the tribal groups of the continent and the part they played in the early period of our history and the history of the States immediately to the north and south of us" (Introduction). It is arranged first by states of the United States, followed by Canada, West Indies, Mexico, and Central America. Information on each tribe includes the origin of the tribal name and a brief list of the more important synonyms, the linguistic connections of the tribe, its locations, its history, its estimated and actual population at different periods, and the "connection in which it is noted, particularly, the extent to which its name has been perpetuated geographically." A substantial bibliography and a detailed index complete the work.

197. Bureau of American Ethnology. **The Indians of the Southeastern United States.** By John R. Swanton. GPO, 1946. 1,053 pp. (Bulletin 137.) LC 46-26581. (Repr.: Greenwood Press, $53.25.) **SI2.3:137.**
This is a comprehensive work concerning the general history of the Indian tribes of the southeastern United States. For the most part, it is arranged alphabetically by tribal names. Separate sections deal with specific areas such as clothing, housing, food, the influence of language, and so on. It includes a 25-page bibliography and a very detailed index.

198. Department of Commerce. **Federal and State Indian Reservations and Indian Trust Areas.** GPO, 1974. 604 pp. illus. S/N 003-011-00076-3. $12. **C1.8/3:In2.**
This is a state-by-state descriptive list and directory of federal and state Indian reservations and trust areas. It lists the tribes, population, labor force, educational status, land status, and information on history, culture, government, economy, climate, transportation, community facilities, and recreation.

199. Smithsonian Institution. **Handbook of North American Indians.** William G. Sturtevant, gen. ed. GPO, 1978- . LC 77-017162. E77.H25. 970/.004/97. OCLC 3414504. **SI1.20/2:vol.**

Vol. 6. **Subarctic.** 1981. 853 pp. S/N 047-000-00374-1. $25.

Vol. 8. **California.** 1978. 800 pp. S/N 047-000-00347-4. $25.

Vol. 9. **Southwest.** 1979. 701 pp. S/N 047-000-00361-0. $23.

Vol. 10. **Southwest.** 1983. 884 pp. S/N 047-000-00390-3. $25.

Vol. 15. **Northeast.** 1978. 924 pp. S/N 047-000-00351-2. $27.

When completed, this series will be a twenty-volume encylopedic summary of the prehistory, history, and cultures of the aboriginal peoples of North America.

South American Indians

200.   Bureau of American Ethnology. **Handbook of South American Indians.** Ed. by Julian Haynes Steward. 7 vols. GPO, 1946-59. (Bulletin 143.) (Repr.: Cooper Square Publications, $30/vol.) **SI2.3:143.**

Vol. 1. **The Marginal Tribes.** 1946.

Vol. 2. **The Andean Civilizations.** 1946.

Vol. 3. **The Tropical Forest Tribes.** 1948.

Vol. 4. **The Circum-Caribbean Tribes.** 1948.

Vol. 5. **The Comparative Ethnology of South American Indians.** 1949.

Vol. 6. **Physical Anthropology, Linguistics and Cultural Geography of South American Indians.** 1950.

Vol. 7. **Index.**

This extensive work was prepared with the cooperation of the Department of State. It includes bibliographies and glossaries.

201.   Smithsonian Institution. **Great Tzotzil Dictionary of San Lorenzo Zinacantan.** By Robert M. Laughlin. GPO, 1975. 598 pp., illus. (Smithsonian contributions to anthropology no. 19.) S/N 047-001-00115-0. $16. **SI1.33:19.**

This is an extensive dictionary of the Mayan language, Tzotzil, spoken by Indians in Chiopas, the southernmost state of Mexico. Words are given in Tzotzil-English and English-Tzotzil.

Economics and Business

GENERAL WORKS

Bibliographies

202. Bureau of Labor Statistics. **Productivity: A Selected Bibliography**. GPO, 1958- . Irregular. (Bulletin series.) **LC2.3:nos. vary**.
These bibliographies list and annotate books and articles on productivity published during the years covered. The publications cited deal with concepts and methods, measurement, sources of change, and relations between productivity and economic variables such as wages and employment. The bibliography for 1965-71 is Bulletin 1776, for 1971-75 is Bulletin 1933, and for 1976-78 is Bulletin 2051. Earlier bibliographies on productivity include Bulletins 1226 (1958) and 1514 (1966).

203. Department of Commerce. **Commerce Publications Update: A Biweekly Listing of Latest Titles from the U.S. Department of Commerce**. GPO, 1980- . Biweekly. OCLC 06504692. S/N 003-000-80004-1. $31/yr. **C1.24/3:date**.
This report lists publications and press releases issued by the Department of Commerce during the preceding two weeks and highlights publications of special interest. It provides the latest figures in nineteen key areas of business and economic activity, including personal income, consumer prices, employment, and housing.

204. Department of Commerce. **United States Department of Commerce Publications**. GPO, 1952. 795 pp. LC 52-60731. Z1223.C75. 016.35382. OCLC 581233. **C1.2:P96**.
This is a comprehensive bibliography of Department of Commerce publications issued from 1790 to 1950, arranged by agency. Serial and monographic publications are included, but ephemeral items such as press releases are not. It is indexed by subjects.

_____. **Supplement**. GPO, 1951/52-1971. Annual. **C1.2:P96/supp**.

205. Department of Commerce. **United States Department of Commerce Publications: Catalog and Index**. GPO, 1972-78. Annual. LC 73-645569. Z1223.C75 suppl. 015/.73. OCLC 1788167. **C1.54/2:yr**.
The title of this publications catalog has varied slightly over the years.

206. Department of Commerce. **Publications Catalog of the U.S. Department of Commerce**. GPO, 1979-83. Annual. LC 81-642636. Z1223.C75 suppl. 015.73/0534/05. OCLC 07543407. 1982 ed. S/N 003-000-00583-6. $6. **C1.54/2-2:yr.**

This is a listing of Department of Commerce publications from the previous year compiled from the *Monthly Catalog*. The Department of Commerce announced that it planned to discontinue publication of the catalog with the 1982 edition.

207. Small Business Administration. **Small Business Bibliographies**. IA, 1958- . Irregular. OCLC 2254770. Single copies are available free from the Small Business Administration, P.O. Box 15434, Fort Worth, TX 76119. **SBA1.3:nos.**

These short bibliographies list key references for many business management topics. Another SBA series is the *Management Aid Series* (SBA1.32:nos.). These free pamphlets recommend methods for handling management problems and business functions. The SBA *Starting Out Series* (SBA1.35:nos.) consists of one-page fact sheets about financial and operating requirements for selected businesses.

Dictionaries

208. Department of Commerce. Office of Federal Statistical Policy and Standards. **Correlation between the United States and International Standard Industrial Classifications**. IA, 1979. 101 pp. (Technical paper no. 1.) OCLC 5963239. **C1.73:1.**

209. Office of Management and Budget. **Standard Industrial Classification Manual**. GPO, 1972 (repr. 1983). 649 pp. S/N 041-001-00066-6. $15. **PrEx2.6/2:In27/972.**

_____. **Supplement**. GPO, 1978 (repr. 1983). 15 pp. OCLC 08735503. S/N 003-005-000176-0. $2.75. **PrEx2.6/2:In27/972/supp.**

This manual classifies and defines industries by the type of activity they perform. It lists industries and their standard industrial classification (SIC) codes. The supplement contains additions, deletions, and errata.

210. Social and Economics Statistics Administration. **Dictionary of Economic and Statistical Terms**. GPO, 1973. 83 pp. LC 73-600838. **C56.2:Ec7/972.**

This is designed primarily for regular users of Bureau of Economic Analysis data. The contents cover national income and product accounts, balance of payments accounts, economic and statistical indicators, demographic and social terms, and economic and statistical terms. There is a single index to all terms.

Directories

211. Bureau of Industrial Economics. **Franchise Opportunities Handbook**. GPO, 1972- . Annual. LC 79-640923. HF5429.3.F694. 381/.13/02573. OCLC 02430498. 1983 ed. S/N 003-008-00191-2. $7. **C62.14:yr.**

This is a directory of franchisors who do not discriminate because of race, color, or national origin in the availability, terms, or conditions of their franchises. Information for each listing is supplied by the franchisor and summarizes the terms, requirements, and conditions under which a franchise is available.

212. National Institute for Occupational Safety and Health. **Occupational Safety and Health Directory.** IA, 1980. 38th ed. LC 80-640336. HD7653.026. 363.1/17/02573. OCLC 3743204. **HE20.7102:Oc1/4/980.**
The directory lists the names, titles, addresses, and telephone numbers of key personnel in the National Occupational Safety and Health Administration and the Occupational Safety and Health Review Commission. It also lists state and local agencies responsible for worker safety and health. It continues the *Directory of Government Occupational Safety and Health Personnel.*

213. Small Business Administration. **Directory of State Small Business Programs.** IA, 1979. LC 80-647935. HD2346.U5D57. 353.9/382048/025. OCLC 06440789. **SBA1.2:D62/3/980.**
This is a descriptive listing of state programs and officials designed to reach out to small business, as well as those able to relate to the daily problems and operations of small business. It does not list every service available in each state, but gives state-by-state descriptions of unique programs.

Statistics

214. Bureau of the Census. **Graphic Summary of the 1977 Economic Censuses.** GPO, 1981. 128 pp. LC 81-001210. HC106.7.G7. 330.973/0926c219. OCLC 77283617. S/N 003-024-02946-4. $7. **C3.2:Ec7/6.**
Data collected in the quinquennial economic census have been summarized graphically in charts and maps. Intended to be a visual supplement to the basic tabular economic census publications, this source depicts highlights of major economic sectors from 1967 to 1977. This is an especially valuable summary volume for libraries not receiving the numerous printed reports for the individual economic censuses, since it offers an overview and highlights in an easy to understand format.

215. Bureau of the Census. **Guide to Industrial Statistics.** By John Berube. GPO, 1978. 105 pp., illus. HD9724.U52 1977. 338/.0973. OCLC 2599378. **C3.6/2:In2/978.**
This is a revision of the 1964 edition. The industrial statistics program of the Bureau of the Census includes the integrated output of the *Current Industrial Reports*, the *Annual Survey of Manufactures*, the quinquennial *Census of Manufactures*, the *Census of Mineral Industries*, and special or supplemental surveys. This guide gives information on locating specific data and tables from these sources, describes each of the Bureau's industrial statistical programs, and defines data items used in these publications. It also gives a complete summary of all industrial energy-related data collected by the Bureau of the Census.

216. Bureau of Economic Analysis. **Business Conditions Digest.** GPO, 1972- . Monthly. LC 72-621004. HC101.A12. 330.9/73/092. OCLC 02452279. S/N 003-001-80002-1. $44/yr. **C59.9:date.**
This periodical presents almost five hundred economic indicators in a form convenient for analysts with different approaches to the study of current business conditions and prospects (i.e., the national income model, the leading indicators, and anticipations and intentions), as well as for analysts who use combinations of these approaches.

217. Bureau of Economic Analysis. **Business Statistics.** GPO, 1951- . Biennial. OCLC 01227582. 1982 ed. S/N 003-010-00124-1. $8. **C59.11/3:yr.**
This biennial supplement to the *Survey of Current Business* (entry 220) presents historical data for the approximately twenty-six hundred series appearing in each monthly issue of the *Survey.* It contains data on national income and product

accounts, U.S. international transactions, business sales, expenditures and inventories, banking, transportation, and other industries and commodities on an annual basis from 1947, quarterly from 1968, and monthly since 1975. An appendix gives pre-1975 monthly or pre-1968 quarterly data for over three hundred important series. Series data not included are in previous editions of this statistical compilation.

218. Bureau of Economic Analysis. **Long Term Economic Growth, 1860-1970**. GPO, 1973. 311 pp. LC 73-600130. S/N 003-024-00014-8. $6.50. **C56.102: Ec7/860-970**.

This statistical compendium is a valuable guide for research in the history of American business and economic growth. It contains data, charts, and graphs of twelve hundred series showing growth and development of the U.S. economy. Data cover output, distribution of income, productivity, utilization of labor and capital, education, other national economic and social series, regional and industry trends, international comparison, and growth rate triangles.

219. Bureau of Economic Analysis. **National Income and Product Accounts of the United States, 1929-76: Statistical Tables**. GPO, 1981. 447 pp. OCLC 2784007. S/N 003-010-00101-1. $10. **C59.11/4:In2/929-76**.

A supplement to the *Survey of Current Business* (entry 220), this major statistical publication presents tables with the full set of estimates from a 1976 comprehensive benchmark revision of the national income and product accounts of the United States. It includes definitions underlying the national income and product aggregates.

220. Bureau of Economic Analysis. **Survey of Current Business**. GPO, 1921- . Monthly. HC101.A13. 330.5. OCLC 01697070. S/N 003-010-80001-1. $50/yr. **C59.11:vol./nos.**

This is an indispensable source for information on trends in industry and the business situation in the United States, outlook, and other information relevant to the business world.

221. Bureau of Industrial Economics. **U.S. Industrial Outlook**. GPO, 1960-. Annual. OCLC 07707121. 1983 ed. S/N 003-008-00188-2. $11. **C62.17:yr.**

Industry reviews and forecasts are given for two hundred industries, with industry profiles, trends, and projection tables, and trade data. Also, there is an analysis of forty-five rapid growth industries and their prospects, selected industries ranked by annual percent change in shipments, and industry shipments of all manufacturing industries. The *Outlook* follows the standard industrial classification (SIC) system.

222. Bureau of Labor Statistics. **Productivity Measures for Selected Industries**. GPO, 1981- . Annual. (Bulletin series.) OCLC 08681662. 1982 ed. (Bulletin 2189) S/N 029-001-02793-1. $6.50. **L2.3:nos. vary**.

Tables and charts show output per employee hour and per employee since 1954 for selected industries in the federal government productivity measurement program. Indexes showing the relationship between gross production, employment, and hours for private businesses, nonfarm business, manufacturing, and nonfinancial corporate sectors are given in BLS quarterly press releases, in *Productivity and Costs*, in the *Monthly Labor Review*, and in *Employment and Earnings*. This continues *Productivity Indexes for Selected Industries*.

223. Congress. Joint Economic Committee. **Economic Indicators**. GPO, 1948- . Monthly. OCLC 01567401. S/N 052-070-80001-1. $27/yr. **Y4.Ec7:Ec7/date**.

This includes information on prices, wages, production, business activity, purchasing power, credit, money, and federal finance.

224. Congress. Joint Economic Committee. **Supplement to Economic Indicators, 1980: Historical and Descriptive Background.** GPO, 1980. 8th ed. 148 pp., illus. OCLC 07769490. S/N 052-070-05453-1. $5.50. **Y4.Ec7:Ec7/980/supp.**
This explains in nontechnical language the data published in the monthly *Economic Indicators.*

225. Internal Revenue Service. **Statistics of Income (SOI) Bulletin.** GPO, 1981- . Quarterly. LC 81-649949. OCLC 07904895. S/N 048-004-80003-9. $14/yr. **T22.35/4:date.**
This gives statistics from individual and business income tax returns in text, tables, and graphs.

226. Internal Revenue Service. **Statistics of Income: Individual Income Tax Returns.** GPO, 1918- . Annual. LC 61-37567. HJ4652.A252. 336.240973. OCLC 3620154. 1981 ed. S/N 048-004-01861-6. $5.50. **T22.35/2:In2/yr.**
Statistical estimates are based on a stratified probability sample of individual income tax returns. Statistics are given on number of returns filed and the sources of income reported in those classified by marital status and by size of adjusted gross income, deductions and exemptions, tax liability and tax credits, data from taxpayers age 65 or older, and data classified by states. Other reports in the *Statistics of Income* series cover business and corporate income tax returns.

227. President. **Economic Report of the President Transmitted to the Congress.** GPO, 1947- . Annual. LC 47-032975. HC106.5.A272. 330.973. OCLC 01193149. 1984 ed. S/N 040-000-00476-9. $8. **Pr40.9:yr.**
The full text of the President's report to Congress on the economic condition of the nation is presented. Economic policies are described and their intent is explained. Statistical tables are included. The SuDocs classification number changes with each President. The major portion of the publication is the Annual Report of the Council of Economic Advisors.

See also SB 152.

BUSINESS MANAGEMENT

228. Department of Labor. **The Practice of Management: Selected Recent References.** GPO, 1980. 101 pp. OCLC 6910646. S/N 029-000-00406-4. $5. **L1.34:M31/5.**
Citations are given to books, government publications, and journal articles published between 1970 and 1980 related to personnel management, public administration, and general principles of management.

229. National Aeronautics and Space Administration. **Management: A Continuing Bibliography with Indexes.** NTIS, 1978- . Annual. (NASA SP-7500.) OCLC 4848488. **NAS1.21:7500(nos.).**
The bibliography cites and annotates reports and journal articles about program, contract, and personnel management and management techniques. Items cited were announced in *Scientific and Technical Aerospace Reports* (STAR).

230. Office of the Federal Register. **Guide to Record Retention Requirements.** GPO, 1955- . Annual. OCLC 02481622. **GS4.107/a:R245/yr.**
This handy guide for industry, business, and the general public contains summaries of record retention regulations, which were compiled from laws in the *U.S. Statutes at Large* and rules of various federal agencies. The guide explains what records must be

kept, who must keep them, and how long they must be kept. Each summary contains a reference to the full text of the law or regulation. The index lists the categories of persons, companies, and products affected by federal record retention requirements.

231. Office of Personnel Management. Library. **Personnel Literature**. GPO, 1941- . Monthly. LC 79-644985. Z7164.C81U45683. 016.3501. OCLC 04792386. S/N 006-000-80002-3. $25/yr. **PM1.16:vol./nos.**

This is a monthly listing of materials about personnel administration that were received in the Office of Personnel Management Library. The library also publishes the annual *Personnel Bibliography* series, which lists subject bibliographies compiled from *Personnel Literature*.

232. Small Business Administration. **Catalog of Federal Paperwork Requirements by Industry Group**. GPO, 1979. 723 pp. OCLC 5962699. S/N 045-000-00168-7. $18. **SBA1.2:P19/2.**

The catalog identifies by type of requirement and indexes by three-digit SIC code all business-related federal reporting and recordkeeping requirements. The sections are: reports and recordkeeping requirements by industry group; business-related federal tax forms; procurement-related, compliance-related, and international business-related paperwork related to application for federal benefits.

See also SB 202 and SB 300.

COMMERCE AND TRADE

Foreign Commerce

233. Bureau of the Census. **Foreign Commerce and Navigation of the United States**. GPO, 1867-1965. Irregular. LC 7-19228rev.2. **C3.159:yr.**

This work contains summary data on foreign trade by year; exports and general imports by month; and exports and imports by continent, world area, and country of destination or country of origin. Historical data on foreign trade can also be found in *Foreign Commerce Yearbook* (C18.26/2:948-951) and *Commerce Yearbook* (C18.26:922-932).

234. Bureau of the Census. **Guide to Foreign Trade Statistics**. GPO, 1967- . Annual. LC 74-642459. HF105.B73A. 382/.0973. OCLC 1792725. 1983 ed. S/N 003-024-05766-2. $4.75. **C3.6/2:F76/yr.**

The content and format of individual reports, tabulations, computer tapes, and microfiche on exports, imports, and shipping statistics are described in this guide to sources of foreign trade statistics and the content and arrangement of data. This source explains the scope of these statistics and gives illustrations of the content and arrangement of the data presented in individual foreign trade reports and tabulations. An overview of the history of foreign trade statistics and references to additional sources of historical trade are given in *Historical Statistics of the United States*.

235. Bureau of the Census. **U.S. Foreign Trade Statistics: Classifications and Cross-Classifications, 1980**. GPO, 1981. Looseleaf. LC 80-600166. OCLC 07958525. **C3.2:F76/2/980.**

This is a compilation of the basic schedules of commodity and geographic trade classifications currently being used in the compilation and publication of U.S. foreign trade statistics. This 1980 edition updates information in the 1974 edition and in the 1978 edition of the *Correlations of Selected Export and Import Classifications Used in*

Compiling U.S. Foreign Trade Statistics. Classifications are those in effect through 1980.

See also SB 123.

Manufacturing

236. Bureau of the Census. **Annual Survey of Manufactures.** GPO, 1949- . Annual. LC 52-60884. **C3.24/9:yr.**
The annual survey of manufactures, which is conducted each year not covered by the Census of Manufactures, provides current statistics on key measures of manufacturing activity. Statistics are given for industry groups and individual industries and for geographic divisions, states, large SMSAs, and large industrial counties and cities. Statistics include employment, payroll, value of shipments for classes of products, expenditures for plants and equipment, value of inventories, energy data, value of fixed assets, and labor costs. Preliminary editions in parts are published in paper and superseded by bound cumulative annual volumes.

237. Bureau of the Census. **Census of Manufactures.** GPO, 1810- . Quinquennial.
Since 1809 the *Census of Manufactures* has provided detailed statistics on manufacturing activities for small geographic areas, individual industries, products shipped, and materials consumed. Two types of statistics are provided: (1) general statistics (number of establishments, employment, payroll, work hours, cost of materials, shipment values, capital expenditures, and inventories), and (2) quantity and value of materials consumed and products shipped. Data are published in printed reports and are also available on computer tape.

This census was taken decennially from 1810 to 1900, quinquennially from 1900 to 1919, and biennially from 1919 to 1939. Publication was discontinued during World War II, and was resumed for the years 1947, 1954, 1958, 1963, and 1967. Under legislation enacted in 1964, this census is now taken quinquennially in years ending in 2 and 7.

238. Domestic and International Business Administration. **Guide to Federal Data Sources on Manufacturing.** GPO, 1977. 197 pp. **C57.2:M31.**
This guide to manufacturing statistics includes those on economic indicators, classifications, manufacturing characteristics, production, employment, foreign trade, prices, and finance. It describes the types of data available in particular publications, their timeliness and detail, and selected definitions, and differentiates between selected sources.

Merchant Vessels and Ports

239. Coast Guard. **Merchant Vessels of the United States.** GPO, 1924/25- . Annual. OCLC 04057799. 1981 ed. 2 vols. S/N 050-012-00198-7. $47. **TD5.12/2:yr.**
American merchant vessels and yachts with uncanceled marine documents (registers, enrollments and licenses, or licenses) are listed. The information given about each vessel includes signal and radio call letters, tonnage, size, year built, horsepower, name of owner, and home port. It is updated by the *Monthly Supplement to Merchant Vessels of the United States* and continues *Annual List of Merchant Vessels of the United States ... and List of Vessels Belonging to the U.S. Government with Distinguishing Signals.*

240. Defense Mapping Agency. Hydrographic/Topographic Center. **World Port Index**. (H. O. Publication 150.) IA, 1984. 9th ed. 313 pp. LC 58-60168. OCLC 06928389. **D5.317:150/6**.

The index provides the location, characteristics, known facilities, and available services of selected ports, shipping facilities, and oil terminals around the world. It consists largely of tables of information, with some charts.

241. National Archives and Records Service. **List of American-Flag Merchant Vessels That Received Certificates of Enrollment or Registry at the Port of New York, 1789-1867**. Comp. by Forrest B. Holdcamper. 2 vols. IA, 1968. (Special list 22.) **GS4.7:22**.

The *Special Lists* series published by the National Archives is part of their records description program. These lists describe in detail the contents of groups of records, that is, series of records that deal with the same subject or government agency.

This list contains the names of more than twenty-six thousand American-flag merchant vessels that received certificates of enrollment or registry at the port of New York during the years 1789 to 1867. It is arranged alphabetically by the name of the vessel, containing the following information for each: tonnage, rig, place and date built, and first New York certification. There is an index of compound names.

Tariff

242. International Trade Commission. **Tariff Schedules of the United States, Annotated**. GPO, 1962- . Annual. OCLC 2252867. S/N 049-000-81001-6. $45/yr. (Subscription includes basic looseleaf manual plus supplements for an indeterminate period.) **ITC1.10:yr**.

This compilation of the legal text of the tariff schedules of the United States with amendments and statistical annotations is used in the classification of imports for rate of duty and for statistical purposes.

Transportation

243. Interstate Commerce Commission. **Transport Statistics in the United States**. GPO, 1888- . Annual. LC 5-11209. **IC1.25:yr./pt**.

This source is published in separate volumes for railroads, electric railways, water carriers, oil pipelines, motor carriers, freight forwarders, and private car lines. It is issued in sections as parts and punched for binders.

COMMUNICATIONS

General Works

244. Federal Communications Commission. **Statistics of Communications Common Carriers**. GPO, 1957- . Annual. OCLC 1777225. 1982 ed. S/N 004-000-00429-9. $8. **CC1.35:yr**.

Common carriers covered are telephone, telegraph, and communications satellites. Financial and operating statistics are given for the year covered. Similar statistics have been issued annually since 1939.

245. National Technical Information Service. **A Directory of Computer Software Applications: Communications, 1970-January 1979.** NTIS, 1979. 82 pp. (PB-289 952). OCLC 4844995. **C51.11/5:C73**.

The directory cites communication reports that list computer programs and/or their documentation. Software listed is related to topics such as satellite communications, radio wave propagation, communication networks, frequency allocation, speech intelligibility and processing, digital communications, signal and message processing, and communication theory. It contains bibliographic data, abstracts, and subject and corporate author indexes. The computer programs and documentation listed may be purchased from NTIS in hard copy or microfiche.

Broadcasting

246. Foreign Broadcast Information Service. **Broadcasting Stations of the World.** GPO, 1946- . Irregular. LC 47-32798. **PrEx7.9:yr./pt.**

This source covers broadcast stations all over the world but excludes those in the United States that broadcast on local channels. It has four parts: "Amplitude Modulation Broadcasting Stations by Country and City," "Amplitude Modulation Broadcasting Stations by Frequency," "Frequency Modulation Broadcasting Stations," and "Television Stations."

Postal Guides

247. Postal Service. **International Mail.** GPO, 1970- . Irregular. OCLC 2784635. S/N 039-000-81002-6. $34. (Subscription includes basic looseleaf manual plus supplements for an indeterminate period.) **P1.10/5:date**.

Details are given about postage rates, services, prohibitions, import restrictions, and other conditions governing mail to other countries.

248. Postal Service. **National Five Digit Zip Code and Post Office Directory.** GPO, 1981- . Annual. LC 82-641753. HE6361.N37. 383/.145. OCLC 08135572. 1984 ed. S/N 039-000-00269-8. $9. **P1.10/8:yr.**

Post offices are listed by states, alphabetically, and by classes, and zip codes are given for each. Also included is a list of post offices by zip code, and zip code listing by state and city, and by street address in larger cities. Beginning with the 1979 edition, the *National Zip Code Directory* was combined with the *Directory of Post Offices* (P1.10.4:yr.).

CONSUMER INFORMATION GUIDES

249. Office of the Special Assistant for Consumer Affairs. **Consumer's Resource Handbook.** Ed. by Midge Shubow. GPO, 1980. 76 pp. OCLC 6071320. **Pr39.15:C76**.

The handbook is designed to guide consumers through the maze of federal, state, and local government agencies to identify the right one to assist with complaints about goods or services. It gives addresses, phone numbers (some toll-free), and descriptions of responsibilities and includes information on consumer laws and rights.

MACHINE READABLE DATA

250. National Technical Information Service. **A Directory of Computer Software Applications: Administration and Management, August 1978-October 1980.** NTIS, 1981. 592 pp. (PB81-113 409). OCLC 07065178. **C51.11/5:Ad6/978-80.**
The directory cites computer programs and/or their documentation in the fields of administration and management. Software listed pertains to personnel management, inventory management, urban planning, logistics, management information systems, and program planning and control. Bibliographic data and abstracts and subject and corporate author indexes are provided. This updates PB-283714, which covered the period 1970-July 1978. The computer programs and documentation listed may be purchased from NTIS in hard copy or microfiche.

ECONOMIC DEVELOPMENT PROGRAMS

251. Office of Management and Budget. **Catalog of Federal Domestic Assistance.** GPO, 1971- . Irregular. LC 73-600118. HC110.P63U53a. 338.973. OCLC 02239457. S/N 041-001-81001-3. $36. (Subscription includes basic manual plus supplements for indeterminate period.) **PrEx2.20:date.**
This is a government-wide listing of programs, projects, services, and activities providing benefits or assistance to Americans. The programs included are available to state and local governments; U.S. territories and possessions; private, public, and quasi-public organizations; specialized groups; and individuals. It is also available on machine readable magnetic tape, which may be purchased from NTIS.

EMPLOYMENT AND LABOR

General Bibliographies

252. Labor-Management Services Administration. **Employee Relations Bibliography: Public, Nonprofit, and Professional Employment.** By Terrence N. Tice. GPO, 1978. 162 pp. OCLC 4291728. **L1.34:Em7.**
This partially annotated list of 2,724 references from 1967 to 1977 covers virtually all the significant English-language material on public employment relations related to contracts between employers and employees in the United States and Canada. The focus is on collective bargaining, dispute resolution, and their analogues where the law provides for neither. Name and subject indexes are provided.

Labor Areas

253. Bureau of Economic Analysis. **BEA Economic Areas: Component SMSAs, Counties, and Independent Cities.** GPO, 1978. 293 pp. OCLC 4353077. **C59.2:Ec7/pt.1,2.**
Bureau of Economic Analysis (BEA) economic areas are nodal functional areas used in regional economic analysis. Each is composed of an economic node (an SMSA or similar area that serves as a center of economic activity) and the surrounding counties. Each area includes the homes and workplaces of its labor force. This publication lists the geographic composition of BEA economic areas for the entire United States.

254. Employment and Training Administration. **Directory of Important Labor Areas.** IA, 1943- . Irregular. LC 43-14218. OCLC 4284538. **L37.2:D62/yr.**
This is a consolidated listing of the geographic boundaries of all labor areas covered by the Employment and Training Administration's area classification program. A labor area is a geographic area composed of a central city or cities and the surrounding territory within commuting distance. This directory is useful for identifying the boundaries of specific labor areas, the labor area covering a specific locality, or the labor supply classification of any community if used in conjunction with a current issue of *Area Trends and Unemployment.*

Labor-Management Relations

255. Bureau of Labor Statistics. **Directory of National Unions and Employee Associations.** GPO, 1971-79. Biennial. (Bulletin series.) LC 73-641250. HD6504.A15. 331.8802573. OCLC 1785101. 1979 ed. (Bulletin 2079.) S/N 029-001-02503-3. $6. **L2.3:nos. vary.**
This directory lists national and state unions and employee organizations, their addresses, and officers. Included are pertinent statistics on memberships as well as short summaries on recent developments in the field. The listing excludes certain federal service organizations. The information is provided by the groups. It continues the *Directory of National and International Labor Unions in the United States.* Other previous titles were *Directory of A.F.L. Unions* (1939-42), *Directory of C.I.O. Unions* (1939-42), and *Directory of Labor Unions in the United States* (1943-54).

256. National Center for Productivity and Quality of Working Life. **Directory of Labor-Management Committees.** GPO, 1978. 2d ed. 211 pp. OCLC 3957582. S/N 052-003-00522-1. $7. **Y3.P94:2L11/2/978.**
Labor-management committees are listed alphabetically by state and then by city. Entries include employers and unions, date of committee origin, number of employees affected, committee type, and coverage by a provision in the union contract. Information is also given on committee structure and history, issues handled and results, and names and addresses of contact people.

Labor Organizations

257. Employment Standards Administration. **Labor Offices in the United States and Canada.** IA, 1979- . Irregular. (Bulletin 177.) HD4814.U3. 350/.83/097. OCLC 1784590. **L36.3:177/nos.**
This is a directory of federal, state, and provincial offices and agencies in the United States and Canada with administrative responsibility for labor or labor-related functions. It gives addresses, telephone numbers, and names of selected personnel.

Occupational Safety

258. National Institute for Occupational Safety and Health. **Industrial Noise Control Manual.** By Paul Jensen, Charles R. Jokel, and Laymon N. Miller. GPO, 1978. 336 pp., illus. OCLC 4750227. **HE20.7108:N69/978.**
Practical information is given on noise control techniques, with case histories of successful projects in industry and a comprehensive discussion of practical applications of noise control in industry. The manual presents basic information on understanding, measuring, and controlling noise. It is written for people with little or no background in noise control. An extensive bibliography is included.

See also SB 213.

Statistics

259. Bureau of Labor Statistics. **BLS Handbook of Methods**. 2 vols. GPO, 1982-83. 198 pp. (Bulletin 2134.) HD8064.U54. 331.0973. OCLC 09180068. S/N 029-001-02729-0 (vol. 1). $6.50. S/N 029-001-002795-8 (vol. 2). $2. **L2.3: 2134-1,2**.
Volume 1 of the handbook provides explanations of the methods used in Bureau of Labor Statistics (BLS) programs of collection, analysis, and presentation of statistics, to give readers an understanding of the nature of the statistical data the BLS produces. It gives a history of each major program, its purpose, definitions of terms, explanation of concepts, and sources of additional information. Volume 2 gives information on the consumer price index with a detailed description of its construction.

260. Bureau of Labor Statistics. **Employment and Earnings**. GPO, 1969- . Monthly with annual supplement. OCLC 02610713. S/N 029-001-80002-9. $31/yr. **L2.41/2:date**.
This monthly periodical gives statistics on employment and earnings at the national level, for individual states, and for over two hundred areas. It includes household and establishment data, seasonably and not seasonably adjusted, and provides timely analyses of labor force development.

261. Bureau of Labor Statistics. **Employment and Earnings: States and Areas, 1939-[year]**. GPO, 1962- . Annual. (Bulletin 1370.) 1982 ed. 2 vols. (L2.3: 1370-17/v.1,2.) S/N 029-001-02800-8. $11 (set). **L2.3:1370-nos**.
A companion to the national data book *Employment and Earnings: United States*, this compilation gives annual averages for total employment, weekly earnings, weekly hours, and hourly earnings for each state, the District of Columbia, and 240 labor areas. It also gives industry data submitted by state agencies. The statistics included in recent volumes are based on the 1972 edition of the *Standard Industrial Classification Manual*.

262. Bureau of Labor Statistics. **Employment and Earnings: United States, 1909-[year]**. GPO, 1960- . Annual. (Bulletin 1312.) **L2.3:1312-nos**.
This is a compendium of detailed industry statistics on the U.S. nonagricultural work force and a comprehensive data book on national-level statistics. It gives annual averages for total employment, weekly earnings, weekly hours, and hourly earnings. The 1979 edition, covering 1909-78, was the first historical volume based on the 1972 edition of the *Standard Industrial Classification Manual* and the first to include seasonally adjusted data on women workers. This volume provides national data only. Similar information for states, the District of Columbia, and 240 labor areas is provided in *Employment and Earnings: States and Areas* (entry 261). Current statistics are available in the monthly *Employment and Earnings* (entry 260).

263. Bureau of Labor Statistics. **Handbook of Labor Statistics**. GPO, 1924/26- . Annual. (Bulletin series.) HD8051.A62. 331/.0973. OCLC 01768204. 1983 ed. (Bulletin 2175.) S/N 029-001-02756-7. $9.50. **L2.3/5:nos. vary**.
This is a one-volume compilation of the major statistical series produced by the Bureau of Labor Statistics, with some related series from other agencies and foreign countries. Tables show the earliest reliable and consistent data and are arranged under economic subject headings. Preceding the tables are technical notes describing major statistical programs and identifying the tables derived from each program. Tables cover employment, unemployment, earnings, and other topics at the national level with some state and area data.

264. Bureau of Labor Statistics. **Labor Force Statistics Derived from the Current Population Survey: A Databook**. 2 vols. GPO, 1982. 1,290 pp. (Bulletin 2096.) LC 81-607902. HD5724.L19. 331.11/0973. OCLC 07577058. S/N 029-001-02721-4 (vol. 1). $14. S/N 029-001-02722-2 (vol. 2). $12. **L2.3:2096/v.1,2.**

These two volumes provide a comprehensive historical collection of national statistical data derived from the current population survey conducted by the Bureau of the Census, 1948-81.

265. Bureau of Labor Statistics. **Monthly Labor Review**. GPO, 1918- . Monthly. Illus. HD8051.A78. 331.0973. OCLC 0534258. S/N 029-001-80003-7. $24/yr. **L2.6:vol./nos.**

Articles concern employment, the labor force, wages, prices, worker satisfaction, social indicators, and labor abroad. Regular features include a review of industrial relations developments, court decisions in labor cases, book reviews, and current labor statistics.

266. Bureau of Labor Statistics. **Perspectives on Working Women: A Databook**. GPO, 1980. 105 pp. (Bulletin 2080.) OCLC 7053620. S/N 029-001-02527-1. $5.50. **L2.3:2080.**

In a format that is primarily tables, this source summarizes data on the characteristics of working women in the United States. It includes data on the socioeconomic status of women.

267. Central Intelligence Agency. National Foreign Assessment Center. **Handbook of Economic Statistics**. GPO, 1981- . Annual. LC 79-644495. HA155.U54a. 330.9/04. OCLC 04654549. 1983 ed. S/N 041-015-00156-6. $14. **PrEx3.10/7: CPAS yr.-10006.**

Statistics are given for selected noncommunist countries and all communist countries since 1960. They cover economics, foreign trade and aid, energy, minerals, metals, and others. Statistics have been collected from official government sources, international organizations, and CIA estimates. Maps, charts, and tables are included.

268. Employment and Training Administration. **Factbook on Youth**. GPO, 1980. 147 pp. (Youth knowledge development report no. 2.5.) OCLC 7355789. S/N 029-014-00128-7. $6.50. **L37.19/2:2.5.**

Charts, tables, and graphs depict key information on youth employment and general background data on youths fourteen to twenty-four years old.

269. Office of Personnel Management. Intergovernmental Personnel Programs. **State Salary Survey**. IA, 1979- . Annual. LC 76-649838. JK2474.A3. 331.2/813539. OCLC 02734528. **PM1.2:St2/2/yr.**

These annual surveys of state salaries are designed to help states determine salaries. The survey covers 31 occupational categories, with 104 titles generally described as administrative, professional, or technical. Three benchmark-level salaries are described for most occupations: beginning, experienced or supervisory, and administrative. Descriptions give definition, degree of supervision and responsibility, examples of duties, and qualifications.

See also SB 44, SB 45, SB 64, and SB 233.

FINANCE AND BANKING

270. Board of Governors of the Federal Reserve System. **Federal Reserve Bulletin**. IA, 1915- . Monthly. LC 15-26318. HG2401.A15. OCLC 01606526. **FR1.3:date.**
Complete data are given on the current financial situation and outlook in the United States, including summary information and national and international statistics.

271. Board of Governors of the Federal Reserve System. **Historical Chart Book**. IA, 1949- . Annual. LC 80-640320. **FR1.30/2:yr.**
This annual publication contains long-range charts that supplement the quarterly *Federal Reserve Chart Book* on financial and business statistics. It covers such topics as bank reserves and reserve bank credit, liquid assets and money supply, commercial banks, government finance, business finance, agriculture, consumer financing, and prices. Some charts show figures as far back as 1900.

272. Securities and Exchange Commission. **Directory of Companies Required to File Annual Reports with the Securities and Exchange Commission under the Securities Exchange Act of 1934: Alphabetically and by Industry Groups**. GPO, 1959- . Annual. OCLC 6389168. 1983 ed. S/N 046-000-00129-0. $8.50. **SE1.27:yr.**
This is a directory of companies whose stocks are listed on national exchanges and which have registered under the Securities Exchange Act of 1934. Part 1 lists companies alphabetically by name with code number to industrial groups and SEC docket numbers. Part 2 lists companies by nine major industrial groups and subgroups.

See also SB 128.

INSURANCE

Retirement

273. Bureau of Labor Statistics. **Digest of Selected Pension Plans**. GPO, irregular. OCLC 2786296. **L2.99:date.**
The digest summarizes the features of selected pension plans for employees under collective bargaining and selected pension plans for salaried workers. It is updated by continuing supplements and cumulated irregularly.

See also SB 285.

Social Security

274. Social Security Administration. **Annotated Readings in Social Security**. By Carole H. Whitney. GPO, 1982. 600 pp. LC 82-600648. OCLC 09157405. S/N 017-070-00386-9. $12. **HE3.38:R22/2.**
This annotated bibliography with author and subject indexes supersedes *Basic Readings in Social Security*, last published in 1970.

275. Social Security Administration. **Author, Title, and Subject Index to the Social Security Bulletin, 1938-79**. GPO, 1982. 132 pp. OCLC 08448044. S/N 017-070-00375-3. $6. **HE3.3/5:938-79.**

The *Social Security Bulletin* has been the official journal for social security program statistics and research results since 1938. This cumulative index covers 1938-79 and has author, title, and subject indexes with a separate index to statistical tables.

276. Social Security Administration. **Four Decades of International Social Security Research: A Bibliography of Studies by the Social Security Administration, 1937-80**. By Lois S. Copeland. GPO, 1981. 74 pp. LC 81-600023. OCLC 07956450. S/N 017-070-00368-1. $5.50. **HE3.38:R31/4/937-80**.
This is a history of the efforts by the Social Security Administration to keep the public informed about foreign social insurance activities.

277. Social Security Administration. **Social Security Bulletin: Annual Statistical Supplement**. GPO, 1955- . Annual. OCLC 01939422. S/N 017-070-80001-7. $6.50 (separate). **HE3.3/3:yr**.
Detailed statistics are provided for each year. Monthly data are included in the "Current Operating Statistics" section of the monthly *Social Security Bulletin*. This is included with an annual subscription to the *Social Security Bulletin* ($28.75/yr.) or may be purchased separately.

278. Social Security Administration. **Social Security Handbook: Retirement Insurance, Survivors Insurance, Disability Insurance, Health Insurance, Supplemental Security Income, Black Lung Benefits**. GPO, 1982. 7th ed. 457 pp. OCLC 08082609. S/N 017-070-00366-4. $7.50. **HE3.6/3:So1/3/982**.
This edition reflects social security legislation and regulations through December 31, 1981 and describes how the programs listed in the title operate and the benefits available from each.

279. Social Security Administration. **Social Security Programs throughout the World**. GPO, 1958- . Biennial. (Research report series.) 1983 ed. (HE3.49:59.) S/N 017-070-00408-3. $9. **HE3.49:nos. vary**.
This comprehensive survey of social security systems worldwide, issued periodically since 1937, highlights the principal features of social security programs in 128 countries.

See also SB 165.

MARKETING

General Works

280. Industry and Trade Administration. **Measuring Markets: A Guide to the Use of Federal and State Statistical Data**. By Theodore A. Nelson. IA, 1979. 101 pp. OCLC 5587270. S/N 003-009-00326-1. $5.50. **C57.8:M34/979**.
This guide to using government data in market research includes case studies showing uses of data in market measurement, and a bibliography of major federal and state statistical sources. It describes types of markets, sales goals, market potential, sales territories, and market research data, as well as five major types of market research data: population, income, employment, sales, and taxes.

See also SB 125.

MINING

281. Bureau of Mines. **Dictionary of Mining, Minerals and Related Terms**. Comp. by Paul W. Thrush. GPO, 1968 (repr. 1978). 1,269 pp. LC 68-67091. S/N 024-004-00002-3. $27. **I28.2:D56**.

This extensive volume defines terms frequently used in mineralogy and related sciences and serves as a comprehensive and authoritative standard reference source for the mining industry. It contains about 55,000 terms (both technical and layman's) and 150,000 clear, concise definitions. It excludes most petroleum, natural gas, and legal terminology except the very general, and includes terminology from the entire English-speaking world, noting country of origin. Sources are given for each definition and a list of authorities and sources is included in the back of the book. A list of geological abbreviations is also given.

282. Bureau of Mines. **List of Bureau of Mines Publications and Articles, January 1 [year] to December 31 [year]**. GPO, 1960- . Annual. LC 61-64978. Z6736.U759. 016.622. OCLC 01953370. 1982 ed. S/N 024-004-02121-7. $3.50. **I28.5:yr**.

This source contains both subject and author indexes to Bureau of Mines publications. It updates two earlier publications, *List of Publications Issued by the Bureau of Mines from July 1, 1910 to January 1, 1960* and *List of Journal Articles by Bureau of Mines Authors Published July 1, 1910 to January 1, 1960*, and cumulates Bureau of Mines monthly *New Publications* (I28.5/2:date).

283. Fish and Wildlife Service. **Atlas of Western Surface-Mined Lands: Coal, Uranium, and Phosphate**. By A. Kent Evans, E. W. Uhleman, and P. A. Eby. IA, 1978. 373 pp. OCLC 4476495. **I49.2:Su7**.

Tables of data are given on all coal, uranium, and phosphate surface mines of over ten acres, operating before 1976 in the western United States. Data on each mine include geographic location and locating instructions, ownership, reclamation, dates of operation, area affected, and current land use and vegetation.

284. Geological Survey. **United States Mineral Resources**. By Donald A. Brobst and Walden P. Pratt. GPO, 1973. 722 pp. (Professional paper 820.) LC 73-600060. S/N 024-001-00307-4. $19. **I19.16:820**.

This is the Geological Survey's first overall assessment of mineral resources since 1952. Each chapter covers a mineral commodity and gives an overview of knowledge about its geology, an appraisal of resources, and an assessment of possibilities of finding additional deposits.

285. President's Commission on Coal. **Coal Data Book**. GPO, 1980. 235 pp. OCLC 6168334. S/N 052-003-00738-0. $8. **Pr39.8:C63/C63/2/980**.

This consists largely of tables, charts, and graphs, with some accompanying narrative depicting data on coal production and consumption. Data sources are given.

See also SB 151.

OCCUPATIONS

General Works

286. Employment and Training Administration. **Guide to Local Occupational Information**. By Igor Sheremeteff. GPO, 1976. 5th ed. 163 pp. OCLC 2177922. **L37.8:In3**.

287. Office of Education. **Women in Nontraditional Occupations: A Bibliography**. IA, 1977. 189 pp. OCLC 3042624. **HE19.128:W84**.

This annotated bibliography lists publications focusing on women's employment in nontraditional fields. It includes overview publications, plus those on women in skilled vocational occupations and professional occupations, sources of additional information, and sources of materials.

See also SB 270.

Career Guides

288. Bureau of Labor Statistics. **Occupational Outlook Handbook**. GPO, 1949- . Biennial. (Bulletin series.) OCLC 01773253. 1984-85 ed. (Bulletin 2205.) S/N 029-001-02765-6. $8.50. **L2.3/4:yr.**

Current, comprehensive information on work today and job prospects for tomorrow is given. Profiles of about two hundred fifty occupations include information on job duties, working conditions, level and places of employment, education and training, advancement opportunities, job outlook, earnings, and related occupations. Occupations are grouped according to the *Standard Occupational Classification Manual*, 1980 edition. There is also an index referenced to the most recent edition of the *Dictionary of Occupational Titles*.

289. Bureau of Labor Statistics. **Occupational Outlook for College Graduates**. GPO, biennial. (Bulletin series.) HF5382.5.U5033. OCLC 01074040. 1980-81 ed. (Bulletin 2076.) S/N 029-001-02322-7. $8. **L2.3:nos. vary.**

This is a guide to careers in a broad range of occupations that require a college degree.

290. Bureau of Labor Statistics. **Occupational Projections and Training Data: A Statistical and Research Supplement to the 1982-83 Occupational Outlook Handbook**. GPO, 1982. 129 pp. (Bulletin 2202.) LC 80-649629. HD5723.U54c. 331.12/0973. OCLC 05133145. S/N 029-001-02733-8. $6. **L2.3:2202.**

Detailed statistics are presented on current and projected occupational employment, with related information on occupational supply and demand, including estimates of job openings.

291. Employment and Training Administration. **Career Opportunities in Art Museums, Zoos, and Other Interesting Places**. GPO, 1980. 166 pp., illus. (Occupational and career information series, no. 4.) OCLC 6977120. S/N 029-014-00123-6. $7. **L37.16:4.**

This source provides a brief introduction to museums, museum work, and training needed for this type of work, followed by occupational descriptions. These include an overview of the occupation, education, training, personal characteristics needed, physical demands and environmental conditions, where to find jobs, and opportunities. A bibliography and sources for additional information are given.

292. Employment and Training Administration. **Criminal Justice Careers Guidebook**. GPO, 1982. 184 pp., illus. OCLC 8949101. S/N 029-014-00200-3. $7. **L37.8:J98.**

A wide range of criminal justice occupations are described, with sources of additional information. The guidebook is useful in counseling high school and college students and the general public.

293. Employment and Training Administration. **Environmental Protection Careers Guidebook**. GPO, 1980. 205 pp. OCLC 6996011. S/N 029-014-00205-4. $7.50. **L37.8:En8**.

An overview and detailed descriptions of activities, responsibilities, and education and training requirements for major environmental protection occupations are presented.

294. Employment and Training Administration. **Health Careers Guidebook**. GPO, 1979 (repr. 1984). 4th ed. 221 pp., illus. OCLC 5428603. S/N 029-014-00343-2. $7.50. **L37.8:H34**.

This source gives descriptions of jobs, training, and opportunities in areas of health care, along with information on financial aid for training and education.

295. Office of Education. **Career Guidance in the Arts and Humanities: Activities, Information and Resources for Grades 7-12: Dance, Music, Theater and Media, Visual Arts and Crafts, Writing, Humanities**. By Phyllis Ritvo. GPO, 1976. 188 pp. OCLC 2720450. S/N 017-080-01644-3. $7. **HE19.108:C18**.

This practical how-to guide helps counselors and teachers aid students in grades 7-12 to look realistically at themselves and at careers in dance, music, theater, media, visual arts, crafts, writing, and the humanities. It includes student activities, suggestions for traditional career education counseling, lists of information sources, and specifics on preparing for these careers.

296. Office of Education. **Exploring Careers in the Humanities: A Student Guidebook**. By Jean Workman. GPO, 1976. 175 pp., illus. OCLC 2778091. S/N 017-080-01649-4. $6.50. **HE19.108:Ex7/8**.

The guide gives very readable profiles of what to expect (both good and bad) from careers as teachers, historians, archivists, anthropologists, economists, geographers, political scientists, sociologists, language specialists, lawyers, museum workers, philosophers, ministers, and special librarians.

297. Office of Education. **Exploring Theater and Media Careers: A Student Guidebook**. By Michael Allosso. GPO, 1976. 138 pp., illus. OCLC 2744941. S/N 017-080-01640-1. $6.50. **HE19.108:Ex7/6**.

This is an introduction to careers in theater, film, and television categorized by type of activity: performance, writing, production, business, and education/criticism.

298. Office of Education. **Exploring Visual Arts and Crafts Careers: A Student Guidebook**. By Sheila Dubman, Ellen Andrews, and Mary Lewis Hansen. GPO, 1976. 162 pp., illus. OCLC 2684560. S/N 017-080-01641-9. $6.50. **HE19.108:Ex7/4**.

This title and others in the student guidebook series present occupational information at about the ninth-grade reading level. Each is a practical overview of what to expect from specific types of careers, giving the pluses and minuses of these careers and information on how to prepare for them.

299. Office of Education. **391 Ways to Explore Arts and Humanities Careers; Classroom Activities in Dance, Music, Theater and Media, Visual Arts and Crafts, Writing, Humanities**. By Mary Lewis Hansen. GPO, 1976. 164 pp. OCLC 2720381. S/N 017-080-01643-5. $6.50. **HE19.108:Ex7/8**.

This source provides learning activities, teaching strategies, and 391 activities to help students in grades 7-12 to explore careers in the humanities. It is supplemented by the student guidebook series.

Counseling

300. National Institute of Education. **Key Resources in Career Education: An Annotated Guide.** By David V. Tiedeman, Marilyn Schreiber, and Tyrus R. Wessell. IA, 1976. 408 pp., illus. OCLC 2864329. **HE19.208:R31.**
Listings of information about career education include bibliographic information, availability, levels, populations, purpose, contents, and comments.

Occupational Titles

301. Department of Commerce. Office of Federal Statistical Policy and Standards. **Standard Occupational Classification Manual.** GPO, 1980. 547 pp. S/N 003-005-00187-5. $17. **C1.8/3:Oc1/980.**
This is the first revision of the manual published in 1977, which is expected to be in use throughout the 1980s. The standard occupational classification provides a mechanism for cross-referencing and aggregating occupation-related data collected in social and economic statistical reporting programs. It provides a coding system and nomenclature for identifying and classifying occupations. The occupational groupings include a list of *Dictionary of Occupational Titles* (4th ed.) titles descriptive of the group.

302. Employment Service. **Conversion Table of Code and Title Changes, Third to Fourth Edition, Dictionary of Occupational Titles.** GPO, 1979. 389 pp. S/N 029-013-00082-9. $9.50. **L37.302:Oc1/conversion.**
This is a guide to converting codes and titles from the 3d edition to the 4th edition of the *Dictionary of Occupational Titles.*

303. Employment Service. **Dictionary of Occupational Titles.** GPO, 1977 (repr. 1984). 4th ed. 1,371 pp. OCLC 3568261 S/N 029-013-00079-9. $23. **L37.302: Oc1.**

    _____. **Supplement.** GPO, 1982. 50 pp. S/N 029-014-00208-9. $4.50. **L37.2:Oc1/2/982/supp.**
The 4th edition of this major reference work gives data for over twelve thousand occupations, arranged alphabetically and by industry, with a glossary of technical terms. Its supplement contains titles, codes, and definitions for occupations that emerged since 1977 or that were inadvertently omitted in the 1977 publication.

304. Employment and Training Administration. **Selected Characteristics of Occupations Defined in the Dictionary of Occupational Titles.** GPO, 1981. 479 pp. OCLC 7185169. S/N 029-014-00202-0. $9.50. **L37.2:Oc1/2/supp.**
This source supplements the information about jobs and occupational characteristics provided in the *Dictionary of Occupational Titles.* It provides additional data on training time, physical demands, and environmental conditions for each job defined in the dictionary.

REAL ESTATE

305. Bureau of the Census. **Census of Housing.** GPO, 1940- . Decennial. **C3.224/3:yr.**
A census of housing has been part of the decennial censuses since 1940. Data collected include rooms, plumbing, facilities, tenure, telephone, heating, water sources, fuels, automobiles, and shelter costs for homeowners. Data are available in printed reports, microfiche, and on computer tapes.

TAXES

306. Internal Revenue Service. **Tax Guide for Small Business: Income, Excise, and Employment Taxes for Individuals, Partnerships and Corporations.** GPO, 1956- . Annual. OCLC 7199878. **T22.19/2:Sm1/yr.**

This is a guide to the tax laws for sole proprietorships, partnerships, corporations, and Subchapter S corporations. It contains sections on business organization and accounting practices, tax aspects of accounting for the assets used in a business, figuring business income for tax purposes, rules for selling or exchanging assets, tax credits, and more.

307. Internal Revenue Service. **Your Federal Income Tax for Individuals.** GPO, 1944- . Annual. OCLC 5961475. **T22.44:yr.**

This publication is designed to help persons file federal income tax returns. It explains how to prepare forms, what exemptions and deductions are allowed, what income is taxable, how to determine income and deductions from investment properties, how to determine capital gains and losses, and other regulations. Examples are provided to make the rules more easily understood, and explanations are written clearly and concisely. A detailed index facilitates the use of this handy publication.

308. National Institute of Education. **Tax Wealth in Fifty States.** By D. Kent Halstead. GPO, 1978. 255 pp. HJ2385.H34. 336.2/00973. OCLC 3345378. **HE19.202:T19.**

———. **Supplement.** 1977. OCLC 588416. S/N 017-080-02076-9. $7.50. **HE19.202:T19/977/supp.**

This publication provides a simple scheme for annual computation of state and local government tax capacity and effort, and gives comparative measures of fiscal capacity effort, along with data on collected revenue.

See also SB 195.

Education

GENERAL WORKS

309. National Center for Education Statistics. **A Classification of Educational Subject Matter**. GPO, 1978. 223 pp. (State educational records and reports series, handbook no. 11.) OCLC 4290867. S/N 017-080-01876-4. $7.50. **HE19.308/2:11.**
A single, comprehensive recording and reporting scheme was commissioned by the National Center for Education Statistics for use throughout the United States. This is a classification of educational subject matter from pre-elementary through postdoctoral levels. It is not a classification of instructional programs, but a single coherent system for classifying subject matter regardless of level of instruction, institution, or source of support.

Bibliographies

General Works

310. Commission on Civil Rights. **Fair Textbooks: Resource Guide**. GPO, 1979. 430 pp. (Clearinghouse publication no. 61.) OCLC 5958362. **CR1.10:61.**
This is a listing of bias-free educational materials that would be useful in teaching sexual, racial, and other forms of equality. Items are listed under four main categories (material resources, procedural resources, directories, and organizational resources), and subdivided by type of material, subject area applicability, and grade/age level. Items on religious minorities and disabled persons are included.

311. Department of Education. **Resources in Women's Educational Equity**. GPO, 1977- . Irregular. LC 78-643616. Z5815.U5R48. 016.376/973. OCLC 3724473. **ED1.17/2:vol./no.**
This source lists and abstracts materials on women in relation to education, law, careers, sex differences, life styles, and health gleaned from computerized data bases. Nonprint media are included. Subject, author, and institution indexes are provided.

312. National Institute of Law Enforcement and Criminal Justice. **Crime and Disruption in Schools: A Selected Bibliography**. GPO, 1979. 104 pp. OCLC 5783906. **J26.9:C86/4**.

This annotated bibliography focuses on school-based crime and disruption. It lists publications from academic, professional, and government sources dealing with overviews of the problem, student misbehavior, and traditional discipline, school programs, and security of school buildings, and gives information on how to obtain each item cited. Many are free on microfiche from the National Criminal Justice Reference Service.

313. Office of Education. **Aids to Media Selection for Students and Teachers**. Comp. by Kathlyn J. Moses and Lois B. Watt. GPO, 1976. 128 pp. OCLC 2368240. **HE19.102:M46/2/976**.

This is a selected bibliography of bibliographies and journals that review books, magazines, and audiovisual materials of relevance for elementary and secondary school instructional programs. Publications listed were issued since 1970. Sources for book selection, audiovisual materials, and multiethnic materials are covered.

Dissertations

314. Library of Congress. Catalog Division. **List of American Dissertations Printed, 1912-1938**. 27 vols. GPO, 1913-40. Annual. LC 13-35002. Z5055.U49U5. (Repr.: Kraus, $515.) **LC9.2:D65/yr.**

The contents of each volume in this series include an alphabetical list of dissertations printed during the year, a subject listing of the dissertations, a subject index, and a list of personal authors. In general, about fifty institutions of higher learning are represented.

Office of Education Catalogs

315. Bureau of Education. **List of Publications of the United States Bureau of Education, 1867-1910**. GPO, 1910 (repr. 1940). 57 pp. (Bulletin 1910, no. 3.) **I16.3:910/3-2**.

Miscellaneous publications from the first year of the Bureau of Education (1867) through 1910 are listed. The first section lists annual reports and their contents chronologically. Circulars, bulletins, and other publications are also listed chronologically. An author and subject index is included.

316. Office of Education. **List of Publications of the Office of Education, 1910-36**. GPO, 1937. 158 pp. (Bulletin 1937, no. 22.) **I16.3:937/22**.

Publications of the former Federal Board for Vocational Education (1917-33) are included in one section and Office of Education publications in another. They are chronologically arranged, with indexes to each section.

317. Office of Education. **Publications, 1937-59**. Comp. by Beryl Parke and Zelma E. McIlvain. GPO, 1960. 157 pp. **FS5.211:11001**.

Publications are arranged by type (circulars, bulletins, etc.) and issuing offices, with author, title, and subject indexes.

318. Office of Education. **Publications of the U.S. Office of Education**. GPO, 1959-79. Annual. OCLC 3739860. **HE19.128:P96/yr.**

This is a list of general publications and those dealing with career education, citizen and community education, education for the handicapped, elementary and secondary education, educational equity, higher education, international education, libraries and reading, occupational and adult education, reports, catalogs, and directories.

Machine Readable Data

319. National Center for Education Statistics. **Directory of Federal Agency Education Data Tapes.** GPO, 1976- . Annual. OCLC 6359630. 1980 ed. S/N 017-080-02097-1. $7.50. **HE19.302:Ed8/3/yr.**
A useful resource for users of federal education statistics, the directory identifies and describes data bases available on computer tape from federal agencies that conduct research and maintain data systems. The data bases listed are numeric rather than bibliographic. Entries describe the methodological and substantive aspects of the survey or system from which the data are derived, the general content of each tape, significant characteristics of the data, and a contact person. Technical specifications such as computer language or character code used are not listed.

320. National Institute of Education. Educational Resources Information Center. **ERIC Data Base.**
This machine readable bibliographic data base offers access to education report literature announced in *Resources in Education* since 1966 and journal articles announced in *Current Index to Journals in Education* since 1969. It is available online through Lockheed DIALOG, Systems Development Corporation (SDC), and Bibliographic Retrieval Service (BRS). *The Thesaurus of ERIC Descriptors* (Oryx Press), a controlled vocabulary of educational terms, is a companion resource.

Directories

321. Department of Education. **Catalog of Federal Education Assistance Programs: An Indexed Guide to the Federal Government's Programs Offering Educational Benefits to the American People.** GPO, 1972- . Biennial. 1980 ed. S/N 065-000-00031-8. $9.50. **ED1.29:yr.**
This is a guide to federal government programs offering educational benefits to the general public, states and other political subdivisions, and institutions. The programs listed, extracted from the *Catalog of Federal Domestic Assistance*, support educational services, library services, or professional training and are described in terms of type of assistance, purpose, eligibility, and where to apply.

322. Department of Education. **Directory of Education Associations.** GPO, 1977- . Annual. LC 78-640957. L901.E335. 370/.6/273. OCLC 03503905. 1980-81 ed. S/N 065-000-00094-6. $5.25. **ED1.30:yr.**
The directory lists names, addresses, and telephone numbers of educational associations and identifies their chief officers and official publications.

323. Department of Education. **Educators with Disabilities: A Resource Guide.** GPO, 1981. 153 pp., illus. OCLC 07625864. S/N 065-000-00104-7. $6.50. **ED1.8:D63/4.**
This directory of over nine hundred educators in higher education and elementary and secondary schools who have disabilities gives name, address, telephone number, TTY number, degrees, position, nature of disability and age at which disability occurred, and areas of interest for consultant or resource work.

324. National Center for Education Statistics. **Education Directory: Local Education Agencies**. GPO, 1980- . Annual. LC 80-649901. L901.E35. 370/.25/73. OCLC 06962953. 1980 ed. S/N 065-000-00071-7. $6. **ED1.111/2:yr.**

This annual directory of local public school systems in the United States gives unit name, county, location of superintendent, zip code, grade span, number of students, and number of schools. This title continues *Education Directory: Public School Systems*. It has been published in various formats since 1895 and is also available as a machine readable data base through the Data Systems Branch, National Center for Education Statistics, 400 Maryland Ave., S.W., Washington, DC 20202; (301) 436-7944.

325. National Center for Education Statistics. **Education Directory: State Education Agency Officials**. GPO, 1971- . Annual. LC 77-644255. L901.E36. 370/.25/73. OCLC 03125846. 1981 ed. S/N 065-000-00125-0. $4.25. **ED1.111/3:yr.**

This is a listing of principal state education officers with titles, addresses, and phone numbers. It continues *Education Directory: State Governments* and has been published in various formats since 1895.

Statistics

326. Department of Education. **National Center for Education Statistics.**

The center collects and disseminates statistics related to education in the United States and in other countries. Center staff will provide statistical information in response to queries by telephone, letter, or personal visit and provide consulting services on the availability and use of education statistics. The center also releases numerous handbooks, statistical compilations, reports, and other publications. A short list of these publications is available free of charge from the center (*NCES Publications*, 13 pp.).

Selected data from the center, the Bureau of the Census, and the Department of Education are available in computerized form. The *NCES Directory of Computer Tapes* (29 pp.) lists the tapes available for sale from NCES, identifies the year of collection, and lists selected variables. Both publications are available from the Statistical Information Office, National Center for Education Statistics, 400 Maryland Ave., S.W., Washington, DC 20202; (202) 254-5213.

327. National Center for Education Statistics. **Condition of Education**. GPO, 1975- . Annual. LC 75-643861. L112.N377a. 370/.973. OCLC 02241465. 1984 ed. S/N 065-000-00200-1. $7. **ED1.109:yr.**

This annual statistical report analyzes current issues at all levels of education and societal trends that affect education. It is a congressionally mandated report summarizing trends and developments for educational institutions, participants, and personnel such as enrollments, achievement, and economic outcomes. Data are presented in text, tables, charts, and graphs. The 1982 edition has a cumulative index to the contents of the 1979-82 editions.

328. National Center for Education Statistics. **The Condition of Education for Hispanic Americans**. By George H. Brown et al. GPO, 1980. 268 pp. OCLC 6845334. S/N 065-000-00023-7. $8. **ED1.102:H62.**

This compilation of data on the education of Hispanic Americans relates their sociological, demographic, and employment characteristics to educational attainment.

329. National Center for Education Statistics. **Digest of Education Statistics**. GPO, 1962- . Annual. OCLC 03133477. 1983-84 ed. S/N 065-000-00191-8. $6.50. **ED1.113:yr.**

This title provides a statistical profile of American education from pre-kindergarten through graduate school. Subjects covered include number of schools and colleges, teachers, and graduates; enrollment; educational attainment; finances; libraries; international education; and research and development.

330. National Center for Education Statistics. **Projections of Education Statistics to [year].** GPO, 1981- . Biennial. OCLC 07724707. 1980-81 ed. 2 vols. S/N 065-000-00144-6 (vol. 1). $6. S/N 065-000-00151-9 (vol. 2). $4.75. **ED1.120:yrs.**
Statistics are projected for elementary and secondary schools and institutions of higher education for enrollments, graduates, teachers, and expenditures. The projections are based on data from the National Center for Education Statistics. Many of these are available for states in the *Digest of Education Statistics*. Time series data are included with the projections to illustrate overall trends. A discussion of methodology is included.

See also SB 83.

COMPARATIVE EDUCATION

331. Library of Congress. Science and Technology Division. **Mainland China Organizations of Higher Learning in Science and Technology and Their Publications: A Selected Guide.** Comp. by Chi Wang. GPO, 1961. 104 pp. LC 61-60070. AS448.U5. Free from the Central Services Division, Library of Congress, Washington, DC 20540. **LC33.2:C44/3.**
This is a directory of societies and other organizations, colleges and universities, government agencies with specific functions, and libraries. Relevant publications of each are listed.

ELEMENTARY AND SECONDARY EDUCATION

General Works

Bibliographies

332. Head Start Bureau. **An Annotated Bibliography of Children's Picture Books: An Introduction to the Literature of Head Start's Children.** By Geraldine L. Wilson. GPO, 1978. 85 pp., illus. OCLC 4966618. **HE23.1111:C43.**
This is an annotated bibliography of literature for young children from and about cultural and racial communities. The items listed were chosen as part of a balanced list of materials for various cultural groups. A how-to section on storytelling, ordering and buying books, and other topics is included.

Directories

333. Head Start Bureau. **Directory of Full Year Head Start Programs, Summer Head Start Programs, Head Start Parent and Child Centers.** IA, 1978. 145 pp. OCLC 4714188. **HE23.1102:D62.**

This is a directory of grantees authorized to operate Head Start programs, with addresses, arranged by cities within each state.

See also SB 196.

HIGHER EDUCATION

Bibliographies

334. National Institute of Education. **Higher Education Planning: A Bibliographic Handbook.** Ed. by D. Kent Halstead. GPO, 1979. 539 pp. Z5814.U7H53. 016.3781/07. OCLC 4504102. **HE19.208:H53.**

This is a selective bibliography of "high quality" literature on state and national planning for higher education. Items are arranged under twenty-two topics and have long annotations.

335. Office of Education. **The College Presidency, 1900-1960: An Annotated Bibliography.** Comp. by Walter Crosby Eells and Ernest V. Hollis. GPO, 1961. 143 pp. **FS5.253:53008.**

This is a bibliography of seven hundred publications on the college president's duties and responsibilities for special phases of administration, qualifications, personal factors, and biographies. Entries are numbered and annotated and there is an author index.

Directories

336. National Center for Education Statistics. **Colleges and Universities Offering Accredited Programs by Accreditation Field, Including Selected Characteristics.** GPO, 1978. 146 pp. OCLC 4329518. S/N 017-080-01913-2. $6.50. **HE19.302:C68/977-78.**

This summary of selected characteristics of institutions of higher education offering accredited programs is condensed from *Education Directory: Colleges and Universities*. It gives institution name, address, size, control, level, and tuition and is useful for identifying institutions accredited in certain fields, or identifying all professional accreditations held by a particular institution.

337. National Center for Education Statistics. **Education Directory: Colleges and Universities.** GPO, 1975/76- . Annual. OCLC 2575450. 1983-84 ed. S/N 065-000-00201-9. $10. **ED1.111:yr.**

This is a directory of accredited colleges and universities in the United States and outlying areas that offer at least a one-year program of college-level studies leading toward a degree. It gives date of establishment, enrollment, tuition and fees, affiliation, calendar system, levels of degrees offered, types of programs, and administrative officers. It contains no evaluative information.

338. National Center for Education Statistics. **Postsecondary Schools with Occupational Programs.** GPO, 1971- . Biennial. 378/.01/302573. OCLC 10476181. 1982 ed. S/N 065-000-00192-6. $9.50. **ED1.102:Oc1/yr.**

This is a directory of public and private noncollegiate schools offering occupational programs in preparation for specific careers. It also includes two- and four-year colleges and universities offering occupational programs leading to a certificate or degree at less than the baccalaureate level.

339. Office of Education. **Directory of Graduate Deans at United States Universities, 1872-1965**. By John L. Chase. GPO, 1966. 40 pp. **FS5.2:D34/872-965**.
The name of "each individual who has served as the principal administrative officer for graduate work at 186 institutions of higher education in the United States" is given. Schools with degree programs in only a single field or in a restricted area are excluded. Institutions are listed alphabetically within each state, and deans are listed chronologically. The dates when each person was a graduate dean and the person's major field are given. For deans in office at the time of publication, birth dates and the institutions from which their highest degrees were granted are also given. For each school the directory provides the dates of the doctorate and beginning of the graduate school. It is indexed by personal names with institutions in parentheses following the names.

Financial Aid Handbooks

340. Department of Education. **Federal Assistance for Programs Serving the Handicapped**. GPO, 1976- . Annual. LC 79-647376. HV3001.A2F43. 362.4/0456/0973. OCLC 5778185. **ED1.34:yr**.
This handbook lists and describes formula grants to states, project grants and contracts, direct payments, direct loans, guaranteed or insured loans, and nonfinancial assistance.

341. Department of Education. **Federal Student Financial Aid Handbook**. 3 sections. IA, annual. LC 82-640139. LB2337.4.F42. 378.3/0973. OCLC 08054682. **ED1.8:F49/2/yr**.
This is a guide to aid postsecondary institutions that administer major federal student financial aid programs. It is also useful for identifying financial aid programs.

342. Department of Education. **Selected List of Postsecondary Education Opportunities for Minorities and Women**. GPO, 1983. 71 pp. OCLC 09513842. S/N 065-000-00194-2. $2.50. **ED1.42:983**.
Loan, scholarship, and fellowship opportunities in specific fields from government and nongovernment sources are listed, and information is given on seeking general assistance in preparing for pursuit of educational and career goals at the postsecondary level. Information is given on contacts with specific programs to request additional information. Although this publication is aimed at minorities and women, many of the sources listed are open to other students.

Statistics

343. National Center for Education Statistics. **Associate Degrees and Other Formal Awards below the Baccalaureate**. GPO, annual. OCLC 1775962. **HE19.333: date**.
In a format that is primarily tables, this source provides summary data by institutional control and type, sex of recipient, state, type of curriculum, and discipline division and speciality.

344. National Center for Education Statistics. **Earned Degrees Conferred**. GPO, 1948- . Annual. LC 73-647678. LB2381.N24b. 378/.24/0973. OCLC 01713675. **ED1.117:date**.
A detailed listing of degrees conferred in each academic field by each institution during the year is arranged by state. This title provides data on baccalaureate and higher

degrees. For data on awards below the bachelor's level, see the companion volume, *Associate Degrees and Other Formal Awards below the Baccalaureate* (entry 343).

See also SB 217.

RESEARCH

Directories

345. Smithsonian Institution. **Smithsonian Opportunities for Research and Study in History, Art, Science.** IA, 1972- . Annual. LC 73-646897. Q11.S8S86. 001.4/3/09753. OCLC 01789143. **SI1.2:R31/yr.**
The Smithsonian Institution offers in-residence appointments for research and study using its facilities and staff. This is a guide for individuals, institutions, and organizations interested in these academic and grant programs.

Details are given about purpose, research fields, eligibility, duration of appointment, application, and deadlines. There are also descriptions of major activities, research resources, and staff interests at the Smithsonian Institution and information about research support units available for use by visiting scientists and scholars.

Research Reports

346. Bureau of Education. **Index to the Reports of the Commissioner of Education, 1867-1907.** GPO, 1909. 103 pp. (Bulletin 1909, no. 7.) **I16.3:909/7.**
The results of early educational studies and other educational papers were contained in the annual reports of the Commissioner of Education. This indexes a total of fifty-seven volumes by author and subject.

347. Head Start Bureau. **A Review of Head Start Research since 1969 and an Annotated Bibliography.** By Ada Jo Mann, Adele V. Harrell, and Maure Hurt, Jr. GPO, 1978. 158 pp. OCLC 3725583. S/N 017-092-00037-5. $7. **HE23.1011:H34.**
This annotated bibliography of research, reviews, and descriptions of Head Start programs includes summaries of research findings in crucial program areas and a discussion of the sources, nature, and scope of the literature.

348. National Institute of Education. **Resources in Education.** GPO, 1975- . Monthly. LC 75-644211. Z5813.R4. 016.370/78. OCLC 02241688. S/N 065-000-80003-9. $95/yr. **ED1.310:vol./nos.**
This is a monthly abstract journal that announces recent research reports, descriptions of outstanding programs, and other documents related to education. It provides current information to keep teachers, administrators, researchers, the public, and other members of the educational community informed about the latest significant educational research findings. It continues *Research in Education*.

349. Office of Education. **Bibliography of Research Studies in Education, 1926/27-1939/40.** 14 vols. GPO, 1929-42. (OE Bulletins.) **I16.3:nos. vary.**
Now only of historical value, this comprehensive bibliography covers the period 1926/27-1939/40, including doctoral dissertations, master's theses, and other pertinent research studies. Arrangement is by broad subject categories and the volumes are well indexed by personal names and corporate bodies as well as by subjects. The following

information is provided: author, title, degree, date of completion, name of institution, and a brief description of the study.

350.   Office of Education. **Office of Education Research Reports, 1956-65: Indexes and Resumes**. 2 vols. GPO, 1967. **FS5.212:12028/12029**.

Reports on research projects sponsored by the Bureau of Research, Office of Education, are cited. The index volume is in four sections: (1) author index, (2) institution index, (3) subject index, and (4) report number index. The second volume, arranged numerically, contains abstracts of the reports.

Geography

GENERAL WORKS

351.   Board on Geographic Names. **Gazetteers**. GPO, 1955-74.
Each gazetteer deals with a specific country or geographic region. Official place names
are given as authorized for use by the federal government.

       Afghanistan. 1971. **I33.8:ct**.

       Albania. 1961. 2d ed. **I33.8:8/2**.

       Algeria. 1972. **I33.8:ct**.

       Angola. 1956. **I33.8:20**.

       Antarctica. 1966. 2d ed. **I33.8:14**.

       Arabian Peninsula. 1961. **I33.8:54**.

       Argentina. 1967. **I33.8:103**.

       Australia. 1957. **I33.8:40**.

       Austria. 1962. **I33.8:66**.

       Belgium. 1963. **I33.8:73**.

       Bolivia. 1955. **I33.8:4**.

       Brazil. 1963. **I33.8:71**.

       British East Africa. 1955. **I33.8:1**.

       British Honduras. 1956. **I33.8:16**.

       British Solomon Islands. 1974. **I33.8:ct**.

       British West Indies and Bermuda. 1955. **I33.8:7**.

       Bulgaria. 1964. **I33.8:64**.

       Burma. 1966. **I33.8:96**.

       Burundi. 1964. **I33.8:84**.

       Cambodia. 1974. 2d ed. **I33.8:ct**.

       Cameroon. 1962. **I33.8:60**.

       Central African Republic. 1962. **I33.8:64**.

       Ceylon. 1960. **I33.8:49**.

Chad. 1962. I33.8:65.

Chile. 1967. I33.8:6.

China, Republic of, 1974. I33.8:ct.

Colombia. 1964. I33.8:86.

Congo, Republic of (Brazzaville). 1962. I33.8:61.

Congo, Republic of (Leopoldville). 1964. I33.8:80.

Cuba. 1963. 2d ed. I33.8:30/2.

Dahomey. 1965. I33.8:91.

Denmark and the Faeroe Islands. 1963. I33.8:53.

Dominican Republic. 1972. I33.8:ct.

Ecuador. 1957. I33.8:36.

Egypt. 1959. I33.8:45.

Fiji, Tonga, and Nauru. 1974. I33.8:ct.

Finland. 1962. I33.8:62.

France. 1964. I33.8:83.

French West Indies. 1957. I33.8:34.

Gabon. 1968. I33.8:107.

Germany, East. 1959. I33.8:43.

Germany, Federal Republic of. 1960. I33.8:47.

Greece. 1955. I33.8:11.

Guatemala. 1965. I33.8:94.

Guinea. 1965. I33.8:90.

Haiti. 1973. 2d ed. I33.8:ct.

Hawaiian Islands. 1956. I33.8:24.

Hong Kong and Macao. 1972. I33.8:ct.

Indian Ocean. 1957. I33.8:32.

Iran. 1956. I33.8:19.

Iraq. 1957. I33.8:37.

Israel. 1970. I33.8:114.

Italy. 1956. I33.8:23.

Ivory Coast. 1965. I33.8:89.

Japan. 1955. I33.8:12.

Jordan. 1971. I33.8:ct.

Kenya. 1964. I33.8:78.

Korea, South. 1965. I33.8:95.

Laos. 1973. 2d ed. I33.8:ct.

Lebanon. 1970. I33.8:115.

Liberia. 1968. I33.8:106.

Libya. 1973. 2d ed. I33.8:ct.

Madagascar. 1955. I33.8:2.

Malawi. 1970. I33.8:113.

Malaysia, Singapore, and Brunei. 1971. 2d ed. I33.8:10.

Mali. 1965. I33.8:93.

Malta. 1971. I33.8:ct.

Mauritania. 1966. I33.8:100.

Mexico. 1956. I33.8:15.

Mongolia. 1970. I33.8:116.

Morocco. 1970. I33.8:112.

Mozambique. 1960. I33.8:109.

New Calendonia. 1974. I33.8:ct.

New Hebrides. 1974. I33.8:ct.

Nicaragua. 1956. I33.8:25.

Niger. 1966. I33.8:99.

Norway. 1963. I33.8:77.

Panama and the Canal Zone. 1969. I33.8:110.

Paraguay. 1957. I33.8:35.

Portugal and Cape Verde Islands. 1961. I33.8:50.

Portuguese Guinea. 1968. I33.8:105.

Puerto Rico, Virgin Islands, etc. 1958. I33.8:38.

Rhodesia and Nyasaland. 1956. I33.8:17.

Rio Muni, Fernando Po, and Sao Tome e Principe. 1962. I33.8:63.

Rwandi. 1964. I33.8:85.

Senegal. 1965. I33.8:88.

Sierra Leone. 1966. I33.8:101.

South Atlantic. 1957. I33.8:31.

South Pacific. 1957. I33.8:39.

Southern Rhodesia. 1973. I33.8:ct.

Southwest Pacific. 1956. I33.8:29.

Spain and Andorra. 1961. I33.8:51.

Spanish Sahara. 1969. I33.8:108.

Sudan. 1962. I33.8:68.

Surinam. 1974. I33.8:ct.

Sweden. 1963. I33.8:72.

Tanzania. 1965. I33.8:92.

Thailand. 1966. I33.8:97.

Tunisia. 1964. I33.8:81.

Turkey. 1960. I33.8:46.

Uganda. 1964. I33.8:82.

Upper Volta. 1965. I33.8:87.

Uruguay. 1956. I33.8:21.

USSR. 7 vols. 1970. 2d ed. I33.8:42.

Venezuela. 1961. I33.8:56.

Vietnam, North. 1964. I33.8:79.

Vietnam, South. 1971. 2d ed. **I33.8:58**.

Zambia. 1972. **I33.8:ct**.

Zanzibar. 1964. **I33.8:76**.

352. Bureau of Land Management. **Glossaries of BLM Surveying and Mapping Terms**. GPO, 1980. 2d ed. 114 pp. OCLC 07327065. S/N 024-011-00149-2. $5.50. **I53.2:G51/3**.

353. Defense Mapping Agency. **Gazetteers: Names Approved by the United States Board on Geographic Names**. IA, 1979- . **D5.319:ct**.

> **Costa Rica**. 1983. 2d ed.
>
> **Djiboui**. 1983.
>
> **El Salvador**. 1982.
>
> **Ethiopia**. 1982.
>
> **Honduras**. 1983. 2d ed.
>
> **Indonesia**. 1982.
>
> **North Korea**. 1983.
>
> **Pakistan**. 1983. 3d ed.
>
> **People's Republic of China**. 1979.
>
> **Somalia**. 1982.
>
> **Syria**. 1983. 2d ed.
>
> **Undersea Features**. 1981. 3d ed.
>
> **Yugoslavia**. 1983.

354. Defense Mapping Agency. Hydrographic/Topographic Center. **Glossary of Mapping, Charting, and Geodetic Terms**. IA, 1981. 4th ed. 264 pp. OCLC 8830330.

355. Library of Congress. Geography and Map Division. **Guide to the History of Cartography: An Annotated List of References on the History of Maps and Mapmaking**. IA, 1973. 96 pp. LC 73-9776. Z6021.R57. 016.5269'8. OCLC 662132. Free from the Central Services Division, Library of Congress, Washington, DC 20540. **LC5.2:H62/2/973**.

This is an annotated list of general works, with references to individual countries and to specialized aspects of cartography. It includes cartobibliographies and other aids to the cartographic history of the United States and its states. Most of the cited titles are monographs.

356. Library of Congress. Geography and Map Division. **A List of Geographical Atlases in the Library of Congress with Bibliographical Notes**. 8 vols. GPO, 1909-74. LC 9-35009. Z6028.U56. Volumes 2 and 5-8 are free from the Central Services Division, Library of Congress, Washington, DC 20540. (Other volumes are out of print.) **LC5.2:G29/v.1-8**.

Atlases are described in detail, with tables of contents for many volumes. Volumes 1-6 list a total of 10,254 titles. Volumes 1 and 2 are a complete list of atlases held by the Library of Congress up to 1909, with author and subject index. Volumes 3 and 4 list new additions to the collection with a cumulative author index in volume 4. The remaining volumes are: (5) world atlases; (6) Europe, Asia, Africa, Oceania, and the polar regions of the ocean; (7) western hemisphere and countries of North and South America; and (8) index to volume 7.

357.   National Science Foundation. **Geographic Names of the Antarctic.** By Fred G. Alberts. GPO, 1981. 981 pp. S/N 038-000-00471-9. $17. **NS1.2:An8/4.**
The names given are approved by the U.S. Board on Geographic Names and the Secretary of the Interior for features in Antarctica and the area extending north to the Antarctic Convergence.

See also SB 102 and SB 183.

THE AMERICAS

General Works

358.   Library of Congress. **List of Maps of America in the Library of Congress Preceded by a List of Works Relating to Cartography.** By P. Lee Phillips. GPO, 1901. 1,137 pp. LC 1-24175. Z881.U5. (Repr.: Burt Franklin, $46.50.)
The list includes both maps published separately and those in books and atlases, with a comprehensive bibliography on the literature of cartography.

359.   Library of Congress. **Maps and Charts of North America and the West Indies, 1750-1789: A Guide to the Collections of the Library of Congress.** Comp. by John R. Sellers and Patricia M. VanEe. GPO, 1981. 495 pp. LC 80-607054. Z6027.N68U54. 016.912/7. OCLC 06223077. S/N 030-004-00020-5. $17. **LC1.6/4:M32/2/750-789.**
This is one of three annotated guides to the three main types of original nonbook materials in the Library of Congress's Revolutionary-era holdings: manuscripts, graphics, and maps. It is a comprehensive list of the Geography and Map Division's holdings of maps and charts of North America and the West Indies for the years 1750-89. The items listed can be examined in the Geography and Map Division, and photographic copies of many of them may be ordered from the Library of Congress.

Latin America

360.   Department of State. **Boundaries of the Latin American Republics: An Annotated List of Documents, 1493-1943 (Tentative Version).** By Alexander Marchant. GPO, 1944. 386 pp. (Inter-American series, no. 24.) **S1.26:24.**
Documents published from 1493 to 1943 on the boundaries of Latin American countries are arranged in two major sections: in chronological order, and by geographic or boundary name. A third section contains a substantial bibliography.

United States

General Works

361.   Geological Survey. **Maps for America: Cartographic Products of the U.S. Geological Survey and Others.** By Morris M. Mordecai. GPO, 1981. 2d ed. 265 pp., illus. LC 81-607878. GA405.T46. 526/.0973. S/N 024-001-03449-2. $15. **I19.2:M32/12/981.**
This comprehensive look at mapping serves as a guide to the uses and types of maps available from the U.S. Geological Survey and other agencies. Included is a short

history of mapping in the United States. An index, a glossary, and an address list of supply agencies are also found in this profusely illustrated volume. The first edition was published in 1979 as a U.S. Geological Survey centennial volume, 1879-1979.

Altitudes

362. Geological Survey. **A Dictionary of Altitudes in the United States**. Comp. by Henry Gannett. GPO, 1906. 4th ed. 1,072 pp. (Bulletin 274.) **I19.3:274.**
The dictionary is arranged by states and cities, in tabular form, with authority and elevation of localities given in feet above sea level.

Atlases

363. Geological Survey. **National Atlas of the United States**. 1970. 431 pp. LC 79-654043. **I19.2:N21a.**
This is the first national atlas of the United States and one of the most significant works ever published by the U.S. government. Unfortunately, it has not been reprinted as a single volume since 1970, and it is now out of print in book format. Selected individual maps have been published as separate sales publications, however, and a price list is available from the Geological Survey.

Prepared by the Geological Survey with the cooperation of more than eighty federal agencies and more than two dozen colleges, universities, and commercial firms, this atlas was designed to be of "practical use to decision makers in government and business, planners, research scholars and others needing to visualize country-wide distributional patterns and relationships between environmental phenomena and human activities."

It contains 756 maps, and hundreds of insets, under the following headings: General Reference, Physical, Historical, Economic, Socio-cultural, Administrative, Mapping and Charting, and the World. Of particular interest to businessmen engaged in international commerce are maps showing foreign service and U.S. foreign trade areas. The economic maps include many comparable to those found in the *Rand McNally Commercial Atlas and Marketing Guide*, which has long been unique in this area. The section entitled "Administrative Maps" shows the changing face of regional administration of the federal government as well as public lands such as national parks, forest, and wilderness areas. A detailed subject index is included at the beginning of the atlas, with an index of over forty-one thousand places at the end.

364. Library of Congress. Map Division. **United States Atlases: A List of National, State, County, City, and Regional Atlases in the Library of Congress**. Comp. by Clara Egli LeGear. 2 vols. GPO, 1950-53. LC 50-62950. Z881.U5 1950at. (Repr.: Vol. 1, Arno, $18. Vol. 2 out of print.) **LC5.2:Un35/v.1,2.**
Over seven thousand atlases (published from 1776 to 1953) are included in classified arrangement with an author index. Volume 2 includes approximately two thousand atlases not in the Library of Congress collection, with U.S. library locations provided. This source is particularly useful for its descriptions of state, county, and city atlases published during the last quarter of the nineteenth century and the early twentieth century.

Boundaries

365. Bureau of Land Management. **Surveys and Surveyors of the Public Domain, 1785-1975.** By Lola Cazier. GPO, 1976. 228 pp., illus. OCLC 2969721. S/N 024-011-00083-6. $8. **I53.2:Su7/785-975.**
This is a narrative history of cadastral surveys performed to identify boundaries between federal land and private or local government-owned lands since 1785. It discusses the surveyors, the history of public land surveys, and survey laws. Black-and-white photographs and some maps are included.

366. Geological Survey. **Boundaries, Areas, Geographic Centers and Altitudes of the United States and the Several States with a Brief Record of Important Changes in Their Territory and Government.** By Edward M. Douglas. GPO, 1930. 4th ed. 265 pp. (Bulletin 817.) **I19.3:817.**
This is a historical overview of the changes in boundaries of the states and territories of the United States. Refererences to original sources and maps are provided. Previous editions were published in 1885 (1st), 1900 (2d), 1904 (3d), 1906 (3d, repr. with corrections), and 1923 (3d ed., rev. and enl.). It is updated by the following entry.

367. Geological Survey. **Boundaries of the United States and the Several States.** By Franklin K. Van Zandt. GPO, 1966. 291 pp., illus. (Bulletin 1212.) **I19.3:1212.**
This source provides information on areas, boundaries, altitudes, and geographic centers. It includes ready reference information about U.S., state, and territorial boundaries with data on the source and marking as well as related data on altitudes, geographic centers, and so on.

Maps

368. Geological Survey. **National Cartographic Information Center.**
The National Cartographic Information Center (NCIC) is a unit of the U.S. Geological Survey that exists to help the public find maps of all kinds, as well as much of the data and materials used to compile and print them. It is the public's primary source of cartographic information. The NCIC deals not only with federal, but also with state, local, and private cartographic information. It sells maps and data products, provides research and information services, and provides information about numerous federal agencies engaged in mapping.

The NCIC operates five regional offices and has established affiliated offices with many state governments. Its headquarter's address is: National Headquarters, National Cartographic Information Center, U.S. Geological Survey, 507 National Center, Reston, VA 22092; (703) 860-6045.

369. Library of Congress. Geography and Map Division. **Fire Insurance Maps in the Library of Congress: Plans of North American Cities and Towns Produced by the Sanborn Map Company: A Checklist.** GPO, 1981. 773 pp., illus. LC 80-607938. Z6026.I7U54. 016.912/73. OCLC 06491015. S/N 030-004-00018-3. $32. **LC5.2:F51.**
This checklist describes some fifty thousand editions of fire insurance maps in the Sanborn Map Co. collection of the Library of Congress. This collection is a uniform series of large-scale maps depicting the commercial, industrial, and residential sections of about twelve thousand cities and towns in the United States, Canada, and Mexico. The maps, dating from 1867 to the present, show the size, shape, construction, fire walls, window and door locations, sprinkler systems, and types of roofs of buildings. They show widths and names of streets, property boundaries, building use, and house

and block numbers. "Sanborn maps are thus an unrivaled source of information about the structure and use of buildings in American cities." Entries give city, county, date of edition, number of streets, and comments.

370. Library of Congress. Geography and Map Division. **Land Ownership Maps: A Checklist of Nineteenth-Century United States County Maps in the Library of Congress.** GPO, 1967 (repr. 1978). 86 pp. LC 67-60091. Z6027.U5U54. S/N 030-004-00004-3. $5. **LC5.2:L22.**

371. Library of Congress. Geography and Map Division. **Maps Showing Explorers' Routes, Trails and Early Roads in the United States: An Annotated List.** Comp. by Richard S. Ladd. GPO, 1962. 137 pp. LC 62-60066. **LC5.2:Ex7.**
This is a highly selective bibliography, indexed by names and geographic areas.

372. Library of Congress. Geography and Map Division. **Panoramic Maps of Anglo-American Cities: A Checklist of Maps in the Collections of the Library of Congress, Geography and Map Division.** By John R. Hebert. GPO, 1974. LC 73-18312. Z6027.U5U54 1974. S/N 030-004-00011-6. $5.50. **LC5.2:An4.**
This is a checklist of "bird's-eye views," nonphotographic representations that depict cities in forty-seven states, the District of Columbia, and Canada. The list of 1,117 panoramic maps in the Library of Congress's collections is invaluable, since it provides access to the largest collection of these maps in North America.

373. Library of Congress. Maps and Charts Division. **The Lowery Collection: A Descriptive List of Maps of Spanish Possessions within the Present Limits of the United States, 1502-1820.** Ed. by Phillip Lee Phillips. GPO, 1912. 567 pp. **LC5.2:L95.**
This comprehensive work is arranged chronologically with extensive annotations and indexed by authors, titles, and general subjects.

374. National Archives and Records Service. **Guide to Cartographic Records in the National Archives.** By Charlotte Ashby et al. GPO, 1971. 444 pp. LC 76-611061. **GS4.6/2:C24.**

SOVIET UNION

375. Library of Congress. Reference Department. **Soviet Geography: A Bibliography.** Ed. by Nicholas R. Rodionoff. 2 vols. IA, 1951. 668 pp. LC 51-62891. Z2506.U58. (Repr.: Greenwood Press, $40.25.)
Part 1 covers USSR geography by subjects; part 2, administrative, natural, and economic regions. Publications are primarily in Russian, with U.S. library locations.

History and Area Studies

GENERAL WORKS

376.   Central Intelligence Agency. **The World Factbook**. GPO, 1981- . Annual. LC
81-641760. OCLC 07390695. 1984 ed. S/N 041-015-00157-4. $11. **PrEx3.15:yr.**
Current summaries on world nations describe aspects of the land, water, people,
government, economy, communications, and defense. Each brief profile includes a map
of the country. This is a good source of information on small and Third World
countries. It continues *National Basic Intelligence Factbook*.

377.   Department of the Army. **Country Study Series**. (DA pamphlet 550-series.)
D101.22:550-nos. vary.
The *Country Study* Series replaced the Army's *Area Handbook* Series in 1978. Each title
in the series focuses on a foreign country and is written to provide basic insight and
understanding of the society with a dynamic rather than a static portrayal. Each title
describes a country's economic, national security, political, and social systems and
institutions, their interrelationships, and how they are shaped culturally. Each is written
by a multidisciplinary team of social scientists. The studies focus on historical, cultural,
political, and socioeconomic characteristics of the society, with emphasis on the people.

Many *Country Studies* are listed in this chapter in the sections that follow. The studies
are revised and updated irregularly. They are usually reprinted by GPO when the stock
of sales publications is exhausted. For a list of in-print titles, stock numbers, and prices
see SB-166. An alphabetic list of over one hundred countries for which studies have
been completed follows:

> **Afghanistan.** DA Pamphlet 550-65.
>
> **Albania.** DA Pamphlet 550-98.
>
> **Algeria.** DA Pamphlet 550-44.
>
> **Angola.** DA Pamphlet 550-59.
>
> **Argentina.** DA Pamphlet 550-73.
>
> **Australia.** DA Pamphlet 550-169.

Austria. DA Pamphlet 550-176.

Bangladesh. DA Pamphlet 550-175.

Belgium. DA Pamphlet 550-170.

Bolivia. DA Pamphlet 550-66.

Brazil. DA Pamphlet 550-20.

Bulgaria. DA Pamphlet 550-168.

Burma. DA Pamphlet 550-61.

Burundi. DA Pamphlet 550-83.

Cambodia (Khmer Republic). DA Pamphlet 550-50.

Cameroon, United Republic of. DA Pamphlet 550-166.

Ceylon. DA Pamphlet 550-96.

Chad. DA Pamphlet 550-159.

Chile. DA Pamphlet 550-77.

China, People's Republic of. DA Pamphlet 550-60.

China, Republic of. DA Pamphlet 550-63.

Congo, Democratic Republic of (Congo Kinshasa). DA Pamphlet 550-67.

Congo, People's Republic of (Congo Brazzaville). DA Pamphlet 550-91.

Costa Rica. DA Pamphlet 550-90.

Cuba. DA Pamphlet 550-152.

Cyprus. DA Pamphlet 550-22.

Czechoslovakia. DA Pamphlet 550-158.

Ecuador. DA Pamphlet 550-52.

Egypt. DA Pamphlet 550-43.

El Salvador. DA Pamphlet 550-150.

Ethiopia. DA Pamphlet 550-28.

Finland. DA Pamphlet 550-167.

Germany. DA Pamphlet 550-29.

Germany, East. DA Pamphlet 550-155.

Germany, Federal Republic of. DA Pamphlet 550-173.

Ghana. DA Pamphlet 550-153.

Greece. DA Pamphlet 550-87.

Guatemala. DA Pamphlet 550-78.

Guinea. DA Pamphlet 550-174.

Guyana. DA Pamphlet 550-82.

Haiti. DA Pamphlet 550-164.

Honduras. DA Pamphlet 550-151.

Hungary. DA Pamphlet 550-165.

India. DA Pamphlet 550-21.

Indian Ocean Territories. DA Pamphlet 550-154.

Indonesia. DA Pamphlet 550-39.

Iran. DA Pamphlet 550-68.

Iraq. DA Pamphlet 550-31.

Israel. DA Pamphlet 550-25.

Italy. DA Pamphlet 550-182.

Ivory Coast. DA Pamphlet 550-69.

Jamaica. DA Pamphlet 550-177.

Japan. DA Pamphlet 550-30.

Jordan. DA Pamphlet 550-34.

Kenya. DA Pamphlet 550-56.

Korea, North. DA Pamphlet 550-81.

Korea, South. DA Pamphlet 550-41.

Laos. DA Pamphlet 550-58.

Lebanon. DA Pamphlet 550-38.

Libya. DA Pamphlet 550-85.

Malagasy Republic. DA Pamphlet 550-163.

Malawi. DA Pamphlet 550-172.

Malaysia. DA Pamphlet 550-45.

Mauritania. DA Pamphlet 550-161.

Mexico. DA Pamphlet 550-79.

Mongolia. DA Pamphlet 550-76.

Morocco. DA Pamphlet 550-49.

Mozambique. DA Pamphlet 550-64.

Nepal, Bhautan, and Sikkim. DA Pamphlet 550-35.

Nicaragua. DA Pamphlet 550-88.

Nigeria. DA Pamphlet 550-157.

Oceania. DA Pamphlet 550-94.

Pakistan. DA Pamphlet 550-48.

Panama. DA Pamphlet 550-46.

Paraguay. DA Pamphlet 550-156.

Peripheral States of the Arabian Peninsula. DA Pamphlet 550-92.

Persian Gulf States. DA Pamphlet 550-185.

Peru. DA Pamphlet 550-42.

Philippines. DA Pamphlet 550-72.

Poland. DA Pamphlet 550-162.

Portugal. DA Pamphlet 550-181.

Romania. DA Pamphlet 550-160.

Rwanda. DA Pamphlet 550-84.

Saudi Arabia. DA Pamphlet 550-51.

Senegal. DA Pamphlet 550-70.

Sierra Leone. DA Pamphlet 550-180.

Singapore. DA Pamphlet 550-184.

Somalia. DA Pamphlet 550-86.

South Africa. DA Pamphlet 550-93.

Southern Rhodesia. DA Pamphlet 550-171.

Soviet Union. DA Pamphlet 550-95.

Spain. DA Pamphlet 550-179.

Sudan. DA Pamphlet 550-27.

Syria. DA Pamphlet 550-47.

Tanzania. DA Pamphlet 550-62.

Thailand. DA Pamphlet 550-53.

Trinidad and Tobago. DA Pamphlet 550-178.

Tunisia. DA Pamphlet 550-89.

Turkey. DA Pamphlet 550-80.

Uganda. DA Pamphlet 550-74.

Uruguay. DA Pamphlet 550-97.

Venezuela. DA Pamphlet 550-71.

Vietnam, North. DA Pamphlet 550-57.

Vietnam, South. DA Pamphlet 550-55.

Yemen. DA Pamphlet 550-183.

Yugoslavia. DA Pamphlet 550-99.

Zaire. DA Pamphlet 550-67.

Zambia. DA Pamphlet 550-75.

Zimbabwe. DA Pamphlet 550-171.

378. Department of State. Bureau of Public Affairs. **Background Notes on the Countries of the World.** GPO, 1980- . Monthly. OCLC 07437325. S/N 044-000-91001-8. $32/yr. **S1.123:ct.**

These short factual pamphlets about approximately 160 countries and territories include information on land, people, history, government, political conditions, economy, and foreign relations.

The subscription service includes updated or new *Background Notes* (without binder) published irregularly during a twelve-month period beginning at the time of the subscription. A complete set of all currently available issues may be purchased for $34 (S/N 044-000-91214-7). A binder in which to file the Notes may be purchased for $3.75 (S/N 044-000-99608-1). SB 093 contains a list of in-print issues with stock number and price for individual issues.

379. Library of Congress. **A Century of Photographs, 1846-1946: Selected from the Collections of the Library of Congress.** GPO, 1980. 211 pp., illus. LC 79-21624. TR6.U62D572. 779/.074/0153. OCLC 5497409. S/N 030-000-00117-6. $20. **LC1.2:P56/5/846-946.**

Since 1946 the Library of Congress has collected photographs as primary sources of historical research. The collection contains close to nine million photographic prints, negatives, transparencies, and stereographs. This title provides descriptive and interpretative essays on the collections, as well as 263 representative images showing the range and beauty of the collections.

ARCHEOLOGY

380. National Park Service. **Remote Sensing: A Handbook for Archeologists and Cultural Resource Managers.** By Thomas R. Lyons and Thomas Eugene Avery. GPO, 1977. 110 pp., illus. 930/.1/028. S/N 024-005-00688-5. $6. **I29.9/2:Se5.**
The handbook presents basic principles of remote sensor data gathering, handling, and interpretation for cultural resource managers and archeological and historical investigators. Photographs, bibliography, and glossary are included.

GENEALOGY

381. Bureau of the Census. **Heads of Families at the First Census, 1790.** 12 vols. GPO, 1907-09. (Repr.: Genealogical Publishing Co., 22 vols., individually priced.) **C3.ll:ct.**
This work contains lists of people of any given surname who were living in a particular town in the year 1790. It contains data from Maine, New Hampshire, Vermont, Massachusetts, Rhode Island, Connecticut, New York, Pennsylvania, Maryland, Virginia, North Carolina, and South Carolina.

382. Library of Congress. **Genealogies in the Library of Congress: A Bibliography.** Ed. by Marion J. Kaminkow. 2 vols. IA, 1972. LC 74-187078. Z5319.U53. OCLC 315166. (Repr.: Magna Carta, $150.)

      _____. Vol. 3. **Supplement, 1972-76.** IA, 1976. 285 pp. (Repr.: Magna Carta, $25.)
This title supersedes *American and English Genealogies in the Library of Congress* (2d ed., 1919). It is a bibliographic guide to genealogical materials held by the Library of Congress. European, Canadian, Australian, and Latin American families are listed. Names are grouped by pronunciation and are identified by given name, place of residence, and dates. Manuscripts are not included in the guide.

AFRICA

General Works

383. Department of the Army. **Africa, Problems and Prospects: A Bibliographic Survey.** GPO, 1978. 577 pp., illus. (DA pamphlet 550-17-1.) Z3501.U47 1977. 016.96. OCLC 3379905. S/N 008-020-00712-9. $13. **D101.22:550-17-1.**
This analytical literature survey aims to assess Africa's problems and prospects. Annotated citations, appendixes, and maps provide data ranging from the strategic importance of Africa as a continent to the political, economic, sociological, and military aspects of African states.

384. Library of Congress. **Introduction to Africa: A Selective Guide to Background Reading.** By Helen F. Conover. GPO, 1952. 237 pp. LC 52-60007. Z3501.U53. (Repr.: Greenwood Press, or Negro Universities Press, $16.75.)
This is a highly selective annotated guide for the nonspecialist interested in background reading on Africa in general and the specific countries. It is now primarily of historical value.

385. Library of Congress. **Islam in Sub-Saharan Africa: A Partially Annotated Guide.** Comp. by Samir M. Zoghby. GPO, 1976. 318 pp. LC 76-7050. Z7835.M6Z63. 297/.0967. OCLC 2091493. S/N 030-001-00068-1. $14. **LC1.12/2:Is4.**
This is a partially annotated bibliography of publications related to Islam in Sub-Saharan Africa through 1974; North Africa is not covered. Items focus on Islam and Muslim populations and are arranged by historical periods. Works included deal with the Islamization of this area; Muslim populations and their social, political, and religious structure; the impact of Islam and Arabic culture on converted peoples; resistance of Muslims to European imperial designs; and Islam's role in political relations between Muslim states in the twentieth century.

386. Library of Congress. **A List of American Doctoral Dissertations on Africa.** GPO, 1962. 69 pp.
The list covers dissertations from universities in the United States and Canada from the late 1800s until 1960/61. It is arranged alphabetically by authors, indexed by key words in titles. For coverage through 1965, see Doris M. Cruger, *A List of American Doctoral Dissertations on Africa Covering 1961/62 through 1964/65* (University Microfilms, Ann Arbor, MI, 1967).

387. Library of Congress. General Reference and Bibliography Division. African Section. **Africa South of the Sahara: A Selected, Annotated List of Writings, 1951-1956.** Comp. by Helen F. Conover. IA, 1957. LC 57-60035. Z3501.U55. **LC2.2:Af8.**

388. Library of Congress. General Reference and Bibliography Division. African Section. **North and Northeast Africa: A Selected Annotated List of Writings, 1951-1957.** Comp. by Helen F. Conover. GPO, 1957. 182 pp. LC 57-60062. Z3501.U57. (Repr.: Greenwood Press, or Negro Universities Press, $15.) **LC2.2:Af8/2.**
This is a highly selective list of three hundred fifty publications of interest to the layman.

See also SB 284.

Algeria

389. Department of the Army. **Algeria: A Country Study.** Ed. by Harold D. Nelson. GPO, 1979. 3d ed. 370 pp., illus. (DA pamphlet 550-44.) LC 79-13466. DT275.A593 1979. 965/.05. OCLC 5328278. S/N 008-020-00791-9. $11. **D101.22:550-44/3.**
For a description of the *Country Study* series *see* entry 377.

Angola

390. Department of the Army. **Angola: A Country Study.** Ed. by Irving Kaplan. GPO, 1979. 286 pp., illus. (DA pamphlet 550-59.) LC 79-21789. S/N 008-020-00816-8. $11. **D101.22:550-59/2.**
For a description of the *County Study* series *see* entry 377.

Egypt

391. Department of the Army. **Egypt: A Country Study**. Ed. by Richard F. Nyrop. GPO, 1983. 4th ed. 362 pp., illus. (DA pamphlet 550-43.) LC 83-600110. DT46.E32 1983. 962/.05. S/N 008-020-00956-3. $8. **D101.22:550-43/4**.
For a description of the *Country Study* series *see* entry 377.

Ethiopia

392. Department of the Army. **Ethiopia: A Country Study**. Ed. by Harold D. Nelson. GPO, 1981. 396 pp., illus. (DA pamphlet 550-28.) LC 81-7928. DT378.E73 1981. 963/.06. OCLC 07555434. S/N 008-020-00870-2. $12. **D101.22:550-28/3**.
For a description of the *Country Study* series *see* entry 377.

Libya

393. Department of the Army. **Libya: A Country Study**. Ed. by Harold D. Nelson. GPO, 1979. 3d ed. 350 pp., illus. (DA pamphlet 550-85.) LC 79-024183. DT215.N97 1979. 961/.2. OCLC 5676518. S/N 008-020-00817-6. $11. **D101.22: 550-85/3**.
For a description of the *Country Study* series *see* entry 377.

Morocco

394. Department of the Army. **Morocco: A Country Study**. Ed. by Harold D. Nelson. GPO, 1978. 4th ed. 410 pp., illus. (DA pamphlet 550-49.) S/N 008-020-00762-5. $12. **D101.22:550-49/3**.
For a description of the *Country Study* series *see* entry 377.

Nigeria

395. Department of the Army. **Nigeria: A Country Study**. Ed. by Harold D. Nelson. GPO, 1982. 376 pp., illus. (DA pamphlet 550-157.) S/N 008-020-00913-0. $12. **D101.22:550-157/3**.
For a description of the *Country Study* series *see* entry 377.

Somalia

396. Department of the Army. **Somalia: A Country Study**. GPO, 1982. 3d ed. 373 pp., illus. (DA pamphlet 550-86.). LC 82-16401. DT401.5.S68 1982. 967/.73. OCLC 08786054. S/N 008-020-00926-1. $13. **D101.22:550-86/3**.
For a description of the *Country Study* series *see* entry 377.

South Africa

397. Department of the Army. **South Africa: A Country Study**. Ed. by Harold D. Nelson. GPO, 1981. 494 pp., illus. (DA pamphlet 550-93.) LC 81-19155. S/N 008-020-00892-3. $12. **D101.22:550-93/2**.
For a description of the *Country Study* series *see* entry 377.

Tanzania

398. Department of the Army. **Tanzania: A Country Study**. Ed. by Irving Kaplan. GPO, 1978. 344 pp., illus. (DA pamphlet 550-62.) LC 78-10304. S/N 008-020-00767-6. $11. **D101.22:550-62/2**.
For a description of the *Country Study* series *see* entry 377.

Tunisia

399. Department of the Army. **Tunisia: A Country Study**. Ed. by Harold D. Nelson. GPO, 1979. 2d ed. 326 pp., illus. (DA pamphlet 550-89.) DT245.A55 1979. 309.1/61/1. OCLC 5101437. S/N 008-020-00792-7. $11. **D101.22:550-89/2**.
For a description of the *Country Study* series *see* entry 377.

Zaire

400. Department of the Army. **Zaire: A Country Study**. Ed. by Irving Kaplan. GPO, 1979. 332 pp., illus. (DA pamphlet 550-67.) LC 79-9987. S/N 008-020-00776-5. $11. **D101.22:550-67/2**.
For a description of the *Country Study* series *see* entry 377.

Zambia

401. Department of the Army. **Zambia: A Country Study**. Ed. by Irving Kaplan. GPO, 1979. 308 pp., illus. (DA pamphlet 550-75.) LC 79-21324. S/N 008-020-00814-1. $11. **D101.22:550-75/3**.
For a description of the *Country Study* series *see* entry 377.

Zimbabwe

402. Department of the Army. **Zimbabwe: A Country Study**. GPO, 1983. 2d ed. 360 pp., illus. (DA pamphlet 550-171.) LC 83-011946. DT962.Z55 1983. 968.91/04. OCLC 09622411. S/N 008-020-00964-4. $8. **D101.22:550-171/2**.
For a description of the *Country Study* series *see* entry 377.

ASIA AND THE MIDDLE EAST

Asia

General Works

403. Library of Congress. Orientalia Division. **Southeast Asia: An Annotated Bibliography of Selected Reference Sources in Western Languages.** Comp. by Cecil Hobbs. GPO, 1964. Rev. and enl. ed. 180 pp. LC 63-60089. Z3321.U524 1964. (Repr.: Greenwood Press, $17.50.) **LC17.2:As4/3/964.**

Contained in this general bibliography are 535 entries. The first edition (1952) was titled *Southeast Asia: An Annotated Bibliography of Selected Reference Sources.* This edition lists publications in chapters by specific geographic areas. Lengthy annotations are both descriptive and critical. It is indexed by authors, titles, and subjects.

404. Library of Congress. Reference Department. **Indochina: A Bibliography of the Land and People.** Comp. by Cecil C. Hobbs et al. IA, 1950. 367 pp. LC 51-60006. Z3321.U53 1950. (Repr.: Greenwood Press, $23.50.) **LC29.2:In2.**

This major bibliography cites works in Western, Russian, and some oriental languages which deal with many aspects of life and society in Indochina.

Afghanistan

405. Department of the Army. **Afghanistan: A Country Study.** Ed. by Harvey H. Smith. GPO, 1973 (repr. 1978). 453 pp., illus. (DA pamphlet 550-65.) LC 73-600084. S/N 008-020-00461-8. $13. **D101.22:550-65/2.**

For a description of the *Country Study* series *see* entry 377.

China

406. Bureau of Economic Analysis. **The Provinces of the People's Republic of China: A Political and Economic Bibliography.** By John Phillip Emerson et al. GPO, 1976. 734 pp. (International population statistics reports, series P-90, no. 15.) LC 76-600034. OCLC 2710343. **C59.13/2:90/25.**

This is a bibliography of major sources on political and economic development in the provinces of the People's Republic of China. It gives author, title, description, name of source that carried the item (newspapers, periodicals, and other publications), availability of English translations, and U.S. libraries holding a copy of the original Chinese text.

407. Department of the Army. **China: An Analytical Survey of Literature.** GPO, 1978. 4th ed. 231 pp., illus. (DA pamphlet 550-9-1.) Z3106.U45 1977. 016.32715. OCLC 2373370. S/N 008-020-00629-7. $9. **D101.22:550-9-1.**

This annotated bibliographic survey of literature on China, 1971-76, is based on classified publications from the Army Library in the Pentagon.

408. Department of the Army. **China: A Country Study.** Ed. by Rinn-Sup Shinn and Frederica M. Bunge. GPO, 1981. 3d ed. 622 pp., illus. (DA pamphlet 550-60.) LC 81-12878. DS706.C489 1981. 951. OCLC 07738928. S/N 008-020-00888-5. $12. **D101.22:550-60/3.**

For a description of the *Country Study* series *see* entry 377.

409. Department of the Army. **Communist China: A Bibliographic Survey**. GPO, 1971. 253 pp. (DA pamphlet 550-9.) **D101.22:550-9**.
This updates two earlier bibliographies published by the Army: *Communist China: Ruthless Enemy or Paper Tiger: A Bibliographic Survey* (1962) and *Communist China, a Strategic Survey: A Bibliography* (1966). It covers a wide range of source materials on a number of subjects including China's nuclear threat, global ambition and objectives, foreign policy and international relations, cultural revolution, and military posture. Full-color maps are included.

Indonesia

410. Department of the Army. **Indonesia: A Country Study**. Ed. by Frederica M. Bunge. GPO, 1983. 4th ed. 343 pp., illus. (DA pamphlet 550-39.) LC 83-015446. OCLC 10266252. S/N 008-020-00965-2. $8. **D101.22:550-39/4**.
For a description of the *Country Study* series *see* entry 377.

411. Library of Congress. General Reference and Bibliography Division. **Netherlands East Indies: A Bibliography of Books Published after 1930, and Periodicals after 1932 Available in U.S. Libraries**. GPO, 1945. 208 pp. LC 45-36052. Z3276.U62. Free from the Central Services Division, Library of Congress, Washington, DC 20540. **LC2.2:N38/2/945**.
Books on many subjects in many languages are listed, with locations of copies in U.S. libraries. The work is indexed by authors.

Japan

412. Library of Congress. Photoduplication Service. **Checklist of Archives in the Japanese Ministry of Foreign Affairs, Tokyo, Japan, 1868-1945: Microfilmed for the Library of Congress, 1949-1951**. Comp. by Cecil H. Uyehara. IA, 1954. 262 pp. LC 53-60045.
Official Japanese documents are listed in chronological order within chapters by historical periods. A detailed index is provided.

Korea

413. Library of Congress. Reference Department. **Korea: An Annotated Bibliography**. 3 vols. GPO, 1950. LC 50-62963. Z3316.U6 1950a. **LC29.2:K48/v.1-3**.
   Vol. 1. **Publications in the Western Languages**. Comp. by Helen D. Jones and Robin Walker. 155 pp.
   Vol. 2. **Publications in the Russian Language**. Comp. by Albert Parry, John T. Dorosh, and Elizabeth Gardner Dorosh. 84 pp.
   Vol. 3. **Publications in Far Eastern Languages**. 167 pp.
This is a bibliography of materials on Korea in the Library of Congress collection.

Laos

414. Department of the Army. **Laos: A Country Study**. Ed. by Donald P. Whitaker. GPO, 1972 (repr. 1979). 338 pp., illus. (DA pamphlet 550-58.) LC 72-600173. S/N 008-020-00467-7. $11. **D101.22:550-58/2**.
For a description of the *Country Study* series *see* entry 377.

North Korea

415. Department of the Army. **North Korea: A Country Study**. Ed. by Frederica M. Bunge. GPO, 1981. 3d ed. 333 pp., illus. (DA pamphlet 550-81.) LC 81-22915. DS932.N66 1981. 951.9/3. OCLC 08170181. S/N 008-020-00908-3. $11. **D101.22:550-81/3**.

For a description of the *Country Study* series *see* entry 377.

North Vietnam

416. Department of the Army. **North Vietnam: A Country Study**. Ed. by Harvey H. Smith. GPO, 1967 (repr. 1981). 508 pp., illus. (DA pamphlet 550-57.) S/N 008-020-00202-0. $13. **D101.22:550-57**.

For a description of the *Country Study* series *see* entry 377.

South Korea

417. Department of the Army. **South Korea: A Country Study**. GPO, 1982. 3d ed. 331 pp., illus. (DA pamphlet 550-41.) LC 82-11385. DS902.S68 1982. 951.9/5. OCLC 08553965. S/N 008-020-00921-1. $12. **D101.22:550-41/4**.

For a description of the *Country Study* series *see* entry 377.

Thailand

418. Department of the Army. **Thailand: A Country Study**. Ed. by Frederica M. Bunge. GPO, 1980. 5th ed. 382 pp., illus. (DA pamphlet 550-53.) LC 80-23075. DS563.5.H46 1980. 959.3. S/N 008-020-00859-1. $11. **D101.22:550-53/4**.

For a description of the *Country Study* series *see* entry 377.

Middle East

General Works

419. Board on Geographic Names. **Yeman Arab Republic: Official Standard Names Approved by the United States Board on Geographic Names**. IA, 1976. 124 pp. DS247.Y42D43 1976. 915.3/32. OCLC 2924287. **I33.8:Y3**.

420. Department of the Army. **Middle East, the Strategic Hub: A Bibliographic Survey of the Literature**. GPO, 1979. 284 pp., illus. (DA pamphlet 550-16-1.) LC 78-606111. Z3013.U495 1978. 016.956. OCLC 74209633. S/N 008-020-00768-4. $8.50. **D101.22:550-16-1**.

Annotated references on the Middle East were prepared by the staff of the Army Library in the Pentagon. Items reflect both friendly and unfriendly viewpoints, and are available from the Army Library. Maps and background notes are included.

421. Library of Congress. Orientalia Division. **American Doctoral Dissertations on the Arab World, 1883-1974**. Ed. by George Dimitri Selim. GPO, 1976. 2d ed. 173 pp. LC 76-7391. Z3013.S43 1976. 016.909/09/74927. OCLC 2119373. **LC1.12/2:Ar1/883-974**.

_____. **Supplement**. GPO, 1983. 213 pp. LC 82-600200. Z3013.S43 1976 Suppl. S/N 030-000-00145-1. $9. **LC41.2:Ar1/975-81/supp.**
This second edition lists mostly dissertations accepted between 1968 and 1974. The first edition (1970) covered those accepted by U.S. and Canadian universities between 1883 and 1968 on all subjects related to the Arab world. Entries are not annotated. The supplement lists dissertations accepted between 1975 and 1981, plus many before 1975 not previously reported.

422. Library of Congress. Orientalia Division. **The Arabian Peninsula: A Selected, Annotated List of Periodicals, Books and Articles in English.** GPO, 1951. 111 pp. LC 51-600030. Z3026.U53. (Repr.: Greenwood Press, $15.75.)
This is a list of over seven hundred titles in English.

See also SB 286.

Iran

423. Library of Congress. General Reference and Bibliography Division. **Iran: A Selected and Annotated Bibliography.** Comp. by Hafez F. Farman. GPO, 1951. 100 pp. LC 52-60003. Z3366.U53 1951. (Repr.: Greenwood Press, $14.) **LC2.2:Ir1.**
A supplement to this bibliography was published in Washington by the Embassy of Iran (1958).

Iraq

424. Department of the Army. **Iraq: A Country Study.** Ed. by Richard F. Nyrop. GPO, 1979. 3d ed. 320 pp., illus. (DA pamphlet 550-31.) LC 79-024184. DS70.6.S6 1979. 956.7. OCLC 5706644. S/N 008-020-00818-4. $11. **D101.22: 550-31/3.**
For a description of the *Country Study* series *see* entry 377.

Israel

425. Department of the Army. **Israel: A Country Study.** Ed. by Richard F. Nyrop. GPO, 1979. 2d ed. 414 pp. illus. (DA pamphlet 550-25.) DS126.5.A695 1979. 956.94/05. OCLC 4982924. S/N 008-020-00790-1. $12. **D101.22:550-25/2.**
For a description of the *Country Study* series *see* entry 377.

426. Library of Congress. African and Middle Eastern Division. **Diplomatic Hebrew: A Glossary of Current Terminology.** Comp. by Lawrence Marwick. GPO, 1980. 188 pp. LC 79-12383. JX1226.M3. 327/.2/03. OCLC 4857847. S/N 030-001-00091-5. $11. **LC41.2:H35.**
The glossary provides a Hebrew-English vocabulary, an acronyms list, and a bilingual listing of international associations, bureaus, institutes, councils, and treaties.

Jordan

427. Department of the Army. **Jordan: A Country Study**. Ed. by Richard F. Nyrop. GPO, 1980. 3d ed. 310 pp., illus. (DA pamphlet 550-34.) LC 80-607127. DS153.A67 1980. 956.95/04. OCLC 6357829. S/N 008-020-00839-7. $11. **D101.22:550-34/3**.
For a description of the *Country Study* series *see* entry 377.

Syria

428. Department of the Army. **Syria: A Country Study**. Ed. by Richard F. Nyrop. GPO, 1979. 268 pp., illus. (DA pamphlet 550-47.) LC 79-607771. S/N 008-020-00813-3. $11. **D101.22:550-47/3**.
For a description of the *Country Study* series *see* entry 377.

Turkey

429. Department of the Army. **Turkey: A Country Study**. Ed. by Richard F. Nyrop. GPO, 1980. 3d ed. 370 pp., illus. (DA pamphlet 550-80.) LC 80-607042. OCLC 6093545. S/N 008-020-00832-0. $12. **D101.22:550-80/3**.
For a description of the *Country Study* series *see* entry 377.

430. Library of Congress. Orientalia Division. **Turkey — Politics and Government: A Bibliography, 1938-1975**. Comp. by Abraham Bodurgil. GPO, 1978. 156 pp. LC 78-10790. Z2850.B64. 016.9561. OCLC 4495897. **LC17.2:T84/938-75**.
A supplement to *Ataturk and Turkey: A Bibliography, 1919-1938* (1974), this bibliography covers the period from the death of Kemal Ataturk in 1938 to 1975. It emphasizes publications in various languages which cover Turkey's politics and government, social and economic conditions, religion, geography, and international relations. Half of the 2,020 references are in Turkish, 731 in English, and the rest in other languages. It is organized by subject and is not annotated.

EUROPE

General Works

431. Library of Congress. European Affairs Division. **Introduction to Europe: A Selective Guide to Background Reading**. Comp. by Helen F. Conover. GPO, 1950. 201 pp. LC 50-62973. Z2000.U6 1950. (Repr.: Greenwood Press, $15.) **LC31.2:Eu7/4**.

_____. **Supplement, 1950-55**. GPO, 1955. 181 pp. Available to U.S. libraries and institutions from the Central Services Division, Library of Congress, Washington, DC 20540. **LC31.2:Eu7/4/supp. 950-55**.
This is a highly selective, annotated guide for the layman interested in background reading on Europe in general and the specific countries. It is now primarily of historical value.

Bulgaria

432. Library of Congress. Slavic and Central European Division. **Bulgaria: A Bibliographic Guide.** By Martin V. Pundeff. GPO, 1965. 98 pp. LC 65-60006. Z2896.P8. (Repr.: Arno, $10.) **LC35.2:B87/2.**
The guide contains a bibliographic survey of many facets of Bulgarian life (social conditions, politics, history). Part 2 contains a complete bibliography of the works discussed. There are 1,243 entries, with library locations provided. There is no index.

Cyprus

433. Department of the Army. **Cyprus: A Country Study.** Ed. by Frederica M. Bunge. GPO, 1980. 3d ed. 306 pp., illus. (DA pamphlet 550-22.) LC 80-607041. DS54.A3K43 1980. 956.45. OCLC 6093544. S/N 008-020-00831-1. $11. **D101.22:550-22/3.**
For a description of the *Country Study* series *see* entry 377.

Czechoslovakia

434. Department of the Army. **Czechoslovakia: A Country Study.** Ed. by Richard F. Nyrop. GPO, 1982. 381 pp., illus. (DA pamphlet 550-158.) LC 82-1716. S/N 008-020-00911-3. $12. **D101.22:550-158/2.**
For a description of the *Country Study* series *see* entry 377.

435. Library of Congress. Slavic and Central European Division. **Czechoslovakia: A Bibliographical Guide.** By Rudolf Sturm. GPO, 1967. 157 pp. LC 68-60019. Z2136.S7. Free from the Central Services Division, Library of Congress, Washington, DC 20540. **LC35.2:C99/2.**
Materials included will be used primarily by "librarians building their collections relating to Czechoslovakia, specialists dealing with the area in depth; and ... general readers with only occasional and less specialized interests." Part 1 is a discussion of the publications under form and subject headings (bibliographies, social conditions, etc.) with numbers to refer to part 2, an alphabetical listing. National Union Catalog (NUC) symbols are provided to show libraries in which the publications may be found. Books published earlier than 1914 are not included.

Germany

436. Library of Congress. Slavic and East European Division. **East Germany: A Selected Bibliography.** Comp. by Arnold H. Price. GPO, 1967. 2d ed. 133 pp. LC 67-61608. Z2244.E38P7. Free to U.S. libraries and institutions from the Central Services Division, Library of Congress, Washington, DC 20540. **LC35.2:G31/967.**
The first edition (1959) was compiled by Fritz T. Epstein. This edition cites 833 works, mostly German, dealing with conditions in the Soviet zone of Germany and the Soviet sector of Berlin. Brief descriptive annotations are provided.

437. National Archives and Records Service. **Guides to German Records Microfilmed at Alexandria, VA.** Comp. by the American Historical Association. IA, 1958. Irregular. D735.A58. OCLC 1951101. **GS4.18:nos.**

These guides are a series of finding aids for National Archives microfilms of records seized during World War II of German central, regional, and local government agencies, of military commands and units, and of the Nazi Party and its affiliated organizations. All microfilms are available for use at the National Archives or may be purchased from the National Archives Publications Sales Branch.

Romania

438. Congress. House. **Hungarians in Rumania and Transylvania: A Bibliographical List of Publications in Hungarian and West European Languages Compiled from the Holdings of the Library of Congress**. By Elmer Bako and William Solyom-Fekete. GPO, 1969. 192 pp. (House document 91-34.) **91-1:H.doc.134**.
This extensive bibliography contains 2,056 citations to works written by Hungarian and Western European authors pertaining to Hungarians in Rumania and Transylvania. Works are arranged in thirteen subject sections covering general reference sources, history, economics, politics, literature, religion, and other topics. It is limited to materials in the Library of Congress collection. An author index is provided.

439. Department of the Army. **Romania: A Country Study**. Ed. by Eugene K. Keefe. GPO, 1972 (repr. 1979). 320 pp., illus. (DA pamphlet 550-160.) LC 72-600095. S/N 008-020-00433-2. $11. **D101.22:550-160**.
For a description of the *Country Study* series *see* entry 377.

440. Library of Congress. Slavic and Central European Division. **Rumania: A Bibliographic Guide**. By Stephen A. Fischer-Galati. GPO, 1963. 75 pp. LC 63-60076. Z2921.U5. (Repr.: Arno, $8.) **LC35.2:R86**.
Part 1 of this guide is a bibliographic essay in which the works are discussed, within various subject areas, in relation to others on that subject. Part 2 is a numbered listing of those works with complete bibliographic citations. The guide primarily lists monographs and periodical titles in Rumanian. It provides NUC symbols for location of copies. It is not indexed.

Soviet Union

441. Bureau of the Census. Foreign Demographics Analysis Division. **Population Projections by Age and Sex for the Republics and Major Economic Regions of the U.S.S.R., 1970-2000**. By Godfrey S. Baldwin. GPO, 1979. 130 pp. (International population reports, series P-91, no. 26.) OCLC 5651470. **C3.186:P91/26**.

442. Department of the Army. **USSR: Analytical Survey of the Literature**. GPO, 1973. 4th ed. 232 pp. (DA pamphlet 550-6-1.) Z2491.U44 1976. 016.947085. OCLC 1819387. S/N 008-020-00624-6. $8. **D101.22:550-6-1**.
This is an annotated bibliography of materials on Soviet military objectives, programs, external relations, and interaction with other countries on a wide range of issues. The materials cited are in the Army Library in the Pentagon.

See also SB 279.

Yugoslavia

443. Department of the Army. **Yugoslavia: A Country Study**. GPO, 1982. 2d ed. 363 pp., illus. (DA pamphlet 550-99.) LC 82-11632. DR1214.Y83 1982. 949.7. OCLC 08626570. S/N 008-020-00920-2. $12. **D101.22:550-99/2**.

For a description of the *Country Study* series *see* entry 377.

LATIN AMERICA

General Works

Archives

444. National Archives and Records Service. **Guide to Materials on Latin America in the National Archives of the United States**. Comp. by George S. Ulibarri and John P. Harrison. GPO, 1974. 489 pp. **GS4.6/2:L34a/974**.

Bibliographies

445. Library of Congress. **Latin America in Soviet Writings: A Bibliography**. Comp. by Leo Okinshevich. Ed. by Robert G. Carlton. 2 vols. Publ. for the Library of Congress. Baltimore: Johns Hopkins University Press, 1966. (Hispanic Foundation publications.) LC 66-16039. Z1601.O55.

> Vol. 1. 1917-58. 257 pp. $25.
>
> Vol. 2. 1959-64. 311 pp. $25.

This bibliography supersedes *Latin America in Soviet Writings, 1945-1958* (LC, 1959) and includes approximately six thousand more entries. Arranged by broad subjects, it lists items originally written in Russian and Russian translations of works related to Latin America. It is indexed by authors.

Biographies

446. Library of Congress. Hispanic Foundation. **National Directory of Latin Americanists: Biographies of 2,695 Specialists in the Social Sciences and Humanities**. IA, 1972. 2d ed. 683 pp. (Hispanic Foundation bibliographic series, no. 12.) LC 75-37737. Z2685.H5 no.12. Free from the Central Services Division, Library of Congress, Washington, DC 20540. **LC24.7:12**.

This is a revision of the 1966 version of this title, providing biographical information on U.S. specialists in the Latin American field. Entries are alphabetic and contain such information as name, birth date and place, major discipline, degrees (including honorary degrees), professional career, fellowships, honors, awards, membership in professional and honorary organizations, research specialties and interests, publications (limited to three), language knowledge and degree of proficiency, linguistic studies, and home and office address. The "Index of Subject Specialties" lists names of people within each major area.

Caribbean Islands

447. American Historical Association. **A Guide for the Study of British Caribbean History, 1763-1834, Including the Abolition and Emancipation Movements.** By Lowell Joseph Ragatz. GPO, 1932. 725 pp. (Annual report 1930, vol. 3.) **SI4.1:930/v.3.**
This comprehensive bibliography lists books, periodical articles, unpublished manuscripts, government publications, and pamphlets, arranged by subjects with annotations for most entries. It is indexed by author, title, and subject.

Costa Rica

448. Department of the Army. **Costa Rica: A Country Study.** Ed. by Howard I. Blutstein. GPO, 1970 (repr. 1981). 338 pp., illus. (DA pamphlet 550-90.) LC 79-608713. S/N 008-020-00340-9. $10. **D101.22:550-90.**
For a description of the *Country Study* series *see* entry 377.

Dominican Republic

449. Department of the Army. **Dominican Republic: A Country Study.** Ed. by Thomas E. Weil. GPO, 1973 (repr. 1982). 276 pp., illus. (DA pamphlet 550-54.) LC 73-600179. S/N 008-020-00484-7. $11. **D101.22:550-54/2.**
For a description of the *Country Study* series *see* entry 377.

Nicaragua

450. Department of the Army. **Nicaragua: A Country Study.** GPO, 1983. 308 pp., illus. (DA pamphlet 550-88.) LC 82-013833. FN1523.N569 1983. 972.85. OCLC 08688568. S/N 008-020-00932-6. $12. **D101.22:550-88/2.**
For a description of the *Country Study* series *see* entry 377.

Panama

451. Department of the Army. **Panama: A Country Study.** Ed. by Richard F. Nyrop. GPO, 1981. 3d ed. 300 pp., illus. (DA pamphlet 550-46.) LC 80-29255. F1563.A63 1980. 927.87. OCLC 07176670. S/N 008-020-00868-1. $11. **D101.22: 550-46/2.**
For a description of the *Country Study* series *see* entry 377.

Peru

452. Department of the Army. **Peru: A Country Study.** Ed. by Richard F. Nyrop. GPO, 1981. 3d ed. 330 pp., illus. (DA pamphlet 550-42.) LC 81-3456. F3408.P4647 1981. 985/.063. OCLC 07460483. S/N 008-020-00869-9. $11. **D101.22:550-42/3.**
For a description of the *Country Study* series *see* entry 377.

OCEANIA

Antarctica

453. Department of the Navy. Bureau of Aeronautics. **Antarctic Bibliography.** GPO, 1951. 147 pp. (NAVAER 10-35-591.) LC 52-60435. **D202.2:An8.**
A classified list of 5,500 entries in five major sections: biological sciences, geophysical sciences, geographical sciences, geographical exploration, and other topics. There is an author index.

454. Library of Congress. Science and Technology Division. **Antarctic Bibliography, 1951-1961.** GPO, 1970. 349 pp. LC 74-606139. **LC33.9:951-61.**
This bibliography fills in the gap between the Navy's *Antarctic Bibliography* (entry 453) and the series with the same title published on an irregular basis by the Library of Congress. This title, which provides retrospective coverage, was continued in 1965 by *Antarctic Bibliography* (entry 455).

455. Library of Congress. Science and Technology Division. **Antarctic Bibliography.** GPO, 1965- . Irregular. LC 65-061825. Z6005.P7A55. OCLC 1064353. **LC33.9:vol.**

Vol. 1. 1965. 506 pp.

Vol. 2. 1966. 523 pp.

Vol. 3. 1968. 491 pp.

Vol. 4. 1970. 491 pp.

Vol. 5. 1972. 499 pp. S/N 030-018-00013-3. $16.

Vol. 6. 1974. 467 pp. S/N 030-018-00015-0. $16.

Vol. 7. 1975. 456 pp. S/N 030-018-00016-8. $16.

Vols. 1-7/Index. 1977. 792 pp. S/N 030-018-00018-4. $20.

Vol. 8. 1977. 500 pp. S/N 030-018-00017-6. $17.

Vol. 9. 1978. 498 pp. S/N 030-018-00019-2. $17.

Vol. 10. 1979. 498 pp. S/N 030-018-00020-6. $17.

Vol. 11. 1981. 474 pp. S/N 030-018-00021-4. $16.

Vol. 12. 1983. 496 pp. S/N 030-018-00022-2. $17.

Vols. 8-12/Index. 1984. 766 pp. S/N 030-018-00023-1. $21.

Sponsored by the Office of Antarctic Programs, National Science Foundation, this is a continuing bibliography, with indexes, for current Antarctic literature published since 1962. A companion source, *Antarctic Bibliography* (entry 454), provides retrospective coverage, while *Current Antarctic Literature* provides monthly updates. This source gives abstracts and indexes of current Antarctic literature arranged in fourteen categories: general, biological sciences, cartography, expeditions, geological sciences, ice and snow, logistics, equipment and supplies, medical sciences, meteorology, oceanography, atmospheric physics, terrestrial physics, and political geography.

456. Office of Naval Operations. **National Interest in Antarctica: An Annotated Bibliography.** By Robert D. Hayton. GPO, 1960. 137 pp. **D207.11:An8.**
Entries are arranged by countries of origin or by international organizations as publishers. They represent the "relevant material of international law, foreign policy, economic exploitation, strategic significance, world politics, explorations, and

expeditions affecting national claims, and analogous rivalries and considerations" (Introduction). The work is indexed by authors and titles.

Arctic

457. Department of Defense. **Arctic Bibliography**. Prep. by the Arctic Institute of North America. 12 vols. GPO, 1953-65. Annual. LC 53-61783. **D1.22:1-12**.
The twelve volumes contain 76,725 abstracts of works on all areas of study in the nineteenth and twentieth centuries, with emphasis on those written by the scientists and explorers themselves. Each volume contains two main sections: (1) an alphabetic listing by author with numbered entries, full bibliographic citations, and abstracts; and (2) a subject-geographic index. Publications in foreign languages are included with their titles translated into English.

Ryukyu Islands

458. Department of the Army. **Ryukyu Islands: A Bibliography**. By Norman D. King. GPO, 1967. 105 pp. (DA pamphlet 550-4.) **D101.22:550-4**.
This general guide to 2,108 works in English on Okinawa and the Ryukyu Islands includes citations to books, periodical articles, and government documents, most of them annotated, arranged alphabetically by author under broad subject. It is indexed by authors.

UNITED STATES

Archives

459. Library of Congress. **A Guide to the Microfilm Collection of Early State Records**. Ed. by Lillian A. Hamrick. IA, 1950. 762 pp. LC 50-62956. Z1223.5.A1U47. **LC1.2:M58**.

———. **Supplement**. 1951. 130 pp.
This guide, produced jointly by the Library of Congress and the University of North Carolina, is an index to reels of microfilms of early state records. It is arranged first by type of publication (legislative proceedings, laws, court records, etc.) and then chronologically.

460. Library of Congress. Manuscript Division. **Guide to Manuscripts Relating to American History in British Depositories**. Ed. by Grace Gardner Griffin. GPO, 1946. 313 pp. LC 46-27863. **LC4.2:Am3**.
This is actually a checklist of reproductions as reflected in the Library of Congress holdings. The material is arranged by locations, that is, by the library or other depository where the original is located. A detailed index facilitates use of this guide.

461. National Archives and Records Service. **Administration of Modern Archives: A Select Bibliographic Guide**. By Frank B. Evans. IA, 1971. 213 pp. LC 70-609042. **GS4.17/3:Ad6**.
This bibliography covers many phases of archival management under two main sections: "Introduction to Archives Administration," which covers topics such as archival concepts, terminology and principles, archivists, librarians, and manuscript

curators, and "Survey of Archival Functions," covering, among other topics, preservation and arrangement of archives and problems of archival management as well as specific types of archival records (i.e., sound records, oral history, cartographic records, and still pictures). Within each chapter are "recommended," "suggested," and "additional" readings, including books, pamphlets, and journal articles. The "additional readings" section of each chapter is in bibliographic essay form, which will aid the user in determining what works would best suit his or her needs. The work includes a subject index, but, regrettably, no author or title index.

462. National Archives and Records Service. **Catalog of National Archives Microfilm Publications.** IA, 1974. OCLC 1294422. **GS4.17/2:974.**
The National Archives has been selectively microfilming national records of high research value since 1940. This catalog lists and describes the many series of records available as microfilm publications. It replaces the 1968 edition, *List of National Archives Microfilm Publications.*

463. National Archives and Records Service. **Guide to the National Archives of the United States.** GPO, 1974. 884 pp. LC 74-600038. S/N 022-003-00908-6. $21. **GS4.6/2:N21.**
This guide lists and describes all official records of the United States government (except presidential papers and historical manuscripts held in presidential libraries) added to the National Archives through June 1970. This is the most comprehensive NARS finding aid, and the first revision of this title published since 1948, when *Guide to the Records in the National Archives* was published.

464. National Archives and Records Service. **Preliminary Inventories.** GPO, 1941- . Irregular. **GS4.10:nos.**
Each number is a detailed list of the archival records of a particular agency or department.

465. National Historical Publications and Records Commission. **Directory of Archives and Manuscript Repositories in the United States.** IA, 1978. 905 pp. **GS4.14:Ar2.**
This is a directory of 2,675 repositories of historical research materials in the United States, District of Columbia, Puerto Rico, Canal Zone, Virgin Islands, and Northern Marianas Trust Territory. Information given for each institution includes address and telephone number, hours of service, user fees, access restrictions, and holdings. The historical source materials held by these repositories include photographs, sound recordings, machine readable files, films, architectural drawings, and microfilms.

466. Smithsonian Institution. Archives. **Guide to the Smithsonian Archives.** IA, 1978. 298 pp. LC 78-602649. Q11.S8S8 1978. 027.5753. OCLC 04532081. **SI1.34:2.**

467. Works Progress Administration. Historical Records Survey. **Bibliography of Research Projects Reports: A Checklist of Historical Records Survey Publications.** IA, 1943. Rev. ed. 110 pp. (Technical series. Research and records projects bibliography no. 7.) **FW4.23:7.**
This bibliography lists inventories of regional archives (including states, counties, cities, and towns). It also lists church archive publications, vital statistics, microform publications and records, and some unpublished works. A series of publications was issued by the Works Progress Administration for each class or group included in this bibliography. For a complete listing of these publications, see *Guide to the Official Publications of the New Deal Administration* and its supplements covering 1933-36, and *Unemployment Relief Documents: A Guide to Official Publications*, both by Jerome K. Wilcox.

General History and Area Studies

468. American Historical Association. **Writings on American History.** GPO, 1902- . Annual. (Annual report, vol. 2.) LC 4-18261. OCLC 4055133. **SI4.1:yr.**
Publisher and place vary. Since 1952 (beginning with the volume for 1948), the National Historical Publications and Records Commission assumed responsibility for preparation of this bibliography, but it is still published as volume 2 of the Annual Report of the American Historical Association. The series began in 1904 with a volume covering historical writings of 1902. Volumes for 1904-05 and 1941-47 have not been published. Each volume contains three major sections: the historical profession, the United States, and regions of the United States. Parts 1 and 2 are subdivided by topic, part 3 geographically. The aim of this series is to include any work of research value concerning the history of the United States from earliest times to the present. Omitted are newspapers, historical fiction, juvenile works, archeological reports, and genealogical works. It includes a list of serials cited and an index. There is a substantial time lag between coverage and publication year; for example, the volume for 1959, which was contained in the annual report for 1961, was not published until 1969.

469. Library of Congress. **Guide to the Diplomatic History of the United States, 1775-1921.** By Samuel Flagg Bemis and Grace Gardner Griffin. GPO, 1935. 979 pp. LC 35-26001. (Repr.: Peter Smith, $17.50.) **LC1.2:D62.**
This comprehensive work on U.S. diplomatic history for the period 1775 to 1921 will be valuable for research in international diplomatic history as well. The bibliography lists both published works and unpublished manuscripts, including those in foreign languages. Two indexes to over five thousand items—collections of personal papers, and authors—facilitate use of this guide.

470. Library of Congress. **United States Local Histories in the Library of Congress: A Bibliography.** Ed. by Marion J. Kaminkow. 5 vols. IA, 1975. LC 74-25444. Z1250.U59 1975. 016.973. OCLC 1365920. (Repr.: Magna Carta, vols. 1-4, $250; vol. 5, $25.)
This inventory of local history holdings in the Library of Congress is grouped by geographic area, and then by author. It provides bibliographic information with some summaries of contents; genealogies are omitted.

471. Library of Congress. American Folklife Center. **Folklife and the Federal Government: A Guide to Activities, Resources, Funds, and Services.** Comp. by Linda C. Coe. GPO, 1977. 147 pp. (Publications of the American Folklife Center, no. 1.) LC 78-54261. GR37.C63. 353.008/5. OCLC 3915417. S/N 030-000-00091-9. $5.50. **LC39.9:1.**

472. Library of Congress. General Reference and Bibliography Division. **A Guide to the Study of the United States of America: Representative Books Reflecting the Development of American Life and Thought.** By Donald H. Mugridge and Blanche P. McCrum. GPO, 1960. 1,194 pp. LC 60-60009. Z1215.U53. **LC2.2: Un3/4.**

———. **Supplement, 1956-1965.** GPO, 1976. 526 pp. 016.973. OCLC 2175634. S/N 030-001-00042-7. $18.
This guide is a monumental annotated bibliography of important books on all aspects of Americana. It serves as an introduction to representative books that reflect the development of life and thought in the United States, by annotating important works in thirty-two fields of endeavor. The main volume includes works published through 1955, the supplement through 1965. An extensive index is included in both volumes.

473. National Historical Publications and Records Commission. **Publications Catalog**. IA, 1976. 87 pp. Z1236.U618. 016.973. OCLC 4279269.
When established by an act of Congress in 1974, the commission was charged with collecting and preserving important historical materials for future generations to study, and editing and publishing the papers of outstanding Americans and other important documents. This catalog and its supplements list and describe the commission's print and microform publications. These include the Adams Papers, First Congress, Franklin Papers, Hamilton Papers, Jefferson Papers, Madison Papers, and the Ratification of the Constitution, plus over two hundred other publications.

474. National Park Service. **National Historic Landmarks: A Preservation Program of the National Park Service**. IA, 1976. 150 pp., illus. OCLC 2591098. **I29.2:L23/4.**
This is a state-by-state listing of national historic landmarks, with location, dates, and a short statement of the significance of each.

475. National Park Service. **National Register of Historic Places**. GPO, 1969- . Biennial. LC 76-010861. S/N 024-005-00645-1 (Vol. 1, 1976, 961 pp.). $22. S/N 024-005-00747-4 (Vol. 2, 1979, 638 pp.). $19. **I29.76:yr.**
This listing of properties on the national register by state and by county is heavily illustrated, with addresses and brief descriptions of architecture and construction. Volume 1 describes properties included through 1974, volume 2 through 1976.

476. National Portrait Gallery. **Fifty American Faces from the Collection of the National Portrait Gallery**. By Margaret C. S. Christman. GPO, 1978. 256 pp., illus. N7593.C49 1982. 760. OCLC 3730317. **SI11.2:Am3/5.**
These fifty portraits selected from the permanent collection of the National Portrait Gallery show people who have significantly contributed to the history, development, and culture of the United States. Portraits are accompanied by biographical profiles.

477. National Portrait Gallery. **National Portrait Gallery: Permanent Collection Illustrated Checklist**. GPO, 1982. 320 pp., illus. LC 80-20329. N857.8.A66. 704.94/2/09730740153. **SI11.2:C41/982.**
This is a listing of the portraits of important individuals in American history, development, and culture. It is arranged alphabetically by subject and gives birth and death dates, portrait date, size, medium, and catalog number.

478. Smithsonian Institution. **Bibliography of American Historical Societies (the United States and the Dominion of Canada)**. By Appleton P. C. Griffin. GPO, 1907. 2d ed., rev. and enl. 1,374 pp. (American Historical Association, Annual Report 1905, vol. 2.) **SI4.1:905/v.2.**
This is a comprehensive guide to materials published by historical societies in the United States and Canada through 1905. Arrangement is by society names with the contents of their publications listed. The work is indexed by author and subject with a separate index to biographies.

History by Periods

Revolutionary

479. Department of the Army. Center of Military History. **War of the American Revolution**. By Robert W. Coakley. GPO, 1975. 257 pp., illus. LC 74-31183. S/N 008-029-00091-1. $7. **D114.2:Am3**.
This introduction and reference volume, which distills scholarship on the Revolutionary War, is meant to serve as a ready reference for dates, places, and other facts. It includes a brief narrative history of the war, a chronology of military events, and a bibliography of over a thousand items.

480. Department of the Navy. Naval History Division. **Naval Documents of the American Revolution**. Ed. by William Bell Clark. GPO, 1964- . Irregular. LC 64-60087. OCLC 00426774. **D207.12:vol**.

> Vol. 1. 1964. 1,451 pp. S/N 008-046-00035-2. $24.
>
> Vol. 2. 1966. 1,463 pp. S/N 008-046-00036-1. $24.
>
> Vol. 3. 1968. 1,486 pp. S/N 008-046-00037-9. $24.
>
> Vol. 4. 1969. 1,580 pp. S/N 008-046-00038-7. $25.
>
> Vol. 5. 1970. 1,486 pp. S/N 008-046-00046-8. $24.
>
> Vol. 6. 1972. 1,641 pp. S/N 008-046-00052-2. $26.
>
> Vol. 7. 1976. 1,463 pp. S/N 008-046-00066-2. $24.
>
> Vol. 8. 1980. 1,206 pp. S/N 008-046-00080-8. $26.
>
> Complete set (8 vols.) S/N 008-046-00106-5. $177.

This collection is a compilation of original and other documents from 1774 to 1777 which illustrate the role of the sea in the American Revolution. It gives full text, writer, date, and source of the material. Maps and drawings are included.

481. Library of Congress. **The American Revolution in Drawings and Prints: A Checklist of 1765-1790 Graphics in the Library of Congress**. Comp. by Donald H. Cresswell. GPO, 1975. 455 pp., illus. LC 73-017405. E209.U54 1975. 769/.4/99733. OCLC 0730766. S/N 030-001-00050-8. $16. **LC1.2:Am3/9**.
This is a checklist of 921 contemporary pictures of the American Revolution in the Library of Congress's collections. Graphics created between 1765 and 1790 are presented in five categories: portraits, events, views, cartoons and allegories, and weapons and implements. Information given includes title, artist, date, process, size, and annotation.

482. Library of Congress. **American Revolution: Selected Reading List**. GPO, 1968. 39 pp. LC 68-67236. Z1238.U62. Free from the Central Services Division, Library of Congress, Washington, DC 20540. **LC1.12/2:R32**.
This bibliography cites books dealing with the period from the beginning of the controversy with Great Britain to the postwar years of the 1780s. It was published as a contribution to the Bicentennial of the American Revolution. Citations are listed under broad subjects with separate sections for biographies, personal narratives and documentary sources, children's literature, and fiction. There is an author index.

483. Library of Congress. **Letters of Delegates to Congress, 1774-1789**. Ed. by Paul H. Smith. GPO, 1977- . Irregular. LC 76-2592. JK1033.L47. 328.73. OCLC 2020737. **LC1.34:vol**.

Vol. 1. August 1774-August 1775. 1976. 751 pp. S/N 030-000-00076-5. $18.

Vol. 2. September-December 1775. 1977. 585 pp. S/N 030-000-00077-3. $15.

Vol. 3. January-May 15, 1776. 1978. 735 pp. S/N 030-000-00083-8. $18.

Vol. 4. May 16-August 15, 1776. 1979. 688 pp. S/N 030-000-00103-6. $18.

Vol. 5. August 16-December 31, 1776. 1979. 767 pp. S/N 030-000-00111-7. $19.

Vol. 6. January 1-April 1777. 1981. 760 pp. S/N 030-000-00101-0. $19.

Vol. 7. May-September 18, 1777. 1981. 749 pp. S/N 030-000-00107-9. $15.

Vol. 8. September 19, 1777-January 31, 1778. 1981. 745 pp. S/N 030-000-00119-2. $17.

Vol. 9. February 1-May 31, 1778. 1982. 872 pp. S/N 030-000-00140-1. $19.

Vol. 10. June 1-September 30, 1778. 1983. 795 pp. S/N 030-000-00151-6. $27.

Documents included were written by delegates to Congress and bear on their congressional tasks, 1774-89. This is a new, expanded edition of the original *Letters of Members of the Continental Congress*, edited by Edmund C. Burnett (1921-36).

484. Library of Congress. **Manuscript Sources in the Library of Congress for Research on the American Revolution.** GPO, 1975. 372 pp. LC 74-5404. Z1238.U57 1975. OCLC 867944. S/N 030-003-00011-0. $14. **LC1.2:M31/3.**
The Library of Congress is one of the world's foremost repositories of original source material on the American Revolution. This guide describes all manuscript material from 1763 to 1789 that is available for research. The collections described include original documents, photostats, transcripts, and microfilm copies.

485. Library of Congress. General Reference and Bibliography Division. **Periodical Literature on the American Revolution: Historical Research and Changing Interpretations, 1895-1970; A Selective Bibliography.** Comp. by Ronald M. Gephart. GPO, 1971. LC 74-609228. Z1238.G4. Free from the Central Services Division, Library of Congress, Washington, DC 20540. **LC2.2:Am3/3/895-970.**
This bibliography was compiled to provide students, teachers, scholars, and librarians with a convenient guide to essays and periodical literature about the Revolutionary period. It is a representative list of studies that have appeared in periodicals, festschriften, and collections of essays or lectures.

486. National Archives and Records Service. **Index: The Journals of the Continental Congress, 1774-1789.** GPO, 1976. 429 pp. S/N 022-000-00126-4. $11. **GS4.2: C76/2/774-89.**

487. National Archives and Records Service. **Index: The Papers of the Continental Congress, 1774-1789.** By John P. Butler. 5 vols. GPO, 1978. LC 78-023783. Z1238.B87. 973.3/12/016. OCLC 4493262. S/N 022-002-00065-1. $115 (set). **GS4.2:C76/3/774-89/v.1-5.**
All papers of the Continental Congress, except the journals, are included in this comprehensive index. The papers indexed date from the first meeting of the Continental Congress in 1774, and are available in the National Archives. All people and important places and subjects are indexed in one alphabetic sequence, followed by a chronological document listing all the materials. The papers also include the records of the Confederation Congresses and of the Constitutional Convention, all contained in Record Group 360. Records of the Continental Congress in other record groups are not included.

488. National Portrait Gallery. **The Dye Is Now Cast: Road to American Independence, 1774-76.** By Lillian B. Miller. GPO, 1975. 328 pp., illus. LC 74-24843. S/N 047-001-00121-4. $12. **SI11.2:Am3/4.**

This is a catalog of an exhibition that illustrates and describes the historic events of the American Revolution, 1774-76.

Civil War

489. Army Military History Institute. **Era of the Civil War, 1820-1876.** By Louise Arnold and Richard Sommers. GPO, 1982. 710 pp. (Special bibliography series, no. 11.) OCLC 09277488. S/N 008-029-00123-3. $13. **D114.14:11/2.**

This bibliography of the institute's collection on the Civil War includes articles on its manuscript holdings and on the U.S. Army Military History Institute museum collection.

490. Library of Congress. **The Civil War in Motion Pictures: A Bibliography of Films Produced in the United States since 1897.** Comp. by Paul C. Spehr. GPO, 1961. 109 pp. LC 61-60074. **LC34.2:C49.**

Over eight hundred entries are listed in three sections: (1) principal sources, (2) theatrical and educational motion pictures, and (3) newsreels. Physical descriptions and annotations are provided for each. There are indexes by subjects, authors, and variant titles.

491. Library of Congress. Geography and Map Division. **Civil War Maps: An Annotated List of Maps and Atlases in Map Collections of the Library of Congress.** Comp. by Richard W. Stephenson. GPO, 1961. 138 pp. LC 61-60061. Z6027.U5U55. (Repr.: Greenwood Press, $16.75. Sterling $11.95, cloth; $6.95, paper, $12 with the paperbound *Hotchkiss Map Collections*.) **LC5.2:C49.**

Seven hundred maps, most of them prepared by or for the Union Army, are described. Each entry gives the following information: title, author, imprint, size, and description. The index includes references to battles, subjects, geographic areas, publishers, and personal names. Note should be made of a similar publication issued by the National Archives, *Civil War Maps in the National Archives* (GPO, 1964. 127 pp. **GS4.2:C49**).

492. National Archives and Records Service. **Guide to Federal Archives Relating to the Civil War.** By Kenneth W. Munden and Henry Putney Beers. GPO, 1962. 721 pp. **GS4.6/2:C49.**

This is an indispensable guide for scholarly study of the Civil War, describing extant official records related to the war. It is arranged by departments with a very detailed subject index.

493. National Archives and Records Service. **Guide to the Archives of Government of the Confederate States of America.** By Henry Putney Beers. GPO, 1968. 536 pp. **GS4.6/2:C76.**

This is a descriptive guide to the extant official records of both the U.S. government and the government of the Confederate States of America. It lists records of the states of the Confederacy followed by those of the central government in Richmond including Congress, the Judiciary, the Presidency, and the Departments of State, Treasury, War, Navy, Post Office, and Justice. It is indexed by subjects.

494. National Archives and Records Service. **Military Operations of the Civil War: A Guide-Index to the Official Records of the Union and Confederate Armies, 1861-1865.** 5 vols. GPO, 1968-80. LC 73-604454. E470.U63. 973.73. OCLC 0196186. **GS4.21:v.1-5.**
This is a 5-volume guide to the printed documentation on the Civil War available in the 127-volume War Department compilation *Official Records of the Union and Confederate Armies, 1861-1865.* Volume 1 is a general guide to the 127-volume set, the original index volume, and the atlas volume. The remaining four volumes are indexes to and lists of Civil War operations recognized in the *Official Records, Armies.*

See also SB 192.

World Wars I and II

495. Army Military History Institute. **The Era of World War II: General Reference Works, Bibliography.** 4 vols. GPO, 1977-79. (Special bibliographic series, no. 16.) OCLC 3588616. **D114.14:16/v.1-4.**
This four-volume set lists the institute's holdings on World War II. Items are listed under subject categories alphabetized by author's name, with no annotations. The four volumes are: (1) General Reference Works, Bibliography; (2) The War in the Pacific; (3) The Eastern and Balkan Fronts, the Axis Forces in Europe; and (4) Mediterranean and Western Europe Theaters of Operation.

496. Department of the Army. Office of the Chief of Military History. **United States Army in World War II: Chronology, 1941-1945.** Comp. by Mary H. Williams. GPO, 1960 (repr. 1978). 660 pp. (Special studies.) S/N 008-029-00015-6. $18. **D114.7:C46.**
This chronology of World War II emphasizes the ground action of American armed forces. It presents the sequence of events from the first bombs dropped on Pearl Harbor to the Japanese surrender. It contains a very detailed index. A list of in-print titles in the *United States Army in World War II* series may be found in SB 098.

497. National Archives. **Handbook of Federal World War Agencies and Their Records, 1917-1921.** GPO, 1943. 666 pp. LC 43-50551. **AE1.6:W19/917-21.**
This is an important source listing government agencies and their functions as part of the World War I effort. It lists twenty-four hundred permanent and emergency bodies (with less emphasis on those existing before the war) and omits those concerned with office management or those created only to aid superior agencies. The agency, listed by key word, is followed by the superior department, date of creation, date of abolition, functions, and descriptions of records. Most records described are housed in the National Archives. Important agencies are given fuller treatment, including references to pertinent congressional publications.

498. National Archives and Records Service. **Records of World War II.** 2 vols. GPO, 1950. **GS4.2:R24/2/v.1,2.**
This counterpart to *Handbook of Federal World War Agencies and Their Records* (entry 497) is intended as a guide to materials that will be useful for reseach, particularly in the planning and administration of national defense activities. Volume 1 includes records of civilian agencies, and volume 2 of military agencies. The period of time covered is generally from 1939 until demobilization in 1945. For each agency listed the following information is given: date of establishment, notes on previous history, general summary, objectives, termination or transfer to another agency, and extent of records. Volume 1 contains an index to shortened titles. Volume 2 contains a complete index.

Law

GENERAL WORKS

499. Administrative Office of the United States Courts. **United States Court Directory**. GPO, 1978- . Semiannual. LC 78-645528. KF8700.A19U55. 347/.73/1025. OCLC 04010539. 1984 ed. S/N 028-004-00048-6. $7.50. **Ju10.17: date**.
Court judges are listed with telephone numbers and addresses. District courts, bankruptcy courts, tax court, courts of appeals, and supreme courts are covered.

500. Department of the Interior. **Handbook of Federal Indian Law with Reference Tables and Index**. By Felix S. Cohen. GPO, 1942. 662 pp. LC 42-38386. (Repr.: AMS Press, $25.) **I48.6:In2**.
This handbook, although somewhat dated, sorts and explains the vast array of laws, treaties, judicial rulings, and the like which pertain to American Indians. "If one who seeks to track down a point of federal Indian law finds in this volume relevant background, general perspective and useful leads to the authorities, the handbook will have served the purpose for which it was written" (Introduction). A very detailed index is provided.

501. Department of Justice. **Register: Department of Justice and Courts of the United States**. GPO, 1871- . Annual. LC 3-11924. OCLC 04179076. **J1.7:no**.
This directory of officials of federal courts and related agencies gives name, office, date of appointment, and other information.

502. Judicial Conference of the United States. Bicentennial Committee. **Judges of the United States**. GPO, 1983. 700 pp. S/N 028-004-00056-7. $20. **Ju10.2: J89/4/983**.
This is a biographical directory that includes every federal judge of the United States from 1789 to 1978. Biographical data include birth and death dates and places, schools attended, nominations for appointment, employment, and family. This directory will be periodically updated.

503. Library of Congress. Congressional Research Service. **Digest of Public General Bills and Resolutions**. GPO, 1936- . Two cumulative issues during each session of Congress, with irregular supplements and a final edition at the conclusion of

each session. LC 79-611725. KF18.L5. OCLC 01777235. **LC14.16:Cong.-sess./no.**

The digest was first prepared for the second session of the 74th Congress and has been prepared for all subsequent sessions and Congresses. Its purpose is to furnish a brief summary of essential features of public bills and resolutions and changes made therein during the legislative process. It also indicates committee action, floor action taken by either body of Congress, and enactments. The cumulative issues are divided into seven parts: (1) Status of Measures Receiving Action, (2) Public Laws, (3) Digest of Public General Bills and Resolutions, (4) Sponsor Index, (5) Subject Index, (6) Specific Title Index, and (7) Identical Bill Index.

BIBLIOGRAPHIES

504. Children's Bureau. **Legal Bibliography for Juvenile and Family Courts.** By William H. Sheridan and Alice B. Freer. GPO, 1966. 46 pp. **FS14.112:L52.**

_____. **Supplement 1.** GPO, 1967. 34 pp.

_____. **Supplement 2.** GPO, 1968. 38 pp.

_____. **Supplement 3.** GPO, 1970. 36 pp.

Designed for judges, probation officers, law enforcement personnel, counsel, and other professional persons in the field of delinquency and the law, this bibliography cites journal articles and specific cases. It is arranged alphabetically in each chapter, with chapters on specific subjects. There are no indexes.

505. Library of Congress. **The Coutumes of France in the Library of Congress: An Annotated Bibliography.** GPO, 1977. 80 pp. LC 76-608412. S/N 030-001-00083-4. $9.50. **LC1.12/2:C83.**

French "coutumes" are comparable to English common law.

506. Library of Congress. **A Guide to the Law and Legal Literature of....** (Subseries in the Latin American series.) **LC1.16:nos.**

No. 3. **Cuba, the Dominican Republic and Haiti.** By Crawford M. Bishop and Anyda Marchant. IA, 1944. 276 pp. LC 44-41173.

No. 4. **Colombia.** By Richard C. Backus and Phanor J. Eder. IA, 1943. 222 pp. LC 44-41777. Z6458.C7B3.

No. 12. **Bolivia.** IA, 1947. 110 pp. LC 47-32662. OCLC 768396.

No. 13. **Mexican States.** IA, 1947. 180 pp. LC 47-32154. OCLC 1247215.

No. 16. **Venezuela.** IA, 1947. 128 pp. LC 47-46281. OCLC 766307.

No. 18. **Ecuador.** IA, 1947. 100 pp. LC 47-31689. OCLC 767018.

No. 26. **Uruguay.** IA, 1947. 123 pp. LC 48-50049. OCLC 768391.

No. 28. **Chile, 1917-1946.** IA, 1947. 103 pp. LC 48-50091. OCLC 768374.

No. 32. **Argentina, 1917-1946.** IA, 1948. 180 pp. LC 48-45659. OCLC 768384. Available to U.S. libraries and institutions from the Central Services Division, Library of Congress, Washington, DC 20540.

No. 38. **A Revised Guide to the Law and Legal Literature of Mexico.** IA, 1973. 463 pp. LC 72-12763. OCLC 52080. Free from the Central Services Division, Library of Congress, Washington, DC 20540.

No. 39. **Peru: A Revised Guide.** By David M. Valderrama. IA, 1976. 296 pp. LC 75-619395. OCLC 1975675. Free from the Central Services Division, Library of Congress, Washington, DC 20540.

507. Library of Congress. **Law Volumes Microfilmed by the Library of Congress.** Comp. by Kimberly W. Dobbs. IA, 1980. 280 pp. LC 80-600085. KF4.D6. 026.34. OCLC 6490951. **LC1.12/2:L41**.

508. Library of Congress. **Legal Codes of the Latin American Republics.** GPO, 1942. 95 pp. (Latin American series, no. 1.) LC 42-38829. **LC1.16:1**.

509. Library of Congress. Latin American, Portuguese and Spanish Division. **Nomenclature and Hierarchy: Basic Latin American Legal Sources.** By Rubens Medina and Cecilia Medina-Quiroga. GPO, 1979. 123 pp. LC 79-14005. OCLC 5007223. S/N 030-013-00008-5. $8.50. **LC24.2:N72**.
This is the first guide of its type ever published on basic Hispanic legal sources, and it fills a significant gap in foreign legal research aids. It covers the basic instruments of legislative and high executive issuance in the eighteen Hispanic nations of Latin America and in Brazil and Haiti.

510. Library of Congress. Law Library. **Anglo-American Legal Bibliographies: An Annotated Guide.** By William L. Friend. GPO, 1944. 166 pp. LC 44-41314. Z663.5.A5. (Repr.: AMS Press, $10; Rothman, $15.) **LC10.2:An4**.
The guide lists many bibliographies but omits those devoted exclusively to American statutory materials and those which are library catalogs.

511. Library of Congress. Law Library. **The Canon Law Collection of the Library of Congress: A General Bibliography with Selective Annotations.** Comp. by Dario C. Ferreira-Ibarra. GPO, 1981. 210 pp. LC 81-607964. 016.2629. OCLC 07555441. S/N 030-000-00123-1. $11. **LC42.9:C16**.
This bibliography with selective annotations lists the canon law holdings of the Library of Congress Law Library and classifies them by subject. It was developed to provide canon law researchers with a simple, comprehensive, and functional reference book, and to aid legal historians, writers, and students interested in tracing canon law research.

CIVIL RIGHTS

512. Commission on Civil Rights. **American Indian Civil Rights Handbook.** GPO, 1980. 2d ed. 71 pp. (Clearinghouse publication 35.) OCLC 6878677. S/N 005-000-00245-1. $4.75 **CR1.10:35/2**.
This handbook describes the basic rights of American Indians both on and off reservations. It explains federal law related to freedom of belief and expression, fair treatment by police and the courts, child custody, employment, voting, and other civil rights.

513. Commission on Civil Rights. **Civil Rights Directory.** IA, 1981. LC 74-610026. KF4755.A83. 323-4/0973s. OCLC 02239734. **CR1.10:15/4**.
The directory lists federal, state, and local government and private organizations engaged in civil rights activities. It gives phone number, address, name of head, and a short description.

CONSTITUTION

514. Congress. House. **The Constitution of the United States of America, as Amended: Analytical Index, Unratified Amendments.** GPO, 1977 (repr. 1982). 79 pp. (House document 95-256.) S/N 052-071-00545-5. $4.50. **X95-2: doc.256**.

The text of the Constitution and amendments is given together with the dates of ratification, information regarding proposed amendments that were never ratified by the states, and a detailed analytic index of the Constitution and the amendments with references to articles, sections, and clauses.

515. Congress. Senate. Committee on Rules and Administration. **Constitution of the United States, Analysis and Interpretation: Annotations of Cases Decided by the Supreme Court of the United States.** GPO, 1984. KF4527.J39 1984. S/N 052-071-00674-5.

The Constitution is presented with citations to important cases concerning it, given clause by clause. It also contains a section on acts of Congress that were declared unconstitutional. This is often referred to as the *Annotated Constitution*. It is indexed and has a table of cases.

INTERNATIONAL LAW

Digests

516. Department of State. **Digest of International Law.** By John Bassett Moore. 8 vols. GPO, 1906. (House document 551, 56th Congress, 2d session.) **Congressional Serial Set 4202-4206.**

This is based largely on materials before 1901, with some coverage of the years 1901-06. Volume 8 is a complete index.

517. Department of State. **Digest of International Law.** By Green H. Hackworth. 8 vols. GPO, 1940-44. **S7.12:v.1-8.**

This continuation of Moore's *Digest* is based on materials since 1906. Volume 8 contains a detailed index and a list of cases.

518. Department of State. **Digest of International Law.** By Marjorie M. Whiteman. 15 vols. GPO, 1963-73. LC 63-62002. **S7.12/2:v.1-15.**

This fifteen-volume series continues the international law digests of Hackworth and Moore. Volume 15 is a complete index.

519. Department of State. Office of the Legal Advisor. **Digest of the United States Practice in International Law.** GPO, 1974- . Annual. LC 79-645897. JX21.R68. 341/.0973. OCLC 04916863. 1979 ed. S/N 044-000-01937-0. $22. **S7.12/3:yr.**

This series of annual digests emphasizes completed rather than ongoing action. It embodies not only practice as regards other nations, but also the domestic foreign policy law of the United States.

Treaties

520. Department of State. **Treaties and Other International Agreements of the United States of America, 1776-1949.** Ed. by Charles I. Bevins. 13 vols. GPO, 1969-76. LC 70-600742. **S9.12/2:v.1-13.**

This series supersedes earlier compilations by William M. Malloy, C. F. Redmond, Edward J. Trenwith, and Hunter Miller. It contains the text of all treaties and international agreements of the United States prior to the starting point of the current *United States Treaties* series. Volume 13 is a general index.

521. Department of State. **Treaties in Force: A List of Treaties and Other International Agreements of the United States in Force on [date].** GPO, 1956- . Annual. LC 56-61604. 1984 ed. S/N 044-000-02018-1. $9.50. **S9.14:yr.**
Listed are all treaties as well as other international agreements between the United States and foreign countries which are in force on January 1 of each year and which have been made by the President.

522. Department of State. **Treaties and Other International Acts Series.** GPO. 1946- . Irregular. LC 46-006169. JX235.9.A32. 341.273. OCLC 01774183. S/N 044-000-81003-4. $89/yr. **S9.10:1501-nos.**
This source contains the text of treaties and international agreements entered into by the United States with other countries. Each number contains the text of a single treaty or agreement. Publication of the series began with number 1501. It is cited as TIAS.

523. Department of State. **United States Treaties and Other International Agreements.** GPO, 1952- . Annual. OCLC 01307767. **S9.12:vol./pt.**
This series contains the official text of treaties and other international agreements entered into by the United States since January 1, 1950, beginning with TIAS 1501, at which time the treaties ceased to be published in the *Statutes at Large.* It cumulates in bound volumes the slip treaties which were originally published in TIAS. It is cited as UST.

See also SB 191.

REGULATIONS

524. Office of the Federal Register. **Code of Federal Regulations.** GPO, 1938- . Revised annually. OCLC 07288624. S/N 022-003-81001-3 (paper). $550/yr. S/N 022-003-81004-8 (microfiche). $200/yr. (Subscription includes new and revised volumes issued during the year.) **GS4.108:title/pt./yr.**
This is a codification of the general and permanent rules issued by executive departments, federal regulatory agencies, and the President. The Code is divided into fifty titles that represent broad areas subject to federal regulation. It is updated by the daily issues of the *Federal Register* and is cited as CFR.

525. Office of the Federal Register. **Code of Federal Regulations: CFR Index and Finding Aids.** GPO, 1977- . Annual. OCLC 04828101. 1984 ed. S/N 022-003-95320-5 (paper). $17. S/N 022-003-98610-3 (microfiche). $2.25. **GS4.108:ind./yr.**
This volume includes tables of CFR titles with breakdowns into chapters and parts; a list of CFR sections affected, divided into yearly units; and a subject/agency index for regulations codified in the CFR. Subjects used in the index are taken from the thesaurus developed by the Office of the Federal Register and published in the *Federal Register* on February 17, 1981 (46 FR 12618).

526. Office of the Federal Register. **Federal Register.** GPO, 1936- . Daily (Monday through Friday, except legal holidays). LC 36-26246. S/N 022-003-80001-8 (paper). $300/yr. S/N 022-003-80006-9 (microfiche). $175/yr. (Subscription includes Index and List of CFR Sections Affected.) **GS4.107:vol./no.**
This is the official publication vehicle for public regulations and legal notices issued by federal executive agencies and independent agencies. It is required by law that presidential proclamations and Executive Orders, federal agency documents of general applicability and legal effect, documents required to be published by acts of Congress, and other agency documents of public interest be published in the *Federal Register*. Final

rules published in the *Federal Register* update the most recently published CFR volumes.

527. Office of the Federal Register. **Federal Register Index.** GPO, monthly. OCLC 02505035. S/N 022-003-80004-2. $18/yr. (also included in *Federal Register* subscription). **GS4.107:vol./no./ind.**
Each monthly issue is cumulative. The December issue is the annual cumulative index.

528. Office of the Federal Register. **The Federal Register: What It Is and How to Use It; A Guide for the User of the Federal Register-Code of Federal Regulations System.** GPO, 1980. 132 pp., illus. OCLC 6283311. S/N 022-003-01041-6. $6. **GS4.6/2:F31/980.**
This is a guide to using the *Federal Register* and related publications which was developed for use in educational workshops conducted by the Office of the Federal Register. It provides an introduction to the *Federal Register* and the federal rulemaking process.

529. Office of the Federal Register. **LSA: List of CFR Sections Affected.** GPO, 1977- . Monthly, with quarterly cumulations. OCLC 04509194. S/N 022-003-80003-4. $20/yr. (also included in *Federal Register* subscription). **GS4.108/3: date.**
This is a list of rules and proposed rules added or amended since the latest revision of the *Code of Federal Regulations*, with a reference to the issue of the *Federal Register* in which the addition or amendment was published. Issues cumulate each quarter; there is no annual cumulation. A current list is published in each issue of the *Federal Register* so that by using it along with the most recent LSA the researcher can identify the latest edition and amendment of a rule.

STATUTES

530. Congress. House. Committee on the Judiciary. **United States Code.** GPO, 1926- . Sexennial. LC 65-61024. 1982 ed. 17 vols. S/N 052-001-81001-5. $550 (set). **Y1.2/5:yr./vol.**

_____. **Supplement.** GPO, 1940- . Annual. OCLC 05003916.
This consolidation and codification of the general and permanent laws of the United States is arranged according to subject matter under fifty titles. The official compilation of U.S. laws in force, the Code (cited as USC) gives the current status of laws as amended. New editions have been published every six years since 1934, with annual cumulative supplements published after the conclusion of each session of Congress. A short pamphlet, *How to Find U.S. Statutes and U.S. Code Citations* (GS4.102:St2/yr.), aids users in quickly and easily identifying up-to-date and accurate citations to the *Statutes at Large* and the *U.S. Code*. See SB 197 for prices of individual volumes of the seventeen-volume 1982 edition.

531. Library of Congress. Law Library. **Index Analysis of the Federal Statutes (General and Permanent Law) 1789-1873; 1873-1907.** By Middleton G. Beaman, George Scott, and A. K. McNamara. 2 vols. GPO, 1911. **LC10.5:v.1,2.**

532. Library of Congress. Legislative Reference Service. **Index to the Federal Statutes, 1874-1931: General and Permanent Law Contained in the Revised Statutes of 1874 and Volumes 18-46 of the Statutes at Large.** By Walter H. McClenon and Wilfred C. Gilbert. GPO, 1943. 1,432 pp. **LC14.2:F31.**

The first volume of *Index Analysis* (entry 531) for the period 1789-1873 covers legislation before the *Revised Statutes*, which was published in volumes 1-17 of the *Statutes at Large*. It includes a table of repeals and amendments. The second volume is superseded by the *Index to Federal Statutes*, which covers volumes 18-46 of the *Statutes at Large* and the *Revised Statutes* of 1874.

533. Library of Congress. Legislative Reference Service. **State Law Index: An Index and Digest to the Legislation of the States of the United States of America.** 12 vols. GPO, 1929-49. LC 30-2750. **LC14.5:v.1-12.**

Volume 1 of this biennial covered the years 1925 and 1926, and the last volume (volume 12) the years 1947 and 1948. It is arranged by subject. Within each subject are subheadings for each state with legislation on that subject listed chronologically.

534. Office of the Federal Register. **United States Statutes at Large.** GPO, 1873- . Annual. LC 7-35353. **GS4.111:vol.**

Volumes 1-17 (1789-1873) were published by Little, Brown. As laws are enacted they are published individually and called "slip laws" (GS4.110:cong./no.). The *Statutes at Large* (cited Stat.) supersedes the slip laws for each session of Congress and contains the full text of all laws and resolutions passed during that session arranged chronologically by date of approval. Each volume is indexed by personal names and subjects. Treaties were included until 1949, and are now published in *United States Treaties and Other International Agreements* (entry 523). The laws published in *Statutes at Large* are codified in the *United States Code* (entry 530).

Political Science

COMMUNISM

535.   Congress. House. Committee on Un-American Activities. **World Communist Movement: Selective Chronology, 1818-1957.** Comp. by the Library of Congress. Legislative Reference Service. 4 vols. GPO, 1960-67. 1,001 pp. **Y4.Un1/2:C73/114/v.1-4.**

The purpose of this chronology is to record in a very general way some of the developments, trends, and events of the world communist movement from the birth of Karl Marx in 1818 until the end of December 1957.

536.   Department of State. Bureau of Intelligence and Research. **World Strength of Communist Party Organizations.** GPO, 1948- . Annual. LC 56-60986. **S1.111:yr.**

Statistical and analytical reviews of world communist parties in and out of power are provided. The arrangement is alphabetic within geographic regions, excluding the Communist Party of the United States. Information includes date of last election; vote totals for communist, noncommunist left, center, conservative, and others; percentage figures of total votes; number and percentage of seats in government; and estimated party membership. A useful checklist provides brief details with page references to complete reviews.

537.   United States Information Agency. **Problems of Communism.** GPO, 1952- . Bimonthly. S/N 025-000-80001-0. $16/yr. **IA1.8:vol./nos.**

This source provides analyses and background on current theoretical and political aspects of world communism. The emphasis is on policies and aims of the Soviet Union and Communist China.

IMMIGRATION

538.   Immigration and Naturalization Service. **Immigration Literature: Abstracts of Demographic, Economic and Policy Studies.** Comp. by Jeannette H. North and Susan J. Grodsky. GPO, 1979. 89 pp. OCLC 5417860. **J21.16:Im6.**

This annotated bibliography focuses on the demographic, economic, and policy aspects of migration to and from the United States during 1965 to 1978. Subject matter covered includes demographic studies of recent migration, economic studies, "brain drain" studies, and policy studies.

539. Immigration and Naturalization Service. **Statistical Yearbook of the Immigration and Naturalization Service.** GPO, annual. OCLC 07063193. **J21.2:St2/yr.**
Statistical data are given on immigration, nationality, and related activities of the Immigration and Naturalization Service during the fiscal year.

See also SB 69.

INTERNATIONAL RELATIONS

General Works

Bibliographies

540. Congress. Senate. Committee on Governmental Affairs. **Bibliography: Nuclear Proliferation.** Comp. by the Congressional Research Service. GPO, 1978. 159 pp. OCLC 3980294. **Y4.G74/9:N88/3.**
This sourcebook of essential materials on nuclear proliferation includes national and international statistical data, a bibliography, analytical papers on the production of plutonium, and a glossary of terms.

541. Department of State. **Publications of the Department of State: October 1, 1929 to January 1, 1953.** GPO, 1954. 507 pp. **S1.30:929-53.**

———. **January 1, 1953-December 31, 1957.** GPO, 1958. 230 pp. **S1.30:953-57.**

———. **January 1, 1958-December 31, 1960.** GPO, 1961. 116 pp. **S1.30:958-60.**
The three successive issues listed above give a complete listing of the numbered publications of the Department of State from October 1, 1929 to December 31, 1960. New publications are listed regularly in the monthly *Department of State Bulletin.* A helpful guide to Department of State publications is *Major Publications of the Department of State: An Annotated Bibliography* (1977, 27 pp., S1.71:200/3).

542. Department of State. **The United States and Russia: The Beginning of Relations, 1765-1815.** Ed. by Nina N. Bashkina et al. GPO, 1980. 1,184 pp., illus., maps. LC 80-607939. E183.8.R9U59. 327.73047.19. OCLC 6627803. S/N 022-002-00068-6. $34. **S1.2:R92/3/765-815.**
This is a collection of documents on Russian-American relations between the latter eighteenth century and the early nineteenth century.

543. Department of State. Bureau of Public Affairs. **Selected State Department Publications.** IA, 1980- . Quarterly. OCLC 06591103. **S1.30/3:St2/date.**
This is a list of selected publications from the Department of State during the time period covered.

544. Library of Congress. **A Guide to Bibliographic Tools for Research in Foreign Affairs.** Comp. by Helen F. Conover. GPO, 1958. 2d ed. with suppl. 160 pp. LC 58-60091. Z6461.U49 1948. (Repr.: Greenwood Press, $13.75.)
The guide contains 351 entries in three sections: (1) general reference, (2) reference sources for international studies, and (3) specialized sources. Lengthy descriptive annotations and author-title-subject indexes are provided.

Dictionaries

545. Department of State. Library. **International Relations Dictionary**. By Carol A. Becker. GPO, 1980. 2d ed. 80 pp. (Department and foreign service series 221.) OCLC 07563770. S/N 044-000-01853-5. $5. **S1.69:221-2**.
Intended to complement standard international relations works, this volume identifies and describes terms, phrases, acronyms, catchwords, and abbreviations used in the conduct of foreign affairs.

Directories

546. Department of State. **Biographic Register**. GPO, 1869-1974. Annual. (Department and foreign service series 69.) LC 9-22072. **S1.69:126/nos**.
This directory provides "information and background on personnel of the Department of State and the Foreign Service, and other Federal Government Agencies that participate in the field of foreign affairs." It includes biographies for ambassadors, ministers, foreign service officers, reserve officers, chiefs of overseas missions, and employees of comparable grade in the Agency for International Development, Peace Corps, United States Information Agency, and Foreign Agricultural Service. Civil Service employees of the Department of State in grade GS-12 and above are included. For each individual the following information is given: place of birth, college, degree, military service, State Department assignments and dates, rank, and foreign languages in which that individual has received a rating of at least "S-3" through examinations at the Foreign Service Institute.

547. Department of State. **Diplomatic List**. GPO, 1893- . Quarterly. LC 10-16292. S/N 044-000-80003-9. $13/yr. **S1.8:date**.
This directory lists foreign diplomats stationed in the United States in order of rank by country. Information for each person includes Washington, DC address and telephone number, and names of any other members of the family living in Washington. National holidays are listed under the name of the country. Ambassadors are also listed by order of precedence with their date of presentation of credentials, the dean of the diplomatic corps, and a special list of countries with temporary chancery addresses.

548. Department of State. **Employees of Diplomatic Missions**. GPO, quarterly. OCLC 01768339. S/N 044-000-80004-7. $9.50/yr. **S1.8/2:date**.
This source lists the names and addresses of alien employees of foreign missions in Washington, DC who are not listed in the *Diplomatic List*.

549. Department of State. **Foreign Consular Offices in the United States**. GPO, 1932- . Annual. (Department and foreign service series 128.) LC 32-26478. 1983 ed. S/N 044-000-01965-5. $6.50. **S1.69:128/no**.
This is a complete, official listing of the foreign consular offices in the United States, their jurisdictions, and recognized personnel.

550. Department of State. Office of External Research. Bureau of Intelligence and Research. **University Centers of Foreign Affairs Research: A Directory**. GPO, 1968. 139 pp. LC 68-60080. **S1.2:Un3**.
This is one in a number of Department of State directories of centers engaged in international studies. This directory is focused on "U.S. university-affiliated centers which have as their main purpose social science research in foreign affairs ... [and] includes only those university research programs and projects which are organized in easily identified centers or institutes." It is arranged alphabetically by name of the university

and gives a complete description of each program. A chronology of the development of foreign affairs research centers forms an appendix.

Sources

551. Department of State. **Foreign Relations of the United States**. GPO, 1861- . Annual. LC 10-3793. JX233.A3. 327.73. OCLC 1768341. **S1.1:yr./vol.**

This is the official record of U.S. foreign policy and diplomacy. This monumental series, issued since 1861, includes "all documents needed to give a comprehensive record of the major foreign policy decisions within the range of the Department of State's responsibilities, together with appropriate materials concerning the facts which contributed to the formulation of the policies." Each volume covers only certain countries within a given year. Documents are arranged chronologically under each country. Each volume contains diplomatic communications between the U.S. and foreign governments, and between the Department of State and American diplomatic personnel. These include comprehensive and objective sections of major memoranda, diplomatic notes, telegrams, and other basic papers. The result is the most extensive and nearly current publication of diplomatic papers in the world. Volumes are published at least twenty-five years after the documents were written in order to accomplish declassification processing. A general index covering the years 1861 to 1899 was published in 1902, and one covering the period 1900 to 1918 was published in 1940. For a list of in-print volumes see SB 210.

552. Department of State. Bureau of Public Affairs. **Atlas of United States Foreign Relations**. By Harry F. Young. GPO, 1983. 96 pp., illus. LC 83-600517. S/N 044-000-01973-6. $5. **S1.3/a:At6/comp.**

The atlas provides basic information about U.S. foreign relations for easy reference and as an educational tool. Comprising about one hundred maps and charts, it is divided into six sections dealing with foreign relations machinery, international organization, elements of the world economy, trade and investment, development assistance, and U.S. national security. These sections were originally published in the *Department of State Bulletin* in 1981 and 1982 and have been reprinted separately. They were updated and revised for this single volume.

Texts

553. Congress. House. Committee on Foreign Affairs. [and] Senate. Committee on Foreign Relations. **Legislation on Foreign Relations through [year]**. GPO, annual. 1983 ed. S/N 052-070-05906-1 (vol. 1). $18. S/N 052-070-05907-9 (vol. 2). $18. **Y4.F76/2:L52/yr./vol.**

This source contains legislation, Executive Orders, and related materials on foreign assistance, agricultural commodities, the Peace Corps, arms control and disarmament, the Department of State, and information and educational and cultural exchange programs. It is republished with amendments and additions at the end of each session of Congress.

See also SB 75 and SB 210.

Disarmament

554. Arms Control and Disarmament Agency. **Documents on Disarmament**. GPO, 1961- . Annual. LC 60-64408. OCLC 966148. 1980 ed. S/N 002-000-00083-1. $14. **AC1.11/2:yr.**
Documents on the nonproliferation treaty and other aspects of disarmament and arms control are arranged chronologically. Principal organizations and conferences and people involved in the field are listed. There is also a bibliography and a complete subject index.

UNITED STATES GOVERNMENT

General Works

555. Bureau of the Census. **Guide to the 1977 Census of Governments**. GPO, 1980. 273 pp. (1977 Census of Governments, vol. 7.) LC 78-17414. OCLC 6629288. S/N 003-024-01625-7. $8. **C3.145/4:977/v.7.**
The guide provides a summary description of each subject volume in the 1977 Census of Governments reports series, as well as contents pages and table formats for each volume.

556. Bureau of Land Management. **Public Land Statistics**. GPO, 1962- . Annual. LC 79-647223. HD183.B87a. 333.1/0973. OCLC 01197130. **I53.1/2:yr.**
Tables of data are presented for public lands, land disposition and use, forest life, outdoor recreation and wildlife, range management, conservation and development, minerals classification and investigation operations, protection, surveys (including off-shore surveys), and government administration and finance.

557. Civil Service Commission. **Official Register of the United States: Persons Occupying Administrative and Supervising Positions in Legislative, Executive and Judicial Branches of Federal Government in the District of Columbia**. GPO, 1816-1959. Annual. LC 8-35096. **CS1.31:yr.**
Although lack of appropriations brought an end to the *Official Register*, it remains an important historical source of government personnel. It was published by the Department of State from 1816 to 1861; Department of the Interior, 1861 to 1905; Bureau of the Census, 1907 to 1932; and Civil Service Commission, 1933 to 1959. Known as the "Blue Book," it was issued biennially from 1816 to 1921 and annually thereafter. It was not published from 1922 to 1924.

It is arranged by departments or agencies, listing principal employees with the following information for each: reported birthplace, official title, place employed, and salary. Prior to 1925 it included all officers, agents, clerks, and other employees of bureaus, offices, commissions, and institutions connected with the federal government and paid from the U.S. Treasury. After 1925 only principal administrators were listed. There is a complete name index in each volume.

558. Department of State. Office of the Historian. **The Eagle and the Shield: A History of the Great Seal of the United States**. By Richard S. Patterson and Richardson Dougall. GPO, 1976. 637 pp., illus. (Department and foreign service series 161.) OCLC 4268298. S/N 044-000-01543-9. $19. **S1.69:161.**
This detailed, illustrated history of the Great Seal of the United States spans two centuries.

559.　Federal Election Commission. **Election Directory**. NTIS, 1978- . Annual. LC
　　78-648244. JK2021.E43. 329/.0025/73. OCLC 04394207. **Y3.El2/3:14/yr.**
The directory describes the composition, functions, and duties of each state agency
responsible for voter registration, election administration, campaign finance, and
campaign disclosure regulation. It also gives addresses and telephone numbers for
federal and state officials with election-related duties, and lists chairpersons of election
committees in state legislatures, state legislative reference services, and officers of associations of election officials.

560.　General Accounting Office. **Federal Information Sources and Systems: A Direc-
　　tory Issued by the Comptroller General**. GPO, 1980. 1,196 pp. LC 78-647191.
　　Z7165.U5F44. 016.353. OCLC 02847138. S/N 020-000-00183-6. $20. **GA1.22:
　　In3/980.**
This source was developed to provide Congress with a single directory that identifies
and describes federal sources and systems maintained by almost a hundred executive
agencies. It also contains fiscal, budgeting, and program-related information.

561.　Office of the Federal Register. **Privacy Act Issuances ... Compilation**.
　　GPO, 1976- . Annual. LC 77-647783. KF5753.A329F4. 342/.73/085. OCLC
　　03084918. **GS4.107/a:P939/2/yr./vol.**
This is a directory of records kept by federal agencies about individuals. It gives
descriptions of the record systems in each federal agency, along with the agency rules
for helping individuals who request information about their records.

562.　Office of the Federal Register. **The United States Directory of Federal Regional
　　Structure**. GPO, 1979- . Annual. OCLC 06922593. **GS4.119:yr.**
This directory identifies field offices of federal departments and agencies, lists key
personnel, addresses, and telephone numbers, and provides regional maps and tables.

563.　Office of the Federal Register. **United States Government Manual**. GPO,
　　1935- . Annual. LC 73-646537. JK421.A3. 353. OCLC 01788884. 1984/85 ed.
　　S/N 002-003-01109-9. $12. **GS4.109:yr.**
The "official handbook of the Federal Government," this publication is really a
directory of agencies in the legislative, judicial, and executive branches. It summarizes
agency responsibilities and gives names, addresses, and telephone numbers. It also
includes information on quasi-official agencies, international organizations, boards,
committees, and commissions. Appendixes cover abolished and transferred agencies,
abbreviations and acronyms, agency organization charts, and agencies appearing in the
Code of Federal Regulations. There are name, subject, and agency indexes.

564.　Office of Management and Budget. **Budget in Brief**. GPO, 1951- . Annual.
　　1985 ed. S/N 041-001-00272-3. $2.50. **PrEx2.8/2:yr.**
This concise, nontechnical overview of the President's proposed budget features charts,
summaries, and historical tables. Other budget publications are listed below. For latest
editions, see SB 204.

565.　Office of Management and Budget. **Budget of the United States Government**.
　　GPO, 1923- . Annual. 1985 ed. S/N 041-001-00270-7. $12. **PrEx2.8:yr.**
This work contains the President's budget message and an overview of his budget
proposals, with explanations of spending programs in terms of national needs, agency
missions, and programs, and the impact of the budget on the economy. It also gives a
description of the budget process as a whole.

566. Office of Management and Budget. **Budget of the United States Government: Appendix**. GPO, 1923- . Annual. 1985 ed. S/N 041-001-00271-5. $19. **PrEx2.8: yr./app.**

The most detailed budget document, the appendix gives the following information for each agency: proposed wording for appropriations legislation, budget tables for each account, new legislative proposals, explanations of the work to be done and the funds needed, proposed general provisions, and schedules of permanent positions.

567. Office of Management and Budget. **Budget of the United States Government: Special Analyses**. GPO, annual. 1985 ed. S/N 041-001-00273-1. $7.50. **PrEx2.8/5:yr.**

These special analyses are designed to highlight specified program areas or provide other significant presentations of the federal budget data.

568. Office of Management and Budget. **Major Themes and Additional Budget Details**. GPO, annual. 1985 ed. S/N 041-001-00274-0. $8. **PrEx2.8:yr./themes.**

This supplementary report to the budget documents highlights the ways in which the budget implements major themes of the President's program and describes specific programmatic changes and their effects.

See also SB 141.

Armed Forces

General Works

569. Department of the Army. Center of Military History. **Guide to the Study and Use of Military History**. Ed. by John E. Jessup, Jr. and Robert W. Coakley. GPO, 1979. 507 pp., illus. LC 78-606157. E181.G85. 973/.07/2. OCLC 4131480. S/N 008-029-00105-5. $9. **D114.12:St9.**

570. Department of the Army. Center of Military History. **Guide to United States Army Museums and Historic Sites**. By Norman Miller Carey, Jr. GPO, 1975. 116 pp., illus. LC 75-619315. S/N 008-029-00561-4. $5.50. **D114.2:M97/975.**

This is a state-by-state guide to sixty-four U.S. Army museums with information on other military-related museums outside the Army.

571. Department of the Army. Center of Military History. **Secretaries of War and Secretaries of the Army: Portraits and Biographical Sketches**. GPO, 1982. 186 pp., illus. LC 80-020122. E176.B42. 353.62/092/2. OCLC 06603916. S/N 008-029-00116-1. $12. **D114.2:Se2.**

This source gives biographies and color portraits of the Secretaries of War and Secretaries of the Army from Henry Knox of George Washington's administration to John O. Marsh, Jr. of the Reagan administration, as well as a brief introduction to Army history, illustrated with drawings and photographs of buildings.

572. Department of the Army. Office of the Adjutant General. **American Decorations: A List of Awards of the Congressional Medal of Honor, the Distinguished Service Cross, and the Distinguished Service Medal Awarded under Authority of the Congress, 1862-1926**. GPO, 1927. 845 pp.

_____. **Supplements 1-5, January 1, 1927-June 30, 1941**. GPO, 1927-41.

For more up-to-date information, consult *Laws Authorizing Issuance of Medals and Commemorative Coins* (entry 631).

573.   Department of the Army. Office of the Chief of Military History. **American Military History**. Ed. by Maurice Matloff. GPO, 1973 (repr. 1983). 729 pp., illus. LC 76-600410. S/N 008-029-00089-0. $19. **D114.2:M59/973**.

This is a survey of American military history from colonial times to the Vietnam conflict in 1968.

574.   Military Academy. **Preliminary Guide to the Manuscript Collection of the U.S. Military Academy Library**. Comp. by J. Thomas Russell. West Point, NY: IA, 1968. 260 pp. (USMA Library bulletin no. 5.) **D109.10:5**.

Issued as an aid to researchers, collectors, and librarians, this guide contains citations to the manuscript holdings in the library of the U.S. Military Academy before October 1967, including both analyzed and unanalyzed collections. It describes collections in terms of physical space, type of documents, how acquired, and names of people and subjects prominent in the collection.

See also SB 98 and SB 131.

Army

575.   Army Military History Institute. **God Save the Queen: A Bibliography of the British and Commonwealth Holdings**. By Lawrence James-Alexander Lentz. Carlisle Barracks, PA: IA, 1979. 390 pp. (Special bibliographic series, no. 18.) OCLC 4978593. **D114.14:18**.

This is a list of the holdings of the U.S. Army Military History Institute related to the Army's involvement with British forces. Most of the books listed are available through interlibrary loan. There are no annotations.

576.   Army Military History Institute. **United States Army Unit Histories**. By George S. Pappas. Rev. and updated by Elizabeth Snoke and Alexandra Campbell. 2 vols. GPO, 1978. (Special bibliographic series, no. 4.) OCLC 3902141. S/N 008-029-00104-7 (vol. 1). $7. S/N 008-029-00106-3 (vol. 2). $7.50. **D114.14: 4/2/v.1,2**.

This two-volume bibliography of unit histories located in the U.S. Army Military History Institute includes regular Army, National Guard, and Army Reserve histories dated from 1914 to the present. A detailed user's guide and cross-reference table are provided. Omitted from the list are Army Air Corps, Army Air Force, and U.S. Air Force unit histories.

577.   Congress. House. **Historical Register and Dictionary of the United States Army from Its Organization September 29, 1789 to March 2, 1903**. Comp. by Frances B. Heitman. 2 vols. GPO, 1903. (House document 446, 57th Congress, 2nd session.) **Congressional Serial Set 4535, 4536**.

This source contains lists of Army officers, battles, forts and other military installations, and statistics.

578.   Department of the Army. **Army Register**. GPO, 1813- . Annual. LC 4-18250. OCLC 2954957. **D102.9:yr**.

The register is issued in the following three volumes: (1) U.S. Army Active and Retired List; (2) Army of the United States and Other Retired Lists; and (3) Officers Honorary Retired List.

579.   Department of the Army. **The Role of the Reserve in the Army: A Bibliographic Survey of the U.S. Army Reserve**. GPO, 1977. 107 pp., illus. (DA pamphlet 140-7.) Z6725.U4226 1977. 016.3553/7/0973. OCLC 2819197. **D101.22:140-7**.

This bibliography covers the many aspects of the Army Reserve. Each citation includes an abstract and full bibliographic information. The twenty-nine appendixes include statistics, charts, and maps. Information on foreign army reserves is included.

580. Department of the Army. Office of the Adjutant General. **Theses and Dissertations in the Holdings of the Army Library: A List of Titles.** GPO, 1966. 3d ed. 101 pp. (Special bibliographies no. 20.) **D102.28:20.**

This classified bibliography lists 836 theses and dissertations on various aspects of military science.

581. Military Academy. **The Centennial of the U.S. Military Academy at West Point, N.Y., 1802-1902.** Ed. by Edward S. Holden. 2 vols. GPO, 1904. **W12.2:C33/v.1,2.**

Volume 1 includes addresses and histories. Noteworthy features of volume 2, "Statistics and Bibliographies," are a bibliography of publications by West Point graduates and a list of graduates. This was also issued as House document 789, 58th Congress, 2nd session (Congressional Serial Set 4750, 4751).

582. National Museum of History and Technology. **United States Army Headgear to 1854: Catalog of United States Army Uniforms in the Collections of the Smithsonian Institution. Volume 1.** By Edgar M. Howell and Donald E. Kloster. GPO, 1969. 75 pp., illus. (Bulletin 269.) LC 73-601. **SI3.3:269.**

This is the first in a projected series on Army dress based on collections of the Museum of History and Technology. Specifically, it is a descriptive, critical, and documentary catalog of the regular establishment through 1854. Other volumes will cover headgear from 1854 to the present, uniforms, and footwear. Pictures of the headgear are provided, as are detailed narrative descriptions, regulations for wear, and source notes for each item. The appendix lists makers of headgear and dates. A bibliography is also provided.

Navy

583. Department of the Navy. Naval Historical Center. **Dictionary of American Naval Fighting Ships.** Ed. by James L. Mooney. 8 vols. GPO, 1959-81. LC 60-060198. OCLC 2794587. **D207.10:v.1-8.**

> Vol. 1. A-B. 1959 (repr. 1983). 369 pp. S/N 008-046-00041-7. $17.
>
> Vol. 2. C-F. 1963 (repr. 1983). 615 pp. S/N 008-046-00007-7. $18.
>
> Vol. 3. G-K. 1968 (repr. 1981). 902 pp. S/N 008-046-00008-5. $32.
>
> Vol. 4. L-M. 1969 (repr. 1981). 771 pp. S/N 008-046-00009-3. $19.
>
> Vol. 5. N-Q. 1970 (repr. 1983). 639 pp. S/N 008-046-00051-4. $18.
>
> Vol. 6. R-S. 1976 (repr. 1981). 751 pp. S/N 008-046-00056-5. $19.
>
> Vol. 7. T-V. 1981. 755 pp. S/N 008-046-00100-6. $18.
>
> Vol. 8. W-Z. 1981. 597 pp. S/N 008-046-00101-4. $17.
>
> Vols. 1-8 (set). S/N 008-046-00105-7. $142.

This series includes histories of almost ten thousand ships that have served the U.S. Navy and, before that, the Continental Navy. Its purpose is to "give the concise facts about every ship so that it may be a ready reference for those who have served in the ships and for the student, writer, and many others." The descriptions of each ship include tonnage, length, beam, draft, speed, armament and class, and, where known, the builder, sponsor, launching and commission dates, date of acquisition by the Navy, first commanding officer, and a concise operational history. Each volume also includes a bibliography, appendixes for various types of ships in the modern and historic Navy, and illustrations. Short biographies of the naval leaders after whom ships were named are also included. The last volume includes a guide to the entire series.

584. Department of the Navy. Naval History Division. **U.S. Naval History Sources in the United States.** Comp. and ed. by Dean C. Allard, Martha L. Crawley, and Mary W. Edmison. GPO, 1979. 235 pp., illus. LC 79-600070. OCLC 6082146. **D207.2:N22.**

585. National Archives and Records Service. **List of Log Books of U.S. Navy Ships, Stations, and Miscellaneous Units, 1801-1947.** Comp. by Claudia Bradley et al. IA, 1978. 562 pp., illus. (Special list 44.) Z6835.U5U43 1978. 016.973s. OCLC 3728731. **GS4.7:44.**

This is an inventory, with descriptions, of individual records in the National Archives holdings of approximately seventy-three thousand log books of U.S. Navy ships, stations, and miscellaneous units between 1801 and 1947. Entries give vessel or station name, dates covered by the log books, and number of log books.

Air Force

586. Department of the Air Force. Office of the Directorate of Personnel Program Actions. **Air Force Register.** GPO, annual. OCLC 09289645. 1982 ed. S/N 008-070-00481-0. $16. **D303.7:yr.**

Regular and reserve Air Force officers on active duty are listed.

Congress

General Works

587. Congress. **Congressional Record.** GPO, 1873- . Daily (when Congress is in session). LC 12-36438. OCLC 02437919. S/N 052-000-80001-3. $218/yr. **X/a.Cong.-sess.:nos.**

Published daily while Congress is in session, the *Congressional Record* is revised and issued in bound volumes for each year (or session of a Congress). Page numbers in the daily and bound editions differ. The daily editions use three separate numbering systems with the following letter prefixes: H (for House proceedings), S (for Senate proceedings), and E (for extension of remarks). Pages in the bound volume are numbered in a single sequence. It contains the record of debates and proceedings in Congress, messages to Congress, and records of voting. Users should be aware that speeches and debates are not necessarily verbatim. Members may edit and alter their remarks, or insert remarks without actually presenting them on the floor. A black bullet designates speeches that were inserted into the Record without having been delivered on the floor. However, absence of the bullet does not necessarily mean that the whole speech was actually delivered on the floor; only the first few sentences may have been read aloud.

588. Congress. **Congressional Record Index: Proceedings and Debates of Congress.** GPO, 1873- . Biweekly. OCLC 02428236. Included with subscription to daily *Congressional Record.* **X/a.Cong.-sess.:nos./ind.**

This subject and name index to the *Congressional Record* includes a History of Bills and Resolutions section, arranged by bill number, which leads to information on all stages of bills from introduction to defeat or passage. When the index section is cumulated for the bound edition, the page numbers are changed to reflect the single numbering sequence of the bound volumes.

589. Congress. House. **Calendars of the U.S. House of Representatives and History of Legislation.** GPO, daily (when Congress is in session). LC 52-63188. J47.A3. 328.73. OCLC 1768279. S/N 052-070-81001-7. $200 per session. **Y1.2/2:date.**
This is a source of up-to-date information on the status of legislation in both the House and Senate. Legislative histories are given by bill number; information is given on bills that required a conference; and the status of major bills is summarized. A cumulative index is included in each Monday issue.

590. Congress. Senate. **Public Documents of the First Fourteen Congresses, 1789-1817: Papers Relating to Early Congressional Documents.** By Adolphus W. Greeley. GPO, 1900. 903 pp. (Senate document 428, 56th Congress, 1st session.) **Congressional Serial Set 3879.**
This is a chronologic listing of publications with notes that describe the documents and cite library locations of the originals. A supplement was published in 1904 in the annual report of the American Historical Association, volume 1.

591. Library of Congress. Manuscript Division. **Members of Congress: A Checklist of Their Papers in the Manuscript Division, Library of Congress.** Comp. by John J. McDonough. GPO, 1980. 217 pp. LC 78-606102. Z1236.U613 1980. 016.32873/092/2. OCLC 4131493. S/N 030-003-00019-5. $10. **LC4.2:C76/2.**

See also SB 201.

Biographical Sources

592. Congress. Joint Committee on Arrangement for the Commemoration of the Bicentennial. **Women in Congress, 1917-1976.** By Susan J. Tolchin. GPO, 1976. 112 pp., illus. OCLC 2687322. **Y4.B47:W84.**
This source gives biographical sketches and photographs of women who have served in the House of Representatives and the Senate between 1917 and 1976.

593. Congress. Joint Committee on Printing. **Congressional Pictorial Directory.** GPO, 1953- . Biennial. LC 68-61223. OCLC 1239852. Ed. for 98th Congress. S/N 052-070-05818-8. $6. **Y4.P93/1:1P/cong.**
The title varies: *Congressional Picture Directory, Pocket Congressional Directory.* The directory contains small black-and-white photographs of the President, Vice President, House and Senate members (arranged by state), officers of the House and Senate, and chaplains and officials of the Capitol.

594. Congress. Joint Committee on Printing. **Official Congressional Directory.** GPO, 1887- . Biennial. LC 6-35330. OCLC 01239877. 1983-84 ed. S/N 052-070-05832-3. $12. **Y4.P93/1:1/cong.**
This official directory presents short biographies of each of the members of the Senate and the House, listed by states and districts, respectively. Additional data on each of the lawmakers are also included, such as committee memberships, terms of service, administrative assistant and/or secretary, room, and telephone number. The directory also lists officials of the federal courts, the military establishments, and other federal departments and agencies including the District of Columbia government; governors of the states and territories; foreign diplomats; and members of the press, radio, and television galleries. A description of the Capitol building, its grounds and floor plans, is included, as are maps depicting congressional districts for each state.

595. Congress. Senate. **Biographical Directory of the American Congress, 1774-1971.** GPO, 1971 (repr. 1977). 1,972 pp. (Senate document 92-8.) S/N 052-071-00249-9. $40. **X92-1:S.doc.8.**

The directory has been published irregularly since 1859, when it was titled *Dictionary of the U.S. Congress and General Government.* It was first published with the present title in 1928. This volume is the eleventh edition of this valuable work.

It is an authoritative directory that contains more than 10,800 short biographies of senators and representatives elected to the Continental Congress (1774-88) and to the Congress of the United States from the first through the ninety-first Congress (1789-1971). Also included are lists of the officers of the executive branch of government from the administration of George Washington through that of Richard Nixon; the delegates to the Continental Congress; and all members of Congress up to 1971. For the first time, this edition contains biographies of presidents who have never served as members of Congress.

All entries include places and dates of birth, summaries of education, capsule histories of nonpolitical careers, political campaigns and elections, household moves, post-elective careers, places and dates of death, and places of interment.

Congressional Districts

596. Bureau of the Census. **Congressional District Atlas: Districts of the ... Congress.** GPO, 1960- . Biennial. OCLC 01768235. 1983 ed. S/N 003-024-05005-6. $12. **C3.62/5:yr.**

The atlas provides maps of congressional district boundaries and listings of the congressional districts in which counties and incorporated municipalities within states are located.

597. Bureau of the Census. **Congressional District Data Book.** GPO, 1961- . Irregular. **C3.134/2:C76/date.**

This title, a supplement to the *Statistical Abstract of the United States,* presents population, housing, and election statistics for the states, congressional districts, and places of ten thousand or more inhabitants. This series, published at irregular intervals, was begun to provide congressmen with a handy reference to the statistical data in each district. Materials are drawn from censuses of population, business, agriculture, and so on and from private sources. Supplements for each state are issued in the event of redistricting.

Hearings

598. Congress. House. Library. **Index to Congressional Committee Hearings in the Library of the United States House of Representatives prior to January 1, 1951.** Comp. by Russell Saville. GPO, 1954. 485 pp. LC 38-26099. **Y1.2:H35/951.**

599. Congress. House. Library. **Supplemental Index to Congressional Committee Hearings, January 3, 1949 to January 3, 1955 (81st, 82nd, and 83rd Congress) in the Library of the United States House of Representatives.** Comp. by John A. Cooper. GPO, 1956. 127 pp. LC 38-26099. **Y1.2:H35/955.**

600. Congress. Senate. Library. **Index of Congressional Committee Hearings (Not Confidential in Character) prior to January 3, 1935 in the United States Senate Library.** GPO, 1935. 1,056 pp. LC 35-26894. (Repr.: Kraus, $54.) **Y1.3: H35/2/935.**

601. Congress. Senate. Library. **Cumulative Index of Congressional Committee Hearings (Not Confidential in Character) from the 74th Congress (January 3, 1935) through the 85th Congress (January 1959) in the United States Senate Library.** Comp. by Richard D. Hupman et al. GPO, 1959. 823 pp. LC 59-61946. **Y1.3:H35/2/959.**

    _____. Supplement 1. **86th Congress (January 7, 1959) through the 87th Congress (January 3, 1963).** GPO, 1963. 762 pp.

    _____. Supplement 2. **88th Congress (January 3, 1963) through the 89th Congress (January 3, 1967).** Comp. by Carmen Carpenter. GPO, 1967. 664 pp.

    _____. Supplement 3. **90th Congress (January 2, 1967) through the 91st Congress (January 2, 1971).** GPO, 1971.

    _____. Supplement 4. **92nd Congress (January 21, 1971) through the 92nd Congress (December 20, 1974).** GPO, 1977. OCLC 2252800.

    _____. Supplement 5. **93rd Congress (January 14, 1975-October 1, 1976).** OCLC 3163375.

    _____. Supplement 6. **94th Congress (January 4, 1977-October 15, 1978).** Z1223.A1U56CA. OCLC 04990872.

    _____. Supplement 7. **95th Congress (January 15, 1979-December 16, 1980).** GPO, 1984. (S.pub. 98-16.) **Y1.2:H35/2/980/supp.7.**

These indexes are of value primarily to those seeking information about the actual publication of hearings. Citations are to numbers assigned in the House and Senate libraries and are thus not applicable to other libraries. Hearings are indexed by subject, by committee, and by bill numbers. These lists are not comprehensive, but they are fairly complete, especially for recent years.

Legislative Procedure

602. Congress. House. **Constitution, Jefferson's Manual, and Rules of the House of Representatives of the United States.** GPO, 1824- . Biennial. LC 6-17027. (Issued as a House document.) OCLC 4966825. **Y1.1/7:nos. vary.**

Popularly known as the *House Manual*, this publication is issued for each Congress. It contains the texts of the Constitution and *Jefferson's Manual* plus the rules of the House of Representatives with notes and annotations showing the history and interpretations of the rules. This is the fundamental source for the parliamentary procedures used by the House. Prepared by Thomas Jefferson while he was Vice President, much of this work is still applicable in the House.

603. Congress. House. Committee on Standards of Official Conduct. **Ethics Manual for Members and Employees of the U.S. House of Representatives.** By Jack Maskell. GPO, 1981. 234 pp. OCLC 07414703. **Y4.St2/3:Et3/981.**

604. Congress. Senate. Committee on Rules and Administration. **Senate Manual.** GPO, 1820- . Biennial. LC 1-9223. (Issued as a Senate document.) **Y1.1/3:nos. vary.**

The *Senate Manual* contains the standing rules, orders, laws, and resolutions affecting the business of the U.S. Senate, the Articles of Confederation, and the Constitution of the United States. Issued for each Congress, the manual also contains rules of conduct for the Senate, lists of presidents pro tempore of the Senate from the first to the current Senate, presidential election electoral vote counts since 1789, lists of senators, lists of Supreme Court justices since 1789, and more.

Presidents

605. Congress. House. **A Compilation of the Messages and Papers of the Presidents, 1789-1897.** By James D. Richardson. 10 vols. GPO, 1896-99. (House miscellaneous document 210, 53rd Congress, 2nd session.) **Congressional Serial Set 3265/v.1-10.**

606. Congress. Senate. **Nomination and Election of the President and Vice President of the United States, Including the Manner of Selecting Delegates to National Political Conventions.** By Thomas M. Durbin and Michael V. Setzinger. GPO, 1980. 420 pp. LC 80-602313. KF4910.D87 1980. OCLC 06177638. S/N 052-002-00038-9. $7.50. **Y1.3:P92/4/980.**

This is a compilation of constitutional provisions, federal and state laws, and rules of the Democratic and Republican parties governing the nomination and election of the President and Vice President of the United States. It lists the dates of state primaries, describes delegate selection for the national conventions, and abstracts laws related to minor and new parties, independent candidates, and corrupt practices.

607. Congress. Senate. **Presidential Vetoes, 1789-1976.** GPO, 1978. 533 pp. OCLC 4251351. **Y1.3:V64/2/789-976.**

This is a comprehensive listing of presidential vetoes of legislation enacted by the first through the ninety-fourth Congresses, 1789-1976. It is also intended to aid in studies of the executive-legislative branch relationship and its system of checks and balances. It is arranged chronologically by Congress and bill number, with action by Congress after the veto, if any, and references to the *Congressional Record*. There is an index of names and subjects.

608. Library of Congress. General Reference and Bibliography Division. **John Fitzgerald Kennedy, 1917-1963: A Chronological List of References**. GPO, 1964. 68 pp. LC 64-60056. Z8462.8.U5. Free from the Central Services Division, Library of Congress, Washington, DC 20540. **LC2.2:K38.**

Works by or about President Kennedy are arranged chronologically from 1940 to 1963. Author, title, and subject indexes are included.

609. Library of Congress. General Reference and Bibliography Division. **Presidential Inaugurations: A Selected List of References.** GPO, 1969. 3d ed., rev. and enl. LC 76-602825. Z1249.P7F7 1969. Free from the Central Services Division, Library of Congress, Washington, DC 20540. **LC2.2:P92/3/969.**

This bibliography presents a selected list of references compiled to serve as a guide to useful information on inaugural ceremonies and festivities from 1789 to the late 1960s.

610. Library of Congress. General Reference and Bibliography Division. **The Presidents of the United States, 1789-1962: A Selected List of References.** Comp. by Donald H. Mugridge. GPO, 1963. 159 pp. LC 63-61781. Z1249.P7U63. Free from the Central Services Division, Library of Congress, Washington, DC 20540. **LC2.2:P92/4/789-962.**

This bibliography lists works about the presidency and vice-presidency in general, presidential elections, and individual Presidents from Washington through Kennedy. It includes an author-title index and a subject index.

611. Library of Congress. Manuscript Division. **Presidents' Papers Index Series.** GPO, 1960- . Irregular. **LC4.7:ct.**

An index is included with the purchase of positive microfilm of the following manuscript groups from the Photoduplication Service, Library of Congress,

Washington, DC 20540. All indexes may be purchased separately as well. Those not in print can be supplied as electrostatic prints. Estimates of cost should be requested from the Photoduplication Service. In-print indexes are for sale by the GPO. Indexes listed below are out of print unless indicated otherwise.

Index to the Abraham Lincoln Papers. 1960. 124 pp. LC 60-60014.
Z8505.U53.

Index to the Andrew Jackson Papers. 1967. 111 pp. LC 67-60014.
Z8443.U53.

Index to the Andrew Johnson Papers. 1963. 154 pp. LC 62-60007.
Z8455.567.U5.

Index to the Benjamin Harrison Papers. 1964. 333 pp. LC 64-60010.
Z6616.H28U5.

Index to the Calvin Coolidge Papers. 1965. 34 pp. LC 65-60004.
Z6616.C78U5.

Index to the Chester A. Arthur Papers. 1961. 13 pp. LC 60-60076.
Z8045.03.U5.

Index to the Franklin Pierce Papers. 1962. 16 pp. LC 60-60077.
Z8689.9.U5.

Index to the George Washington Papers. 1964. 294 pp. LC 64-60052.
Z8950.U64.

Index to the Grover Cleveland Papers. 1965. 345 pp. LC 64-60012.
Z6616.C6U5.

Index to the James A. Garfield Papers. 1973. 422 pp. LC 73-9594.
Z6616.G34U5. S/N 030-003-00014-4. $11.

Index to the James K. Polk Papers. 1969. 91 pp. LC 67-60016.
Z6616.P595U5.

Index to the James Madison Papers. 1965. 61 pp. LC 63-60034.
Z8540.U53.

Index to the James Monroe Papers. 1963. 25 pp. LC 62-60006.
Z8587.8.U5.

Index to the John Tyler Papers. 1961. 10 pp. LC 60-60078. Z6616.T95U5.

Index to the Theodore Roosevelt Papers. 3 vols. 1969. 1,322 pp.
LC 68-60026. Z6616.R73U5.

Index to the Thomas Jefferson Papers. 1976. 155 pp. LC 74-13958.
Z6616.J4U5. 1976.

Index to the Ulysses S. Grant Papers. 1965. 83 pp. LC 64-60011.
Z6616.G76U5.

Index to the William H. Harrison Papers. 1960. 10 pp. LC 60-60012.
Z8387.97.U5.

Index to the William Howard Taft Papers. 6 vols. 1972. LC 70-60096.
Z6616.T18U6.

Index to the William McKinley Papers. 1963. 482 pp. LC 63-60031.
Z6616.M18U5.

Index to the Woodrow Wilson Papers. 3 vols. 1973. LC 73-7658.
Z6616.W53U59 1973. S/N 030-003-00013-6. $32 (set).

Index to the Zachary Taylor Papers. 1960. 9 pp. LC 60-60013.
Z8863.5.U5.

612. National Archives and Records Service. Franklin D. Roosevelt Library. **Era of Franklin Delano Roosevelt: A Selected Bibliography of Periodical and Dissertation Literature, 1945-66**. Comp. by William J. Stewart. Hyde Park, NY: IA, 1969. 175 pp. LC 70-602361. **GS4.17/3:R67/945-66**.

This bibliography excludes publications that are concerned purely with military operations, newspaper articles, and unsigned articles. It is divided into four sections: (1) Franklin D. Roosevelt; (2) New Deal; (3) World War II; and (4) Archives, Bibliography, and Historiography. Annotations give the scope and nature of the work without evaluative or critical comment. It is indexed by authors and subjects with a list of serials cited.

613. National Park Service. **The Presidents: From the Inauguration of George Washington to the Inauguration of Gerald R. Ford: Historic Places Commemorating the Chief Executives of the United States**. GPO, 1976. 598 pp., illus. (National survey of historic sites and buildings, vol. 20.) E159.U55 1976a. 973/.092/2. OCLC 2403247. **I29.2:H62/9/v.20**.

This source gives biographical sketches of U.S. Presidents from George Washington to Gerald R. Ford, with portraits and other illustrations as well as a survey of historical places commemorating the Presidents.

614. National Portrait Gallery. **If Elected: Unsuccessful Candidates for the Presidency, 1796-1968**. GPO, 1973. 312 pp. LC 73-1304. S/N 047-006-00008-2. $14. **SI11.2:P92/2/796-968**.

A catalog accompanying an exhibition at the National Portrait Gallery, this source provides portraits and brief reviews of the ideologies and campaigns of unsuccessful presidential candidates of major political parties. It details ten crucial elections and their implications for American history.

615. Office of the Federal Register. **Codification of Presidential Proclamations and Executive Orders, January 20, 1961-January 20, 1981**. GPO, 1981. 988 pp., illus. LC 79-642776. KF70.A473. 348/.73/1. OCLC 04826797. S/N 022-002-00097-0. $10. **GS4.113/3:961-81**.

This is an editorial codification, not intended to serve as a definitive legal authority. Proclamations and executive orders issued during the period 1961-81 that have general applicability and continuing effect are arranged according to fifty subject chapters similar to those in the *U.S. Code* and the *Code of Federal Regulations*. All amendments in effect on January 20, 1981 are incorporated into the text of each proclamation and executive order.

616. Office of the Federal Register. **Public Papers of the Presidents of the United States**. GPO, 1958- . Annual. LC 58-061050. J80.A283. 353.03. OCLC 1198154. **GS4.113:yr**.

This series, begun in 1958, includes retrospective volumes back to 1945 (Harry S. Truman) plus volumes for the Hoover administration (1929-33). It was the first official publication of presidential papers since 1899. Volumes give a record of the activities of the President during each year by providing the text of messages to Congress, speeches, news conferences, and selected press releases.

617. Office of the Federal Register. **Weekly Compilation of Presidential Documents**. GPO, 1965- . Weekly. LC 65-009929. J80.A284. OCLC 01769543. S/N 022-003-80002-6. $96/yr. **GS4.114:date**.

This source contains the text of statements, messages, speeches, transcripts of news conferences, and other presidential materials released by the White House each week. Each issue includes a cumulative index to prior issues for the year. Separate indexes are published quarterly, semiannually, and annually. Each issue also has lists of laws approved by the President, nominations submitted to the Senate, and a checklist of White House releases.

618.   White House Historical Association. **The Presidents of the United States of America**. GPO, 1981. 87 pp., illus. LC 81-81182. S/N 066-000-00002-8. $6.50. **Y3.H62/4:2P92**.

One-page biographies and full-page official portraits (in color) are provided for each President through Ronald Reagan.

First Ladies

619.   White House Historical Association. **The First Ladies**. GPO, 1981. 3d ed. 91 pp., illus. LC 81-52061. S/N 066-000-00004-4. $6.50. **Y3.H62/4:2F51**.

Biographies and pictures are provided for each First Lady of the White House.

See also SB 106.

Recreation and Hobbies

OUTDOOR RECREATION

620. Bureau of Outdoor Recreation. **Guides to Oudoor Recreation Areas and Facilities**. GPO, 1973. 79 pp. S/N 024-016-00064-1. $5.50. **I66.15:G94/973**.
This list of national, regional, and state guidebooks to outdoor recreation gives publisher's address and price.

621. Forest Service. **National Forest Vacations**. GPO, 1960. (USDA program aid 1037.) **A1.68:1037/2**.
This is a popular directory aimed at vacationers or "outdoors people" in general. It gives general information such as locations, acreage, and address to write for further information for the following: camping and picnicking, winter sports, resorts and summer homes, national forest wildernesses, trails, roads, water sports, hunting and fishing, and other pastimes. It also gives a state-by-state guide to national forests, including attractions and facilities, exact location, and nearby towns for each. It includes a list of general rules and the addresses of the regional foresters in the district offices in the United States.

622. National Park Service. **Access National Parks: A Guide for Handicapped Visitors**. GPO, 1978. 197 pp., illus. E160.U644 1977. 917.3/04/9260240816. OCLC 3327039. S/N 024-005-00691-5. $6.50. **I29.9/2:H19/2**.
The accessibility of facilities, services, and interpretive programs in almost three hundred areas of the National Park System are described. Addresses, telephone numbers, elevation of some areas, availability of first aid and medical care, descriptions of special programs, wheelchair access, and other information are given.

623. National Park Service. **Index of the National Park System and Related Areas**. GPO, 1982. 94 pp. LC 80-648554. OCLC 05778314. S/N 024-005-00829-2. $4.75. **I29.103:982**.
U.S. national parks, monuments, preserves, lakeshores, seashores, rivers, battlefield parks and sites, and battlefields described. This state-by-state guide gives address, description, size, and date of establishment.

624. National Park Service. **Land and Water Conservation Funds Grant Manual**. GPO, 1983. Looseleaf. OCLC 09437450. S/N 024-016-81001-5. $45. (Subscription includes basic manual plus supplements for indeterminate period.) **I29.107:983**.

The manual aids in the administration of grants made under the Land and Water Conservation Fund Act of 1965 and serves as a guide to states and local governments with details of procedures for obtaining federal assistance.

625. National Park Service. **Lesser-Known Areas of the National Park System**. GPO, 1980. 70 pp., illus. OCLC 07616454. S/N 024-005-00794-6. $4.50. **I29.9/2:P21/980**.

This is a state-by-state list of forests, desert canyons, seashores, lakeshores, Indian ruins, and other historical sites that are less frequented by visitors.

626. National Park Service. **Visitor Accommodations, Facilities, and Services Furnished by Concessioners in the National Park System**. GPO, 1976/77- . Biennial. OCLC 6436101. 1980-81 ed. S/N 024-005-00777-6. $5. **I29.2: Ac2/2/yr**.

Lodgings and other facilities and services provided for visitors are listed by park name.

See also SB 170.

STAMP COLLECTING

627. Fish and Wildlife Service. **Duck Stamp Data**. GPO, 1981. Looseleaf. OCLC 04095283. S/N 024-010-81001-7. $12. (Subscription includes basic manual plus supplement for indeterminate period.) **I49.93:934-81**.

Of special interest to hunters and philatelists, this publication provides photo enlargements and background information for each annual migratory bird hunting stamp issued during the period 1934-80.

628. Postal Service. **United States Postage Stamps**. GPO, 1970 (repr. 1973). Biennial supplements. 287 pp. LC 27-27645. S/N 039-000-00224-8 (covering 1847-1970). $8.50. S/N 039-000-00267-1 (includes basic and supplements 1-7 for stamps issued 1847-1980). $21. Supplements 1-7 also sold separately. **P4.10:970**.

This official U.S. Postal Service guide and its supplements give illustrated descriptions of all U.S. postage and special service stamps issued since July 1, 1847. Detailed descriptions are given of the history and dimensions of each stamp, including designers, engravers, date of issue, and number in first issue. Tables with statistics for stamps issued since 1933 are included. Illustrations are in black and white.

See also SB 11.

COINS AND MEDALS

629. Bureau of the Mint. **Domestic and Foreign Coins Manufactured by Mints of the United States, 1937-1980**. GPO, 1981. 178 pp. OCLC 08328020. S/N 048-005-00025-0. $4.50. **T28.1/a:C666/2/793-980**.

This is a complete historical record of the coins manufactured by the U.S. Mint from 1793 to 1980. Tables show total coins manufactured by year and class (gold, silver, minor, or clad). Each presentation is delineated by both number of pieces and face value. The second section enumerates coins manufactured for foreign governments, 1876 through 1980, and gives the text of major coin legislation, 1792-1978.

630. Bureau of the Mint. **Medals of the United States Mint Issued for Public Sale**. GPO, 1972. 318 pp. LC 74-602460. S/N 048-004-00497-6. $12. **T28.2: M46/2/972.**

This catalog of medals issued by the U.S. Mint and available for sale to the public gives front and back photographs of each medal and a chronology of events in the lives of the people they memorialize.

631. Congress. House. **Laws Authorizing Issuance of Medals and Commemorative Coins**. GPO, 1960- . Irregular. LC 60-60111. **Y1.2:M46/yr.**

This source gives the full text of laws, plus lists of individuals receiving awards.

See also SB 198.

Sociology

GENERAL WORKS

632. Department of Health, Education and Welfare. Project Share. **The Project Share Collection, 1976-1979**. IA, 1979. 891 pp. OCLC 5844068. **HE1.18:P94**.
This is a cumulative volume of abstracts published by Project Share, a clearinghouse for improving the management of human services. Included are eighteen hundred abstracts of publications on planning, management, and delivery of human services from the Project Share automated data base.

633. Department of Health and Human Services. Project Share. **Catalog of Human Services Information Resource Organizations: An Exploratory Study of Human Services Information Clearinghouses**. IA, 1980. 343 pp. (Human services monograph series, no. 15.) LC 81-600516. OCLC 6975340. **HE1.54:15**.
The catalog provides descriptive profiles of 157 national, regional, and state organizations that disseminate information to researchers, practitioners, administrators, and the general public. Organizations listed are clearinghouses, information analysis centers, special libraries, document collections, resource centers, abstracting and indexing services, and diffusion networks. The human services areas covered are civil rights, consumer affairs, education, employment and training, health, income maintenance, safety, and social services. Organizational profiles include address, telephone number, purpose, target clientele, publications, services and fees, and collections.

CRIMINOLOGY

Bibliographies

634. National Institute of Justice. **Citizen Crime Prevention Tactics: A Literature Review and Selected Bibliography**. By J. T. Skip Duncan and John Slone. GPO, 1980. 116 pp. OCLC 6571921. **J28.11:P92**.
Materials listed focus upon steps individuals and groups can take to reduce their vulnerability to crime. It is not a comprehensive bibliography, but lists representative materials and new crime prevention initiatives. Bibliographies, narrative, and lengthy

annotations are given for some entries. Many of the publications cited are available free on microfiche from the National Criminal Justice Reference Service (NCJRS).

635.   National Institute of Law Enforcement and Criminal Justice. **Publications of the National Institute of Law Enforcement and Criminal Justice: A Comprehensive Bibliography**. Comp. by John Ferry, Marjorie Kravitz, and Allie Smith. GPO, 1978. 230 pp. OCLC 4675452. **J26.9:P96/2.**

_____. **Supplement**. GPO, 1979. **J26.9:P96/2/979.**
This comprehensive bibliography is keyed to the research sponsored and published by the National Institute of Law Enforcement and Criminal Justice since 1968.

See also SB 36 and SB 74.

Dictionaries and Thesauri

636.   National Criminal Justice Information and Statistics Service. **Dictionary of Criminal Justice Data Terminology: Terms and Definitions Proposed for Interstate and National Data Collection and Exchange**. GPO, 1976. 119 pp. HV6017.S4 1976. 364/.03. OCLC 2543049. **J1.2:D26.**
The dictionary gives standard names and definitions for communication of criminal justice information and statistics between states and nationally.

637.   National Institute of Justice. **National Criminal Justice Thesaurus: Descriptors for Indexing Law Enforcement and Criminal Justice Information**. IA, 1981. 309 pp. OCLC 7440208. **J28.2:T34/981.**
Terms used to index the literature in the National Criminal Justice Reference Service (NCJRS) data base are listed.

Directories

638.   Bureau of Justice Statistics. **1980 Directory of Automated Criminal Justice Information Systems**. GPO, 1980. 799 pp. LC 81-601018. OCLC 7376927. **J29.8:C86/980.**
A standard work for research on criminal justice information systems, the directory contains indexed lists of the automated criminal justice information systems used by police, courts, corrections, and other justice agencies. Arranged by state jurisdictions, each listing describes the system, contact people, and the current system status. The purpose of the directory is to help criminal justice planners in developing new systems or enhancing existing ones.

639.   National Institute of Law Enforcement and Criminal Justice. **Directory of Criminal Justice Information Sources**. GPO, 1976- . Biennial. LC 79-641184. HV8138.D5. 364/.07. OCLC 08248430. 1981 ed. S/N 027-000-01152-7. $6. **J28.20:yr.**
This source lists criminal justice agencies that offer information resources such as computer literature searches, interlibrary loans, reference, and technical assistance to criminal justice professionals. It gives the sponsor, address, telephone number, user restrictions, establishment date, number of staff, director, contact person, and descriptions of services, activities, and publications.

Manuals

640. Bureau of Justice Statistics. **A Style Manual for Machine-Readable Data Files and Their Documentation**. By Richard C. Roistacher et al. GPO, 1980. 75 pp. OCLC 7003070. **J29.9:SD-T-3**.

641. Federal Bureau of Investigation. **Handbook of Forensic Science**. GPO, 1984. 134 pp., illus. S/N 027-001-00034-3. $5. **J1.14/16:F76/984**.
This is a handbook of modern crime laboratory techniques to aid the on-site investigator in solving crimes, with a discussion of the capabilities and limitations of a crime laboratory.

642. Federal Bureau of Investigation. **The Science of Fingerprints: Classification and Uses**. GPO, 1979. 209 pp. OCLC 5975508. S/N 027-001-00024-6. $7. **J1.14/2:F49/12/979**.
This guide to classification and other phases of fingerprint identification may be of particular interest to those contemplating establishment of fingerprint identification files. There are many photographs and illustrations.

643. National Criminal Justice Information and Statistics Service. **Computer Crime: Criminal Justice Resource Manual**. GPO, 1979. 392 pp. OCLC 5873396. S/N 027-000-00870-4. $10. **J26.8:C86/5**.
Written to aid investigators and prosecutors dealing with computer crime, this manual may also help laymen determine when to use technical expertise and how to interact with the specialists who provide it. It focuses on legal, technical, and investigative aspects of computer crime. It is written for those with little knowledge of the subject as well as for those with extensive technical knowledge.

Statistics

644. Bureau of Justice Statistics. **Sourcebook of Criminal Justice Statistics**. GPO, 1973- . Annual. LC 74-601963. HV7245.N37b. 364/.973. OCLC 2441090. 10th ed. (1982). S/N 027-000-01171-3. $10. **J29.2:SD-SB-no**.
This is a compilation of nationwide criminal justice and related statistics, displayed at the regional, state, or city level. It consists largely of tables. Emphasis is on state and local rather than federal data. Sources of data are noted.

645. Federal Bureau of Investigation. **Uniform Crime Reports: Crime in the United States**. GPO, 1930- . Annual. 1983 ed. S/N 027-001-00035-1. $9. **J1.14/7:yr**.
In this overview of crime nationwide, based on police statistics from states and localities, population size is the only correlate of crime used. Tables show number of offenses reported and cleared, number of arrests for various crimes, and data on law enforcement personnel. Appendixes show ten-year trends.

646. National Criminal Justice Information and Statistics Service. **Criminal Victimization in the United States: A Description of Trends from 1973-1977**. By Richard W. Dodge. GPO, 1973- . LC 75-640532. HV7245.N37a. 362.8/8/0973. OCLC 1798331. **J26.10:SD-NCS-N-10**.

Analysis of Trends

647. National Criminal Justice Information and Statistics Service. **Trends in Expenditure and Employment Data for the Criminal Justice System**. GPO, 1971/74- . LC 79-641198. JK2403.A35. 353.9/08s388.4/364. OCLC 4403191. **J26.10:SD-EE-no.**

Data on costs and employment for U.S. criminal justice activities are summarized, largely in tabular form, with a section giving graphic summaries of federal, state, and local government trends. These statistics were summarized from the annual issues of *Expenditure and Employment Data for the Criminal Justice System*, which present greater detail for states and the largest SMSAs, counties, and cities of the United States.

648. National Institute of Justice. **Data Sources on White-Collar Law Breaking**. By Albert J. Reiss, Jr. and Albert D. Biderman. IA, 1980. 486 pp. OCLC 7289882. **J28.2:D26.**

This is an assessment of the current status of federal statistical information systems related to white-collar crime. It reviews major government data sources useful in research and statistical reporting and summarizes issues in controlling white-collar crime.

649. Office of Juvenile Justice and Delinquency Prevention. **Juvenile Criminal Behavior in the United States: Its Trends and Patterns**. By M. Joan McDermott and Michael J. Hindelang. GPO, 1981. 110 pp. OCLC 7393968. **J26.15/2: V66/2.**

This source relates trends identified from the 1973-77 National Crime Survey victimization data that pertain to criminal behavior of juveniles, youthful offenders, and adults.

ETHNIC GROUPS

650. Bureau of the Census. **Social and Economic Status of the Black Population in the United States: An Historical View, 1790-1978**. GPO, 1980. (Current population reports, series P-23, no. 80.) OCLC 1774175. S/N 003-024-01659-1. $8. **C3.186:P-23/80.**

The history of changes in the demography and social and economic characteristics of blacks in the United States is presented, largely in tables and graphs. Covered are changes in population distribution, income, labor force, employment, education, family composition, mortality, fertility, housing, voting, public office-holding, armed forces personnel, and other aspects.

651. Bureau of Labor Statistics. **Directory of Data Sources on Racial and Ethnic Minorities**. By Earl F. Mellor. GPO, 1975. 83 pp. (Bulletin 1879.) S/N 029-001-01777-4. $5.50. **L2.3:1879.**

This annotated guide to minority group data from various federal agencies lists sources of demographic, social, and economic data about minority groups published by the federal government.

652. Health Resources Administration. **Health Status of Minorities and Low-Income Groups**. By Melvin H. Rudov and Nancy Santangelo. GPO, 1979. 275 pp., illus. OCLC 5580791. S/N 017-022-00673-1. $8. **HE20.6002:H34/6.**

Data, with textual interpretations, related to specific aspects of the health of the disadvantaged, such as chronic diseases and dental health, have been compiled from numerous sources. They provide the "best aggregation of information extant in dealing with this problem area."

653. Library of Congress. **The Negro in the United States: A Selected Bibliography**. Comp. by Dorothy B. Porter. GPO, 1970. 313 pp. LC 78-606085. Z1361.N39P59. S/N 030-000-00044-7. $11. **LC1.12/2:N31**.

654. Library of Congress. American Folklife Center. **Ethnic Recordings in America: A Neglected Heritage**. GPO, 1982. 269 pp., illus. (Studies in American folklife series, no. 1.) LC 80-607133. Z663.117.E73 1982. 789.9/121773. OCLC 06357839. S/N 030-001-00098-2. $13. **LC39.11:1**.

One of the first books on this topic, this source includes an extensive research guide to recordings and record companies. It also includes essays on specific themes and people. Developed from a 1977 conference sponsored by the American Folklife Center, this source "begins the task of defining and assembling the research tools needed for future investigations."

655. National Institute of Mental Health. **Bibliography on Racism, 1972-75**. GPO, 1978. OCLC 4355416. S/N 017-024-00782-0. $10. **HE20.8113:R11/972-75/v2**.

This is a comprehensive listing of all research abstracts related to racism from the computerized data files of the National Clearinghouse for Mental Health Information and the National Institute of Mental Health.

SOCIAL CONDITIONS

Aging

656. Congress. House. Select Committee on Aging. **A Directory of State and Area Agencies on Aging**. GPO, 1982. 140 pp. OCLC 09337889. S/N 052-070-05816-1. $6.50. **Y4.Ag4/2:Ag4/9/982**.

This is a state-by-state listing of state units and area agencies that provide assistance and referral for older Americans. It includes names, addresses, and telephone numbers.

657. Health Care Financing Administration. **Directory of Adult Day Care Centers**. GPO, 1980. 162 pp., illus. OCLC 7143688. S/N 017-062-00124-3. $6. **HE22.202:Ad9/980**.

The directory identifies 618 programs of adult day care across the United States, classified as either restorative, maintenance, or social. Not included are senior center programs, centers providing primarily psychiatric or mental health services for adults of all ages (rather than those for the elderly only), and programs for the mentally retarded. Program information includes name, address, telephone number, director, sponsoring organization, funding sources, program nature, and average daily attendance.

658. National Clearinghouse on Aging. **Inventory of Federal Statistical Programs Relating to Older Persons**. IA, 1979. 113 pp. OCLC 4827919. **HE23.3012:St2**.

This directory of federal statistical activities related to the needs and interests of older people lists statistical surveys or programs on areas such as demography, marital status, living arrangements, income, employment, and other subjects. Information given on each program includes purpose and method of data collection, scope, limitations and reliability of data, lowest level of geography, age detail, frequency of data collection, method of storage, time lag, and availability of data.

See also SB 39.

Children and Youth

659.   Children's Bureau. **Research Relating to Children**. GPO, 1950-79. Irregular. LC 52-60018. **HE19.120:1-42**.
Descriptions of research include abstracts with information about investigators, purpose, subjects, methods, duration, and publications.

660.   Children's Bureau. Clearinghouse on Child Abuse and Neglect Information. **Child Abuse and Neglect Data Base**.
This computerized data base contains citations and abstracts for published literature and audiovisual materials, descriptions of ongoing research projects, program descriptions, and excerpts from state laws, all pertaining to child abuse and neglect. Searches may be requested by mail or telephone: NCCAN, U.S. Children's Bureau, Department of Health and Human Services, P.O. Box 1182, Washington, DC 20013; (703) 558-8222.

661.   National Center on Child Abuse and Neglect. **Annual Review of Child Abuse and Neglect Research**. IA, 1978- . Annual. OCLC 4736668. **HE23.1210/3:yr**.
The review provides an annual summary of recent research in the field of child abuse and neglect. Completed and ongoing research not related to legal matters is summarized to provide a broad overview of the status of research. Projects related to definition, incidence, psychosocial ecology, prevention and treatment, and effects are listed with names of investigators, a short description of methodology, and a short description of findings.

662.   National Center on Child Abuse and Neglect. **Child Abuse and Neglect Audiovisual Materials**. GPO, 1980. 92 pp. OCLC 6545811. S/N 017-092-00070-7. $5.50. **HE23.1210:Au2/980**.
This source lists and describes videotapes, films, slides, multimedia packages, and other audiovisual materials related to the medical, legal, mental health, social welfare, and educational aspects of child abuse and neglect. Materials listed are pulled from the Child Abuse and Neglect Data Base.

663.   National Center on Child Abuse and Neglect. **Child Abuse and Neglect Research: Projects and Publications**. GPO, 1976- . Semiannual. LC 76-648692. HV741.C456. 362.7/1/0973. OCLC 2363357. **HE23.1210/2:date**.
This title lists and describes publications and research projects related to child abuse and neglect. This publication and its companion volume, *Child Abuse and Neglect Programs*, are used to disseminate information in the National Center on Child Abuse and Neglect computerized data files.

664.   National Center on Child Abuse and Neglect. **Interdisciplinary Glossary on Child Abuse and Neglect: Legal, Medical, Social Work Terms**. GPO, 1980. 45 pp. OCLC 6430864. S/N 017-092-00062-0. $4.75. **HE23.1210:G51/980**.
Legal, medical, and social work terms used in child abuse and neglect prevention and treatment programs are included. Definitions are designed to facilitate communication and understanding across disciplines.

665.   National Institute of Justice. **Child Abuse and Neglect: A Literature Review and Selected Bibliography**. By Marian Eskin and Marjorie Kravitz. IA, 1980. 118 pp. OCLC 6276315. **J28.11:C43**.
This is a state-of-the-art review and annotated bibliography on child abuse and neglect. It reviews major historical, legal, social, and medical issues; describes current prevention and treatment programs and legislation; and offers suggestions for research and

future programs. Many of the publications cited are available free on microfiche from the National Criminal Justice Reference Service.

See also SB 35.

Sex Roles

666. National Institute of Education. **Sex Role Socialization/Sex Discrimination: A Bibliography**. By Constantina Safilios-Rotchschild. IA, 1979. 120 pp. OCLC 5933895. **HE19.213:Se9**.
This is a multidisciplinary bibliography on sex role socialization and discrimination covering the period 1960-78. It is comprehensive for 1960-74 and selective for 1975-78. There are no annotations and no subject index. Arrangement is by authors' last names.

667. National Institute of Mental Health. **The Male Sex Role: A Selected and Annotated Bibliography**. By Kathleen E. Grady. GPO, 1979. 196 pp. S/N 017-024-00929-6. $7. **HE20.8113:Se9/2**.
This bibliography describes the relatively small pool of literature on new roles and patterns of behavior for men. Publications cited are annotated. Research studies have short descriptions of subjects, methods, findings, and comments.

Statistics and Demography

GENERAL WORKS

668. Bureau of the Census. **Census '80: Continuing the Factfinder Tradition**. By Charles P. Kaplan and Thomas L. Van Valey. GPO, 1980. 490 pp. LC 80-600007. OCLC 6270187. S/N 003-024-02262-1. $9. **C3.2:C33/34.**
This college-level textbook created by the College Curriculum Support Project of the Bureau of the Census describes the history and organization of the decennial censuses and principles of data collection and tabulation; gives an overview of the 1980 census; and describes uses of 1960 and 1970 census data by planners, businesses, and others.

669. Bureau of the Census. **Factfinder for the Nation (series)**. IA, 1979- . Irregular. Available from the Data User Services Division, Customer Services (Publications), Bureau of the Census, Washington, DC 20233. **C3.252:nos.**
These concise and extremely useful brochures explain categories of Census Bureau data. Each gives an overview of Census Bureau data gathering on a specific topic and cites key references. Number 5 in the series, *Reference Sources*, is a valuable annotated bibliography of over eighty Bureau of the Census reference publications. All are revised periodically.

    1. **Statistics on Race and Ethnicity**. 1981. 4 pp. 25 cents.

    2. **Availability of Census Records about Individuals**. 1983. 4 pp. 25 cents.

    3. **Agricultural Statistics**. 1983. 4 pp. 25 cents.

    4. **History and Organization**. 1979. 12 pp. 30 cents.

    5. **Reference Sources**. 1981. 12 pp. 25 cents.

    6. **Housing Statistics**. 1981. 4 pp. 25 cents.

    7. **Population Statistics**. 1981. 4 pp. 25 cents.

    8. **Census Geography—Concepts and Products**. 1982. 8 pp. 30 cents.

    9. **Construction Statistics**. 1983. 4 pp. 25 cents.

    10. **Retail Trade Statistics**. 1983. 4 pp. 25 cents.

    11. **Wholesale Trade Statistics**. 1983. 4 pp. 25 cents.

    12. **Statistics on Service Industries**. 1983. 4 pp. 25 cents.

13. **Transportation Statistics.** 1983. 4 pp. 25 cents.

14. **Foreign Trade Statistics.** 1978. 4 pp. 25 cents.

15. **Statistics on Manufactures.** 1983. 4 pp. 25 cents.

16. **Statistics on Mineral Industries.** 1983. 4 pp. 25 cents.

17. **Statistics on Governments.** 1983. 4 pp. 25 cents.

18. **Census Bureau Programs and Products.** 1982. 16 pp. 40 cents.

19. **Enterprise Statistics.** 1983. 4 pp. 25 cents.

20. **Energy and Conservation Statistics.** 1980. 4 pp. 25 cents.

21. **International Programs.** 1981. 4 pp. 25 cents.

22. **Data for Small Communities.** 1981. 12 pp. 30 cents.

670. Bureau of the Census. **Guide to Recurrent and Special Governmental Statistics.** GPO, 1976. 205 pp., illus. (State and local government special studies, no. 18.) OCLC 2154210. **C3.145:18.**
The guide summarizes the tables in recent recurrent reports and special studies of the Census Bureau's state and local government statistics program. Recurrent reports provide data on government finances, tax revenue, public employment, and so on. Special studies cover such topics as expenditure and employment data for the criminal justice system and national data needs, such as fire service statistics.

671. Bureau of the Census. **Index to Selected 1970 Census Reports.** By Paul T. Zeisset. GPO, 1974. 354 pp. LC 74-602987. **C3.223:In2/970.**
This is an exhaustive index and cross-reference guide to tables in selected final reports series of the 1970 Census of Population and Housing.

672. Bureau of the Census. **The Methods and Materials of Demography.** By Henry Shryock and Jacob S. Siegel. 2 vols. GPO, 1980. 960 pp., illus. OCLC 6743224. S/N 003-024-02568-0. $20 (set). **C3.2:D39/980/v.1,2.**
This source gives a comprehensive discussion, with illustrations, of current demographic methods and materials. It discusses how population data are gathered, classified, and treated to yield tabulations and summarizing measures that reveal aspects of the composition and dynamics of populations. It includes information on statistically underdeveloped countries and special methods for handling incomplete and inaccurate data.

673. Bureau of the Census. **1980 Census of Population and Housing Users' Guide.** 3 pts. GPO, 1982-83. Looseleaf. LC 82-600138. HA201.1980B. 001.4.33.19. Part A. S/N 003-024-03625-8. $5.50. Part B. S/N 003-024-05004-8. $6. Part C. S/N 003-024-05771-9. $4.25. **C3.223:80-R-1A,B,C.**
This is a multivolume guide to locating and using 1980 census data. Part A, "Text," covers census data subjects; geographic areas; user tapes, maps, and other products; and user services. Part B, "Glossary," provides detailed definitions of terms used for the census and addresses and phone numbers for organizations offering products and services such as tape processing, area profiles, training, and reference assistance. Part C, "Index to Summary Tape Files 1 to 4," describes data available in four series of computer tapes that provide statistics for states, SMSAs, counties, places, census tracts, and other small areas. It provides a subject index to tables in the tape series, along with complete descriptions of the tables. Parts B and C are supplements 1 and 2, respectively, to the guide.

674.　Bureau of the Census. **Reference Manual on Population and Housing Statistics from the Census Bureau.** IA, 1977. 146 pp., illus. OCLC 2990204. **C3.6/2: P81.**

This comprehensive discussion of the 1970 census and subsequent survey reports and data tapes covers limitations and strength of data and skills needed to locate specific data.

675.　Bureau of the Census. **Twenty Censuses: Population and Housing Questions, 1790-1980.** By Frederick G. Bohme. GPO, 1979. 91 pp., illus. LC 79-600181. OCLC 5756224. **C3.2:C33/33.**

The variety of information collected in the population and housing censuses and their evolution are described. The actual questions are reproduced, along with the instructions that were given on the forms.

676.　Department of Commerce. Office of Federal Statistical Policy and Standards. **Revolution in United States Government Statistics, 1926-1976.** By Joseph W. Duncan and William C. Shelton. GPO, 1978. 257 pp. OCLC 4531499. S/N 003-005-00181-6. $7.50. **C1.2:St2/10/926-76.**

Part of a comprehensive review of the federal statistical system, this volume is a history of selected important events in federal statistics during a fifty-year period. A history of ideas rather than events, it focuses on four themes of the statistical revolution: probability sampling, national income and product accounts, mechanization and computers, and coordination.

See also SB 121 and SB 273.

BIBLIOGRAPHIES

677.　Bureau of the Census. **Bureau of the Census Catalog of Publications, 1790-1972.** 2 vols. in 1. GPO, 1974. 911 pp. LC 74-600076. S/N 003-024-00110-1. $8. **C56.222/2-2:790-972.**

This is a comprehensive historical bibliography of sources for Census Bureau statistics from the first census in 1790 to 1972. It comprises two catalogs: the *Catalog of United States Census Publications, 1790-1945*, which lists all materials issued by the bureau and its predecessor organizations during that period, and the *Catalog of Publications, 1946-1972*, which updates the historical compilation and describes more than sixty thousand reports issued by the bureau between January 1946 and December 1972.

678.　Bureau of the Census. **Bureau of the Census Catalog.** GPO, 1980- . Annual. LC 74-644649. Z7554.U5U32. 016.3173. OCLC 01793944. 1984 ed. S/N 003-024-05668-2. $7. **C3.163/3:date.**

The catalog contains abstracts and ordering information for all publications and data files issued during the year. It has been published since 1947; issues from 1947 to 1979 were quarterly (each issue cumulative) with monthly supplements. The *Bureau of the Census Catalog: Monthly Supplement* was discontinued in 1980 and was replaced by the *Monthly Product Announcement* (entry 681).

679.　Bureau of the Census. **Census Bureau Methodological Research: Annotated List of Papers and Reports.** GPO, 1968- . Annual. OCLC 7046339. **C3.163/4: M56/yr.**

Published and unpublished papers, memoranda, and reports on methodological research are listed. Items listed describe research in progress and give research results when available.

680. Bureau of the Census. **Information Privacy and Statistics: A Topical Bibliography.** By Tore Dalenius. IA, 1978. 160 pp. (Working paper 4.) OCLC 4178673. **C3.214:41.**
This unannotated bibliography focuses on privacy in statistical information systems. References deal with sample and census surveys and data banks. Most references are from the United States.

681. Bureau of the Census. **Monthly Product Announcement.** IA, 1981- . Monthly. OCLC 07372650. **C3.163/7:date.**
The announcement is published monthly to inform census data users about newly available publications, microfiche, maps, and computer tapes. It includes order forms.

682. Library of Congress. Census Library Project. **General Censuses and Vital Statistics in the Americas: An Annotated Bibliography.** GPO, 1943. 151 pp. LC 44-40643. (Repr.: Blaine-Ethridge, $12.) **C3.2:C33/10.**
This is an annotated bibliography of the historical censuses and current vital statistics of the twenty-one American republics; the American sections of the British Commonwealth; the American colonies of Denmark, France, and the Netherlands; and the American territories and possessions of the United States.

683. Library of Congress. Census Library Project. **National Censuses and Vital Statistics in Europe, 1918-1939: An Annotated Bibliography.** By Henry J. Dubester. GPO, 1948. 215 pp. LC 48-45672. Z7553.C3U46. **C3.2: C33/12/918-39.**

_____. **Supplement, 1940-1948.** By Henry J. Dubester. GPO, 1948. (Repr.: in 1 vol., Burt Franklin, $13.50.)
The national censuses of forty-two European countries are listed in these publications. Subjects include population, industry, housing, and agriculture.

684. Library of Congress. Census Library Project. **Population Censuses and Other Official Demographic Statistics of Africa (Not Including British Africa): An Annotated Bibliography.** By Henry J. Dubester. GPO, 1951. 53 pp. LC 52-60006. Z7554.A34U5 1950. 016.312. OCLC 1909520. **C3.2:P81/17.**

685. Library of Congress. Census Library Project. **Population Censuses and Other Official Demographic Statistics of British Africa: An Annotated Bibliography.** By Henry J. Dubester. GPO, 1950. 78 pp. LC 50-60396. Z7554.A35U5. OCLC 3990015. **C3.2:P81/16.**

686. Library of Congress. Census Library Project. **State Censuses: An Annotated Bibliography of Censuses of Population Taken after the Year 1790 by States and Territories of the United States.** By Henry J. Dubester. GPO, 1948. 73 pp. LC 48-46440. Z7554.U5U63 1948. (Repr.: Burt Franklin, $18.50.) **C3.2: St2/7/790-948.**
The population censuses taken by the states and territories of the United States after 1790 are listed by state.

687. Library of Congress. Census Library Project. **Statistical Bulletins: An Annotated Bibliography of the General Statistical Bulletins of Major Political Subdivisions of the World.** By Phyllis G. Carter. GPO, 1954, 93 pp. LC 54-60010. Z7552.U64. (Repr.: Greenwood Press, $14.) **LC29.2:St2/2.**
Prepared jointly by the Library of Congress and the Bureau of the Census, this bibliography is arranged by continent and then by country. It includes "periodicals issued by an official agency more frequently than annually" and covers a wide variety of

subjects. Annotations provide information on frequency, type of data regularly appearing, and Washington area locations.

688. Library of Congress. Census Library Project. **Statistical Yearbooks: An Annotated Bibliography of the General Statistical Yearbooks of Major Political Subdivisions of the World**. By Phyllis G. Carter. GPO, 1953. 123 pp. LC 53-60036. Z7552.U65. (Repr.: Greenwood Press, $14.75.) **LC29.2:St2/3**.

This bibliography is arranged alphabetically by continent and country. Entries are annotated with data on the historical background of the yearbooks, the contents of a recent issue, types of statistics usually included, and Washington locations.

CENSUS SCHEDULES

689. National Archives and Records Service. **Federal Population Censuses, 1790-1890**. IA, 1971 (repr. 1979). LC 72-610891. **GS4.2:P81/2/790-890**.

Federal decennial population census schedules contain a wealth of information for historians, social scientists, and genealogists. They contain information on westward expansion, the status of free and slave labor, regional and local history, immigration, and evidence for proving citizenship. This is a catalog of microfilm copies of the schedules, listing over twelve thousand rolls of census microfilm. Listings are chronological under states and counties. Each entry gives information on the number of rolls, contents, and price.

690. National Archives and Records Service. **1900 Federal Population Census: A Catalog of Microfilm Copies of the Schedules**. IA, 1978 (repr. 1979). 84 pp. LC 72-610891. **GS4.2:P81/2/900**.

This catalog lists the 1900 census schedules (on microfilm) and the 1900 Soundex system (reproduced as a separate microfilm publication for each state and territory). The census schedules are arranged by state or territory, then by county. This catalog supplements *Federal Population Census, 1790-1890*, which contains information for ordering copies of the original population schedules for 1790-1890 including the 1880 Soundex.

691. National Archives and Records Service. **The 1910 Federal Population Census**. IA, 1982. LC 72-610891. **GS4.2:P81/2/910**.

This catalog is a finding aid for those wishing to order copies of the 1910 census schedules, the most recent schedules available.

COMPENDIUMS

692. Bureau of the Census. **County and City Data Book**. GPO, 1949- . Irregular. LC 52-4576. OCLC 01184940. 10th ed. (1983). S/N 003-024-05833-2. $24. **C3.134/2:C83/2/yr**.

This *Statistical Abstract* supplement is a compact social and economic profile that provides statistics for each county, 277 standard metropolitan statistical areas (SMSAs), and 910 large cities. It also gives information on standard federal administrative regions, census regions and divisions, and states. Contents are also available on computer tapes from the Bureau of the Census.

693. Bureau of the Census. **Geographical Mobility**. GPO, 1948- . Annual. (Current population reports, series P-20, nos. vary.) OCLC 08638162. 1981-82 ed. (Series P-20, no. 384.) S/N 003-001-90783-6. $5. **C3.186:P-20/nos. vary**.

Mobility trends by age, race, sex, occupation, income, and marital status are given, based on estimates from the current population survey. Data are derived by comparing the location of respondents' residence in two specific years. This continues *Mobility of the Population of the United States.*

694. Bureau of the Census. **Household and Family Characteristics**. GPO, 1947- . Annual. (Current population reports, series P-20, nos. vary.) OCLC 08620642. 1983 ed. (Series P-20, no. 388.) S/N 003-001-90787-9. $7.50. **C3.186:P-20/nos. vary.**

The data presented on changes in the composition, size, and social characteristics of families and households are collected to supplement the monthly current population survey. Estimates are based on interviews with people in about sixty-five thousand sample households. Data are presented at the national level, and at the state and local levels when possible.

695. Bureau of the Census. **Historical Statistics of the United States, Colonial Times to 1970**. 2 vols. GPO, 1975. 1,264 pp. LC 75-038832. HA202.387 1976. 317.3. OCLC 2182988. S/N 003-024-00120-9. $35 (set). **C3.134/2:H62/970/pt.1,2.**

This supplement to the *Statistical Abstract* is a massive two-volume collection of statistics on almost every conceivable aspect of American life from 1610 to 1970. Over 12,500 time series, mostly annual, provide a statistical history of U.S. social, economic, political, and geographic development. Definitions of terms, descriptive text, and source notes to original published sources are included.

696. Bureau of the Census. **International Population Dynamics, 1950-1979: Demographic Estimates for Countries with a Population of 5 Million or More**. GPO, 1980. 258 pp. (International Statistical Program Office, world population series.) OCLC 6526546. S/N 003-024-02503-5. $7.50. **C3.205/3:WP-79(A).**

Demographic data for the eighty-seven largest countries of the world are summarized.

697. Bureau of the Census. **Pocket Data Book, USA**. GPO, 1967- . Irregular. 1979 ed. S/N 003-024-02682-1. $7.50. **C3.134/3:date.**

This portable supplement to the *Statistical Abstract* consists largely of tables and graphs summarizing national data in twenty-five categories, including population, vital statistics, welfare, mining, transportation, and foreign commerce. Many tables show historical data as well as current statistics. This is a quick, easy to use source.

698. Bureau of the Census. **Social Indicators 3: Selected Data on Social Conditions and Trends in the United States**. GPO, 1980. 645 pp. LC 77-608307. OCLC 07624058. S/N 003-024-02683-0. $19. **C3.2:So1/2/979.**

This is a comprehensive graphic collection of statistical data selected and organized to describe current social conditions and trends in the United States. It combines colorful graphs and charts with hard statistics to provide a comprehensive picture of our lives and current social organization. Population and the family, health and nutrition, housing, environment, income, productivity, social security, welfare, and many more subjects are covered.

699. Bureau of the Census. **State and Metropolitan Area Data Book**. GPO, 1979- . Irregular. LC 80-600018. OCLC 77113217. 1982 ed. S/N 003-024-04932-5. $15. **C3.134/5:date.**

This supplement to the *Statistical Abstract* presents statistics for states, SMSAs, census divisions, and regions. Most of the statistics are from the latest available censuses of population, housing, governments, manufactures, retail and wholesale trade, and selected services. The data presented are also available for purchase on one reel of industry-compatible computer tape.

700.   Bureau of the Census. **Statistical Abstract of the United States**. GPO, 1878- .
       Annual. LC 4-18089. HA202.317.3. OCLC 01193890. 1984 ed. S/N 003-024-
       05839-1. $19. **C3.134:yr.**
This is the standard summary of statistics on the social, political, and economic organization of the United States. It is designed to serve as a handy statistical reference volume
and as a guide to other statistical publications and sources. The data given are derived
from numerous government and private statistical sources. The emphasis is on national
data, but many tables give data at the state and census region level, and some give data
for cities and SMSAs. A very comprehensive index is included. From 1878 to 1902 the
Statistical Abstract was prepared by the Bureau of Statistics, Department of the
Treasury; from 1903 through 1911 by the Bureau of Statistics, Department of
Commerce and Labor; from 1912 through 1937 by the Bureau of Foreign and Domestic
Commerce; and since 1938 by the Bureau of the Census.

701.   Bureau of the Census. **Statistical Portrait of Women in the United States: 1978**.
       GPO, 1980. 169 pp. (Current population reports, series P-23, no. 100.) LC
       80-6070. OCLC 1774175. **C3.186:P-23/100.**
This statistical profile of American women during the 1970s is based on data primarily
from U.S. government surveys, censuses, vital statistics, and administrative records. It
includes recent trends (1970-78) in population growth and distribution, longevity,
mortality, health, marital status, living arrangements, housing, fertility, and education
of women in relation to men. Data on black, white, Spanish, American Indian, and
Asian women are presented separately. This report updates *A Statistical Portrait of
Women in the United States* (Current population reports, series P-23, no. 58, April
1976), which presents historical data from 1900.

702.   Bureau of the Census. **World Population [year]: Recent Demographic Estimates
       for the Countries and Regions of the World. Summary**. GPO, 1973- . Annual.
       (International Statistical Program Office, world population series.) 1979 ed.
       S/N 003-024-02686-4. $2.25. **C3.205/3:WP-yr.(B)**.
This source summarizes demographic information for two hundred countries and territories of the world, with aggregated data for the world's regions and subregions. The
Country Demographic Profiles series (C3.205/3:DP-nos.) reports demographic data for
selected countries on age, sex, fertility, mortality, migration, and social and economic
status.

703.   National Center for Health Statistics. **Vital Statistics of the United States**. 3
       vols. GPO, 1937- . Annual. LC 40-26272. OCLC 01168068. **HE20.6210:
       yr./v.1-3.**
Three annual sections are published: (1) Natality; (2) Mortality, issued in two parts; and
(3) Marriage and Divorce. Material covered includes local area statistics and general
trends. Technical appendixes include a discussion of sources, classification and quality
of statistics reported in the volumes, and population tables for computing vital rates.

704.   Public Health Service. **National Center for Health Statistics**.
The National Center for Health Statistics (NCHS) produces data on the health of all
Americans. The center's major data collections are described below:

> **Vital Registration Program:** data on births, deaths, marriages, and divorces
> in the United States.

> **National Survey of Family Growth:** data based on a five-stage probability
> sample of women fifteen to forty-four years old, with children at
> home.

> **Health Interview Survey:** a continuing national sample survey in which
> health data are collected through personal household interviews.

Health Examination Survey: a continuing national sample survey in which health data are collected through physical examinations, tests, and measurements.

Health and Nutrition Examination Survey: collection of data on the nutritional status of Americans through physical examinations, tests, and measurements.

Master Facility Inventory: a comprehensive file of inpatient health facilities in the United States.

Hospital Discharge Survey: a continuing national sample survey of short-stay hospitals in the United States.

National Ambulatory Medical Care Survey: a continuing national probability sample of ambulatory medical encounters.

Data from these surveys and studies are presented in a variety of publications, including the *Vital and Health Statistics Series* (HE20.6209:nos.). Additional data collected by the center are available in public-use data tapes and unpublished tabulations. Two publications describing these products may be requested free of charge: *Catalog of Public Use Data Tapes from the National Center for Health Statistics* and *Data Systems of the National Center for Health Statistics.*

Questions about published and unpublished center data should be sent to: Scientific and Technical Information Branch, Division of Data Services, National Center for Health Statistics, 3700 East-West Highway, Hyattsville, MD 20782.

DIRECTORIES

705. Bureau of the Census. **Directory of Federal Statistics for Local Areas: A Guide to Sources, 1976.** By Mary S. I. Gordon. GPO, 1978. 359 pp. LC 77-26291. S/N 003-024-01553-6. $9. **C3.6/2:St2/2/976.**
This source and its companion volume, *Urban Update*, serve as guides to facts about U.S. cities. Used together, these two volumes describe every table of urban data issued by the federal government — with one hundred kinds of areas from four hundred fifty reports. The directory does not include actual statistics or data analyses, but gives table-by-table descriptions of subjects in statistical reports on cities.

706. Bureau of the Census. **Directory of Federal Statistics for Local Areas: A Guide to Sources — Urban Update, 1977-1978.** Comp. and ed. by John D. McCall, M. Yvonne Wade, and Neil Tillman. GPO, 1980. OCLC 6037840. S/N 003-024-02167-6. $5. **C3.6/2:St2/2/977-78.**
The directory provides table-by-table descriptions of statistical reports issued through 1978 giving urban data for numerous topics. It is not a statistical compendium or analysis of data, but rather a guide to data sources, both published and unpublished, federal and nonfederal. It is a companion to the *Directory of Federal Statistics for Local Areas: A Guide to Sources* (entry 705); the two volumes are linked by a cumulative index to 2,300 terms.

707. Bureau of the Census. **Directory of Non-Federal Statistics for Local Areas: A Guide to Sources, 1969.** By Francine E. Schacter et al. GPO, 1970. 678 pp. LC 76-605082. **C3.6/2:St2/4.**
This is the first directory published by the Census Bureau of nonfederal statistics sources for local areas. Included with the fifty states are the District of Columbia, Guam, Puerto Rico, and the Virgin Islands and some of their component parts. It is intended to direct the user to published sources of nonfederal statistics on social, political, and economic aspects.

708. Department of Commerce. Office of Federal Statistical Policy and Standards. **Federal Statistical Directory**. GPO, 1979. 26th ed. OCLC 1207757. **C1.75:979.**
The statistical data collection and analysis of the U.S. government is decentralized, with statistical activities pursued by numerous individual agencies. This directory, which began in 1946, was produced to facilitate coordination of federal statistical activities and serve as a guide for nongovernment users. For each executive agency and its subunits, the directory lists names, addresses, and telephone numbers of key people involved in statistical programs.

709. National Institute of Child Health and Human Development. Interagency Committee on Population Research. **Inventory and Analysis of Federal Population Research**. IA, 1976/77- . Annual. HB850.5.U5U546. 301.32/07/2073. OCLC 3393233. **HE20.3362/2:yr.**
This annual report on federally sponsored population research includes a description of the activities of the Interagency Committee on Population Research (ICPR), statistical analysis, and lists of projects. Project listings give names of researchers, place of research, federal funding, and length of project.

710. National Institute of Child Health and Human Development. Interagency Committee on Population Research. **Inventory of Private Agency Population Research**. GPO, 1973- . Annual. LC 75-647556. HB850.5.U5156. 301.32072073. OCLC 1983967. **HE20.3362/2-2:yr.**

711. Office of Management and Budget. **Statistical Services of the United States Government**. GPO, 1975. 234 pp. OCLC 2126517. **PrEx2.2:St2/975.**
Government statistical programs are described, with explanations of principal economic and social statistical series, the statistical responsibilities of each agency, and a list of principal statistical publications.

MACHINE READABLE DATA

712. Bureau of the Census. **Directory of Data Files**. By Molly Abrahmowitz and Barbara Aldrich. IA, 1979. 119 pp. LC 79-607025. HA37.U5 1979. 029/.9/3173. OCLC 4931086. For sale by the Data User Services Division, Customer Services (Publications), Bureau of the Census, Washington, DC 20233. $11 (includes updates). **C3.262:979.**
This is a guide to machine readable data available from the Census Bureau. Abstracts for statistics, microdata, and geographic reference data describe file type, structure, scope, subject matter, reference, and related products. Periodic updates announce new files.

713. Bureau of the Census. **Index to 1970 Census Summary Tapes**. By Paul T. Zeisset. GPO, 1973. 215 pp. LC 74-110406. **C3.223:Su6/970/ind.**
The index includes a cross-reference guide to all tabulations in all six counts of the 1970 census summary data, organized alphabetically by subject variables. It is an aid for locating specific tables for specific subjects in the summary tape documentation.

714. Bureau of the Census. International Statistical Programs Center. **Computer Programs for Demographic Analysis**. By Eduardo Arriaga, Patricia Anderson, and Larry Heligman. GPO, 1976. 580 pp. OCLC 2470727. **C3.205/3:TR-2.**
This is a manual of computer programs for analyzing the quality of population data and calculating and estimating demographic parameters. These subroutines are written in Fortran, with documentation presented in a simple, nontechnical style, understandable by inexperienced programmers.

715. National Technical Information Service. **Directory of Federal Statistical Data Files**. NTIS, 1981- . Annual. LC 82-640888. HA37.U113. 025/.0631/02573. OCLC 08157023. **C51.15:yr.**
Major statistical data files available from numerous federal agencies are described.

Urbanology

BIBLIOGRAPHIES

716. Department of Housing and Urban Development. **Housing and Planning References, New Series**. GPO, 1965- . Bimonthly. S/N 023-000-80002-1. $21/yr. **HH1.23/3:date**.

This series was begun as *Housing References*. The title was changed with the old series of *Housing and Planning References* in 1962. It is a bimonthly selection of publications and articles received in the HUD library. Publications are listed by subjects and then by authors, with entry numbers. Geographic and author indexes are included in each issue, but no cumulative indexes are provided.

DIRECTORIES

717. Department of Housing and Urban Development. **Urban Planning Assistance Program: Project Directory**. GPO, 1966. LC 62-6488. **HH1.26:966**.

The directory covers approved projects for the Urban Planning Assistance Program authorized by section 701 of the Housing Act of 1954 as amended. It is divided into seven parts, including urban planning assistance for small areas, for metropolitan and regional areas, and for the state's comprehensive planning, and is arranged in each section by state and planning agency. It gives project number, dates approved and completed, and net amount of federal grant approved and disbursed.

STATISTICS

718. Department of Housing and Urban Development. **Statistical Yearbook**. GPO, 1966-79. Annual. OCLC 02231304. **HH1.38:yr**.

This is a compendium of data on program and financial operations of the Department of Housing and Urban Development, as well as statistical information related to housing and urban activities.

Part Three

Science and Technology

General Works

BIBLIOGRAPHIES

General Bibliographies

719. Library of Congress. Science and Technology Division. **LC Science Tracer Bullet**. 1A, 1972. Irregular. LC 77-647422. Z7401.L14. OCLC 3315419. **LC33.10:nos**.
These are brief literature guides to materials in the Library of Congress on topics of current interest. Because a pathfinder format is used, these bibliographies are selective and arranged with more basic materials first (subject headings, basic texts), building up to more sophisticated sources (abstracts, conference proceedings). As the name of the series implies, these bibliographies are designed to put the user "on target." A free list of titles in the series is available from the Reference Section, Science and Technology Division, Library of Congress, Washington, DC 20540.

720. National Bureau of Standards. **Publications of the National Bureau of Standards, 1901 to June 30, 1947**. GPO, 1948. 375 pp. (NBS circular 460.) LC 48-47112. **C13.4:460**.

_____. **Supplementary List of Publications of the National Bureau of Standards, July 1, 1947 to June 30, 1957**. GPO, 1958. 373 pp. (NBS circular 460.) **C13.4:460/supp**.

721. National Bureau of Standards. **Publications of the National Bureau of Standards, July 1, 1957 to June 30, 1960**. By Betty L. Arnold. GPO, 1961. 391 pp. (NBS special publication 240.) **C13.10:240**.

_____. **Supplement. Publications of the National Bureau of Standards, July 1960 through June 1966**. By Betty L. Oberholtzer. GPO, 1967. 740 pp. **C13.10: 240/supp**.

722. National Bureau of Standards. **Catalog of National Bureau of Standards Publications, 1966-1976**. Ed. by Betty L. Burris and Rebecca J. Morehouse. GPO, 1978. (NBS special publication 535.) S/N 003-003-02010-9 (vol. 1, pts. 1 and 2). $32. S/N 003-003-02011-7 (vol. 2). $30. **C13.10:535/v.1,2**.

This is a consolidated reprint of NBS Special Publication 305, which included publications issued in 1966-67, and its annual supplements 1-8.

723. National Bureau of Standards. **Publications of the National Bureau of Standards ... Catalog**. GPO, 1978- . Annual. LC 80-649921. QC100.U57. 602/.18. OCLC 02575953. Supp. 15 (1983 entries). S/N 003-003-02585-2. $12. (C13.10:305/supp.9-nos).

Supplement 9, which contains entries for 1977, continues NBS Special Publication 535, a consolidated catalog with entries for publications issued in 1966-76.

724. National Technical Information Service. **Appropriate Technology Information for Developing Countries: Selected Abstracts from the NTIS Data File**. NTIS, 1981. 3d ed. 453 pp., illus. (PB81-146052.) LC 81-602971. OCLC 07718813. **C51.2:T22/981.**

This source provides bibliographic information and abstracts from the NTIS data base for publications related to technologies that can be transferred, adapted, and applied in solving local development problems around the world.

See also SB 257.

Machine Readable Data

725. National Technical Information Service. **A Directory of Computer Software**. NTIS, 1983- . Annual. OCLC 09789329. **C51.11/2:yr.**

Federal production of machine readable data files has increased considerably during the past decade. This growth has been accompanied by an increase in public demand for access to these files and for aid in acquiring and using them. This title is a guide to machine readable software and related technical reports available to the public from over a hundred federal agencies. Each entry includes an abstract and availability information. Indexes of agencies, NTIS order numbers or agency numbers, subjects, hardware configuration, and computer language are included. This continues *A Directory of Computerized Data Files and Related Technical Reports* and *A Directory of Computerized Data Files*.

726. National Technical Information Service. **NTIS Bibliographic Data Base**. 1964- .

A companion to the printed index *Government Reports Announcements and Index*, this machine readable data base includes all of the research summaries and bibliographic citations announced by NTIS in its role as the central clearinghouse for government-sponsored research, development, and engineering reports. While it covers numerous disciplines and subject areas, documents listed are primarily from three agencies: Department of Energy, Department of Defense, and National Aeronautics and Space Administration. A free guide to the data base, *A Reference Guide to the NTIS Bibliographic Data Base*, is available from the National Technical Information Service, 5285 Port Royal Road, Springfield, VA 22161. The NTIS Bibliographic Data Base is accessible through commercial vendors (BRS, Lockheed DIALOG, and SDC) or through lease from NTIS.

Periodicals

727. Library of Congress. Science and Technology Division. **Chinese Scientific and Technical Serial Publications in Collections of Library of Congress.** Comp. by Joan Wu. GPO, 1961. Rev. ed. 107 pp. LC 62-60011. Z7403.U536. Free from the Central Services Division, Library of Congress, Washington, DC 20540. **LC33.2:C44/961.**
Titles are listed under broad subjects with full bibliographic citations and variant titles.

728. Library of Congress. Science and Technology Division. **Japanese Scientific and Technical Serial Publications in Collections of Library of Congress.** Comp. by Chi Wang and Jay H. Woo. GPO, 1962. 247 pp. LC 62-60085. **LC33.2:J27.**
This source lists serials in Western languages and in Japanese, including a separate section on indexing services. There is a title index.

729. Library of Congress. Science and Technology Division. **Scientific and Technical Serial Publications of the Soviet Union, 1945-1960.** Comp. by Nikolay T. Zikeev. GPO, 1963. 347 pp. LC 63-61782. Z7403.U5368. **LC33.2:So8/2.**
Over five thousand serials are listed alphabetically by title. For more current information on specific titles, see *Half a Century of Soviet Serials*.

730. Smithsonian Institution. **Catalogue of Scientific Technical Periodicals, 1665-1896, Together with Chronological Tables and a Library Checklist.** By Henry Carrington Bolton. GPO, 1897. 2d ed. 1,247 pp. (Smithsonian miscellaneous collections, vol. 40.) **SI1.7:40.**
"It is intended to contain the principal independent periodicals of every branch of pure and applied science, published in all countries from the rise of this literature to the present time." Part 1 is a corrected reprint of the first edition, listing 4,954 titles. Part 2 contains newer titles. In all, 8,603 entries are included. Arrangement is alphabetical by the first word of the earliest title, with later titles listed. The chronological tables give dates for specific volumes of many of the periodicals. The catalog is indexed by subjects and titles.

Abstract Journals

731. National Technical Information Service. **Government Reports Announcements and Index.** NTIS, 1946- . Semimonthly, with annual cumulation of the index. LC 75-645021. Z7916.G78. 016.6. OCLC 02242215. **C51.9/3:date.**
GRA&I is the major resource for access to unclassified, unlimited technical reports. It indexes and abstracts U.S. and foreign government-sponsored research and development, technical reports, engineering reports, and other analyses prepared by federal agencies, their contractors, or grantees. Because of the varied missions of government agencies and diverse subject content of their technical reports, GRA&I covers topics not only in the hard sciences, but also in the behavioral and social sciences. Citations to reports are arranged under twenty-two major subject categories and numerous subcategories. They are indexed by subjects, personal and corporate authors, contract numbers, and accession/report numbers. GRA&I is computer-searchable through the NTIS Bibliographic Data Base, which includes all research summaries announced by NTIS in machine readable format.

DICTIONARIES

732. National Aeronautics and Space Administration. **NASA Thesaurus**. 2 vols. NTIS, 1982. 1,219 pp. (NASA SP-7050.) **NAS1.21:7050/v.1,2.**
Documents in the NASA scientific and technical information collection are indexed by keywords from this controlled vocabulary. The thesaurus contains over twenty thousand subject entries for all the basic and applied sciences related to aeronautics and space research.

DIRECTORIES

733. Federal Coordinating Council for Science, Engineering, and Technology. **Directory of Federal Technology Transfer**. GPO, 1977. 223 pp. T174.3.U545 1977. 607.273. OCLC 3152409. S/N 052-003-00376-7. $7.50. **PrEx23.10:977.**
Technology transfer involves putting ideas into practical use. This directory was created to increase the use of science and technology in the public sector by identifying program resources and contacts at the federal level for the use of industry and state and local governments. Federal agency programs are described, along with their research base, technology transfer policy and objectives, responsibilities, implementation methods, accomplishments, and user organizations.

734. Library of Congress. National Referral Center. **Directory of Federally Supported Information Analysis Centers**. GPO, 1980. 4th ed. 87 pp. Q223.5.U54 1979. OCLC 6167613. S/N 030-000-00115-0. $5.50. **LC1.31:In3/979.**
Information given for each of 108 centers includes title, address, telephone number, sponsor, when started, number of staff, mission, scope, holdings, publications, services, and qualifications for users.

735. National Bureau of Standards. **Calibration and Related Measurement Services of the National Bureau of Standards**. GPO, 1963- . Irregular. (NBS special publication 250.) LC 63-60099. 1982 ed. S/N 003-003-02446-5. $6. **C13.10:250/no.**
This is an item-by-item descriptive listing of most of the test and calibration work done at the National Bureau of Standards, including fees. It also gives background on the NBS, procedures for requesting tests, and the accompanying reports issued. It is updated by semiannual appendixes. This publication continues *Calibration and Test Services*.

736. National Science Foundation. **Guide to Programs**. GPO, annual. LC 68-061432. Q180.U5A549. 507/.2073. OCLC 01142423. 1984 ed. S/N 038-000-00514-6. $4.75. **NS1.20:P94/yr.**
Designed to summarize information about all support programs of the National Science Foundation, the guide gives a description of the purpose and characteristics of programs, eligibility, deadlines, and sources of additional information.

737. National Technical Information Service. **International Directory of Appropriate Technology Resources**. NTIS, 1978. OCLC 6311042. **C51.2:D63.**
Part 1 lists organizations involved with appropriate technology and gives address, contact person, description of activities and functions, and the existence of a library or publications. Part 2 is a list of publications issued by these organizations. Part 3 is a subject index.

738.   Smithsonian Institution. Science Information Exchange. **Information Services on Research in Progress: A Worldwide Inventory.** NTIS, 1978. 432 pp. (PB-282 045.) **NS1.2:In2/7.**
This directory of worldwide information systems for keeping track of research in progress lists 179 ongoing research information systems in 53 countries, at the operational, pilot, or planning stage. It includes national, subnational, international, and regional systems and is in French and English.

MANUALS AND HANDBOOKS

739.   National Bureau of Standards. **From Sundials to Atomic Clocks: Understanding Time and Frequency.** By James Jespersen and Jane Fitz-Randolph. GPO, 1978. Illus. (NBS monograph 155.) OCLC 3690943. S/N 003-003-01650-1. $7. **C13.44:155.**
This is a layman's introduction to time and frequency. It discusses the generation of time measurement, its uses, distribution, and physical and scientific nature.

740.   National Bureau of Standards. **Time and Frequency User's Manual.** Ed. by George Kamans and Sandra L. Howe. GPO, 1979. 248 pp. (NBS special publication 559.) LC 79-600169. **C13.10:559.**
This manual was written to assist novice and experienced users of time and frequency calibration services available in the United States and the world. Aimed at the level of the casual user who wants to set his watch, the book uses simple explanations and avoids complex derivations or mathematical analysis. It is also useful for those needing to adjust oscillators or perform related scientific measurements. It includes a brief history and description of world time and frequency coordination and describes available services and how to use them.

741.   Office of Naval Research. **The Infrared Handbook.** Ed. by William L. Wolfe and George J. Zissis. GPO, 1978. 1,720 pp., illus. LC 77-90786. OCLC 4964222. **D210.6/2:In3/2.**
This supersedes the *Handbook of Military Infrared Technology* (1965) and includes coverage of new detectors and materials, improved instrumentation techniques, infrared systems, displays, infrared tubes, and experimental charge-coupled device models.

PATENTS

742.   National Technical Information Service. **Catalog of Government Patents.** NTIS, 1981- . Annual. OCLC 07885671. **C51.16:yr.**
The catalog lists thousands of government-owned inventions, many of which are available for licensing. It provides a list of patents with abstracts and some illustrations, arranged according to the Patent and Trademark Office classification system in Part A. Part B indexes inventions by subject and agency. Part C is the weekly abstract newsletter *Government Inventions for Licensing*, which provides information on U.S. government-owned patents and patent applications. Patents issued between 1966 and 1980 were published in five volumes: volumes 1-3 (1966-74) and volumes 4 and 5 (1975-80).

743.   Patent and Trademark Office. **Attorneys and Agents Registered to Practice before the U.S. Patent and Trademark Office.** GPO, 1960- . Irregular. LC 75-648024. KF3165.A3A8. 346/.73/0486025. OCLC 2246063. 1982 ed. 2 pts. S/N 003-004-00594-7. $9 (set). **C21.9/2:yr.**

Names, addresses, and telephone and registration numbers are given for attorneys and agents registered to practice before the U.S. Patent and Trademark Office. Part 1 is an alphabetic listing by name. Part 2 has lists by state and foreign country.

744. Patent and Trademark Office. **Classification Definitions (Patents)**. GPO, quarterly. S/N 003-004-81005-0 (microfiche). $157. (Subscription includes complete set and quarterly changes for an indeterminate period.) **C21.3/2:nos.**

This source gives detailed definitions of the subject matter included or excluded from each class and subclass of the Patent and Trademark Office classification. Patent classes and subclasses are listed, followed by notes and definitions clarifying inclusions and exclusions.

745. Patent and Trademark Office. **Concordance: United States Patent Classification to International Patent Classification**. GPO, 1979. 4th ed. 152 pp. OCLC 5635560. S/N 003-004-00562-9. $6.50. **C21.14/2:C74/980.**

This is a guide for relating the U.S. Patent Classification System to the third edition of the International Patent Classification.

746. Patent and Trademark Office. **Index of Patents Issued from the United States Patent and Trademark Office**. GPO, 1974- . Annual. LC 76-643074. T223.D3. 608/.7/73. OCLC 02441502. **C21.5/2:yr./pt.**

This annual index to information from the *Official Gazette* issues of the past year is issued in two parts. Part 1, *List of Patentees*, is an alphabetic list of persons or companies having new or reissued patents. It also includes lists of design patentees, plant patentees, disclaimers and dedications, and decisions published in the *Official Gazette* and gives the patent number for each patentee. Part 2, *Index of Subjects of Inventions*, is arranged by class and subclass number in accordance with the Patent Office Classification, with patent numbers following these classes. There is a list of class titles in class number order and an alphabetic list of class titles that must be consulted in order to find patents of a particular subject. The index includes supplementary lists of libraries receiving issues of patents, of libraries receiving the *Official Gazette*, and a summary of the number of patents issued annually from 1836 to the present.

747. Patent and Trademark Office. **Index of Trademarks Issued from the United States Patent and Trademark Office**. GPO, 1927- . Annual. LC 75-646550. T223.V4A2. 602/.75. OCLC 2243146. 1981 ed. S/N 003-004-00581-9. $22. **C21.5/3:yr.**

"Includes the registrants of all trademark registrations issued during the year; and also registrants of trademarks published in the *Official Gazette* ..., and registrants of trademark registrations renewed, cancelled, surrendered, amended, disclaimed, corrected, etc. during the year." It is arranged alphabetically by name of registrant with address and registration information.

748. Patent and Trademark Office. **Index to the U.S. Patent Classification**. GPO, 1983. 242 pp. LC 78-643766. 608/.7/012. OCLC 04010459. S/N 003-004-90037-7. $7. **C21.12/2:983.**

This alphabetic subject heading list refers the user to patent classes and subclasses related to each index term; it serves as an initial point of entry when trying to define a patent search in terms of specific classes and subclasses. This title serves as an index to the *Manual of Classification* and continues the *Index to Classification*.

749. Patent and Trademark Office. **Manual of Classification**. GPO, 1982. Looseleaf. OCLC 07639764. S/N 003-004-81001-7. $40. (Subscription includes the basic manual, the current *Index to United States Patent Classification*, and quarterly replacement pages for an indeterminate period.) **C21.12:982.**

This list of all patent class and subclass numbers and their descriptive titles is meant to serve as a list only; the descriptive titles are brief and definitive. Because the manual provides only brief descriptive statements for classes and subclasses, it can be used as a key to *Classification Definitions* by turning to the same class and subclass in the definitions for elaboration.

750. Patent and Trademark Office. **Official Gazette of the United States Patent and Trademark Office: Patents.** GPO, 1872- . Weekly. Illus. LC 75-641794. T223.A23. OCLC 02240595. S/N 003-004-80001-1. $270/yr. (nonpriority). $375/yr. (priority). **C21.5:vol./nos.**
Published weekly since 1872, the gazette contains summaries and drawings of approximately fifteen hundred U.S. patents granted each week. The *Index of Patents* (entry 746) is an annual index of its contents.

751. Patent and Trademark Office. **Official Gazette of the United States Patent and Trademark Office: Trademarks.** GPO, 1971- . Weekly. Illus. LC 75-641793. T223.V13A34. 602/.75. OCLC 2240594. S/N 003-004-80002-0. $238/yr. **C21.5/4:vol./nos.**
This is a listing, with illustrations, of trademarks, trademark notices, marks published for opposition, registrations issued, and index of registrants. The *Index of Trademarks* (entry 747) is an annual index to its contents.

752. Patent and Trademark Office. **Patent Laws.** GPO, 1979. 139 pp. OCLC 2476007. S/N 003-004-00561-1. $6. **C21.7:979.**
This source provides the text of Title 35, U.S. Code, and notes on other statutes related to patents.

753. Patent and Trademark Office. Office of Technology Assessment and Forecast. **Patent Data Base.**
This is a master data base of all U.S. patents, which can be searched by basic elements included in U.S. patents, such as subclass, patent title, inventor's name, or field of search. The Office of Technology Assessment and Forecast will perform custom searches to satisfy specific requests, with the option of various presentation formats such as charts, tables, and graphs. The Patent Data Base is searchable on line through the Bibliographic Retrieval Service (BRS), Lockheed DIALOG, or SDC Search Service. It is also available for lease from NTIS. For information write to the Custom Reports Manager, Office of Technology Assessment and Forecast, U.S. Patent and Trademark Office, Washington, DC 20231, or call (703) 557-2982.

See also SB 21.

STANDARDS

754. National Bureau of Standards. **Directory of Standards Laboratories in the United States.** GPO, 1965- . Irregular. LC 65-61792. **C13.2:St2/2/yr.**
"Designed to fulfill three functions: to serve as a 'classified index' of standards laboratories in this country, providing those seeking information on calibration services with a list of available services; to provide information useful to those offering calibration services; to provide information concerning activities in the standards and calibration field essential to the planning and operation of the National Conference of Standards Laboratories."

Part 1, "Laboratories and Capabilities," lists laboratories alphabetically by name of the parent organization and, in chart form, the areas of calibration with which each works.

Part 2, in similar form, is by areas of capability and keyed to the numbers assigned in Part 1. Part 3 lists the laboratories, names of people from whom information may be obtained, mailing address, availability of services, and number of professional and technical personnel.

755. National Bureau of Standards. **Directory of United States Standardization Activities**. Ed. by Sophie J. Chumas. GPO, 1975. 224 pp. (NBS special publication 417.) LC 75-619012. S/N 003-003-01395-1. $13. **C13.10:417**.

This is a directory of associations with ongoing activities related to developing standards. Private, state, and federal associations and their addresses are listed. It describes the types of work being done and gives affiliations with other standardizing agencies, publications, and other pertinent information.

756. National Bureau of Standards. **Standard Reference Materials**. GPO, 1964- . Irregular. (NBS special publication 260.) LC 64-62975. 1984-85 catalog. S/N 003-003-02558-5. $5.50. **C13.10:260/yr**.

This current list of standard reference materials is arranged in logical sequence, with normal values of certified properties, and provides ordering information. It is supplemented by *Price and Availability Listing of Standard Reference Materials*.

757. National Bureau of Standards. **World Index of Plastic Standards**. Ed. by Leslie H. Breden. GPO, 1971. 445 pp. (NBS special publication 352.) LC 76-172537. QC100.U57 no.352. **C13.10:352**.

This is a keyword-in-context index to the titles of over nine thousand national and international standards for plastics and related materials, in effect through 1970. The standards are published by technical societies, trade associations, government agencies, and military organizations.

758. Office of Federal Supply and Services. **Index of Federal Specifications and Standards, and Commercial Item Descriptions**. GPO, 1979- . Annual. LC 80-643534. JK1679.I53. 353.0082/1. OCLC 05730039. S/N 022-001-81002-9. $29/yr. (Subscription includes basic manual plus cumulative supplements.) **GS2.8/2:date**.

This index includes alphabetic, numerical, and federal supply classification (FSC) listings of federal and interim federal specifications and standards, federal handbooks, and qualified products lists in general use by the federal government. A cumulative list of canceled documents is published on a triennial basis as an appendix to the annual basic index.

See also SB 133, SB 148, and SB 271.

Agriculture

GENERAL WORKS

759. Economics, Statistics, and Cooperative Service. **Chronological Landmarks in American Agriculture**. GPO, 1980. 103 pp. (Agricultural information bulletin 425.) OCLC 6257707. **A1.75:425/2**.

The chronological list of major events in U.S. agricultural history includes inventions, laws, land policy changes, individuals, institutional development, and introduction of new crops and livestock. Event notations give date, description, and a citation to additional information.

760. Farmer Cooperative Service. **Legal Phases of Farmer Cooperatives**. 3 pts. GPO, 1976. (FCS information series, no. 100.) OCLC 2344548. **A89.15:100/sec.1-3**.

This is the fourth revision of Lyman S. Hulbert's work, first published in 1922. It contained the first extensive discussion of legal problems in the organization and operation of cooperatives. This revision gives background on cooperatives and cites developments in law and court decisions that affect their legal status. Section 1, "Sample Legal Documents," describes legal instruments needed to carry on cooperative business and to form and establish a cooperative. Section 2, "Federal Income Taxes," discusses tax legislation that deals specifically with farmer cooperatives. Section 3, "Antitrust Laws," covers cooperatives in relation to monopolies and restraint of trade legislation.

See also SB 161 and SB 162.

Bibliographies

General Bibliographies

761. Department of Agriculture. **List of the Agricultural Periodicals of the United States and Canada Published during the Century July 1810 to July 1910**. By Stephen Conrad Stuntz. Ed. by Emma B. Hawks. GPO, 1941. 190 pp. (USDA miscellaneous publication no. 398.) **A1.38:398**.

Nearly four thousand periodicals are listed in this bibliography, which is an indispensable guide for research in the field of agricultural history.

762. Department of Agriculture. Science and Education Administration. **A Bibliography for Small and Organic Farmers, 1920-1978.** By J. W. Schwartz. IA, 1981. 237 pp. (Bibliographies and literature of agriculture, no. 11.) OCLC 08029778. **A13.11/3:11.**

This is a list of research publications related to the needs of small farmers and organic farmers, with no annotations.

763. Department of Agriculture. Science and Education Administration. **Structure of U.S. Agriculture Bibliography.** Comp. by Ronald C. Wimberly and Charles N. Bebee. IA, 1981. 514 pp. (Bibliographies and literature of agriculture, no. 16.) OCLC 07411323. **A1.60/3:16.**

This is a bibliography of references to scientific and policy materials related to the structure of agriculture. Citations were generated from the AGRICOLA data base, 1970-79.

764. Department of Agriculture. Science and Education Administration. Technical Information Systems. **Bibliography of Agricultural Bibliographies.** IA, 1977. (Bibliographies and literature of agriculture, no. 1.) OCLC 4655722. **A106.110/3:1.**

This source is a categorized listing of bibliographies compiled from the AGRICOLA data base. Entries include bibliographic information but no abstracts.

765. Farm Credit Administration. **Cooperation in Agriculture: A Selected and Annotated Bibliography with Special Reference to Marketing, Purchasing, and Credit.** Comp. by Chastina Gardner. GPO, 1936. 214 pp. (Bulletin 4.) LC 36-26618. **FCA1.3:4.**

766. Farmer Cooperative Service. **Bibliography of Dissertations and Theses on Cooperatives.** Comp. by Wendell McMillan. GPO, 1958. 50 pp. (General reports, no. 42.) **A89.11:42.**

_____. **Bibliography of Dissertations and Theses on Cooperatives.** By Walter Furbay and Wendell McMillan. GPO, 1965. 79 pp. (General reports, no. 130.) **A89.11:130.**

Doctoral dissertations and master's theses are listed in separate sections alphabetically by author. Entries gives title, year, and name of academic institution, indexed by subjects.

767. National Agricultural Library. **Bibliography of Agriculture.** 33 vols. GPO, 1942-70. **A17.18:vol.**

The *Bibliography of Agriculture* is the standard work in the field. It began in 1908 as part of the *Report of the Librarian* and was succeeded in 1926 by *Agricultural Library Notes.* In 1942 the following specialized bibliographies as well as *Agricultural Library Notes* ceased publication and were merged to form *Bibliography of Agriculture: Agricultural Economic Literature* (1927-42; A17.10:nos.); *Current Literature in Agricultural Engineering* (1931-42; A70.7:nos.); *Entomology, Current Literature* (1932-42; A17.14:nos.); *Plant Science Literature: Selected References* (1934-43; A17.11:vol.); *Forestry: Current Literature* (A13.25:vol.); *Commodity Exchange Administration Literature* (1938-39; A59.8:vol.); *Cotton Literature* (1931-42; A17.13:nos.); and *Soil Conservation Literature* (1937-42; A17.15:nos.). In 1970 the National Agricultural Library ceased publishing the *Bibliography of Agriculture*. At that time, the CCM Information Corp. began its publication with no interruption in the bibliography. It is currently being published by Oryx Press.

Each monthly issue is in classified arrangement with personal and organizational indexes. Annual cumulative indexes appear in each December issue. Subject indexing was started in 1966. Approximately 100,000 references are cited each year including books, government documents, and journal articles from the United States, Western Europe, and Russia. Foreign language titles are translated into English but contain a note on the original language. Subjects included cover a wide variety of specialized disciplines, for example, plant science, forestry, agricultural economics, food and nutrition, and animal industry.

768.   National Agricultural Library. **Bibliography on Cooperation in Agriculture.** Comp. by Howard B. Turner and Florence C. Bell. IA, 1948. 178 pp. (Library list 17.) **A17.17:41.**

769.   National Agricultural Library. **Bibliography on Cooperation in Agriculture, 1946-63.** Comp. by Elizabeth G. Davis. IA, 1954. 21 pp. (Library list 41.) **A17.17:41/supp.1.**

770.   National Agricultural Library. **Cooperation in Agriculture, 1954-1964: A List of Selected References.** Comp. by Gene J. Kubal. IA, 1966. 115 pp. (Library list 41.) HD1491.U53K71. OCLC 3941165. **A17.17:14/supp.2.**
Together, the above three bibliographies and entry 765 form a comprehensive record of references in English on all phases of agricultural cooperation throughout the world.

771.   Office of Education. **Summaries of Studies in Agricultural Education.** GPO, 1935. 196 pp. (Bulletin 180.) **I16.54/3:180.**

772.   Office of Education. **Summaries of Studies in Agricultural Education: An Annotated Bibliography of Studies in Agricultural Education with a Classified Subject Index.** GPO, 1942- . Annual. OCLC 1480970. **HE5.281:81002-yr.**
The first issue of this series was published in 1935 and lists approximately four hundred research studies. Entries for new studies are arranged alphabetically by author and provide fairly detailed information covering such aspects as objectives of research, methods used, and significant findings and conclusions. The appended classified index facilitates the use of this bibliographic service, which primarily concentrates on doctoral dissertations, master's theses, and contracted research reports.

773.   Tennessee Valley Authority. National Fertilizer Development Center. **Fertilizer Abstracts.** IA, 1968-82. Monthly with annual index. LC 71-11106. OCLC 2486854. **Y3.T25:36/nos.**
This abstract journal was compiled from articles in technical journals, patents, and miscellaneous scientific and technical reports. Some abstracts were from *Chemical Abstracts*, with permission.

Department of Agriculture Catalogs

774.   Department of Agriculture. **Films of the U.S. Department of Agriculture.** GPO, 1920- . Irregular. (Agriculture handbook 14.) **A1.76:14/yr.**
This annotated listing of films available from the USDA for loan or purchase includes a subject index and list of state film libraries that lend USDA films.

775.   Department of Agriculture. **List of Publications of the United States Department of Agriculture from January 1901 to December 1925 Inclusive.** By Mabel G. Hunt. GPO, 1927. 182 pp. (USDA miscellaneous publication no. 9.) **A1.38:9.**

776. Department of Agriculture. **List of Publications of the United States Department of Agriculture from January 1926 to December 1930 Inclusive.** By Mabel G. Hunt. GPO, 1932. 46 pp. (USDA miscellaneous publication no. 153.) **A1.38:153.**

777. Department of Agriculture. **List of Publications of the United States Department of Agriculture from January 1931 to December 1935 Inclusive.** By Mabel G. Hunt. GPO, 1937. 64 pp. (USDA miscellaneous publication no. 252.) **A1.38:252.**

778. Department of Agriculture. **List of Publications of the United States Department of Agriculture from January 1936 to December 1940 Inclusive.** By Mabel H. Doyle. GPO, 1941. 68 pp. (USDA miscellaneous publication no. 443.) **A1.38:443.**

779. Department of Agriculture. **List of Publications of the United States Department of Agriculture from January 1941 to December 1945 Inclusive.** By Bertha L. Zoeller and Mabel H. Doyle. GPO, 1946. 56 pp. (USDA miscellaneous publication no. 617.) **A1.38:617.**

780. Department of Agriculture. Division of Publications. **List, by Titles, of Publications of the United States Department of Agriculture from 1840 to June 1901 Inclusive.** By R. B. Handy and Minna A. Cannon. GPO, 1902. 216 pp. (Bulletin 6.) **A21.3:6.**

781. Department of Agriculture. Office of Experiment Stations. **List of Bulletins of the Agricultural Experiment Stations from Their Establishment to the End of 1920.** GPO, 1924. 186 pp. (USDA bulletin 1199.) **A1.3:1199.**
This bibliography lists nearly all of the publications of the state agricultural experiment stations from 1875 to 1920. It was continued in other publications up to 1942.

782. Department of Agriculture. Office of Information. **List of Available Publications of the United States Department of Agriculture.** GPO, 1929- . Annual. (List 11.) OCLC 4079823. **A107.12:11/nos.**
Subject areas of publications listed include all aspects of agriculture and animal science, civil defense, conservation, entomology, extension work, forestry, home economics, safety, fire prevention, teaching aids, and visual aids.

783. National Agricultural Library. **Available Bibliographies and Lists.** IA, 1946- . Irregular. (Library list 25.) **A17.17:25/nos.**
Bibliographies and *Library Lists* available from the National Agricultural Library are listed.

784. Rural Electrification Administration. **Current REA Publications.** IA, 1966- . Annual. Looseleaf. **A68.3:ind./yr.**
Current publications of the Rural Electrification Administration's rural telephone program are listed; a subject index is included.

785. Superintendent of Documents. **List of Publications of the Agricultural Department, 1862-1902 with Analytical Index.** Comp. by William Leander Post. GPO, 1904. 623 pp. (Bibliography of U.S. public documents. Departmental list no. 1.) **GP3.10:1.**

Department of Agriculture
Publications Indexes

786. Department of Agriculture. **Index to Departmental Bulletins Numbers 1-1500.** Comp. by Mabel G. Hunt. GPO, 1936. 384 pp. **A1.3:1-1500/ind.**
Departmental Bulletins were published from 1913 to 1927 and then superseded by Technical Bulletins.

787. Department of Agriculture. **Index to Farmers' Bulletin Numbers 1-1750.** 3 vols. GPO, 1920-41. **A1.9:1-1750/ind.**
The Farmers' Bulletin series began in 1889 and individual numbers are published on an irregular basis.

788. Department of Agriculture. **Index to Technical Bulletins Numbers 1-750.** By Mabel G. Hunt. 2 vols. GPO, 1937-41. **A1.36:1-750/ind.**
The Technical Bulletin series began in 1927.

789. Department of Agriculture. Division of Publications. **Index to Authors with Titles of Their Publications Appearing in the Documents of the U.S. Department of Agriculture.** By George F. Thompson. GPO, 1898. 303 pp. (Bulletin 4.) **A21.3:4.**

790. Department of Agriculture. Division of Publications. **Index to the Annual Reports of the U.S. Department of Agriculture for the Years 1837 to 1893.** GPO, 1896. 252 pp. (Bulletin 1.) **A21.3:1.**

791. Department of Agriculture. Division of Publications. **Synoptical Index of the Reports of the Statistician, 1863 to 1894.** By George F. Thompson. GPO, 1897. 258 pp. (Bulletin 2.) **A21.3:2.**

792. Department of Agriculture. Office of Experiment Stations. **Experiment Station Record: General Index to Volumes 1-80, 1889-1939.** 7 vols. GPO, 1903-49. **A10.6/2:vol./ind.**
The record is primarily important to those involved in agricultural research. It includes materials in English and some foreign languages.

793. Department of Agriculture. Office of Information. **Index to the Publications of the U.S. Department of Agriculture, 1901-40.** Ed. by Mary A. Bradley. 4 vols. GPO, 1932-43. **A21.2:In2/2.**
All USDA publications except periodicals issued by the various bureaus are covered.

794. National Agricultural Library. **Serials Currently Received by the National Library of Agriculture, 1975: A Keyword Index.** GPO, 1976. 1,333 pp. OCLC 2534289. **A17.18/2:Se6/975.**
This is a keyword-out-of-context (KWOC) listing of nineteen thousand serials received by the National Agricultural Library. Serials listed deal with animal science, biochemistry, botany, consumer science, economics, entomology, food and nutrition, management, natural resources, technical agriculture, and other related topics. For NAL's holdings of discontinued serials, consult the *Dictionary Catalog of the National Agricultural Library* (1862-1965), the *National Agricultural Library Catalog, Quinquennial Edition* (1966-1970), and the *National Agricultural Library Catalog* (1971-), which also announces new serial holdings.

Farm Products

795. Department of Agriculture. **Bibliography of Potato Diseases through 1945, with Common and Scientific Names.** Comp. by Muriel J. O'Brien and E. L. LeClerg. GPO, 1970. 243 pp. (USDA miscellaneous publication no. 1162.) LC 76-608932. **A1.38:1162.**

The potato is considered our most important vegetable crop, yet when this bibliography was published in 1970 no extensive bibliography of potato diseases was available. This unannotated bibliography lists research papers through 1945, many of which remain classics in the field.

796. Department of Agriculture. **Cotton Boll Weevil (Anthonomus grandis Boh): Abstracts of Research Publications, 1843-1960.** Comp. by Henry A. Dunn. GPO, 1964. 194 pp. (USDA miscellaneous publication no. 985.) **A1.38:985.**

This is a comprehensive source for early research on the cotton boll weevil. It is indexed by authors.

797. Department of Agriculture. **Boll Weevil (Anthonomus grandis Boh): Abstracts of Research Publications, 1961-65.** Comp. by Lucille L. and Norman Mitlin. GPO, 1968. 32 pp. (USDA miscellaneous publication no. 1092.) **A1.38:1092.**

Newer titles are listed with annotations and author and subject indexes.

798. Forest Service. Northeastern Forest Experiment Station. **Population Dynamics of the Gypsy Moth.** Broomall, PA: IA, 1978. 124 pp. (General technical report NE-48.) OCLC 4993854. **A13.88:NE-48.**

This source provides an annotated bibliography of 592 references from the world literature on population dynamics of the gypsy moth and related subjects.

Foreign Agriculture

799. National Agricultural Library. **Publications on Chinese Agriculture prior to 1949.** Comp. by W. J. Logan and P. B. Schroeder. IA, 1966. 142 pp. (Library list 85.) **A17.17:85.**

Approximately one thousand publications pertaining to agriculture in mainland China are listed with annotations and author and title indexes.

History of Agriculture

800. Department of Agriculture. **A Bibliography of the History of Agriculture in the United States.** By Everett E. Edwards. GPO, 1930, 307 pp. (USDA miscellaneous publication no. 84.) (Repr.: Gale, $31.) **A1.38:84.**

This comprehensive work will be useful for research in the history of U.S. agriculture.

801. National Agricultural Library. **Heritage of American Agriculture: A Bibliography of Pre-1860 Imprints.** Comp. by Alan M. Fusonie. IA, 1975. 71 pp. (Library list 98.) LC 75-600876. Z881.U4L5 no.98. 016.63. OCLC 1216838. **A17.17:98.**

This is a selective, unannotated bibliography of pre-1860 publications which identifies pre-Civil War developments in U.S. agriculture.

802. National Agricultural Library. **Historic Books and Manuscripts concerning General Agriculture in the Collection of the National Agricultural Library.** IA, 1967. 94 pp. (Library list 86.) **A17.17:86.**

This important bibliography lists works published in Europe before 1800 and those published in the United States before 1830. It includes complete bibliographic information as well as NAL call number, collation, LC card number, and a brief annotation.

803. National Agricultural Library. **Historic Books and Manuscripts concerning Horticulture and Forestry in the Collection of the National Agricultural Library.** Comp. by Mortimer L. Naftalin. IA, 1968. 106 pp. (Library list 90.) **A17.17:90.**

Titles published prior to 1800 (for European imprints) and 1830 (American imprints) are included, with a few selected works published at a later date. Full bibliographic information is given; including NAL call number, collation, and LC card number. Horticulture books are listed first, alphabetically by author, followed by those on forestry.

Biographical Sources

804. Congress. House. Committee on Agriculture. **Men and Milestones in American Agriculture.** GPO, 1966. 59 pp. LC 66-62982. **Y4.Ag8/1:M52.**

Biographies are provided for Americans who are "considered representative of men and women from every state in the Union and from every walk of life."

805. Department of Agriculture. **Early American Soil Conservationists.** GPO, 1941 (repr. 1966). 61 pp. (USDA miscellaneous publication no. 449.) **A1.38:449.**

Biographies are provided for selected soil conservationists from the eighteenth and nineteenth centuries with a bibliography of works cited.

Directories

806. Agricultural Marketing Service. **Grain Inspection Points under the Grain Standards Act.** IA, 1961- . Irregular. Looseleaf. **A88.2:G76/6/yr.**

This source lists locations of grain inspection services provided regularly under the authority of the U.S. Grain Standards Act.

807. Cooperative State Research Service. **Directory of Professional Workers in State Agricultural Experiment Stations and Other Cooperating State Institutions.** GPO, 1981- . Annual. (Agricultural handbook no. 305.) OCLC 07537305. 1982-83 ed. S/N 001-000-04338-2. $6. **A1.76:305/yr.**

Federal agricultural personnel involved in research and extension and regional directors of state agricultural experiment stations are listed. The bulk of the directory is a state-by-state listing of college and university departments and personnel.

808. Department of Agriculture. **Directory of Agricultural Research.** IA, 1974. 165 pp., illus. **A1.89/3:Ag8/974.**

Agricultural Research Service offices and key personnel in the Washington, DC area, the states, and foreign countries are listed. The index of agricultural specialists refers to the office in which each is located.

809. Department of Agriculture. Statistical Reporting Service. **Directory of Refrigerated Warehouses in the United States.** IA, 1947- . Irregular. (SRS series.) LC 51-60510. **A92.34:nos. vary.**

This directory of refrigerated warehouses throughout the United States which participated in the USDA's survey is organized by states, and then by cities.

810. Food Safety and Inspection Service. **Meat and Poultry Inspection Directory**. GPO, 1977- . Semiannual. OCLC 03260420. S/N 701-034-00000-7. $21/yr. **A110.11:date**.

This is a list of establishments, public stockyards, manufacturers of biological products, pathological laboratories, diagnosticians, and state officials for animal disease control.

Machine Readable Data

811. National Agricultural Library. **AGRICOLA (Agricultural OnLine Access) Data Base**. 1970- .

The AGRICOLA system (formerly called CAIN) provides comprehensive worldwide coverage of the published literature on agriculture and allied subjects as represented in the National Agricultural Library. It contains bibliographic citations to monographs, serial titles, and journal articles selected from six thousand serial titles from January 1970 to the present. It includes the following subfiles:

> **AAEDC**. American Agricultural Economic Documentation Center is jointly sponsored by the American Agriculture Economics Association, Canadian Society for Agriculture Economics, and the U.S. Department of Agriculture.

> **BRU**. Brucellosis file, prepared by the Emergency Programs Information Center, Animal Plant and Health Inspection Service.

> **ENV**. Environmental impact statements of interest to agricultural researchers.

> **FNC**. Food and Nutrition Information Center. The primary emphasis is on human nutrition research and education, food service management, and food technology.

AGRICOLA is available commercially through Lockheed DIALOG, SDC, and BRS. The National Technical Information Center sells AGRICOLA magnetic tapes for an annual fee.

Standards

812. Agricultural Marketing Service. **Grade Names Used in U.S. Standards for Farm Products**. GPO, 1958- . Irregular. (Agriculture handbook 157.) **A1.76:157**.

Grade names are listed for all agricultural products for which U.S. standards have been issued. The information was compiled from the official published standards and checked for accuracy by the commodity division issuing the standards. Products include cotton, dairy products, fruits and vegetables in general, nuts, processed honey and sugar products, grain, beans, peas, rice, hay, straw, livestock, meat, wool, poultry products, tobacco, and naval stores.

Statistics

813. Bureau of the Census. **Census of Agriculture**. GPO, 1840- . Quinquennial. **C3.31/4:date**.

The census of agriculture provides a periodic statistical picture of the nation's farming, ranching, and related activities. Taken every five years, this census provides data on agricultural production, resources, and inventories at the county, state, regional, and national levels. It provides the only set of uniform agricultural data at the county level. Data are released in printed reports, microfiche, and on computer tapes.

814. Department of Agriculture. **Agricultural Statistics.** GPO, 1936- . Annual. OCLC 1773189. 1983 ed. S/N 001-000-04401-1. $13. **A1.47:yr.**
This comprehensive statistical report contains current and historical agricultural data. It provides an annual statistical compilation of agricultural production, supplies, consumption, facilities, costs, and returns. Statistics represent actual counts of items covered, estimates based on surveys, and censuses of agriculture taken every five years.

815. Department of Agriculture. **Agricultural Trade of the Western Hemisphere: Statistical Review, 1963-1973.** IA, 1975. 204 pp. (USDA statistical bulletin 546.) **A1.34:546.**
This review presents dollar amounts for trade of food, beverages, and agricultural raw materials, classified by major Standard International Trade Classification (SITC) groups.

816. Department of Agriculture. **Handbook of Agricultural Charts.** GPO, 1964- . Annual. (Agriculture handbook series.) LC 64-062697. OCLC 02484189. 1983 ed. (A1.76:619.) S/N 001-000-04377-3. $5. **A1.76:nos. vary.**
Charts and tables are given with explanatory text, summarizing data on farms, natural resources, population and rural development, consumers, food and nutrition programs, foreign production and trade, and commodity trends. A supplement has enlargements of the charts and graphs. Any of the charts in the handbook may be ordered in sets on slides or black-and-white prints. Order information is provided.

817. Department of Agriculture. **Wool Statistics and Related Data, 1930-69.** Comp. by Mildred V. Jones. GPO, 1970. 294 pp. (USDA statistical bulletin 455.) LC 70-608952. **A1.34:455.**
Statistics on wool, mohair, and similar hair fibers for 1930-69 are given, with selected data on cotton and man-made fibers. Data summarize production, consumption, foreign trade, and prices, primarily for the United States.

818. Economic Research Service. **U.S. Fats and Oils Statistics, 1961-76.** GPO, 1977. 131 pp. (USDA statistical bulletin 574.) OCLC 3110770. **A1.34:574.**
This compilation of conversion factors and domestic statistics on oilseeds, fats, oils, and their products complements statistics appearing in the *Oil Crops Outlook and Situation* (A93.23/2:nos.). It includes a glossary of terms.

819. Economic Research Service. **U.S. Fresh Market Vegetable Statistics, 1949-75.** IA, 1976. 106 pp. (USDA statistical bulletin 558.) OCLC 2429143. **A1.34:558.**
Production, price, foreign trade, and other benchmark data on the U.S. fresh vegetable industry are provided. This source serves as supplement to the quarterly *Vegetable Outlook and Situation* (A93.12/2:nos.).

820. Economics, Statistics, and Cooperative Service. **Statistics on Cotton and Related Data, 1960-78.** Comp. by Mildred V. Jones. IA, 1979. 145 pp. (USDA statistical bulletin 617.) OCLC 4849307. **A1.34:617.**
This title supersedes *Statistics on Cotton and Related Data, 1920-73* and serves as a statistical handbook to the quarterly *Cotton and Wool Situation* (A93.24/2:nos.). An annual supplement is also published.

821. Federal Energy Administration. **Energy and U.S. Agriculture: 1974 Data Base.** 2 vols. GPO, 1977. OCLC 2897538. **FE1.2:Ag8/974/v.1,2.**

Tables depicting energy in agricultural production are based on an agricultural accounting model with five major dimensions: energy, geography, commodity, time, and function. Volume 1 covers U.S. and state data. Volume 2 provides commodity series of energy tabulations.

See also SB 277.

Yearbooks

822. Department of Agriculture. **Yearbook of Agriculture**. GPO, 1894- . Annual. LC 4-18127. **A1.10:yr**.
Since 1936, each issue of the yearbook has covered one broad subject of general interest. Although not intended to be definitive, the yearbooks are comprehensive in treatment. Many volumes contain bibliographies for further research. Cumulative indexes have been published covering 1894-1915. The following is a list of yearbooks published since 1936.

1936-37. **Better Plants and Animals**. 2 vols.

1938. **Soil and Men**.

1939. **Food and Life**.

1940. **Farmers in a Changing World**.

1941. **Climate and Man**.

1942. **Keeping Livestock Healthy**.

1943-47. **Science in Farming**.

1948. **Grass**. S/N 001-000-00096-9. $15.

1949. **Trees**.

1950-51. **Crops in Peace and War**. S/N 001-000-00098-5. $15.

1952. **Insects**.

1953. **Plant Diseases**. S/N 001-000-00100-1. $16.

1954. **Marketing**. S/N 001-000-00101-9. $13.

1955. **Water**. S/N 001-000-00102-7. $14.

1956. **Animal Diseases**. S/N 001-000-00103-5. $13.

1957. **Soil**.

1958. **Land**. S/N 001-000-00105-1. $13.

1959. **Food**. S/N 001-000-00106-0. $12.

1960. **Power to Produce**. S/N 001-000-00107-8. $14.

1961. **Seeds**.

1962. **After a Hundred Years**. S/N 001-000-00109-4. $13.

1963. **Place to Live**. S/N 001-000-00110-8. $13.

1964. **Farmer's World**. S/N 001-000-00111-6. $13.

1965. **Consumers All**. S/N 001-000-00112-4. $13.

1966. **Protecting Our Food**. S/N 001-000-00113-2. $12.

1967. **Outdoors USA**. S/N 001-000-00114-1. $13.

1968. **Science for Better Living**. S/N 001-000-00115-9. $13.

1969. **Food for Us All**. S/N 001-000-00116-7. $9.

1970. **Contours of Change**. S/N 001-000-01053-1. $13.

1971. **Good Life for More People.** S/N 001-000-01459-5. $13.

1972. **Landscape for Living.** S/N 001-000-02441-8. $12.

1973. **Handbook for the Home.** S/N 001-000-02960-6. $12.

1974. **Shopper's Guide.** S/N 001-000-03300-0. $11.

1975. **That We May Eat.** S/N 001-000-03471-5. $9.

1976. **Face of Rural America.** S/N 001-000-03521-5. $16.

1977. **Gardening for Food and Fun.** S/N 001-000-03679-3. $12.

1978. **Living on a Few Acres.** S/N 001-000-03809-5. $13.

1979. **What's to Eat?** S/N 001-000-04041-3. $8.50.

1980. **Cutting Energy Costs.** S/N 001-000-04173-8. $12.

1981. **Will There Be Enough Food?** S/N 001-000-04257-2. $7.

1982. **Food from Farm to Table.** S/N 001-000-04298-0. $12.

1983. **Using Our Natural Resources.** S/N 001-000-04387-1. $7.

FORESTRY

Bibliographies

823. Department of Agriculture. **A Selected Bibliography of North American Forestry.** Comp. by E. N. Munns. 2 vols. GPO, 1940. (USDA miscellaneous publication no. 364.) **A1.38:364.**
This standard work lists items published in North America since 1930 in classified arrangement. It is indexed by authors.

824. Forest Service. Northeastern Forest Experiment Station. **A Bibliography on Forest Genetics and Forest Tree Improvement, 1954-55.** 2 vols. GPO, 1956-57. (Station papers 77 and 90.) **A13.42/16:77,90.**

825. Forest Service. **A Bibliography on Forest Genetics and Forest Tree Improvement, 1956-57.** Comp. by Jonathan W. Wright and Raymond F. Finn. GPO, 1960. 85 pp. (USDA miscellaneous publication no. 808.) LC 60-61127. **A1.38:808.**

826. Forest Service. **A Bibliography on Forest Genetics and Forest Tree Improvement, 1958-59.** Comp. by Jonathan W. Wright and Paul O. Rudolf. GPO, 1962. 93 pp. (USDA miscellaneous publication no. 906.) LC 60-61127. **A1.38:906.**
The bibliography was compiled from standard botanical and forestry sources such as *Bibliography of Agriculture* and *Biological Abstracts*. It is arranged alphabetically by author with subject indexes.

827. Forest Service. **Economics of Forestry: A Bibliography for the United States and Canada, 1960-62.** By F. Rumsey. GPO, 1965. 45 pp. (USDA miscellaneous publication no. 1003.) **A1.38:1003.**
Together with entry 830, these bibliographies list nearly nine thousand items on the economics of forestry. None were issued covering the years 1955-59.

828. Forest Service. **Forest Service Films Available on Loan for Educational Purposes**. GPO, 1962- . Irregular. OCLC 5307861. **A13.2:F48**.
This source lists and describes films available from the Forest Service for loan or for sale. It is indexed by title.

829. Forest Service. Pacific Southwest Forest and Range Experiment Station. **Fifty Years of Forestry Research: Annotated Bibliography of the Pacific Southwest Forest and Range Experiment Station, 1926-1975**. Comp. by Vincent P. Aitro. Berkeley, CA: IA, 1977. 250 pp. (General technical report PSW-23.) OCLC 3644546. **A13.88:PSW-23**.
This is an annotated list of publications issued during the first fifty years of the Pacific Southwest Forest and Range Experiment Station, the research branch of the Forest Service in California and Hawaii. The 2,905 publications cited allow tracing of both the growth of the station and trends in forestry and forestry research.

830. National Agricultural Library. **Economics of Forestry: A Bibliography for the United States and Canada, 1940-47**. Comp. by Frances J. Flick and Elizabeth P. Brown. GPO, 1950. 126 pp. (Library list 52.) **A17.17:52**.

———. **Supplement, 1948-1952**. Comp. by Frances J. Flick. GPO, 1955. 136 pp. **A17.17:52/supp.1**.

———. **Supplement, 1953-54**. Comp. by Mary Jackman et al. GPO, 1959. 45 pp. **A17.17:52/supp.2**.

See also SB 86.

Directories

831. Forest Service. **Forest Service Organizational Directory**. GPO, annual. OCLC 01978365. **A13.36:Or3/2/yr**.
Names, addresses, and telephone numbers of individuals in the Forest Service Washington office, state and private forestry areas, regions, and research units are given. This is not a directory of all Forest Service personnel; it lists people responsible for units, key functions, lines of work, and research projects.

832. Forest Service. **Forestry Schools in the United States**. GPO, 1951- . Irregular. LC 52-60486. **A13.2:Sch6/yr**.
Forestry schools are listed alphabetically by state with complete address and official name of academic department. A brief statement for each school gives such information as the degrees granted, major areas of concentration, special requirements, and accreditation by the Society of American Foresters.

Handbooks

833. Forest Service. **Digest of State Forest Fire Laws**. GPO, 1979. 330 pp. OCLC 5398432. S/N 001-001-99489-8. $10. **A13.2:St29/3**.
This digest of state forest fire laws is organized by subject categories. It also includes air pollution laws with relevance to forest fire control.

834. Forest Service. **Eastern Forest Insects**. By Whiteford L. Baker. GPO, 1972. 642 pp., illus. (USDA miscellaneous publication no. 1175.) LC 76-607316. **A1.38:1175**.

This guide to the identification, distribution, host relationships, and life histories of insects occurring in the eastern forests of the United States includes new information available since the 1940 publication of *Insect Enemies of the Eastern Forests*.

835. Forest Service. **A Guide to Common Insects and Diseases of Forest Trees in the Northeastern United States**. GPO, 1979. 127 pp., illus. (Northeastern Area NA-FR-4.) OCLC 5976992. S/N 001-001-00501-1. $6. **A13.102:4**.
This is an identification guide to forest insects and diseases, with some information on weather factors, vertebrate animals, nematodes, and mites. Entries are arranged by the type of trees the insects prey upon and describe and show color photographs of the insects. Common names are used whenever possible. A glossary is included.

836. Forest Service. **Western Forest Insects**. By R. L. Furniss and V. M. Carolin. GPO, 1977 (repr. 1980). 654 pp., illus. (USDA miscellaneous publication no. 1339.) LC 76-600049. S/N 001-000-03618-1. $22. **A1.38:1339/2**.
This supersedes *Insect Enemies of Western Forests*, 1938.

Machine Readable Data

837. Forest Service. Pacific Southwest Forest and Range Experiment Station. **Directory of Selected Forestry-Related Bibliographic Data Bases**. Berkeley, CA: IA, 1979. (General technical report PSW-34.) **A13.88:PSW-34**.

HOME ECONOMICS

838. Agricultural Research Service. **Cheese Varieties and Descriptions**. GPO, 1978. 151 pp. (Agriculture handbook 54.) OCLC 3782268. S/N 001-000-03737-4. $5.50. **A1.76:54/978**.
An expanded version of *Varieties of Cheese: Descriptions and Analyses*, first published in 1908, this mini-encyclopedia of cheese describes characteristics and methods of production. Over three hundred cheese types are listed in dictionary format, with selected references.

839. Children's Bureau. **Homemaker Services: History and Bibliography**. By Maud Morlock. GPO, 1964. 116 pp. (Bureau publication no. 410.) **FS14.111:410**.
Part 1 is a brief summary of the historical development of homemaker services. Part 2 lists 517 bibliographic citations under broad subjects, with detailed annotations. There are author and subject indexes.

840. Department of Agriculture. **Composition of Foods**. GPO, 1978- . Looseleaf. (Agriculture handbook 8.) **A1.76:8-nos**.

> **Baby Foods**. 1978. (Agriculture handbook 8-3.) S/N 001-000-03900-8. $8.
>
> **Breakfast Cereals**. 1982. (Agriculture handbook 8-8.)
> S/N 001-000-04283-1. $7.
>
> **Dairy and Egg Products**. 1976. (Agriculture handbook 8-1.)
> S/N 001-000-03635-1. $7.
>
> **Fats and Oils**. 1979. (Agriculture handbook 8-4.) S/N 001-000-03984-9. $7.
>
> **Fruits and Fruit Juices**. 1982. (Agriculture handbook 8-9.)
> S/N 001-000-04287-4. $9.

> **Pork Products**. 1983. (Agriculture handbook 8-10.) S/N 001-000-04368-4.
> $7.50.
>
> **Poultry Products**. 1979. (Agriculture handbook 8-5.)
> S/N 001-000-04008-1. $9.50.
>
> **Sausages and Luncheon Meats**. 1980. (Agriculture handbook 8-7.)
> S/N 001-000-04183-5. $6.
>
> **Soups, Sauces and Gravies**. 1980. (Agriculture handbook 8-6.)
> S/N 001-000-94114-2. $8.
>
> **Spices and Herbs**. 1977. (Agriculture handbook 8-2.) S/N 001-000-03646-7.
> $6.50.

These handbooks, each covering a major food group, give tabular reference data for specific types of foods. Each page gives the nutrient profile of a single food item—for 100 grams, a cup, a tablespoon, and a pound. Food values are provided for refuse, energy, proximate composition, seven minerals, nine vitamins, fatty acids, cholesterol. phytosterols, and eighteen amino acids. Values are given for the foods in raw, processed, and prepared state.

841.   Department of Agriculture. **Home Economics Research Report**. GPO, 1957- .
        Irregular. **A1.87:nos**.
Both technical and nontechnical works on all aspects of home economics research are listed. Such topics as textiles and clothing, child care, foods and nutrition, and family finances and budgeting are covered.

842.   Department of Agriculture. Office of Governmental and Public Affairs.
        Popular Publications for the Farmer, Suburbanite, Homemaker, Consumer.
        GPO, 1944- . Irregular. (List no. 5.) LC 59-22775. OCLC 08412307.
        A107.12:5.
This is a handy bibliography with wide appeal. Many of the publications listed are available free from the Department of Agriculture.

843.   National Agricultural Library. **Food Science and Technology: A Bibliography
        of Recommended Materials**. Ed. by Richard E. Wallace. IA, 1978. 231 pp.
        OCLC 3816844. **A106.110:F73**.
The bibliography is useful for building a basic collection in any of fourteen subject areas: basic food science and technology; economics and statistics; nutrition; marketing; advertising; packaging; beverages; fruits, vegetables, and nuts; starch, sweeteners, and confectionery; cereals and bakery products; fats and oil; dairy products and egg products; spices, herbs, flavorings, and food additives; and fish, meat and poultry. No annotations are given.

HORTICULTURE

844.   Agency for International Development. **Handbook of Tropical and Subtropical
        Horticulture**. By Ernest Mortensen and Ervin T. Bullard. GPO, 1970. 186 pp.,
        illus. OCLC 1534387. **S18.8:H78/970**.
This handbook was designed to meet the needs of the Agency for International Development, the Peace Corps, and other U.S. personnel involved in foreign assistance programs and to fill the need for consolidated information in ready reference form for the nonspecialist. It is arranged under broad headings such as "Fruits and Tree Crops," "Vegetable Crops," "Insect Control and Vegetables," and "Equipment Supplies and Materials." Names and addresses of sources of plant material, vegetable seed sources, equipment materials, and supplies are given. There is also a handy section on conversion factors, and a bibliography of general reference sources.

845. Agricultural Research Service. **Annotated Index of Registered Fungicides and Nematicides: Their Uses in the United States.** By Edward P. Carter, Daniel O. Betz, and Charles T. Mitchell. GPO, 1969. 1,392 pp. LC 73-604359. **A77.302:F96.**

The purpose of this publication is to "give those persons responsible for providing recommendations for the use of fungicides and nematicides information relating to active ingredients, formulations and patterns of use that have been accepted for Federal registration, and for which labels bearing adequate directions and cautions for the protection of the public are available in channels of trade."

846. Agricultural Research Service. **Insecticides from Plants: A Review of the Literature, 1941-53.** Comp. by Martin Jacobson. GPO, 1958. 299 pp. (Agriculture handbook 154.) **A1.76:154.**

The review includes literature published from 1941 to 1953 with plants grouped by families. It is in classified arrangement with a special chapter on literature cited and is indexed by subjects.

847. Environmental Protection Agency. **Pesticides Abstracts.** GPO, 1974- . Monthly with annual index. LC 74-643215. RA1270.P4H4. 632/.95/04205. OCLC 01793271. **EP5.9:vol./nos.**

Abstracts cover the major worldwide literature on the effects of pesticides and review over two thousand U.S. and foreign sources. Maps are included. This continues *Health Aspects of Pesticides: Abstract Bulletin.*

848. National Agricultural Library. **Sunflower: A Literature Survey, January 1960-June 1967.** Comp. by Merne H. Posey. IA, 1969. 133 pp. (Library list 95.) LC 70-603089. **A17.17:95.**

Intended as a general survey with no attempt at selectivity, this bibliography includes references to material on various aspects of sunflower cultivation and growth in the United States and abroad. It contains listings of books and articles on the growth and uses of the sunflower and on the production of sunflower oil and its by-products. It is arranged alphabetically by author with very brief annotations and is indexed by authors (including joint authors) and subjects.

849. National Agricultural Library. **Toxicity of Herbicides to Mammals, Aquatic Life, Soil Micro-organisms, Beneficial Insects and Cultivated Plants, 1950-65.** Comp. by Patricia A. Condon. IA, 1968. 161 pp. (Library list 87.) **A17.17:87.**

Citations are listed alphabetically by author under broad subjects with author and title indexes.

850. Naval Facilities Engineering Command. **Herbicide Manual for Noncropland Weeds.** GPO, 1971. 205 pp., illus. **D209.14:H41.**

This manual contains practical instructions for the classification, use, and application of herbicides; detailed information regarding specific weed species and site situations; and unique characteristics and properties of specific herbicides suggested for noncropland use.

WILDLIFE MANAGEMENT

851. Council on Environmental Quality. **The Evolution of National Wildlife Law.** GPO, 1977. 485 pp. OCLC 2890451. S/N 041-011-00033-5. $8.50. **PrEx14.2:W64/2.**

This source provides a description and analysis of the evolution and relationships of over a hundred treaties, international agreements, federal statutes, executive orders, and federal regulations related to protection and conservation of wildlife. It covers the legal framework within which wildlife laws developed, major themes of legislation, an examination of three recent comprehensive laws, and an analysis of recent trends.

852. Department of Agriculture. **Beekeeping in the United States.** GPO, 1981. 193 pp., illus. (Agriculture handbook 335.) OCLC 7061654. S/N 001-000-04137-1. $7.50. **A1.76:335/980.**

This is a detailed handbook for beekeepers, which discusses bee behavior, breeding, diseases, and other topics. Not a "beginner's book in the how-to-do-it sense," it does provide beginners and experienced beekeepers with insights into this ancient art.

853. Department of the Interior. Library. **Index to Federal Aid Publications in Sport Fish and Wildlife Restoration and Selected Cooperative Research Project Reports.** IA, 1968. 726 pp. LC 68-62958. **I22.9:F52.**

This cooperative fish and wildlife reference indexing project was initiated in direct response to the expressed needs of federal and state conservation administrators. The purpose of this project was to provide "ready access to the wealth of information contained in the unpublished reports and the publications of the Dingell-Johnson and the Pittman-Robertson programs, as the Federal Aid work in sport fishery and wildlife conservation is popularly known." The proliferation of data necessitated the development of automated reference sources. This index cites published material only, and includes all material available from the beginning of the federal aid programs in the early 1940s through March 1968. Citations are by item numbers under broad subject headings with complete bibliographic data, source, state-federal aid number, list of descriptors, geographic index, and LC classification number for each. There are both English and Latin descriptor indexes, an author index (with corporate authors listed separately at the end), and a geographic index.

854. Fish and Wildlife Service. **Fishery Publications Index, 1955-64; Publications of the Fish and Wildlife Service by Series, Authors, and Subjects.** GPO, 1969. 240 pp. (Circular 296.) LC 76-603664. **I49.4:296.**

This index is a serial list of the numbers issued in each publication series of the Fish and Wildlife Service. Although entries are not annotated, full contents of each publication are listed when several different reports are issued in one volume. Author and subject indexes are included.

855. Fish and Wildlife Service. **Habitat Preservation Abstracts.** IA, 1979- . Irregular. OCLC 6676478. **I49.18:H11.**

Information is given on ecology and technology related to environmental issues affecting fish and wildlife resources and their supporting ecosystems, including coal extraction and conversion, power plants, mineral development, water resource analysis, and information management. It is updated by irregular supplements which are combined with cumulative indexes each year.

856. Fish and Wildlife Service. **National Wildlife Refuges.** GPO, 1955- . Irregular. (Resource publications series.) **I49.66:nos. vary.**

This directory gives data on wildlife refuges maintained as part of the National Wildlife Refuge System. It is arranged alphabetically by state and is well indexed.

857. Fish and Wildlife Service. **Publications of the United States Bureau of Fisheries, 1871-1940.** GPO, 1958. 202 pp. (Special scientific reports—fisheries, no. 284.) **I49.15/2:284.**

858. Fish and Wildlife Service. **Sport Fishery Abstracts.** GPO, 1955- . Quarterly. LC 59-038041. SH1.S82. 799.106173. OCLC 01641708. S/N 024-010-80003-8. $15/yr. **I49.40/2:vol./nos.**
Abstracts of current literature in sport fishery research and management are provided.

859. Fish and Wildlife Service. **Wildlife Abstracts: A Bibliography and Index of the Abstracts in Wildlife Review.** GPO, 1954- . Irregular. OCLC 01561529. 1976-80 ed. 2 vols. S/N 024-010-00644-7. $29 (set). **I49.17/2:yrs.**
This title provides cumulative author, geographic, subject, and systematic indexes to *Wildlife Review*, most recently at five-year intervals.

860. Fish and Wildlife Service. **Wildlife Review.** GPO, 1935- . Quarterly. LC 53-017432. SK351.W58. OCLC 01769882. S/N 024-010-80004-6. $33/yr. **I49.17:vol./nos.**
Wildlife publications issued by the Fish and Wildlife Service are abstracted. Topics such as conservation, plants, and wildlife are included.

861. Fish and Wildlife Service. Bureau of Sport Fisheries and Wildlife. **Bibliography of Research Publications, 1928-1972.** Ed. by Paul H. Eschmeyer and Van T. Harris. GPO, 1974. 154 pp. (Resource publication 120.) **I49.66:120.**
This bibliography resulted from freshwater fishery research and wildlife research sponsored by the Department of the Interior between 1928 and 1972. It is not annotated. Entries are arranged by author under each departmental subunit.

862. Fish and Wildlife Service. Office of Endangered Species. **Liaison Conservation Directory for Endangered and Threatened Species.** IA, 1980. 4th ed. 129 pp. OCLC 6438353. **I49.2:En2/8/980-2.**
This directory of over two hundred fifty federal, state, territorial, and private conservation organizations provides addresses, telephone numbers, and contact people.

863. National Marine Fisheries Service. **Fishery Statistics of the United States.** GPO, 1939- . Annual. (Statistical digest series.) LC 75-640422. SH11.A443. 338.3/72/7092073. OCLC 01798265. **C55.316:nos. vary.**
This is an annual review of U.S. commercial fishery statistics, including volume and value of catches, employment, quantity of gear operated, and number of fishing craft. It also covers processed fish products, freezings, cold storage holdings, and foreign trade and includes drawings of fish and other sea life for identification.

864. National Marine Fisheries Service. **United States Fisheries Systems and Social Science: A Bibliography of Work and Directory of Researchers.** GPO, 1979. 162 pp., maps. OCLC 6139584. **C55.332:So1.**
This source has two parts: a bibliography of unpublished, published, and current reseach among fishermen and in U.S. fishing communities; and a directory of the researchers who have performed this work or who have an interest in these subjects.

865. National Oceanic and Atmospheric Administration. National Marine Fisheries Service. **Fishery Publication Index, 1965-74.** By Mary Ellen Engett and Lee C. Thorson. GPO, 1977. 220 pp. (NOAA technical reports, NMFS circular 400.) OCLC 3082066. **C55.13:NMFS CIRC-400.**
Publications are listed numerically and indexed by author and subject.

866. National Oceanic and Atmospheric Administration. National Marine Fisheries Service. **Fishery Publication Index, 1975-79.** By Lee C. Thorson. GPO, 1981. 117 pp. (NOAA technical reports, NMFS circular 437.) OCLC 07611151. **C55.13:NMFS CIRC 437.**

See also SB 116.

Astronomy

GENERAL WORKS

867. National Aeronautics and Space Administration. **A Bibliography on the Search for Extraterrestrial Intelligence**. By Eugene F. Mallove et al. NTIS, 1978. 132 pp. (NASA reference publication 1021.) OCLC 4757107. **NAS1.61:1021**.

868. National Aeronautics and Space Administration. **Data Bases and Data Base Systems Related to NASA's Aerospace Program: A Bibliography with Indexes**. NTIS, 1981. 511 pp. (NASA SP-7045.) LC 81-603155. OCLC 07899073. **NAS1.21:7045**.
This is a selection of annotated references to unclassified reports and journal articles entered into the NASA scientific and technical information system from 1975 to 1980 in *Scientific and Technical Aerospace Reports* (STAR) and *International Aerospace Abstracts* (IAA).

869. National Aeronautics and Space Administration. **A Meeting with the Universe: Science Discoveries from the Space Program**. GPO, 1981. 221 pp., illus. (EP-177.) OCLC 08433910. S/N 033-000-00836-8. $14. **NAS1.19:177**.
This nontechnical summary of what was learned about the universe as a result of space exploration includes many color photographs.

870. National Aeronautics and Space Administration. **NASA Photography Index**. GPO, annual. **NAS1.43/4:yr**.
This is an index to the photographs available from NASA.

Comets

871. National Aeronautics and Space Administration. **Atlas of Cometary Forms, Structures Near the Nucleus**. GPO, 1969. 128 pp. (NASA SP-198.) **NAS1.21:198**.
"By providing a comprehensive collection of photographs and photoreproductions of worldwide visual observations of comets from 1835 to 1962, this atlas makes available material on which to develop theories both as to the nature of comets and the interactions of comets with the solar corona."

872. National Aeronautics and Space Administration. **Comet Kohoutek: Workshop Held at Marshall Space Flight Center, Huntsville, Alabama, June 13-14, 1974 [With List of References]**. Ed. by Gilmer Allen Gray. GPO, 1975. 272 pp. (NASA SP-355.) **NAS1.21:355.**

The study of Comet Kohoutek has been the most comprehensive and detailed to date. This document provides photographs and text for workshop sessions on tail form, structure, and evaluation; H_2O-related observations; molecules and atoms in the coma and tail; and photometry and radiometry. Appendixes give a list of participants, author index, photograph identification, and comprehensive ephemeris of the comet.

873. National Aeronautics and Space Administration. **The Study of Comets: The Proceedings of IAU Colloquium No. 25, Cosponsored by COSPAR, and Held at Goddard Space Center, Greenbelt, MD, October 28-November 1, 1974**. Ed. by B. Donn et al. 2 pts. GPO, 1976. 1,083 pp. (NASA SP-393.) LC 76-601332. OCLC 2101867. **NAS1.21:393/pt.1,2.**

Planets

874. National Aeronautics and Space Administration. **Advances in Planetary Geology**. NTIS, irregular. (NASA technical memorandum series.) OCLC 08808794. **NAS1.15:nos. vary.**

875. National Aeronautics and Space Administration. **Atlas of Mercury**. By Merton E. Davis et al. GPO, 1978. 128 pp., illus. (NASA SP-423.) OCLC 4142243. S/N 033-000-00695-1. $21. **NAS1.21:423.**

This is a series of photographs of the face of Mercury as seen for the first time as a result of the Mariner 10 mission to Venus and Mercury.

876. National Aeronautics and Space Administration. **A Bibliography of Planetary Geology Principal Investigators and Their Associates, 1980-1981**. Comp. by Joseph M. Boyce. NTIS, 1982. 81 pp. (NASA technical memorandum 84468.) OCLC 08757524. **NAS1.15:84468.**

877. National Aeronautics and Space Administration. **The Martian Landscape**. GPO, 1978. 160 pp., illus. (NASA SP-425.) QB641.V54 1978. 559.9/23/028. OCLC 3868087. **NAS1.21:425.**

Photographs taken of Mars during the Viking landings are presented, along with an anecdotal account of the Viking Program.

878. National Aeronautics and Space Administration. **Mission to Earth: Landsat Views of the World**. By Nicholas M. Short et al. GPO, 1976. 459 pp., illus. (NASA SP-360.) QB637.M57. 910/.02/0222. OCLC 2190153. **NAS1.21:360.**

Landsat color images show the land surface at a scale and resolution that allow many natural and cultural features to be recognized. Forty percent of the images are of the United States. Captions describe well-known geographic points of interest, urban and cultural features, farm and industrial activities, vegetation, and geology. This oversize volume is aimed at a diverse audience: resource specialists, researchers, college and high school teachers, students of geography and geology, outdoorsmen, travelers, and the general public.

Stars

879. Smithsonian Institution. **Smithsonian Astrophysical Observatory Star Catalog: Positions and Proper Motions of 258,997 Stars for Epoch and Equinox of 1950.** 4 pts. GPO, 1966 (repr. 1979). 2,876 pp., illus. S/N 047-000-00006-8. $60 (set). **SI1.2:St2/pt.1-4.**

Part 1. Stars 000-001-073-708 (Bands $+80°$ to $+30°$).

Part 2. Stars 073-709-128-547 (Bands $+20°$ to $+0°$).

Part 3. Stars 128-548-192-333 (Bands $-0°$ to $-20°$).

Part 4. Stars 192-334-258-997 (Bands $-30°$ to $-80°$).

Unidentified Flying Objects

880. Air Force Office of Scientific Research. **UFOs and Related Subjects: An Annotated Bibliography.** By Lynne E. Catoe. GPO, 1969. 401 pp. (AOFSR 68-1656.) (AD 688332.) LC 68-62196. Z5064.F5C37). (Repr.: Gale Research, $36. Also includes *Unidentified Flying Objects.*) **D301.45/19-2:68-1656.**

This is "believed to be the most comprehensive bibliography published" on this subject. It includes books, journal articles, pamphlets, conference proceedings, tapes, original manuscripts of "scholarly intent" in order to make "the bibliography as useful as possible for both scholars and general readers." More than sixteen hundred citations are listed under broad subject headings with annotations ranging in length from one line to several paragraphs. The wide range of fields covered includes the physical sciences, occult sciences, and selected fiction. A separate part contains a selection of recent cartoons on the subject. There is an author index. The 1978 edition of *Unidentified Flying Objects* (Gale Research) includes a supplement dated 1976 by Kay Rodgers.

NAVIGATION

881. Defense Mapping Agency. Hydrographic Center. **American Practical Navigator: An Epitome of Navigation.** 2 vols. IA, 1977. 1,386 pp., illus., maps. (H.O. publication 9.) OCLC 3662622. **D5.317:9/3/v.1,2.**

The first edition of this title was published in 1802 and was revised by Nathaniel Bowditch, the author, several times before his death in 1838. Still commonly referred to as "Bowditch," it is considered the epitome of navigation and has been continuously maintained since 1802. Volume 1 covers fundamentals, piloting and dead reckoning, celestial navigation, the practice of navigation, navigational safety, oceanography, weather, electronics and navigation, and appendixes. Volume 2 gives tables, formulas, data, and instructions for forming many of the computations for dead reckoning, piloting, and celestial navigation.

882. Naval Observatory. Nautical Almanac Office. **The Air Almanac.** GPO, 1952- . Semiannual. LC 52-061239. TL587.A36. 528/.05. OCLC 02257061. July-Dec. 1984 ed. S/N 008-054-00109-2. $12. **D213.7:date.**

This astronomical handbook of data required for air navigation contains data on stars, planets, the moon, and the sky. It is published jointly with Her Majesty's Stationery Office, Great Britain.

883. Naval Observatory. Nautical Almanac Office. **The Astronomical Almanac.** GPO, 1981- . Annual. LC 80-647548. QB8.U6A77. 528. OCLC 6721508. 1984 ed. S/N 008-054-00096-7. $14. **D213.8:yr.**

Precise ephemerides of the sun, moon, planets, and satellites, eclipse data, and data for other astronomical phenomena are provided, with brief explanations. This source is useful for specialists in astronomy, space science, geodesy, surveying, navigation, and other applications. Jointly published with Her Majesty's Stationery Office, it replaces *The American Ephemeris and Nautical Almanac*. Detailed explanations of the bases and derivations of many of the ephemerides are given in *Explanatory Supplement to the Astronomical Ephemeris and to the American Ephemeris and Nautical Almanac* published by Her Majesty's Stationery Office, London.

884. Naval Observatory. Nautical Almanac Office. **The Nautical Almanac for the Year....** GPO, 1960- . Annual. OCLC 01286390. 1985 ed. S/N 008-054-00107-6. $10. **D213.11:yr.**

This almanac contains the astronomical data required for marine navigation and continues *American Nautical Almanac*.

885. Naval Oceanographic Office. **Navigation Dictionary.** GPO, 1969. 2d ed. 292 pp. LC 71-603652. **D203.22:220/969.**

This "comprehensive, authoritative and current dictionary of navigational terms" is designed to serve the needs of the "navigator of any type of craft." Terms in fields related to navigation (i.e., astronomy, meteorology, cartography) are included but defined in the language and from the viewpoint of the navigator. Definitions are clearly understandable for the intelligent, interested layman, and include cross references to related terms. Separate sections cover abbreviations and symbols, and there is a brief bibliography.

See also SB 29.

Biological Sciences

GENERAL WORKS

886. Library of Congress. National Referral Center. **Directory of Information Resources in the United States: Biological Sciences**. GPO, 1972. 577 pp. LC 72-2659. QH303.U5. S/N 030-000-00060-9. $11. **LC1.31:D62/7.**
Each directory in this series gives the organization name, address, telephone number, areas of interest, holdings, publications, and types of information service it is willing to provide.

BOTANY

887. Agricultural Research Service. **Economically Important Foreign Weeds: Potential Problems in the United States**. By Clyde F. Reed. IA, 1977. 746 pp., illus. (Agriculture handbook 498.) OCLC 3053926. **A1.76:498.**
This guide to weed identification to aid in preventing their accidental introduction and establishment includes species descriptions, illustrations, glossary, and bibliography.

888. Agricultural Research Service. **Grass Varieties in the United States**. By A. A. Hanson. GPO, 1972. Rev. ed. 125 pp. (Agriculture handbook 170.) S/N 001-000-02444-2. $6. **A1.76:170/972.**
This guide to named and experimental grasses in the United States is arranged alphabetically by grass name. It gives agencies involved in development of each variety, individuals involved, method of breeding, description, release date, releasing agency, source of seed, and status of certified seed production. There are no illustrations.

889. Agricultural Research Service. **Selected Weeds of the United States**. GPO, 1970 (repr. 1978). 463 pp. (Agricultural handbook 366.) S/N 001-000-00751-3. $11. **A1.76:366.**
This handbook describes 224 species of weeds and shows their geographic distribution.

890. Department of Agriculture. **Geographical Guide to the Floras of the World: An Annotated List with Special Reference to Useful Plants and Common Plant Names**. By Sidney F. Blake. GPO, 1942- . Irregular. (USDA miscellaneous publication nos. 401 and 797.) **A1.38:401,797.**

This annotated bibliography is based on holdings of the National Agricultural Library and includes periodical articles. Volumes are arranged by country and indexed by author and geographic name.

891. Department of Agriculture. **Manual of Grasses of the United States.** By A. S. Hitchcock. Ed. by Agnes Chase. GPO, 1951. 2d rev. ed. 1,051 pp. (USDA miscellaneous publication no. 200.) (Repr.: Peter Smith, $25 for the set.) **A1.38:200/2.**

The manual includes line drawings, identification keys, comprehensive descriptions of species and varieties with both scientific and vernacular names, range of distribution, common uses, and over two hundred pages of synonymy (names of grasses that have previously appeared in the botanical literature).

892. Forest Service. **Atlas of United States Trees.** GPO, 1971- . Irregular. (USDA miscellaneous publication series.) **A1.38:nos. vary.**

> Vol. 1. **Conifers and Important Hardwoods.** By Elbert L. Little. 1971. 10 pp., 310 maps. (USDA miscellaneous publication no. 1146.) S/N 001-000-01026-3. $33.
>
> Vol. 2. **Alaska Trees and Common Shrubs.** 1975. 19 pp., 82 maps. (USDA miscellaneous publication no. 1293.) LC 75-07787. S/N 001-000-03310-7. $6.
>
> Vol. 3. **Minor Western Hardwoods.** 1976. 13 pp., 290 maps. (USDA miscellaneous publication no. 1314.) LC 77-4502. S/N 001-000-03453-7. $18.
>
> Vol. 4. **Minor Eastern Hardwoods.** 1976. 17 pp., 230 maps. (USDA miscellaneous publication no. 1342.) LC 78-80506. S/N 001-000-03641-6. $15.
>
> Vol. 5. **Florida.** 1978. 23 pp., 262 maps. (USDA miscellaneous publication no. 1361.) LC 78-24942. S/N 001-000-03728-5. $6.50.
>
> Vol. 6. **Supplement.** 1981. 37 pp. (USDA miscellaneous publication no. 1410.) S/N 001-000-04242-4. $4.50.

This is an atlas with large maps (and little text) illustrating the natural distribution or range of native tree species of the continental United States. It was planned as a five-volume series; additional volumes on special subjects may be published later. Volume 1 includes an introduction to the series.

893. Forest Service. **Checklist of U.S. Trees: Native and Naturalized.** By Elbert L. Little, Jr. GPO, 1979. 375 pp. (Agriculture handbook 541.) OCLC 5699024. S/N 001-000-03846-0. $13. **A1.76:541.**

This is a compilation of the accepted scientific names and current synonyms, approved common names and other names in use, and the geographic ranges of native and naturalized forest trees in the continental United States. Created to encourage uniform usage of tree names, this checklist is the official standard for tree names in the Forest Service. It is not illustrated.

894. National Agricultural Library. **Linnaeana in the Collection of the National Agricultural Library.** Comp. by Mortimer L. Naftalin. IA, 1968. 43 pp. (Library list 89.) **A17.17:89.**

This is part of a series of bibliographies on the historical books in the National Agricultural Library. It lists monographs that were written by or about the botanist Carl Linnaeus. Citations, arranged chronologically, date from 1735 to 1968 and include a physical description of the book and the NAL call number. It is indexed by authors and subjects.

ZOOLOGY

895. Agricultural Research Service. **A Catalog of the Diptera of America North of Mexico**. GPO, 1965. 1,696 pp. (Agriculture handbook 276.) **A1.76:276**.
This complete catalog of the order Diptera (common houseflies, mosquitoes, etc.) provides references to every known name from 1758 through 1962. Over twenty-five thousand entries are listed. The catalog also contains a detailed bibliography, a list of periodicals, and a name index.

896. Department of Defense. **Poisonous and Venomous Marine Animals of the World**. By Bruce W. Halstead. 3 vols. GPO, 1965-70. LC 65-60000. **D1.2: M33/v.1-3**.
This guide was compiled to "provide a systematic organized source of technical data on marine biotoxicology covering the total world literature from antiquity to modern times" (Preface). Volume 1 covers invertebrates, and volumes 2 and 3 cover vertebrates.

897. Department of the Navy. Bureau of Medicine and Surgery. **Poisonous Snakes of the World: Manual for Use by United States Amphibious Forces**. By Granville M. Moore. GPO, 1968 (repr. 1979). 212 pp., illus. S/N 008-045-00009-7. $12.50. **D206.6/3:Sn1**.
This is an illustrated guide for recognition of the poisonous snakes on each continent, with information on avoiding snakebite, recognizing snake venom poisoning, and treating snakebite.

898. Fish and Wildlife Service. **Migration of Birds**. By Frederick C. Lincoln. Rev. by Steven R. Peterson. GPO, 1979. 119 pp., illus. (Circular 16.) OCLC 5271908. S/N 024-010-00484-3. $6. **I49.4:16/2**.
Frederick C. Lincoln's classic work was first published in 1935, and the revised edition was out of print for years. This updated reissue incorporates new research and illustrations. It is essentially a review of the literature on bird migration through the early 1970s, with an extensive bibliography and color illustrations.

899. Forest Service. **Cavity-Nesting Birds of North American Forests**. By Virgil E. Scott et al. GPO, 1977. 112 pp., illus. (Agriculture handbook 511.) OCLC 3915666. S/N 001-000-03726-9. $5.50. **A1.76:511**.
Habitat, cavity requirements, and food for eighty-five bird species that nest in cavities of dead or dying trees are described. There are color illustrations of each species and maps showing their distribution.

900. Forest Service. **Wood-Inhabiting Insects in Houses**. By Harry B. Moore. IA, 1979. 133 pp., illus. OCLC 6068912. **A13.2:In7/8**.
This guide for homeowners discusses characteristics of signs of infestation, prevention, inspection, and control of wood-destroying insects.

901. National Museum of History and Technology. **Bibliography and Index to the Scientific Contributions of Carl J. Drake for the Years 1914-67**. By Florence A. Ruhoff. GPO, 1968. 81 pp. (Bulletin 267.) LC 68-60954. **SI3.3:267**.
This complete bibliography of the works of entomologist Carl J. Drake is arranged chronologically by date of publication. It includes an index by order, family, genus, and species of the insects he studied.

902. Public Health Service. **Pictorial Keys to Anthropods, Reptiles, Birds and Mammals of Public Health Significance**. GPO, 1969. 192 pp. **FS2.60/7:Ar7/2**.

These thirty pictorial keys were devised by the Public Health Service to teach animal identification to people not specially trained in taxonomy. It covers centipedes, scorpions, ants, earwigs, termites, bats, and other animals of public health significance. Drawings and diagrams are in black and white and vary in format. Schools and libraries, as well as public health trainees, should find these keys to be useful references.

903. Smithsonian Institution. **Bibliography of Catalogs, Lists, Faunal and Other Papers on Butterflies of North America, North of Mexico Arranged by State and Province.** By William D. Field, Cyril F. dos Passos, and John H. Masters. GPO, 1974. 104 pp. (Smithsonian contributions to zoology 157.) LC 73-7549. QL1.S54 no.157. 591.'.08s. **SI1.27:157.**

This is a selective guide to manuals, guides, species lists, and other publications about the butterflies of North America, north of Mexico. Citations are listed by geographic area and include Canada and Greenland. Arrangement is alphabetic by author, with no annotations.

904. Smithsonian Institution. **Monotremes and Marsupials: Reference for Zoological Institutions.** By Larry R. Collins. GPO, 1973. 323 pp., illus. LC 73-5963. QL737.M3C65. 599'.1. S/N 047-000-00263-0. $10. **SI1.2:M75/2.**

This is a comprehensive manual on the care, maintenance, and display of captive monotremes and marsupials. Information given includes species distribution, history in captivity, reproduction, development of the young, parasites, torpidity, enclosure specifications, and diet. The manual includes photographs and a bibliography.

CRYOGENICS

905. National Bureau of Standards. **Publications and Services of the Cryogenics Division, National Bureau of Standards, 1953-1977.** By D. J. Frizen and J. R. Mendenhall. GPO, 1978. 102 pp. (NBS technical note 1005.) OCLC 4152483. S/N 003-003-01920-8. $5.50. **C13.46:1005.**

This is a bibliography of publications, with subject and author indexes. It also lists thermodynamic properties charts, bibliographies, and miscellaneous reports related to cryogenics, along with a description of the NBS Cryogenics Division.

Chemistry

GENERAL WORKS

906. National Technical Information Service. **A Directory of Computer Software Applications: Chemistry, 1970-May 1978.** NTIS, 1978. 114 pp. (PB-280 217.) OCLC 4179616. **C51.11/5:C42/970-78.**
Reports in chemistry that list computer programs and/or their documentation are cited. Software listed pertains to topics such as chemical engineering, analytical chemistry, and physical chemistry. Applications emphasize thermodynamic properties, activation analysis, spectroscopic analysis, orbital and kinetic theory, and pollution control. Bibliographic data and abstracts and subject and corporate author indexes are provided. The computer programs and documentation listed may be purchased from NTIS in hard copy or microfiche.

907. Smithsonian Institution. **Select Bibliography of Chemistry, 1492-1892.** By Henry Carrington Bolton. GPO, 1893. 1,212 pp. (Smithsonian miscellaneous collections, vol. 36.) **SI1.7:36.**

908. Smithsonian Institution. **[Supplement, 1492-1897].** GPO, 1899. 489 pp. (Smithsonian miscellaneous collections, vol. 39.) **SI1.7:39.**

909. Smithsonian Institution. **[Supplement, 1492-1897. Academic Dissertations].** GPO, 1901. 534 pp. (Smithsonian miscellaneous collections, vol. 41.) **SI1.7:41.**

910. Smithsonian Institution. **[Supplement, 1492-1902].** GPO, 1904. 462 pp. (Smithsonian miscellaneous collections, vol. 44.) **SI1.7:44.**
Volume 1 covers the period "from the rise of the literature to the close of 1892," the "independent works and their translations, and does not, as a rule, include academic dissertations or so-called 'reprints' or 'separates'. No attempt has been made to index the voluminous literature of periodicals except in the section of Biography" (Preface). Arrangement is by types of work, that is, bibliographies, dictionaries, history of chemistry, biographies, chemistry, pure and applied, alchemy, and periodicals. There is a very detailed subject index.

Volume 2 is a supplement of works published from 1892 to 1897 and is arranged with the same sections as volume 1. Volume 3 is a bibliography devoted exclusively to academic dissertations of universities in France, Germany, Russia, and the United States. Volume 4 is a supplement of works published from 1897 to 1902, arranged as in volume 1, with dissertations included in a separate section.

ELEMENTS AND COMPOUNDS

Gases

911. Bureau of Mines. **Helium: Bibliography of Technical and Scientific Literature from Its Discovery (1868) to January 1, 1947.** Comp. by Henry P. Wheeler, Jr. and Louise B. Swenarton. GPO, 1952. 76 pp. (Bulletin 484.) LC 52-60982. **I28.3:484.**

912. Bureau of Mines. **Helium: Bibliography of Technical and Scientific Literature from January 1, 1947 to January 1, 1962.** Comp. by Harold W. Lipper and Carla W. Cherry. GPO, 1968. 525 pp. (Information circular 8373.) **I28.27:8373.**

913. Bureau of Mines. **Helium: Bibliography of Technical and Scientific Literature, Including Papers on Alpha-Particles.** GPO, 1969- . Annual. (Information circular series.) **I28.27:nos. vary.**
Citations related to helium and alpha-particles from twelve scientific and technical abstract publications are listed.

914. Public Health Service. **Carbon Monoxide: A Bibliography with Abstracts.** GPO, 1966. 40 pp. (Public health bibliography series, no. 68.) **FS2.21:68.**
This bibliography, international in scope, covers the literature on carbon monoxide from 1880 to 1966. It is arranged by subject with author and geographic indexes.

Isotopes

915. Atomic Energy Commission. **Radioisotopes in World Industry: Abstracts of Selected Foreign Literature.** NTIS, 1961. 141 pp. **Y3.At7:22/TID-6613.**

_____. **Supplement 1.** NTIS, 1961. 120 pp.

_____. **Supplement 2.** NTIS, 1962. 129 pp.

_____. **Supplement 3.** NTIS, 1962. 131 pp.

_____. **Supplement 4.** NTIS, 1963. 163 pp.

_____. **Supplement 5.** NTIS, 1964. 123 pp.

Metals

916. Bureau of Mines. **Bibliography of Zirconium.** GPO, 1957. 281 pp. (Information circular 7771.) **I28.27:7771.**

_____. **Supplement.** GPO, 1958. 216 pp. **I28.27:7830.**

_____. **Supplement.** GPO, 1962. 99 pp. **I28.27:8048.**

The main volume in this series covers the literature about zirconium and hafnium published from 1907 to 1957. References to periodicals, published reports, and patents are included. Each volume has a detailed subject index.

MACHINE READABLE DATA

917.   National Library of Medicine. **CHEMLINE® (Chemical Dictionary Online).** This is a machine readable data file of 900,000 names for chemical substances, representing 450,000 unique compounds. CHEMLINE, created by the NLM in collaboration with Chemical Abstracts Service (CAS), contains such information as CAS registry numbers, molecular formulas, preferred chemical nomenclature, and generic and trivial names. The file may be searched by any of these elements and also by nomenclature fragments and ring structure information, making chemical structure searches possible.

Eleven regional medical libraries, each responsible for a geographic area, coordinate NLM's online search services in the United States. For information on the Online Center nearest you write to Office of Inquiries and Publications Management, National Library of Medicine, 8600 Rockville Pike, Bethesda, MD 20209. In addition, CHEMLINE may be searched from computer terminals at institutions with access to NLM's MEDLINE.

Data Processing

BIBLIOGRAPHIES

918. National Bureau of Standards. **Computer Literature Bibliography, 1946-1963**. Comp. by W. W. Youden. GPO, 1965. 464 pp. (NBS special publication 266.) LC 64-62989. **C13.10:266**.

    _____. **Computer Literature Bibliography, 1964-1967**. Comp. by W. W. Youden. GPO, 1968. 381 pp. (NBS special publication 309.) **C13.10:309**.
Together, the above two bibliographies cite over eleven thousand books, journal articles, and conference proceedings and reports. In each volume, the bibliography is in classified arrangement with author and title indexes.

919. National Bureau of Standards. **Data Abstraction, Databases, and Conceptual Modelling: An Annotated Bibliography**. By Michael L. Brodie. GPO, 1980. 75 pp. (NBS special publication 550-59.) OCLC 6338062. S/N 003-003-02179-2. $5. **C13.10:550-59**.
This is a comprehensive, annotated bibliography on conceptual modeling of dynamic systems of complex data, with emphasis on data abstraction. It lists publications related to programming languages, data base management, artificial intelligence, and software engineering. Items listed deal with terminology, basic concepts, research problems, approaches to data modeling, the integration of approaches, and specification, representation, and verification issues that arise in the design, development, and maintenance of data base applications.

COMPUTER PROGRAMS

920. General Services Administration. Office of Information Resources Management. **Federal Software Exchange Catalog**. NTIS, 1977- . Quarterly. OCLC 3454211. **GS12.14:date**.
This catalog contains abstracts of computer software and documentation submitted by federal agencies to the Federal Software Exchange Center; it includes subject, hardware, and language indexes. Any software listed may be purchased from the center, and technical assistance in implementing software in local systems is available from General Services Administration regional offices listed in the catalog.

921. National Aeronautics and Space Administration. **Computer Program Abstracts**. IA, 1969-81. Quarterly. LC 76-604507. QA76.C5716. 651.8. OCLC 01564604. **NAS1.44:date**.

This source, now discontinued, provided abstracts of documented computer programs developed by or for NASA and the Department of Defense.

922. National Bureau of Standards. **Guide to Computer Program Directories**. Comp. by Addie G. Chattic. GPO, 1977. 167 pp. (NBS special publication 500-22.) LC 77-017610. QC100.U57 no.500-22. 602/.1S. OCLC 3414247. S/N 003-003-01867-8. $6.50. **C13.10:500-22**.

The National Bureau of Standards is responsible for activities that improve the effectiveness of computer use in the federal government. This title contains abstracts of materials in the NBS collection of computer catalogs and directories, which list computer software available from private organizations, universities, and government agencies.

923. National Technical Information Service. **A Directory of Computer Software Applications: Minicomputers and Microcomputers, August 1977-1980**. NTIS, 1980. 189 pp. (PB80-105513.) **C51.11/5:M66/977-80**.

Reports on minicomputers and microcomputers that list computer programs and/or their documentation are cited. Software listed pertains to topics such as electronics, computer graphics, computer-aided instruction, pattern recognition, mathematical modeling, and computer systems programs. The directory provides bibliographic data and abstracts and subject and corporate author indexes. It updates the 1977 edition (PB-272 972), which covered 1970-77. The computer programs and documentation listed may be purchased from NTIS in hard copy or microfiche.

DICTIONARIES

924. Department of the Air Force. 7602nd Air Intelligence Group. **Chinese-English Automation and Computer Technology Dictionary**. San Francisco, CA: IA, 1979. LC 81-602498. OCLC 97598027. **D301.2:C44/v.1**.

EQUIPMENT

925. General Services Administration. Office of Information Resources Management. **Automatic Data Processing Equipment Inventory in the United States Government as of the End of Fiscal Year....** GPO, 1976/77- . Annual. OCLC 03838279. 1982 ed. S/N 022-001-00095-7. $12. **GS12.10:yr**.

See also SB 51.

Earth Sciences

GENERAL WORKS

926. Geological Survey. **Computer Software for Spatial Data Handling**. Ed. by D. F. Marble. 3 vols. Reston, VA: IA, 1980. 1,042 pp., illus. OCLC 7707517. **I19.2:C73/4/v.1-3.**
Programs for manipulation and analysis of spatial data from a variety of disciplines and numerous countries are listed. Each entry includes information on the title, purpose, input and retrieval, manipulation, future development, sample, programming basis/operating information, origin, and availability of the program. Contents are as follows: full geographic information systems (volume 1); data manipulation programs (volume 2); and cartography and graphics (volume 3).

927. Geological Survey. **Minerals, Lands and Geology for the Common Defense and General Welfare**. By Mary C. Rabbitt. 2 vols. GPO, 1979-80. OCLC 4811834. S/N 024-001-03151-5 (vol. 1). $11. S/N 024-001-03362-3 (vol. 2). $11. **I19.2:M66/9/v.1,2.**
This is planned to be a four-volume study relating the development of the U.S. Geological Survey to the broader context of U.S. history, geology, and allied sciences. Volume 1 details events in the United States before the Survey's establishment, during the time when geology was developing as a science. It includes black-and-white photographs and an extensive bibliography. Volume 2 covers 1879 to 1904, the first twenty-five years of the Survey. It depicts a "history of geology in relation to the development of public land, Federal-science, and mapping policies and the development of mineral resources in the United States."

928. National Aeronautics and Space Administration. **Earth Resources**. NTIS, quarterly. (NASA SP-7041.) LC 76-646855. Z6033.A8E18. 016.3337. OCLC 02749463. **NAS1.21:7041/nos.**
Selected, annotated references are given to unclassified reports and journal articles related to remote sensing of earth resources by aircraft and spacecraft. References cited were added to the NASA scientific and technical information system and announced in *Scientific and Technical Aerospace Reports* (STAR) and *International Aerospace Abstracts*.

See also SB 160.

GEOLOGY

Abstracts

929. Geological Survey. **Abstracts of North American Geology**. GPO, 1966-71.
Monthly. **I19.54:date**.
This is a supplement to the annual *Bibliography of North American Geology* for the
period covered. It contains abstracts of technical papers, books, and maps arranged by
author, with a subject index.

930. Geological Survey. **Geophysical Abstracts**. GPO, 1929-71. Monthly.
I19.43:nos.
This source contained abstracts of international literature pertaining to the physics of
the solid earth, physical methods, geological problems, and geophysical exploration.
Each issue was indexed by author, with annual cumulative author and subject indexes
issued separately. Earlier issues were part of the Bureau of Mines *Information Circulars*
series.

Bibliographies

931. Geological Survey. **Bibliography and Index of U.S. Geological Survey
Publications Relating to Coal, 1882-1970**. By Paul Averitt and Lorreda Lopez.
GPO, 1972. 173 pp. (Bulletin 1377.) LC 72-603449. **I19.3:1377**.

_____. **January 1971-June 1974**. By Flora K. Walker. IA, 1975. 14 pp.
(Circular 709.) **I19.4/2:709**.

932. Geological Survey. **Bibliography of North American Geology**. GPO, 1887-1973.
Annual. (Bulletin series.) **I19.3:nos. vary**.
This title listed publications on the geology of the United States, the rest of America,
Greenland, the West Indies, Guam, and other island possessions. After 1973 it was
incorporated into the *Bibliography and Index of Geology* published by the American
Geological Institute. Cumulative editions that have been published follow.

933. Geological Survey. **Geologic Literature on North America, 1785-1918**. By
John M. Nickles. GPO, 1924. (Bulletin 746,747.) **I19.3:746,747**.

934. Geological Survey. **Bibliography of North American Geology, 1919-1928**. GPO,
1931. 1,005 pp. (Bulletin 823.) **I19.3:823**.

935. Geological Survey. **Bibliography of North American Geology, 1929-1939**. GPO,
1944. (Bulletin 937.) **I19.3:937**.

936. Geological Survey. **Bibliography of North American Geology, 1940-1949**. By
R. R. King et al. 2 vols. GPO, 1957. 2,205 pp. (Bulletin 1049.) **I19.3:1049**.

937. Geological Survey. **Bibliography of North American Geology, 1950-1959**. By
R. R. King et al. 4 vols. GPO, 1965. 4,025 pp. (Bulletin 1195.) **I19.3:1195**.
This standard bibliography in the field of North American geology cites journal articles,
books, professional papers, and entries from *Dissertation Abstracts*. Alphabetical
author lists with detailed subject and geographic indexes are provided. Included along
with continental North America are Hawaii, Guam, Greenland, the West Indies, and
Panama.

938. Geological Survey. **Catalogue and Index of Contributions to North American Geology, 1732-1891.** By Nelson H. Darton. GPO, 1896. 1,045 pp. (Bulletin 127.) **I19.3:127.**
"Includes geologic literature published in North America and such literature on North America (excepting Greenland and Central America) wherever published" (Preface). Publications are listed chronologically within headings for authors and subjects. Some entries are annotated; some include references to reviews in professional journals. A list of subject headings used and a list of serials cited are included.

939. Geological Survey. **New Publications of the Geological Survey.** GPO, 1910- . Monthly. **I19.14/4:nos.**
This title updates the permanent catalogs covering 1879-1961 and 1962-1970 as well as the annual catalogs covering 1971 on.

940. Geological Survey. **Publications of the Geological Survey, 1879-1961.** GPO, 1965. 457 pp. **I19.41/1:879-961.**
This volume is a permanent catalog of books, maps, and charts issued by the Geological Survey through December 1961. It consists of lists by types of publications (bulletins, professional papers, water supply papers, etc.) with subject, geographic, and author indexes.

941. Geological Survey. **Publications of the Geological Survey, 1962-1970.** GPO, 1972. 586 pp. **I19.14:962-70.**
This catalog is a permanent supplement to the 1879-1961 publications catalog. It lists publications issued between 1962 and 1970, as well as reports from the 1879-1961 catalog that have since gone out of print.

942. Geological Survey. **Publications of the Geological Survey.** GPO, 1962- . Annual. OCLC 01260816. **I19.41/1:yr.**
A list of books and maps published during the year, this title supplements the two permanent catalogs (entries 940 and 941). It cumulates entries in the monthly *New Publications of the Geological Survey* (entry 939).

Geologic Names

943. Geological Survey. **Geologic Names of North America Introduced in 1936-1955.** By Druid Wilson et al. GPO, 1957. 622 pp. (Bulletin 1056.) **I19.3:1056-A,B.**
The bulletin supplements *Lexicon of Geologic Names* (entry 945) by adding references to the geological names introduced from 1936 to 1955. It includes continental North America plus Greenland, West Indies, and U.S. territories in the Pacific. The index is by the age of the unit, and by the politico-geographic divisions containing the type locality of the unit.

944. Geological Survey. **Geologic Names of the United States through 1975: A Computer List of Geologic Names in Use in the United States and the Major Elements Necessary for Their Definition.** By R. W. Swanson et al. GPO, 1981. 645 pp., illus. (Bulletin 1525.) LC 81-600167. OCLC 08066336. S/N 024-001-03459-0. $9. **I19.3:1535.**

945. Geological Survey. **Lexicon of Geologic Names of the United States (Including Alaska).** By M. G. Wilmarth. 2 vols. GPO, 1938 (repr. 1957). (Bulletin 896.) **I19.3:896.**
Called simply the "Wilmarth lexicon," this comprehensive work lists geological names followed by pertinent data such as age, thickness, formations, and bibliographic

citations. It also includes entries for Canada, Mexico, West Indies, Central America, and Hawaii, but without detailed definitions.

946. Geological Survey. **Lexicon of Geologic Names of the United States for 1936-1960**. By G. C. Keroher et al. 3 vols. GPO, 1966. 4,341 pp. (Bulletin 1200.) **I19.3:1200**.

947. Geological Survey. **Lexicon of Geologic Names of the United States for 1961-1967**. GPO, 1970. 848 pp. (Bulletin 1350.) **I19.3:1350**.
The above two volumes supplement the Wilmarth lexicon covering the United States, its possessions, the trust territory of the Pacific Islands, and the Panama Canal Zone.

948. Geological Survey. **Lexicon of Geologic Names of the United States for 1968-1975**. By Gwendolyn W. Luttrell et al. GPO, 1981. 342 pp. (Bulletin 1521.) LC 81-607034. QE75.B9 no.1520. 557.3s. OCLC 7283755. S/N 024-001-03396-8. $7.50. **I19.3:1520**.
This source lists new geologic names introduced into the literature between 1968 and 1975 for the United States and its possessions.

Machine Readable Data

949. Geological Survey. **Geoindex**. By Patricia Fulton and Harold Johnson. GPO, 1982. 304 pp., illus. (Professional paper 1172.) LC 82-600504. S/N 024-001-03467-1. $8.50. **I19.16:1172**.
A data base index to geologic maps, this title includes the flowcharts, programs, and operational instructions for the data base management system developed by the Geological Survey to facilitate publication of geologic index maps.

HYDROLOGY

Bibliographies

950. Department of the Interior. Water Resources Scientific Information Center. **A Selected Annotated Bibliography on the Analysis of Water Resources Systems**. IA, 1969- . Irregular. (WRSIC-series). OCLC 3184902. **I1.97:nos. vary**.

951. Geological Survey. **Bibliography of Hydrology of the United States and Canada, 1963**. Comp. by J. R. Randolph and R. G. Deike. GPO, 1966. 166 pp. (Water supply paper 1863.) **I19.13:1863**.

952. Geological Survey. **Bibliography of Hydrology of the United States and Canada, 1964**. Comp. by J. R. Randolph, N. M. Baker, and R. G. Deike. GPO, 1969. 232 pp. (Water supply paper 1864.) **I19.13:1864**.

953. Federal Inter-Agency River Basin Committee. **Annotated Bibliography on Hydrology, 1941-1950 (United States and Canada)**. GPO, 1952. 408 pp. (Notes on hydrologic activities, bulletin 5.) **Y3.F31/13:3/5**.

954. Geological Survey. **Annotated Bibliography on Hydrology and Sedimentation, United States and Canada, 1955-58**. By Henry C. Riggs. GPO, 1962. 236 pp. (Water supply paper 1546.) **I19.13:1546**.

The above comprehensive bibliographies are arranged alphabetically by author, indexed by subjects, and not annotated.

955.   Interagency Committee on Water Resources. **Annotated Bibliography on Hydrology (1951-54) and Sedimentation (1950-54), United States and Canada.** GPO, 1956. 207 pp. (Joint hydrology-sedimentation bulletin no. 7.) **Y3.In8/8: 9/7.**

956.   Interagency Committee on Water Resources. **Annotated Bibliography on Hydrology and Sedimentation, 1959-62 (United States and Canada).** GPO, 1964. 323 pp. (Joint hydrology-sedimentation bulletin no. 8.) **Y3.In8/8:9/8.**

957.   Water Resources Council. **Annotated Bibliography on Hydrology and Sedimentation, 1963-1965 (United States and Canada).** GPO, 1969. 527 pp. (Joint hydrology-sedimentation bulletin no. 9.) **Y3.W29:9/9.**
The above bibliographies comprise a complete guide to the literature of hydrology and sedimentation published in the United States and Canada from 1941 through 1965.

958.   National Archives and Records Service. **United States Hydrographic Office Manuscript Charts in the National Archives, 1838-1908.** Comp. by William J. Heynen. IA, 1978. 250 pp. (Special list 43.) OCLC 3728733. **GS4.7:43.**
The Hydrographic Office of the U.S. Navy, established in 1830, is one of three federal agencies engaged in hydrographic surveying and charting. This list describes 4,910 manuscript hydrographic and oceanographic survey charts and cartographic records in the pre-1908 Hydrographic Office holdings of the National Archives. The basic arrangement of entries is geographic, with indexes to subjects, people, places, and ships. Entries give the date of the original survey or chart compilation or receipt. Other textual and cartographic records in Record Group 37 are described briefly in *Inventory of the Records of the Hydrographic Office* (1971).

Indexes and Abstracts

959.   Department of the Interior. **Water Resources Research Catalog.** GPO, 1965- . Annual. LC 65-61526. TC423.W36. 333.9/1/00973. OCLC 2246507. **I1.94:vol.**
This series presents "summary descriptions of current research on water resources problems," and makes available information on what is being done, by whom, and where. Both federally and privately supported projects are described. It is indexed by subjects, investigators, contractors, and supporting agencies.

960.   Department of the Interior. Water Resources Scientific Information Center. **Selected Water Resources Abstracts.** NTIS, 1968- . Semimonthly. TC1.S45. OCLC 01765362. **I1.94/2:date.**
Abstracts of literature on water resources from the life, physical, and social sciences are presented. The engineering and legal aspects of the characteristics, supply, condition, conservation, control, use, and management of water resources are covered. This is available upon request to federal agencies and their contractors and grantees involved with water resources research.

961.   Geological Survey. Office of Water Data Coordination. **Catalog of Information on Water Data: Index to Water-Data Acquisition.** IA, 1979. LC 76-642056. TD223.U535a. 551.4/8/0974. OCLC 2304643. **I19.42/5:no./yr.**
This is a 21-volume index to the catalog, each volume corresponding to one of 21 water resources regions in the United States. The catalog itself is a computerized data file on water data acquisitions activities in the United States, its territories, and possessions,

and some in Canada and Mexico. The catalog does not contain the data, but tells where data are being collected, the types being acquired, and how they may be obtained. The index is a basic resource for coordination and planning water data programs and aids in determining where data are available. The index presents selected information from the catalog as of 1978.

Thesauri

962. Department of the Interior. **Water Resources Thesaurus: A Vocabulary for Indexing and Retrieving the Literature of Water Resources Research and Development.** GPO, 1981. 3d ed. OCLC 07317607. S/N 024-000-00869-0. $10. **I1.2:W29/2/980.**

METEOROLOGY

963. Library of Congress. **Glossary of Polish-English Meteorological Terms.** Comp. by Doman A. Rogoyski. NTIS, 1968. 301 pp. LC 74-5089. QC854.R63.

964. National Technical Information Service. **A Directory of Computer Software Applications: Atmospheric Sciences, 1970-October 1978.** NTIS, 1978. 114 pp. (PB-285 256.) OCLC 4520992. **C51.11/5:At6.**
Reports related to atmospheric sciences that include lists of computer programs and/or their documentation are cited. Software listed is related to topics such as aeronomy, atmospheric motion, meteorological data processing, weather forecasting, meteorological instruments, physical meteorology, and weather modification. Complete bibliographic data and abstracts are included, as well as subject and corporate author indexes. The computer programs and documentation listed may be purchased from NTIS in microfiche or hard copy.

CLIMATOLOGY

General Works

965. Environmental Data and Information Service. **The Interim Climate Data Inventory: A Quick Reference to Selected Climate Data.** By C. F. Ropelewski. IA, 1980. 176 pp. OCLC 77397486. **C55.202:C61/6.**
This is a listing of American and Canadian climate data sets held in federal and state agencies, private industry, and academic institutions represented at the Climate Data Management Workshop, held at Harpers Ferry, West Virginia, May 1979. Information for each data set includes title, parameters, observation period, place, data type, storage media, volume, and holding center. The listings are also available in machine readable data format from the agency. This "interim" inventory is a prototype for a future comprehensive climate data inventory.

966. National Climatic Center. **Selective Guide to Climatic Data Sources.** By Keith D. Butson and Warren L. Hatch. Asheville, NC: IA, 1980. 142 pp., maps. (Key to meteorological records documentation 4.11.) OCLC 6383325. **C55.219:4.11.**
This guide to published and unpublished climatological data identifies publications in which categories of data (temperature, precipitation, wind, humidity, etc.) may be found. It also lists climatological tables, charts, and graphs given in each publication.

967. National Oceanic and Atmospheric Administration. Environmental Data Service. **Annotated Bibliography of Selected Sources on Climate of India, 1940-71.** By Annie B. Grimes. NTIS, 1973. 146 pp. (NOAA technical memorandum EDS BC-107.) **C55.13/2:EDS BC-107.**

968. National Weather Service. **Selected Worldwide Marine Weather Broadcasts.** GPO, 1982- . Annual. QC994.U63. 551.6/9/162. OCLC 08880316. 1984 ed. S/N 003-017-00517-8. $5.50. **C55.119:yr.**

This title, which continues *Worldwide Marine Weather Broadcasts*, gives information on English-language marine weather broadcasts worldwide, and foreign-language broadcasts when English is not available. Information given includes station name, call sign, broadcast times, radio frequencies, and broadcast contents. It is updated by the *Weekly Notice to Mariners* and the quarterly *Mariners Weather Log*.

Atlases

969. Environmental Science Services Administration. **Climatic Atlas of the United States.** GPO, 1968 (repr. 1984). 80 pp. OCLC 9838075. S/N 003-017-00512-7. $12. **C55.22:C61.**

"The purpose of this atlas is to depict the climate of the United States in terms of the distribution and variation of constituent climatic elements." The climate maps present a series of analyses showing the national distribution of mean, normal, and/or extreme temperatures, precipitation, wind, barometric pressure, relative humidity, dewpoint, sunshine, sky cover, heating degree days, solar radiation, and evaporation.

970. National Climatic Center. **Climatic Atlas of the Outer Continental Shelf Waters and Coastal Regions of Alaska.** By William A. Brower, Jr. 3 vols. Asheville, NC: IA, 1977. Illus. OCLC 3712906. **C55.281:Al1/v.1-3.**

The maps, graphs, and tables in this atlas present a detailed climatic profile of the marine and coastal regions of Alaska. Statistics are provided on wind, visibility, present weather, sea level pressure, temperature, clouds, waves, storm surges, tides, sea ice, surface currents, bathymetry, detailed weather, and aviation weather. The three volumes cover the following areas: the Gulf of Alaska, the Bering Sea, and the Chukchi and Beaufort Seas.

971. National Science Foundation. **Meteorological Atlas of International Indian Ocean Expedition.** GPO, 1972. **NS1.2:In2/5/v.1,2.**

    Vol. 1. **Surface Climate of 1963 and 1964.** By C. S. Ramage et al. 171 pp., illus.

    Vol. 2. **Upper Air.** By C. S. Ramage and C. V. R. Raman. 115 pp. , illus. LC 72-600068.

The International Indian Ocean Expedition (1959-65) was a multinational, multi-disciplinary attempt to study the physical and biological characteristics of the "monsoon" ocean.

972. Naval Weather Service Command. **U.S. Navy Marine Climatic Atlas of the World.** GPO, 1974-81. Rev. ed. OCLC 2127983. **D202.2:At6/v.1-9/974.**

    Vol. 1. **North Atlantic Ocean.**

    Vol. 2. **North Pacific Ocean.**

    Vol. 3. **Indian Ocean.**

    Vol. 4. **South Atlantic Ocean.** S/N 008-042-00069-1. $18.

Vol. 5. **South Pacific Ocean**. S/N 008-042-00070-5. $11.

Vol. 6. **Arctic Ocean**.

Vol. 7. **Antarctic Ocean**.

Vol. 8. **The World**.

Vol. 9. **World Wide Means and Standard Deviations**.
S/N 008-042-00072-1. $31.

This series is widely accepted as an authoritative reference for large-scale operational planning and applied research, by presenting a detailed and useful ocean climatology. Maps and graphs depict winds, surface air temperature, sea surface temperature, humidity, precipitation, visibility, cloud cover, ceiling, pressure, waves, and tropical cyclones.

Statistics

973. National Climatic Center. **Climatological Data, National Summary**. Asheville, NC: IA, 1950- . Monthly with annual summary. OCLC 4447360. **C55.214:date**.
This source provides an overall summary of weather across the nation during the time period covered, along with tables showing extremes of temperature and precipitation by states, storm summary, and other surface data; upper air data; and solar radiation data. State data are given for weather station sites.

974. National Climatic Center. **Comparative Climatic Data for the United States**. IA, 1978- . Irregular. LC 79-644434. OCLC 5629209. **C55.202:C61/2/yr**.
Tables of meteorological elements depicting the climatic conditions at about three hundred U.S. sites include observed data such as record high and low temperatures, snowfall, wind speed, humidity, and sunshine, as well as climatological normals. This source could be easily interpreted by a nonspecialist, especially after reading the explanation of tables.

975. National Climatic Center. **Monthly Climatic Data for the World**. IA, 1948- . Monthly. OCLC 4512269. **C55.211:date**.
Compiled from data gathered at weather stations around the world, the tables in this source show pressure, temperature, vapor pressure, precipitation, amount of sunshine, and upper air data for countries and selected cities.

976. Smithsonian Institution. **World Weather Records**. Comp. by Felix Exner et al. Ed. by H. Helm Clayton. GPO, 1927 (repr. 1944). 1,199 pp. (Smithsonian miscellaneous collections, vol. 79.) LC 27-26885. **SI1.7:79**.

———. **Errata**. GPO, 1929. 29 pp.

977. Smithsonian Institution. **World Weather Records, 1921-30**. Comp. by G. C. Simpson et al. Ed. by H. Helm Clayton. GPO, 1934. 616 pp. (Smithsonian miscellaneous collections, vol. 90.) LC 27-26885. **SI1.7:90**.

978. Smithsonian Institution. **World Weather Records, 1931-40**. Comp. by H. Helm Clayton and Frances L. Clayton. GPO, 1947. 646 pp. (Smithsonian miscellaneous collections, vol. 105.) LC 47-32329. **SI1.7:105**.

979. Weather Bureau. **World Weather Records, 1941-50**. GPO, 1959. 1,361 pp. LC 27-26885. **C30.2:W89/941-50**.

980. Weather Bureau. **World Weather Records, 1951-60.** 6 vols. GPO. LC 27-26885. **C30.2:W89/951-60/v.1-6.**

These volumes form a complete listing of weather records from the earliest times through 1960. Statistics are given in tabular form. The 1951-60 edition is in volumes by geographic areas.

981. National Climatic Center. **World Weather Records, 1961-1970.** GPO, 1979- . OCLC 5998211. **C55.281:W89/961-70/vol.**

Vol. 1. **North America.** 1979. 290 pp. S/N 003-018-00096-2. $7.

Vol. 2. **Europe.** 1979. 488 pp. S/N 003-018-00101-2. $8.

Vol. 3. **West Indies, South and Central America.** 1982. 442 pp. S/N 003-018-00108-0. $8.

This is the sixth issue in this series, which has offered data for ten-year periods from 1920 and before. It provides monthly averages of station pressure, sea level pressure, temperature, and precipitation for weather stations worldwide.

MINERALOGY

982. Bureau of Mines. **Mineral Facts and Problems.** GPO, 1956- . Quinquennial. (Bulletin series.) TN23.U425. OCLC 1779113. **I28.3:nos. vary.**

This standard reference on mineral commodities in the United States and abroad gives information on projected U.S. and world minerals requirements, appraisal of resources and reserves, stockpiles, tariffs and duties, depletion allowances, regulations, and research. Since 1980 this source has covered nonfuel minerals only, because the Department of Energy has responsibility for the fuel data.

983. Bureau of Mines. **Minerals Yearbook.** GPO, 1932- . Annual. LC 33-26551. TN23.U612. 338.2/0973. OCLC 01847412. **I28.37:yr./vol.**

This standard work is a comprehensive review of U.S. and foreign mineralogical and metallurgical developments, techniques, production, and trade. The federal government has reported annually on mineral industry activities through this series since 1882. It discusses the performance of the worldwide mineral industry during the previous year, and gives background information for interpreting developments. In three volumes, it gives information on metallic and nonmetallic mineral commodities important to the U.S. economy; area reports for the states, outlying areas, and Puerto Rico; and the latest mineral data for over 130 foreign countries.

See also SB 99.

OCEANOGRAPHY

General Works

984. Defense Mapping Agency. **Gazetteer of Undersea Features: Names Approved by the United States Board on Geographic Names.** IA, 1981. 3d ed. 125 pp. OCLC 08122798. **D5.319:Un2.**

This source provides a list of names of undersea features of the world, approved by the U.S. Board on Geographic Names. Undersea features are parts of the ocean floor or seabed with measurable relief which can be delimited by relief.

985. Library of Congress. National Referral Center. **Directory of Information Resources in the United States: Geosciences and Oceanography**. GPO, 1981. 395 pp. LC 81-607045. S/N 030-000-00131-1. $8.50. **LC1.31:Oc2**.

This directory is the first in this series issued since 1974. The data base from which the series is compiled is available for online computer searching through DOE/RECON of the Department of Energy. For this directory, "geosciences" and "oceanography" have been broadly defined. Each directory listing gives organization name, address, telephone number, interests, holdings, publications, and types of information services it is willing to share.

986. National Oceanic and Atmospheric Administration. Office of Ocean Engineering. **NOAA Diving Manual: Diving for Science and Technology**. Ed. by James W. Miller. GPO, 1979. 2d ed. 550 pp., illus. LC 79-015578. VM981.U6228 1979. 797.2/3/0235. OCLC 5029060. S/N 003-017-00468-6. $17. **C55.8: D64/979**.

Instructions, recommendations, and advice are given on a broad range of diving conditions and situations. Emphasis is on diving at depths of less than 250 feet. Applied diving technology needed to perform scientific studies and many of the tasks required of the working diver are discussed, with photographs and illustrations.

987. National Oceanographic Data Center. **Computer Programs in Marine Science**. By Mary A. Firestone. GPO, 1976. 225 pp. (Key to oceanographic records documentation 5.) OCLC 2282681. **C55.219/3:5**.

Abstracts of seven hundred computer programs from ten countries give program description, language, hardware, and contact address. Many of these programs are available from NTIS, GPO, and other sources.

See also SB 32 and SB 260.

Dictionaries

988. National Oceanographic Data Center. **Annotated Acronyms and Abbreviations of Marine Science Related International Organizations**. By Charlotte M. Ashby. IA, 1976. 2d ed. 113 pp. OCLC 2174549. **C55.292:Ac7**.

Created to assist marine scientists in identifying acronyms and abbreviations of organizations, programs, projects and expeditions, and miscellaneous terms, this dictionary also defines the terms and describes the names listed. It includes an alphabetic index of the abbreviations and acronyms and a full title index.

Navigation

989. Coast Guard. **Light List**. 5 vols. GPO, 1976- . Annual. LC 82-3992. OCLC 2923471. **TD5.9:vol./yr.**

Vol. 1. **Atlantic Coast of the United States**. Covers 1st, 3d, and 5th Coast Guard Districts.

Vol. 2. **Atlantic and Gulf Coast**. Covers 7th and 8th Coast Guard Districts.

Vol. 3. **Pacific Coast**. Covers 11th, 12th, 13th, 14th, and 17th Coast Guard Districts.

Vol. 4. **Great Lakes**. Covers 9th Coast Guard District.

Vol. 5. **Mississippi River**. Covers 2d Coast Guard District.

These are listings of lights, fog signals, buoys, daybeacons, radio-beacons, and U.S. racon and loran stations on the Pacific coast of the United States and Pacific islands, and those maintained by British Columbia between the U.S. coast and Alaska. They are not intended to substitute for charts and coast pilots used in navigation. The information is updated weekly by the *Notice to Mariners* or the *Local Notice to Mariners*.

990. National Ocean Survey. **United States Coast Pilot**. 9 vols. GPO, 1960- . Annual. OCLC 02406894. **C55.422:vol./ed.**

> Vol. 1. **Atlantic Coast: Eastport to Cape Cod.**
>
> Vol. 2. **Atlantic Coast: Cape Cod to Sandy Hook.**
>
> Vol. 3. **Atlantic Coast: Sandy Hook to Cape Henry.**
>
> Vol. 4. **Atlantic Coast: Cape Henry to Key West.**
>
> Vol. 5. **Atlantic Coast, Gulf of Mexico, Puerto Rico and Virgin Islands.**
>
> Vol. 6. **Great Lakes: Lakes Ontario, Erie, Huron, Michigan and Superior and St. Lawrence River.**
>
> Vol. 7. **Pacific Coast and Hawaii.**
>
> Vol. 8. **Alaska: Dixon Entrance to Cape Spencer.**
>
> Vol. 9. **Pacific and Arctic Coasts; Alaska, Cape Spencer to Beaufort Sea.**

Coast Pilots are a series of nine nautical manuals with information on U.S. coastal and intracoastal waters and the Great Lakes. Most of this information cannot be graphically depicted on standard nautical charts, and is not readily available elsewhere. Subjects covered include navigation regulations, outstanding landmarks, channel and anchorage peculiarities, dangers, weather, ice, freshets, routes, pilotage, and port facilities.

Oceanographic Ships

991. Naval Oceanographic Data Center. **Oceanographic Vessels of the World**. 3 vols. GPO, 1964-66. LC 62-61003. **D203.24:G-2.**
Vessels are listed alphabetically by countries with information such as year built, length, tonnage, displacement, equipment on board, and the like. A glossary, list of abbreviations, a symbol chart, and an index of ships are also included.

992. Naval Oceanography Command. **Oceanographic Ship Operating Schedules**. IA, 1961/62- . Annual. LC 82-5591. OCLC 1761010. **D201.2:Sch2/yr.**
The purpose of this publication is "to encourage coordination of cruises among agencies, increase the direct exchange of information in areas of mutual interest, and where feasible, lead to the accommodation of instrumentation and scientific personnel for certain cruises so that all available platforms are fully utilized."

Tides

993. National Ocean Survey. **Tidal Current Tables: Atlantic Coast of North America**. GPO, 1890- . Annual. OCLC 2458466. **C55.425:yr.**

994. National Ocean Survey. **Tidal Current Tables: Pacific Coast of North America and Asia**. GPO, 1898- . Annual. LC 22-26900. **C55.425/2:yr.**
There are two volumes in this series, which has been published since the 1890s: one for the Atlantic coast and the other for the Pacific coast of the United States. Each gives

daily predictions of times of slack water and of flood and ebb currents, with velocities of strength for the latter.

995. National Ocean Survey. **Tide Tables: High and Low Water Predictions.** 4 vols. GPO, 1853- . Annual. LC 84-43183. OCLC 2458504.

> **East Coast of North and South America, including Greenland. C55.421/2: yr./ed.**

> **West Coast of North and South America, including the Hawaiian Islands. C55.421:yr./ed.**

> **Central and Western Pacific Ocean and Indian Ocean. C55.421/4:yr./ed.**

> **Europe and West Coast of Africa, including Mediterranean Sea. C55.421/3:yr./ed.**

Tide Tables predict the daily times and heights of high and low waters for a number of reference stations. They include, in addition to the tables, a bibliography of publications related to tides and currents and an index map of the tide table coverage.

PALEONTOLOGY

Bibliographies

996. Geological Survey. **A Bibliographic Index of North American Carboniferous Invertebrates.** By Stuart Weller. GPO, 1898. 653 pp. (Bulletin 153.) **I19.3:153.** The first part of this volume contains a list of the titles of references cited, first arranged chronologically and then arranged by authors. Following the bibliography is a tabulation of the genera of each class with the number of species in each genus. The second part is the bibliographic list, in which all North American carboniferous genera of invertebrates have been arranged alphabetically (with species arranged alphabetically under each genus).

997. Geological Survey. **Bibliography and Catalogue of the Fossil Vertebrata of North America.** By Oliver P. Hay. GPO, 1902. 868 pp. (Bulletin 179.) **I19.3:179.**
"The purpose of this bibliography and catalogue is to present a list of all the species of fossil vertebrates which have been described, up to the end of the year 1900, from all that part of the continent of North America lying north of Mexico, and to furnish a guide to the literature relating to all these extinct forms of organized beings" (Preface). The work is arranged by author with subject indexes. It is supplemented by *Second Bibliography and Catalogue of the Fossil Vertebrata of North America* (Washington, DC: Carnegie Institute, 1929-30. 2 vols.) and *Bibliography of Fossil Vertebrates* (New York: Geological Society of America, 1928- . Quinquennial.)

998. Geological Survey. **A Bibliography of Paleozoic Crustacea from 1698 to 1889, including a List of North American Species and a Systematic Arrangement of Genera.** By A. W. Vodges. GPO, 1890. 177 pp. (Bulletin 63.) **I19.3:63.**
Part 1, an author list, includes a brief index of the genera described in each work. Part 2 is a catalog of the North American Paleozoic trilobites. Part 3, the nontrilobitic Paleozoic crustacea, includes a list of species.

Fossil Indexes

999. Geological Survey. **A Catalogue of the Cretaceous and Tertiary Plants of North America.** By F. H. Knowlton. GPO, 1898. 247 pp. (Bulletin 152.) **I19.3:152.**
In this catalog, the entire flora is in one alphabetical arrangement with original data and place of publication for each genus and species. Lists of the most important references are also given for species. A bibliography of sources published in North America is included.

1000. Geological Survey. **A Catalogue of the Mesozoic and Cenezoic Plants of North America.** By F. H. Knowlton. GPO, 1919. 815 pp. (Bulletin 696.) **I19.3:696.**

———. **Supplement, 1919-1937.** By R. S. LaMotte. GPO, 1944. 330 pp. (Bulletin 924.) **I19.3:924.**
This volume excludes Mexico and Greenland in its definition of North America. It gives the original place and date of publication for each genus included, followed by the most important references, especially those that refer to descriptions and figures. Additional information includes a bibliography of sources, index of genera and families, and floral lists. The supplement brings the catalog up to date to 1937 in the same format as the main volume.

1001. Geological Survey. **Index of Generic Names of Fossil Plants, 1820-1965.** By Henry N. Andrews. GPO, 1970. 354 pp. (Bulletin 1300.) LC 76-604645. **I19.3:1300.**
The index includes generic names of fossil plants, exclusive of the diatoms, that have been published from 1820 through 1965. It is based on the Geological Survey's Compendium Index of Paleobotany and its accompanying bibliography. A lengthy bibliography presents the full citations of references indicated in the index.

1002. Geological Survey. **Index of Generic Names of Fossil Plants, 1966-73.** By Anna M. Blazer. GPO, 1975. 54 pp. (Bulletin 1396.) **I19.3:1396.**

1003. Geological Survey. **Index of Generic Names of Fossil Plants, 1974-1978.** By Arthur D. Watt. GPO, 1982. 63 pp. (Bulletin 1517.) LC 80-606811. OCLC 07178058. **I19.3:1517.**

1004. Geological Survey. **Index to the Known Fossil Insects of the World, including Myriapods and Arachnids.** By S. H. Scudder. GPO, 1891. 744 pp. (Bulletin 71.) **I19.3:71.**
This is a compilation of the card catalog kept by the author for twenty years prior to the publication of this volume. Cross references from one form of an insect name to another are provided. Entries under each insect name are chronological.

1005. Smithsonian Institution. **Catalog of the Type Specimens of Invertebrate Fossils.** GPO, 1968- . Irregular. (Smithsonian contributions to paleobiology.) **SI1.30:nos. vary.**
This series lists specimens in the Smithsonian Institution Division of Invertebrate Paleontology. Each issue lists specimens in a specific class.

SEISMOLOGY

1006. Environmental Data and Information Service. **Directory of World Seismograph Stations. Vol. 1. The Americas.** By Barbara B. Poppe. IA, 1980. 465 pp. (World Data Center A for Solid Earth Geophysics report, SE-25.) OCLC 7252587. **C55.220/5:25.**
Stations in the United States, Canada, and Bermuda are listed.

1007. Environmental Data and Information Service. **Earthquake History of the United States.** Ed. by Jerry L. Coffman and Carl A. Von Hake. GPO, 1970 (repr. 1982 with supplement 1971-80). 276 pp. (Publication 41.) S/N 003-017-00507-1. **C55.228:41-1/2.**
A nontechnical history of significant U.S. earthquakes from historical times through 1980, this title describes major, intermediate, and minor earthquakes, and includes a section on Puerto Rico. It is not a complete listing of earthquakes, but only those of intensity V or higher. It includes bibliographies, photographs, and tables.

1008. Geological Survey. **United States Earthquakes.** GPO, 1928- . Annual. LC 75-640209. QE535.2.U6U55. 551.2/2/0973. OCLC 01798128. **I19.65/2:yr.**
This series contains detailed technical information for each earthquake registered in the United States and regions under its jurisdiction during the year. It includes samples of seismographs and tilt-graph readings and photographs, and detailed damage descriptions.

Energy

GENERAL WORKS

Annuals

1009. Energy Information Administration. **International Energy Annual**. GPO, 1979- . Annual. LC 82-641118. OCLC 07138645. **E3.11/20:yr**.
Current data and trends for production, consumption, stocks, imports, and exports for primary energy commodities in over 190 countries are provided. Also included are crude petroleum and petroleum products prices in selected countries.

Bibliographies

1010. Department of Energy. **Energy Education Materials Inventory**. GPO, 1978. 293 pp. OCLC 4369013. S/N 061-000-00183-2. $8.50. **E1.28:HCP/M8685-01**.
This is volume 1 of a systematic listing of energy education materials and reference sources useful in elementary and secondary schools. It provides brief annotations, source and grade level, audiovisual materials, instructional materials, and activities.

1011. Department of Energy. **Passive Solar Design: An Extensive Bibliography**. NTIS, 1979. 199 pp. LC 79-602299. Z5853.S63A15 1978. 016.62147. OCLC 6089667. **E1.28:HCP/M4113-03**.
This is a comprehensive bibliography on passive heating and cooling solar design techniques.

1012. Department of Energy. Solar Energy Research Institute. **Solar Energy Legal Bibliography**. By Dwight Seeley et al. NTIS, 1979. 160 pp. OCLC 5417735. **E1.28:SERI/TR-62-069**.
The bibliography includes abstracts of 160 items published before October 1980 related to solar energy development and the law. Legal barriers and incentives to solar energy development are emphasized. Availability sources are noted. This bibliography is periodically updated in issues of the *Solar Law Reporter*.

See also SB 9, SB 303, SB 304, SB 305, and SB 306.

Indexes and Abstracts

1013. Department of Energy. Technical Information Center. **Energy Abstracts for Policy Analysis.** GPO, 1975- . Monthly. LC 75-644221. TJ163.2.E45. 333.7. OCLC 02241695. S/N 061-000-80003-4. $72/yr. **E1.ll:vol./nos.**
This source focuses on nontechnical and semitechnical documents on energy analysis and development, including programs; policy, legislation, and regulation; social, economic, and environmental impacts; and regional and sectoral analyses. It provides abstracts of congressional, federal agency, state, local, and regional reports and books, periodicals, and publications of industry and academia.

1014. Department of Energy. Technical Information Center. **Energy Research Abstracts.** GPO, 1977- . Semimonthly. LC 78-642308. Z5853.P83U544b. 621. OCLC 03568399. S/N 061-000-80002-6. $165/yr. **E1.17:vol./nos.**
Abstracted and indexed are all technical reports, articles, conference papers and proceedings, books, patents, and theses of the Department of Energy, its laboratories, energy centers, and contractors. Other U.S. government-sponsored publications and international literature in energy areas are also abstracted. Subject areas covered include energy systems, conservation, safety, environmental protection, physical research, biology, medicine, reactor technology, radioactive waste processing and storage, and nuclear fusion technology.

1015. Energy Information Administration. **EIA Data Index: An Abstract Journal.** GPO, 1980- . Semiannual. OCLC 07181609. **E3.27/5:date.**
Individual tables, graphs, and other formatted data reported in Energy Information Administration statistical publications are indexed and abstracted. Subject areas covered include energy production, consumption, price, resource availability, and supply and demand projections.

1016. Energy Information Administration. **EIA Publications Directory: A User's Guide.** GPO, 1980- . Quarterly, with the 4th issue being the annual cumulation. LC 80-645059. OCLC 06307287. **E3.27:date.**
This publication is a merger of *EIA Publications Directory* and *EIA Publications Directory Supplement*. It contains abstracts of Energy Information Administration publications.

1017. National Aeronautics and Space Administration. **Energy.** NTIS, 1974- . Quarterly. (NASA SP-7043.) LC 74-647980. Z7914.F8E53. 016.621042. OCLC 01796233. **NAS1.21:7043(nos.).**
This is a selection of annotated references to unclassified reports and journal articles related to energy sources, solar energy, energy conservation, transport, and storage. Items listed were added to the NASA scientific and technical information system, and announced in *Scientific and Technical Aerospace Reports* (STAR) and *International Aerospace Abstracts*.

1018. National Technical Information Service. **A Directory of Computer Software Applications: Energy, 1977-1980.** NTIS, 1980. 305 pp. (PB80-105497.) OCLC 4016616. **C51.11/5:En2/977-80.**
Computer programs and/or their documentation in energy are cited. Software listed includes applications to solar, geothermal, and nuclear energy; petroleum and natural gas resources; batteries; electrohydrodynamic and magnetohydrodynamic generators; and hydroelectric power production. Applications include simulation and modeling, calculations of future energy requirements, calculations of energy conservation

measures, and computations of economic considerations of energy systems. Bibliographic data and abstracts and subject and corporate author indexes are provided. This updates the 1977 edition (PB-264 200) covering 1974-76. The software listed may be purchased from NTIS in hard copy or microfiche.

Directories

1019. Department of Energy. Office of Consumer Affairs. **Consumer Energy Atlas.** GPO, 1980. 251 pp., illus. LC 80-603744. OCLC 7059547. S/N 061-000-00445-9. $8. **E1.33/2:10879-01.**
An aid to consumers in finding answers to energy-related questions, this publication lists executives, federal and congressional offices, state agencies, national energy organizations, and energy publications.

1020. Department of Energy. Solar Energy Research Institute. **National Solar Energy Education Directory.** By Kevin O'Connor et al. GPO, 1979. 279 pp. OCLC 4856221. **E1.28:SERI/SP-42-141.**

1021. Energy Information Administration. **Energy Information Directory.** GPO, 1980- . Semiannual. LC 80-645421. HD9502.U5UE526. 025.4/933379/0973. OCLC 06168403. **E3.33:date.**
Energy information sources in the Department of Energy and other federal agencies are identified, with individual names and addresses arranged topically.

1022. Federal Energy Administration. National Energy Information Center. **Federal Energy Information Locator System: Energy Information in the Federal Government.** IA, 1976. 458 pp. OCLC 2709116. **FE1.24:976.**
This manual was developed to help people seeking specific energy data to quickly locate relevant agencies, programs, data files, or publications. It may be used as a single directory for energy information being collected by federal agencies. It describes the Federal Energy Information Locator System (FEILS), which identifies sources of energy data in the government and acts as a user's guide to the system.

Machine Readable Data

1023. Department of Energy. **DOE Energy Data Base.**
This data base of world scientific and technical literature on energy covers solar and geothermal energy, fuels, nuclear and fusion energy, electric power engineering, and many other subjects. Abstracts are included. The data base is available on magnetic tape from the National Technical Information Service and from commercial vendors (BRS, SDC, and Lockheed DIALOG). It is also accessible via the Department of Energy's online system, DOE/RECON.

1024. Department of Energy. **FEDEX (the Federal Energy Data Index).**
This is a machine readable bibliographic file containing indexes and abstracts of Energy Information Administration (EIA) publications. The EIA publishes materials related to energy production, consumption, prices, availability of energy resources, and supply and demand projections. Two publications are generated from the FEDEX data file: *EIA Publications Directory: A User's Guide*, which contains abstracts of EIA publications, and *EIA Data Index: An Abstract Journal*, with abstracts of tables and graphs.

FEDEX can be searched online through the Department of Energy DOE/RECON system and commercially through BRS. Individual FEDEX searches are also available through the National Energy Information Center Affiliate, University of New Mexico, 2500 Central Ave., S.E., Albuquerque, NM 87131; (505) 846-2383.

Thesauri

1025. Department of Energy. Technical Information Center. **Energy Information Data Base: Subject Thesaurus**. NTIS, 1979. 864 pp. (DOE/TIC-7000-R4.) OCLC 4371660. **E1.55:979**.
This is a thesaurus of terms in the Department of Energy indexes and abstracts, the DOE Energy Data Base, and DOE/RECON. The terminology reflects the scope of DOE's mission, including terms from the basic sciences, energy resources, conservation, safety, environment, and regulations. Other manuals and guides for the Energy Data Base are: *Serial Titles*, *Energy Categories*, *Permutated Listing*, *Magnetic Tape Description*, and *Guide to Abstracting and Indexing*.

1026. National Technical Information Service. **Integrated Energy Vocabulary, 1976.** NTIS, 1976. 447 pp. (PB-259 000.) OCLC 2782304. **C51.2:V85/976**.
This thesaurus of thirty thousand terms related to energy research and development represents the largest vocabulary of its kind and one of the few integrated energy vocabularies ever compiled.

Engineering

AERONAUTICAL AND SPACE ENGINEERING

General Works

1027.	Library of Congress. National Referral Center. **Directory of Information Resources in the United States: Physical Sciences, Engineering.** GPO, 1971. 803 pp. LC 78-611209. Q223.U526 1971. S/N 030-000-00040-4. $13. **LC1.31:D62/6.**
This is the sixth in the series compiled by the National Referral Center under the general title *Directory of Information Resources in the United States.* It gives name, address, telephone number, areas of interest, holdings, publications, and types of information services available.

See also SB 222 and SB 297.

Abstracts

1028.	National Aeronautics and Space Administration. **A Selected Listing of NASA Scientific and Technical Reports.** IA, 1963- . Annual. (NASA SP series.) LC 64-61468. TL501.U5894. OCLC 3960324. **NAS1.21:nos. vary.**

1029.	National Aeronautics and Space Administration. **Significant NASA Inventions Available for Licensing in Foreign Countries.** GPO, 1981. 137 pp., illus. (NASA SP-7038(06).) S/N 033-000-00821-0. $6. **NAS1.21:7038(06).**
Abstracts are given, with drawings, for NASA-owned inventions available for licensing in certain foreign countries. Each abstract gives a name and address for obtaining further information on the invention. The publication also reprints NASA's foreign patent licensing regulations.

1030. National Aeronautics and Space Administration. Scientific and Technical Information Branch. **Aeronautical Engineering**. NTIS, 1970- . Monthly with annual cumulative index. (NASA SP-7037.) LC 71-613342. Z5063.A2A28. 016.62913. OCLC 01664053. **NAS1.21:7037(nos.).**

Selected, annotated references are given to classified reports and journal articles related to engineering, design, and operation of aircraft and their components. Items listed were added to the NASA scientific and technical information system and announced in *Scientific and Technical Aerospace Reports* (STAR) and *International Aerospace Abstracts*.

1031. National Aeronautics and Space Administration. Scientific and Technical Information Branch. **Scientific and Technical Aerospace Reports**. GPO, 1963- . Semimonthly. LC 64-39060. OCLC 1645472. S/N 033-000-80004-5. $100/yr. (Subscription does not include semiannual and annual cumulative indexes.) **NAS1.9/4:date**.

This title covers all aspects of aeronautics and space research and development, supporting basic and applied research and applications, aerospace aspects of earth resources, energy development, conservation, oceanography, environmental protection, and urban transportation. It abstracts and indexes technical reports of NASA, NASA contractors and grantees, federal government agencies, universities, private firms, and U.S. and foreign institutions; translations in report form; NASA-owned patents and patent applications; and dissertations. It is usually referred to as "STAR." Related resources are NASA/RECON (computerized data base) and the *NASA Thesaurus*.

1032. National Aeronautics and Space Administration. Scientific and Technical Information Branch. **NASA Patent Abstracts Bibliography**. NTIS, 1979- . Semiannual. (NASA SP-7039.) OCLC 04820173. **NAS1.21:7039/(nos.).**

This is an abstract and index to NASA-owned patents and patent applications. The items listed were published in *Scientific and Technical Aerospace Reports* (STAR) since 1969. Patents may be searched by subject, inventors, inventing organization, Patent Office class number, and other identifying numbers.

Bibliographies

1033. Air Force Office of Scientific Research. **Air Force Scientific Research Bibliography, 1959-1965**. 8 vols. GPO, 1961-70. LC 61-60038. **D301.45/19-2:700/v.1-8**.

This series contains "abstracts of all technical notes, technical reports, journal articles, books, symposium proceedings and monographs produced and published by scientists supported in whole or in part by the Air Force Office of Scientific Research."

1034. Library of Congress. Map Division. **Aviation Cartography: A Historico-Bibliographic Study of Aeronautical Charts**. By Walter W. Ristow. GPO, 1960. 2d ed., rev. and enl. 245 pp. LC 60-61621. Z6026.A2U54 1960. Free from the Central Services Division, Library of Congress, Washington, DC 20540. **LC5.2:Av5/960**.

Part 1 is a review of the history of aviation cartography from 1888 through 1959. Part 2 is a bibliography listing 774 works alphabetically by author. The work is indexed by subjects.

1035. Library of Congress. Science and Technology Division. **Space Science and Technology Books, 1957-1961: A Bibliography with Contents Noted**. GPO, 1962. 133 pp. LC 62-60086. Z5064.A8U53. Free from the Central Services Division, Library of Congress, Washington, DC 20540. **LC33.2:Sp1**.

This bibliography lists, by country, works on space law, international cooperation in space exploration, and general works. It is indexed by authors and subjects.

1036. National Advisory Committee for Aeronautics. **Bibliography of Aeronautics, 1909-1932**. 14 vols. GPO, 1921-36. **Y3.N21/5:7/yr.**
Volumes 1-3 covered the years 1909-21. Thereafter, annual volumes were published. It is continued by entry 1041.

1037. National Aeronautics and Space Administration. **Aerospace Bibliography**. GPO, 1982. 7th ed. 140 pp. (EP-48.) S/N 033-000-00866-0. $6. **NAS1.19:48/4**.
This is an annotated bibliography of materials on space flight and space science for use of elementary and secondary school teachers and general adult readers; it gives the reading level for titles. Materials listed were published between 1971 and 1980.

1038. National Aeronautics and Space Administration. **Bibliography of Space Books and Articles from Non-Aerospace Journals, 1957-1977**. By John J. Looney. GPO, 1980. 243 pp. LC 80-601815. Z5065.U5L66. OCLC 6181366. **NAS1.9/2: Sp1/957-77**.
This source represents a first attempt to compile a bibliography of nonspecialized, secondary literature related to NASA and space flight, with an emphasis on pre-1970 literature. It is an unannotated bibliography of articles from nonaerospace science and technology journals and nontechnical literature of the humanities and social sciences. Literature on aeronautics is excluded.

1039. Office of Air Force History. **An Aerospace Bibliography**. Comp. by Samuel Duncan Miller. GPO, 1978. 2d ed. 341 pp. Z6725.U5M54 1978. 016.3584/ 00973. OCLC 3966222. **D301.62/2:Ae8**.
This is a briefly annotated bibliography covering Air Force aviation, military aviation, and aviation in general. It has three appendixes: bibliography of bibliographies, reference works, and guide to documentary collections.

1040. Smithsonian Institution. **Bibliography of Aeronautics**. Comp. by Paul Brockett. GPO, 1910. 940 pp. (Smithsonian miscellaneous collections, vol. 55.) **SI1.7:55**.
This major bibliography on the beginnings of aeronautics covers works published up to 1909. It lists over thirteen thousand books and indexes articles in two hundred periodicals.

1041. Works Progress Administration. **Bibliography of Aeronautics**. 50 pts. GPO, 1936-41. **FW4.29:nos.** and **Y3.W89/2:60/nos.**
This continues entry 1036.

Dictionaries

1042. Library of Congress. **Chinese-English Technical Dictionaries. Volume 1. Aviation and Space**. NTIS, 1969. 694 pp. (AD 681397.) LC 71-600441. TL509.U674.

Machine Readable Data

1043. National Aeronautics and Space Administration. **NASA/RECON**.
The NASA computerized data file provides bibliographic citations for documents related to aeronautics and space worldwide. NASA/RECON is an online, interactive

computerized search and retrieval system, which allows users at remote locations to directly access the NASA central data base. The major publications searchable on NASA/RECON are: *Scientific and Technical Aerospace Reports* (STAR), *International Aerospace Abstracts, Limited Scientific and Technical Aerospace Reports, Computer Program Abstracts*, and *NASA Tech Briefs* plus the NASA contracts data file and the NASA library collection.

History of Aeronautics

1044. National Aeronautics and Space Administration. **Aeronautics and Astronautics: An American Chronology of Science and Technology in the Exploration of Space, 1915-1960**. By Eugene M. Emme. GPO, 1961. 240 pp. **NAS1.2:Ae8/915-60**.
This is a chronology of major achievements in space and aeronautical engineering, technology, and development.

1045. National Aeronautics and Space Administration. **Astronautics and Aeronautics**. GPO, 1963- . Annual. (NASA SP series.) TL521.3.A8A3. OCLC 03490304. **NAS1.21:nos. vary**.
This is a chronology on science, technology, and policy related to aeronautics and space activities.

1046. National Aeronautics and Space Administration. **History of Aeronautics and Astronautics: A Preliminary Bibliography**. NTIS, 1969. 421 pp. (NASA HHR-29.)

1047. National Aeronautics and Space Administration. **Sixty Years of Aeronautical Research, 1917-1977**. By David A. Anderton. GPO, 1978. 89 pp., illus. (EP-148.) OCLC 4477174. S/N 033-000-00736-1. $5.50. **NAS1.19:145**.
This overview of major events in U.S. aeronautical research begins with the construction of the Langley Research Center in 1917, the first federally funded aeronautical research laboratory in the United States. This historical review is written in a popular style and has many photographs.

Space Exploration

1048. Congress. House. Committee on Science and Technology. **Astronauts and Cosmonauts Biographical and Statistical Data**. Prep. by Congressional Research Service. GPO, 1983. 341 pp. S/N 052-070-05856-1. $6. **Y4.Sci2:98/J**.
Data are provided on NASA astronauts active between 1959 and 1983, including astronaut candidates and Soviet cosmonauts, with a black-and-white photograph of each.

1049. National Aeronautics and Space Administration. **Chariots for Apollo: A History of Manned Lunar Spacecraft**. By Courtney G. Brooks, James M. Grimwood, and Lloyd S. Swenson, Jr. GPO, 1979. 538 pp., illus. (NASA SP-4205.) TL789.8.U6A5239. 629.45/4. OCLC 4664449. S/N 033-000-00768-0. $12. **NAS1.21:4205**.
This narrative history of Apollo, the U.S. program to land men on the moon, covers the period from the establishment of NASA to Apollo 11, and the first moon landing in 1969. Phases of spacecraft evolution are covered. It is illustrated, with a detailed bibliography.

CIVIL ENGINEERING

1050. National Bureau of Standards. Institute for Applied Technology. **Standards Referenced in Selected Building Codes**. By Bertram M. Vogel. NTIS, 1976. 427 pp. (NBSIR 76-1140.) OCLC 2637211. **C13.58:76-1140.**
Standards referenced in building codes of the three model building code organizations, the twenty states with mandatory or voluntary codes, and the thirty largest U.S. cities are compiled. Standards, dates, titles, and the codes referencing them are identified.

1051. National Technical Information Service. **A Directory of Computer Software Applications: Civil and Structural Engineering, 1978-September 1980.** NTIS, 1981. 116 pp. (PB80-217540.) OCLC 04179700. **C51.ll/5:C49/978-80.**
Reports in civil and structural engineering that list computer programs and/or their documentation are cited. Software listed pertains to topics such as highway construction, dams, harbor engineering, construction management, soil stabilization, rock mechanics, and the dynamics and statics of structures. Bibliographic information and abstracts and subject and corporate author indexes are provided. The computer programs and documentation listed may be purchased from NTIS in hard copy or microfiche. This continues the 1978 edition (PB-278 125), which covered 1970-March 1978.

ELECTRONICS AND ELECTRICAL ENGINEERING

1052. National Technical Information Service. **A Directory of Computer Software Applications: Electrical and Electronics Engineering, 1970-September 1978.** NTIS, 1978. 126 pp. (PB-284 924.) OCLC 4520862. **C51.11/5:El2.**
Reports on electrical and electronics engineering that list computer programs and/or their documentation are cited. Software cited is related to topics such as computer-aided design and computer-aided analysis of electrical and electronic materials, components, and systems. Bibliographic data and abstracts, as well as subject and corporate author indexes, are included. The computer programs and documentation listed may be purchased from NTIS in hard copy or microfiche.

MARINE ENGINEERING

1053. National Technical Information Service. **A Directory of Computer Software Applications: Marine Engineering, 1970-April 1979.** NTIS, 1979. 60 pp. (PB-294 014.) OCLC 5150156. **C51.11/5:M33.**
Reports related to marine engineering that include lists of computer programs and/or their documentation are cited. Software listed is related to topics such as ship hull design, propeller design, hydrodynamics of ship motion and mooring cables, and ship maintenance management. Bibliographic information and abstracts are included, as well as subject and corporate author indexes. The computer programs and documentation listed may be purchased from NTIS in hard copy or microfiche.

MILITARY AND NAVAL ENGINEERING

1054. Air University. Library. **Air University Library Index to Military Periodicals.** Maxwell Field, AL: IA, 1949- . Quarterly with annual cumulative issues. LC 51-4277. OCLC 02500050. **D301.26/2:date.**
This index is available to libraries only. It is a subject index to periodical articles, including news items and editorials, from English-language military and aeronautical periodicals that are not indexed in other standard periodical indexes. Annual and triennial cumulations are published.

1055. Department of the Air Force. **United States Air Force Dictionary.** Ed. by Woodford Agee Helflin. GPO, 1956. 578 pp. LC 56-61737. **D301.2:D56.**

———. **Addenda.** GPO, 1957. 4 pp.
More than sixteen thousand terms are defined, many with quotations to illustrate the definitions.

1056. Joint Chiefs of Staff. **Department of Defense Dictionary of Military and Associated Terms.** GPO, 1984. OCLC 5385010. S/N 008-004-00020-0. $12. **D5.12:1/11.**
This dictionary was produced to aid standardization and dissemination of military terminology. All terms have Department of Defense or joint service interest and usage, specific military significance, and are not already adequately defined in standard dictionaries. All terms are unclassified and show a code for the agency using them. Weapons terms are for modern weapons only.

1057. National Technical Information Service. **A Directory of Computer Software Applications: Detection and Countermeasures, 1970-July 1979.** NTIS, 1979. 84 pp. OCLC 5357937. **C51.11/5:D48.**
Reports on detection and countermeasures that list computer programs and/or their documentation are cited. Software cited is related to topics such as radar, infrared, acoustic, optical, magnetic, and seismic detection, target acquisition, tracking and signatures, signal processing, detection countermeasures, and nuclear explosion detection. Bibliographic information, abstracts, and corporate author and subject indexes are included. The computer programs and documentation listed may be purchased from NTIS in hard copy or microfiche.

NUCLEAR ENGINEERING

1058. Department of Defense [and] Energy Research and Development Administration. **Effects of Nuclear Weapons.** By Samuel Glasstone and Phillip J. Dolan. GPO, 1977 (repr. 1983). 3d ed. 653 pp., illus. OCLC 3570296. S/N 008-046-00093-0. $17. **D1.2:N88/2.**

1059. Library of Congress. Science and Technology Division. **Nuclear Science in Mainland China: A Selected Bibliography.** By Chi Wang. GPO, 1968. 70 pp. LC 68-62146. Z7144.N8W3. Free to U.S. libraries and institutions from the Central Services Division, Library of Congress, Washington, DC 20540. **LC33.2:C44/4.**
This reference guide consists of a selection of titles of research reports, studies, articles, and other informative materials for preliminary research on nuclear science in Mainland China. Part 1 lists items in Chinese with emphasis on works published between 1950 and

1966. Part 2 contains items in other languages, primarily English, from 1964 to 1967. Items are numbered and listed under broad subject headings. Brief annotations are provided for most entries. There are indexes by authors and subjects and a list of Chinese journals cited.

1060. Oak Ridge National Laboratory. **Nuclear War Survival Skills.** By C. H. Kearny. NTIS, 1979. 244 pp., illus., maps. OCLC 5525694. **E1.28:ORNL-5037.**
This first comprehensive handbook of survival information for untrained citizens wanting to improve their changes of surviving a nuclear attack includes chapters on psychological preparations, warning and communications, evacuation, shelters, and medical care.

See also SB 200.

PUBLIC SAFETY ENGINEERING

Civil Defense

1061. Office of Civil Defense. **Abbreviations and Definitions of Terms Used in Civil Defense Training.** IA, 1971. (MP-51.) **D119.11:51/2.**
This source is for use primarily in OCD national training programs, to "assist in the understanding and standardization of many civil defense terms."

Fire Safety

1062. Fire Administration. **Fire Technology Abstracts.** GPO, 1976- . Bimonthly with annual cumulative index. LC 77-641909. TH9111.F79. 628.9205. OCLC 03220341. **FEM1.109:date.**
Abstracts of applied fire literature from books, journals, reports, patents, codes, and standards are given, primarily in the English language, with selected items from the world fire literature.

1063. Forest Service. **Fire: Summary of Literature in the United States from the Mid-1920s to 1966.** By Charles T. Cushwa. IA, 1968. 117 pp. **A13.63/13-12:F51**.
"This summarizes literature concerning properties, uses, and effects of controlled and uncontrolled fire, from the mid 1920s to the present published mainly in the United States." It is arranged alphabetically by author with a complete subject index, but is not annotated.

1064. National Bureau of Standards. Institute for Applied Technology. **Fire Research Specialists: A Directory.** By Nora H. Jason. NTIS, 1977. 133 pp. (NBSIR 77-1264.) OCLC 3336267. **C13.58:77-1264.**
Specialists in the United States and Canada are listed, with affiliation, address, and telephone number.

Motor Vehicle Safety

1065. National Highway Traffic Safety Administration. **Safety Related Recall Campaigns for Motor Vehicles and Motor Vehicle Equipment, including Tires.** GPO, 1980- . Quarterly with annual cumulations. OCLC 07498758. **TD8.9/2: date.**

Specific recall campaigns are listed by names of companies, with precise descriptions of the motor vehicles being recalled, including model, year, number of vehicles recalled and description of defect. This continues *Motor Vehicle Safety Defect Recall Campaigns.*

Natural Disasters

1066.   Department of Housing and Urban Development. **Directory of Disaster Related Technology, A to Z.** By Ugo Morelli and Maria del Sart. GPO, 1975. 829 pp. LC 75-600019. **HH1.2:D63/5.**
This compendium of research related to disaster preparedness, assistance, mitigation, and hazard reduction of natural disasters covers 1970-75, with abstracts for each citation.

Environmental Sciences

GENERAL WORKS

1067. Department of the Air Force. **Environmental/Socioeconomic Data Sources.** By John Kavaliunas. IA, 1976. 170 pp., illus., maps. OCLC 2831060. **D301.6/5:En8**.
Published jointly by the Air Force and the Census Bureau, this is a guide to statistical sources for environmental and socioeconomic planning and decision making. It discusses which tables and reports may provide the data to answer specific questions.

1068. Department of Defense. **Glossary of Environmental Terms (Terrestrial).** GPO, 1968. 149 pp. (Military standard 1165.) **D7.10:1165**.
The purpose of this glossary is "to facilitate the exchange of information within the broad field of environmental engineering, by providing a common vocabulary for use in this field." It is intended primarily for use by engineers, technicians, contractors, and administrators who are involved in "developmental and testing activities involving an aspect of the terrestrial environment but who are not specialists in the sciences that treat these subjects." Its scope is limited to terms which refer to "environments on the land surfaces of the earth and adjacent portions of the oceans and lower atmosphere that have a direct effect on surface conditions." Definitions are technical and contain source symbols explained in the back of the volume.

1069. Department of the Interior. Office of Library and Information Services. **Information Sources and Services Directory.** IA, 1979. 365 pp. OCLC 4916760. **I1.2:In3/2**.
Information products and services available to the public from the Department of the Interior and its field offices are listed. Information given for each subagency includes address, telephone number, information products and services, subject coverage, time span covered, and geographic coverage. Information products and services listed include specialized library collections, information and referral services, records management, and computer data files.

1070. Environmental Protection Agency. **EPA Environmental Modeling Catalogue.** IA, 1979. 229 pp., illus. OCLC 5365657. **EP1.2:En8/25**.
This compilation of most of the major environmental models used by the EPA includes descriptions of mathematical models for air pollution, water quality, water runoff,

economics, and others. It gives an overview, functional capabilities, basic consumptions, input and output, system resource requirements, applications, contact people, and references.

1071. Environmental Protection Agency. **U.S. Directory of Environmental Sources.** NTIS, 1979. 3d ed. 861 pp. (EPA 840-79-010.) OCLC 2908234. **EP1.2: Un3/10/979.**
This is a directory of sources of environmental information that were registered with the U.S. International Environmental Referral Center. Intended to aid in location of information sources, it lists government, academic, association, and commercial sources, giving address. telephone number, telex and cable, descriptions of available information, funding sources, geographic limitations, and language.

1072. Environmental Protection Agency. Library Systems Branch. **EPA Publications Bibliography.** NTIS, 1977- . Quarterly. Fourth quarterly issue includes annual cumulative indexes. LC 79-644595. Z5863.P7U58a. 016.3637. OCLC 03806538. **EP1.21/7:date.**
Bibliographic citations and abstracts are provided for reports generated by the EPA and added to the NTIS collection. Indexes are by report title, subjects, authors, contract numbers, and accession/report numbers. This updates the *EPA Cumulative Bibliography, 1970-1976* (PB-265 920).

1073. Federal Committee on Research Natural Areas. **A Directory of Research Natural Areas on Federal Lands of the United States of America.** GPO, 1968. 129 pp. LC 68-61218. **Y3.F31/19:9/968.**
More than three hundred natural areas set aside on federal lands for scientific and educational purposes are described. This directory was designed to serve as (1) an inventory of the research natural areas already established, (2) a means of determining what additional areas are needed, and (3) an announcement of the availability of these natural areas for appropriate use of scientists and educators. It is arranged by primary type of area and then alphabetically by name, and includes a list of areas by state and indexes to common names and scientific names.

1074. Fish and Wildlife Service. Office of Biological Services. **Coastal Marsh Productivity: A Bibliography.** By J. D. Bagur. IA, 1977. 300 pp. OCLC 4067608. **I49.18:C64.**
This is an annotated bibliography covering marshes and marsh vegetation, productivity of plants, detritus in the food chain, marsh estuaries as fish haven, and marshes as wildlife habitat and feeding grounds.

1075. National Technical Information Service. **A Directory of Computer Software Applications: Environmental Pollution and Control, 1977-1980.** NTIS, 1980. 200 pp. (PB80-105505.) **C51.11/5:En8.**
Environmental reports that include lists of computer programs and/or their documentation are cited. Software listed is related to topics such as air and water pollution, noise levels, radioactive releases, and solid waste disposal. Bibliographic data and abstracts are included, as well as subject and corporate author indexes. The computer programs and documentation listed may be purchased from NTIS in hard copy or microfiche. This continues the 1977 edition (PB-270 018), which covered 1970-77.

1076. Peace Corps. **Glossary of Environmental Terms: Spanish-English, English-Spanish.** Comp. by Richard E. Saunier. IA, 1976. 202 pp. (Program and training journal reprint series, no. 17.) OCLC 3761707. **AA4.10:17.**

AIR POLLUTION

1077. Library of Congress. Technical Information Division. **Air Pollution Bibliography.** 2 vols. 1957-59. LC 57-60050. Z6673.A4. (Repr.: Kraus, $35.) **LC36.10:Ai7.**
"Consists of references on the administrative, economic, engineering, legal, medical, and physical-chemical aspects of air pollution and its control" (Introduction). Included are works from 1952 through 1957/58. Citations, with abstracts, are arranged by authors with subject, geographic, and author indexes in volume 1 and a cumulative subject index in volume 2.

1078. National Air Pollution Control Administration. **Hydrocarbons and Air Pollution: An Annotated Bibliography.** 2 vols. GPO, 1970. (AP-75.) LC 78-610871. **HE20.1309:75/v.1-2.**
"This bibliography represents an effort to collect, condense and organize the literature on hydrocarbons in relation to air pollution. The approximately 2,300 documents abstracted here ... are from recent literature (1959-1970)" (Introduction). Entries are in classified arrangement with accession number, authors, title, imprint information, and abstract for each citation. The following indexes are included: subject, geographic, author, and title.

1079. Public Health Service. **Air Pollution Publications: A Selected Bibliography.** 3 vols. GPO, 1964-69. 870 pp. LC 63-60159. **FS2.24:Ai7/v.1-3.**
Each volume in this series cites approximately one thousand sources and is in classified arrangement with author and subject indexes.

1080. Public Health Service. **Handbook of Air Pollution.** By James P. Sheehy, William C. Achinger, and Regina A. Simon. GPO, 1968. 259 pp. (PHS publication no. 999-AP-44.) LC 68-62587. **FS2.300:AP-44.**
This work was designed to consolidate the applicable portions of numerous references concerning the characteristics of atmospheric pollutants and data of a general nature such as mathematics and conversion factors.

See also SB 46.

CONSERVATION

1081. Agricultural Research Service. **Abstracts of Recent Published Materials on Soil and Water Conservation.** GPO, 1949- . Irregular. (ARS series.) **A77.15:41-nos.**
This is a source of summaries of recently published information about soil and water conservation. Abstracts cover watershed management, water management, basic soil problems, erosion control, soil management, plant management, economic and social problems, biology, and soil surveys. An author index is provided in each issue since April 1965. A cumulative index for numbers 9-21 was published in 1963 (A77.15:41-59). Numbers 1-8 are indexed separately.

1082. Department of the Interior. **Conservation Yearbooks.** GPO, 1965-79. **I.95:no.**
No. 1. **Quest for Quality.** 1965. 96 pp. S/N 024-000-00022-2. **I1.2:Q3.**
No. 2. **Population Challenge: What It Means to America.** 1966. 80 pp. S/N 024-000-00444-9. $7.
No. 3. **Third Wave: America's New Conservation.** 1967. 128 pp. S/N 024-000-00445-7. $8.50.

No. 4. **Man: An Endangered Species?** 1968. 100 pp. S/N 024-000-00446-5. $7.50.

No. 5. **It's Your World: The Grassroots Conservation Story.** 1969. 96 pp. S/N 024-000-00447-3. $7.50.

No. 6. **River of Life, Water: The Environment Challenge.** 1970. 96 pp. S/N 024-000-00537-2. $7.

No. 7. **Our Living Land: Department of the Interior Environmental Report.** 1971. 96 pp.

No. 8. **Our Environment and Our Natural Resources: Indivisibly One.** 1972. 96 pp.

No. 9. **In Touch with People.** 1973. 128 pp.

No. 10. **Our Natural Resources: The Choices Ahead.** 1974. 130 pp. S/N 024-000-00808-8. $8.50.

No. 11. **America 200: The Legacy of Our Land.** 1976. 160 pp.

No. 12. **Living with Our Environment.** 1978-79. 120 pp. S/N 024-000-00845-2. $8.

1083. Forest Service. **Wilderness Management.** By John C. Hendee, George H. Stankey, and Robert C. Lucas. GPO, 1978. 381 pp., illus. (USDA miscellaneous publication no. 1365.) OCLC 4534654. S/N 001-001-00438-3. $14. **A1.38:1365.**
This is a manual for proper management of wilderness areas, including the national forests, national parks, and wildlife refuges. It is the first manual to focus on wilderness management and the decisions facing wilderness managers. It is not a policy manual, but sets forth principles and basic concepts that apply to all wildernesses.

1084. Forest Service. Northeastern Forest Experiment Station. **Annotated Bibliography on the Ecology and Reclamation of Drastically Disturbed Areas.** By Miroslaw N. Czapowskyj. Broomall, PA: IA, 1976. 98 pp. (General technical report NE-21.) OCLC 2437613. **A13.88:NE-21.**
Important research literature on ecology of lands disturbed by surface mining is compiled, with emphasis on those demonstrating ways to improve the environment and on projects in coal regions of the United States. Abstracts are included.

1085. Soil Conservation Service. **Conservation Districts.** IA, 1973- . Annual. Maps. OCLC 2731644. **A57.2:C76/23/yr.**
Nearly three thousand conservation districts are listed by states, with statistics for acreage, number of farms, and general location (according to counties).

1086. Soil Conservation Service. **Engineering Field Manual for Conservation Practices.** GPO, 1975. 1,070 pp., illus. **A57.6/2:En3/3/975.**

1087. Soil Conservation Service. **National Handbook of Conservation Practices.** GPO, 1977. 278 pp. S/N 001-007-00903-1. $11. **A57.6/2:C76/2/978.**
This source gives official names, definitions, national standards, and specifications or guides to specifications for soil and water conservation. The standards are based on research, field trials, and experience.

See also SB 238.

WASTE DISPOSAL

1088. Environmental Protection Agency. **Directory of Federal Coordinating Groups for Toxic Substances**. IA, 1980. 2d ed. OCLC 6629880. **EP1.79/2:80-008**.
The directory lists committees, task forces, and other groups performing coordinative functions in conjunction with federal toxic substances control and testing agencies, including group members and how to contact them. Federal, state, nonprofit, and private groups are included, but no international groups.

1089. Environmental Protection Agency. **Movement of Hazardous Substances in Soil: A Bibliography**. By Emily D. Capenhaver and Benita K. Wilkinson. 2 vols. NTIS, 1979. OCLC 5961483. **EP1.23/6:600/9-79-024a,b**.
Publications issued between 1970 and 1974 related to disposal of hazardous wastes on land (other than sewage sludge) are included. About half of the entries include abstracts. Volume 1 covers selected metals; volume 2 deals with pesticides.

1090. Geological Survey. **Subsurface Waste Disposal by Means of Wells: A Selective Annotated Bibliography**. By Donald R. Rima, Edith B. Chase, and Beverly M. Myers. GPO, 1971. 305 pp. (Water supply paper 2020.) LC 77-179486. **I19.13:2020**.
"This bibliography was prepared to gather significant references into a single publication that would be a reference source for both scientific and waste-management needs" (Introduction). It contains 692 abstracts compiled from a selective review of the literature through 1959, with subject and geographic indexes.

1091. Interagency Regulatory Liaison Group. **Publications on Toxic Substances: A Descriptive Listing**. GPO, 1979. 96 pp. OCLC 5827644. S/N 052-011-00226-7. $4.50. **Y3.R26/2:10T66**.
This is a bibliography of publications and audiovisual productions on toxic substances in the home, at work, on the farm, and in the environment. Most items cited are free, and each is available from one of four federal agencies: Food and Drug Administration, Occupational Safety and Health Administration, Environmental Protection Agency, and Consumer Product Safety Commission. Most items listed are pamphlets and arc aimed at the general public.

1092. National Highway Traffic Safety Administration. **Emergency Action Guide for Selected Hazardous Materials**. IA, 1978. 75 pp., illus. OCLC 4618495. **TD8.8:H33/978**.
This is a guide to action during the first thirty minutes after a spill of toxic, volatile, gaseous, or flammable material. For each of forty-four materials, a description is given of potential hazards; action for spills, fires, and first aid; evacuation; and water pollution controls.

1093. Public Health Service. **Refuse Collection and Disposal: A Bibliography, 1941-50**. By Ralph J. VanDerwerker and Leo Weaver. GPO, 1951. 90 pp. (Public health bibliography series, no. 4.) LC 53-60514. **FS2.21:4**.

———. **Supplements A-F, 1951-63**. 6 vols. GPO, 1952-67.
Citations are given by authors under broad subjects. Annotations, author, subject, and geographic indexes are also provided.

WATER POLLUTION

1094.   Environmental Protection Agency. **Fish Kills Caused by Pollution: Fifteen-Year Summary, 1961-1975.** IA, 1979. TD223.A26. 626.168. OCLC 1443613. **EP2.24: 961-75.**

This fifteen-year summary of information from federal fish kill publications contains an analysis of voluntarily reported data on number of incidents, number of fish killed, average size of kill, and the largest kills reported. It also gives the number of incidents for each pollution source.

1095.   Environmental Protection Agency. **Fish Kills Caused by Pollution in [year].** IA, 1975- . Annual. LC 79-643529. OCLC 05157062. **EP2.24:yr.**

The annual fish kill reports are based on voluntary reporting by state and local agencies. The reports analyze data on number of incidents, number of fish killed, average size of kills, and details on the largest kills reported. The number of incidents is also listed by pollution source.

1096.   Environmental Protection Agency. **Water Quality Management Directory.** IA, 1980. 4th ed. LC 77-641488. 363.6/1. OCLC 3276577. **EP1.2:W29/35/980.**

Agencies and people directly involved in water quality management programs at state, regional, and local levels are listed, as are recipients of grant awards.

1097.   National Oceanic and Atmospheric Administration. **Marine Ecosystems Analysis Program: Bibliography of New York Bight.** 2 pts. GPO, 1974. 677 pp. LC 74-601342. **C55.26:N42y/pt.1,2.**

The New York Bight is a coastal marine area extending from Long Island to New Jersey, from the coastline to the edge of the Continental Shelf. This retrospective bibliography, with emphasis on 1951-73, focuses on environmental problems facing the New York Bight. Part 1 is a list of citations, with subject descriptors but no annotations. Part 2 provides subject and author indexes. Subjects covered are physical and biological sciences, social aspects, pollution, and industries.

See also SB 50.

Mathematics

1098. Bureau of Land Management. **Standard Field Tables and Trigonometric Formulas**. GPO, 1975. 245 pp. **I53.10:956**.
This is a supplement to the *Manual of Instructions for the Survey of Public Lands in the United States*, including the mathematical tables necessary for the survey. The following types of information are given: units of linear measure; traverse tables; natural and logarithmic sines, cosines, tangents, and cotangents; logarithms of numbers; and many more.

1099. Coast and Geodetic Survey. **Natural Sines and Cosines to 8 Decimal Places**. GPO, 1942. 542 pp. (Special publication 231.) S/N 003-002-00019-5. $17. **C4.19:231**.

1100. Department of the Air Force. **New Tables of Incomplete Gamma-Function Ratio and of Percentage Points of Chi-Square and Beta Distributions**. GPO, 1964. 245 pp. **D301.36/5:G14**.

1101. National Bureau of Standards. **Applied Mathematics Series**. GPO, 1948- . Irregular. **C13.32:nos**.
"Contains mathematical tables, annuals, and studies of special interest to physicists, engineers, chemists, biologists, mathematicians, computers, and others engaged in scientific and technical work."

1102. National Bureau of Standards. **Handbook of Mathematical Functions: With Formulas, Graphs, and Tables**. GPO, 1964 (repr. 1973). Rev. ed. 1,046 pp. (Applied mathematics series, no. 55.) S/N 003-003-00279-8. $24. **C13.32:55**.
This handbook includes every special function normally needed by anyone who uses mathematical tables in his work. This revised edition contains an increase in the number of functions covered and more extensive numerical tables. It gives larger collections of mathematical properties of the tabulated functions. Most people who refer to tables of mathematical functions will find this a valuable aid.

1103. National Technical Information Service. **A Directory of Computer Software Applications: Mathematics, 1970-April 1979**. NTIS, 1979. 175 pp. (PB-293 184.) OCLC 5070671. **C51.11/5:M42**.

Mathematics reports are cited that include listings of computer programs and/or their documentation. Software listed pertains to topics such as algebra, analysis (mathematics), geometry, operations research, and statistical methods. Bibliographic data and abstracts and subject and corporate author indexes are provided. The computer programs and documentation listed may be purchased from NTIS in hard copy or microfiche.

1104. Naval Research Laboratory. **Tables of All Primitive Roots for Primes Less Than 5000**. GPO, 1970. 590 pp. (NRL report 7070.) **D210.8:7070**.

See also SB 24.

Medical Sciences

GENERAL MEDICINE

Audiovisual Materials

1105. Centers for Disease Control. **Media Handbook: A Guide to Selecting, Producing, and Using Media for Patient Education Programs**. By Robert M. Davis. Atlanta, GA: IA, 1978. 126 pp., illus. LC 78-013341. RA440.55.A43 1978. 616/.007/15. OCLC 4194020. **HE20.7208:M46**.
This handbook for hospital staff who must select, produce, and use media for patient education programs gives detailed how-to information for each of eight steps in educational planning: assessing needs; writing objectives; developing content; selecting learning activities; selecting, using, and producing instructional media; and evaluation. It discusses types of media for patient education rather than specific titles.

1106. National Audiovisual Center. **Medical Catalog of Selected Audiovisual Materials Produced by the United States Government**. GPO, 1980. 187 pp. OCLC 6257251. S/N 022-002-00066-0. $7. **GS4.17/6:980**.
This is a partially annotated list of over two thousand medical and allied health audiovisual titles in the National Audiovisual Center (NAC) collection. All are available through purchase, rental, or loan from NAC.

1107. National Institute of Arthritis, Metabolism, and Digestive Diseases. **Audiovisual Materials Catalog**. GPO, 1981. 95 pp. OCLC 07669457. S/N 017-045-00099-7. $5.50. **HE20.3316:Au2**.
The catalog is designed to aid health professionals in locating and selecting appropriate audiovisual materials for patient, public, professional, and paraprofessional education about rheumatic diseases. References have been culled from the Arthritis Clearinghouse Data Base. Acquisition information is given, and abstracts are included.

1108. National Library of Medicine. **National Library of Medicine AVLINE Catalog**. GPO, 1977. 337 pp. R835.U49a. 016.61. OCLC 3248616. S/N 017-052-00183-3. $10. **HE20.3602:Au2/975-76**.
This is a subject list of twenty-four hundred audiovisual instructional materials in the health sciences, cataloged by NLM for its AVLINE (Audiovisuals On-Line) data base

between 1975 and 1976. Later audiovisual citations are listed in the *National Library of Medicine Audiovisuals Catalog*.

1109. National Library of Medicine. **National Library of Medicine Audiovisuals Catalog**. GPO, 1977- . Quarterly with annual cumulation. LC 79-640065. R835.U49b. 016.61. OCLC 04108612. S/N 017-052-80008-6. $20/yr. Annual cumulation separately, $13. **HE20.3609/4:date**.

This quarterly publication identifies hundreds of new nonprint materials through either subject or name/title indexes. Bibliographic information given for each item includes title, producer, medium, sale or loan source, price, and subject descriptors. Instructional audiovisual materials as well as recordings of educational events such as congresses, symposia, and lectures are covered. Abstracts are provided for instructional materials. A companion data base of audiovisual information is called AVLINE (Audiovisuals On-Line). Used to compile this catalog, the data base is searchable online at over eight hundred U.S. institutions with access to NLM's online network.

1110. National Library of Medicine. **National Medical Audiovisual Center Catalog: Films for the Health Sciences**. GPO, 1974- . Annual. OCLC 01112261. 1981 ed. S/N 017-052-00221-0. $8. **HE20.3608/4:yr**.

Listed are over seven hundred 16-mm films that are available on loan from the National Medical Audiovisual Center for use in health professions education. Materials are also available in 3/4-inch videocassettes and videotape. This continues *Public Health Service Film Catalog*.

Bibliographies

Current Bibliographies

1111. Bureau of Community Health Services. **Catalog of Family Planning Materials**. GPO, 1979. 144 pp. S/N 017-026-00076-3. $6.50. **HE20.5102:F21/8**.

This first edition lists print and audiovisual patient education and staff training materials, as well as resources for groups with special needs (adolescents, mentally or physically handicapped, and others).

1112. Department of Energy. Technical Information Center. **Nuclear Medicine: A Bibliography**. 2 vols. NTIS, 1978. 1,033 pp. OCLC 6606792. **E1.28:TID-3319-S8-P1-2**.

References cover publications related to nuclear medicine added to the Department of Energy's information data base since July 1976. Extensive bibliographies and reviews are included. Citations and subject descriptors are given for each item. In some cases phrases that elaborate the title are also included.

1113. John E. Fogarty International Center for Advanced Study in the Health Sciences. **Bibliography of Soviet Sources on Medicine and Public Health in the Union of Soviet Socialist Republics**. By Lee Perkins. GPO, 1975. 235 pp. S/N 017-053-00033-7. **HE20.3711:So8/2**.

This comprehensive bibliography of articles translated from Soviet medical journals emphasizes the period 1965-72.

1114. Library of Congress. **National Library of Medicine Catalog**. 18 vols. IA, 1948-65. Annual. LC 51-60145. **LC3013:yr**.

The title varies: *U.S. Army Medical Library Catalog* (1948-50) and *Armed Forces Medical Library Catalog* (1950-54). Cumulations were published for 1950-54, 1955-59, and 1960-65. It is a supplement to the *Library of Congress Author Catalog* and is superseded by the *National Library of Medicine Current Catalog*.

1115. National Institute of Child Health and Human Development. Interagency Committee on Population Research. **Inventory and Analysis of Federal Population Research**. GPO, 1976/77- . Annual. HB8505.U5U546. 301.32/07/2073. OCLC 3393233. **HE20.3362/2:yr.**
This bibliography covers research publications related to population studies conducted with a health science focus. No abstracts are given. There is a grant and research statistical overview.

1116. National Institute of Neurological and Communicative Disorders and Stroke. **Bibliography of Kuru**. By Michael P. Alpers, D. Carleton Gajdusek, and Steven G. Ono. IA, 1975. 220 pp. **HE20.3513:K96/975.**
This is an unannotated, comprehensive bibliography of literature on Kuru and medical or genetic studies of the people of the Kuru region.

1117. National Library of Medicine. **Bibliography of Medical Translations, January 1959-June 1962**. GPO, 1962. 278 pp. **FS2.209:T68.**

_____. **Supplements, 1962-1964**. GPO, 1962-1966.
Entries contained in *Technical Translations* under the subject headings for medicine and allied sciences are listed.

1118. National Library of Medicine. **National Library of Medicine Current Catalog**. GPO, 1966- . Quarterly. S/N 017-052-80005-1. $31/yr. **HE20.3609/2:date.**

_____. **National Library of Medicine Current Catalog: Annual Cumulation**. GPO, 1966- . Annual. OCLC 02264687. 1982 ed. S/N 017-052-00238-4. $45. **HE20.3609/3:yr.**
This is a bibliographic listing of citations to publications cataloged by the National Library of Medicine. The quarterly issues are noncumulating, arranged by subject and name sections. The annual cumulation also has subject and name sections.

Medical History

1119. Armed Forces Institute of Pathology. **Billings Microscope Collection of Medical Museum, Armed Forces Institute of Pathology**. Ed. by Helen R. Purtle and John A. Ey, Jr. IA, 1974. 2d ed. 244 pp., illus. **D1.16/2:M58.**
This descriptive catalog of the historic Billings collection of nearly seven hundred microscopes provides references to the maker, type and model, and historical significance, plus other details for each instrument listed. Most descriptions are accompanied by a photograph.

1120. National Library of Medicine. **Bibliography of the History of Medicine**. GPO, 1966- . Annual with quinquennial cumulations. 1983 ed. (no. 19). S/N 017-052-00247-3. $7.50. **HE20.3615:nos.**

_____. **1970-1974 Cumulation**. 1976. 1,069 pp. S/N 017-052-00171-0. $24. **HE20.3615:10.**

_____. **1975-1979 Cumulation**. 1981. 1,006 pp. S/N 017-052-00216-3. $22. **HE20.3615:15.**
This selective annual bibliography of recent literature on the history of medicine and related sciences and professions covers all chronological periods and geographic areas.

The series is cumulated every five years. It is prepared from HISTLINE, the National Library of Medicine's computerized data base for the history of medicine. HISTLINE may be searched from computer terminals with access to NLM's MEDLINE.

1121. National Library of Medicine. **A Catalogue of Sixteenth Century Printed Books in the National Library of Medicine**. Comp. by Richard J. Durling. GPO, 1967. 698 pp. LC 67-62303. **FS2.209:Si9**.
This bibliography cites over 4,800 sixteenth-century works that are in the National Library of Medicine collection. Annotations provide physical descriptions of the works (such as defects in the copies) and bibliographic history (including information about authors and editors). Indexes of printers and publishers, a geographic index of printers and publishers, and a short title catalog are also provided.

1122. National Library of Medicine. **Early American Medical Imprints: A Guide to Works Printed in the United States, 1668-1820**. By Robert D. Austin. GPO, 1961. 240 pp. **FS2.209:Im7/668-820**.
This bibliography cites 2,106 medical works published in the United States from 1668 to 1820, including books on general medicine, nursing, dentistry, first aid, pharmacology, veterinary medicine, psychology, and some allied areas such as faith healing and astrology. Locations of copies in U.S. libraries are noted. Entries are arranged alphabetically by authors with a chronological index.

1123. National Library of Medicine. **Highlights in Medicolegal Relations**. Comp. by Jaroslav Nemec. GPO, 1976. 166 pp. OCLC 2749869. S/N 017-052-00170-1. $12. **HE20.3602:M46/3**.
The events and publications included are landmarks in the history of medicolegal relations from ancient times to the present.

1124. National Library of Medicine. **International Bibliography of History of Legal Medicine**. By Jaroslav Nemec. GPO, 1974. 224 pp. LC 74-601572. **HE20.3614: M46**.

1125. National Library of Medicine. **Short Title Catalog of Eighteenth Century Printed Books in the National Library of Medicine**. By John Ballard Blake. GPO, 1979. 501 pp. S/N 017-052-00198-1. $13. **HE20.3614:C28**.
The works included are holdings of the National Library of Medicine's history of medicine collection which were printed between 1701 and 1800. About one-third have not been recorded in either the *Index-Catalogue* or the *National Union Catalog, Pre-1956 Imprints*.

Dictionaries

1126. National Institutes of Health. **Medical and Health Related Sciences Thesaurus**. IA, 1963- . Annual. LC 74-610164. Z695.1.M48U47a. 025.3/361. OCLC 1790929. **HE20.3023:yr**.
This is a list of indexing terms developed for use with CRISP (Computer Retrieval of Information on Scientific Projects), the Public Health Service's research project data file. The thesaurus is also used to index the annual *Research Awards Index* of the Public Health Service. The vocabulary terms cover many diversified areas of medicine, dentistry, mental health, and allied public health.

1127. Public Health Service. **Emergency Health Services Glossary**. GPO, 1969. 101 pp. (Health mobilization series A-10.) LC 71-603695. **FS2.302:A-10**.

"This collection combines, in a single reference document, definitions and abbreviations relating to emergency health and medical services from 21 separate glossaries and other sources." It is designed primarily for use by health and medical professional personnel and others concerned about or involved in the provision of emergency health services. A source symbol is given for each definition and a list of sources appears in the front of the book.

Directories

1128. Bureau of Community Health Services. **Clinical Genetic Service Centers: A National Listing**. IA, 1980. OCLC 6441953. **HE20.5102:G28/2**.
This is a directory of U.S. institutions that provide services in clinical genetics, genetic counseling, prenatal diagnosis, cytogenetics, or biochemical genetics. Entries give address, phone number, contact person, and types of services provided. A supplemental section lists federally funded programs for hemophilia and sickle-cell disease.

1129. Centers for Disease Control. **A Directory of Selected References and Resources for Health Instruction**. By Mary K. Beyrer and Marian K. Solleder. Atlanta, GA: IA, 1982. 3d ed. 246 pp. OCLC 09003954. **HE20.7002:D62**.

1130. Health Care Financing Administration. Health Standards and Quality Bureau. **Medicare/Medicaid Directory of Medical Facilities**. IA, semiannual. OCLC 4606714. **HE22.213:date**.
The listing is alphabetic by state, city within state, and facility name within city. It gives address, information on services and facilities, number of beds, and ownership.

1131. John E. Fogarty International Center for Advanced Study in the Health Sciences. **Soviet Biomedical Institutions: A Directory**. IA, 1974. 553 pp. **HE20.3702:So8/4**.
Research facilities, educational facilities, medical societies, and health care facilities are listed, with name and address, affiliation, director, and a description of research activities. Geographic and subordination indexes and English-Russian listings of names are included. Names of institutions are transliterated.

1132. National Institute on Alcohol Abuse and Alcoholism. **National Directory of Alcoholism Treatment Programs**. GPO, 1961. 244 pp. OCLC 97746090. S/N 017-024-01075-8. $7.50. **HE20.8302:Al1/17**.
The directory lists federal, state, local, and private agencies providing alcoholism and drug treatment services in the United States and its territories. Entries give unit name, address, telephone number, and orientation.

1133. National Institutes of Health. **Associate Training Programs in the Medical and Biological Sciences**. GPO, 1965- . Annual. LC 65-60919. OCLC 04011951. **HE20.3015:yr**.
The purpose of this directory is to "set forth in one place brief descriptions of programs of concern to those interested in Associateships at the National Institutes of Health." It is specifically directed toward physicians and others "undertaking careers in medical or related research, or in academic medicine." It provides general and specific information on associateships.

1134. Office on Smoking and Health. **Directory of On-Going Research in Smoking and Health**. GPO, 1967- . Annual. **HE20.7015:yr**.
The listing covers current research worldwide related to smoking, tobacco, and tobacco use.

Machine Readable Data

1135. Bureau of Health Manpower. **The Area Resource File, ARF: A Manpower Planning and Research Tool.** IA, 1980. 168 pp. OCLC 5701662. **HE20.6602: Ar3/2.**
The Area Resource File (ARF) is a computerized file of health manpower data at the county level. It contains health and socioeconomic data for use in health systems research, analysis, and planning at the national and local levels, and is publicly available. This publication is a guide to the data contained in the file, data formats available for retrieval, and data currently being added or available in the future.

1136. National Center for Health Statistics. **Catalog of Public Use Data Tapes from the National Center for Health Statistics.** Hyattsville, MD: IA, 1980. 61 pp. OCLC 7099888. **HE20.6202:D26.**

1137. National Center for Health Statistics. **Publications and Data Tapes of the National Center for Health Statistics Available from the National Technical Information Service.** Hyattsville, MD: IA, 1978. 260 pp. OCLC 4446431. **HE20.6216:P96.**
This is the first published listing describing some of the publications and data tapes from the National Center for Health Statistics (NCHS) that are available from NTIS. Many are no longer available from NCHS. Bibliographic information, abstracts, descriptors, and NTIS price codes are provided.

1138. National Library of Medicine. **MEDLARS** and **MEDLINE.** 1966- .
MEDLARS (Medical Literature Analysis and Retrieval System) contains citations to health science-related books and journal articles published since 1965. MEDLINE (MEDLARS online) contains citations (and many abstracts) for biomedical journal literature from the current and two previous years, and for chapters and articles from selected monographs. Retrospective files allow searches back to 1966. Coverage is worldwide. In addition to MEDLARS and MEDLINE, the National Library of Medicine maintains data bases in other subject areas, some of which are listed below.

> **Health Planning and Administration**—references to literature on health planning, organization, financing, management, manpower, and related topics.
>
> **CLINPROT (Clinical Cancer Protocols)**—summaries of clinical investigations of new anticancer agents and treatments.
>
> **BIOETHICSLINE**—references to literature on topics such as euthanasia, human experimentation, abortion, and other bioethical topics.
>
> **POPLINE (Population Information Online)**—citations to literature related to population, such as reproductive biology, applied research in contraceptive technology, family planning, and demography.
>
> **Laboratory Animal Data Bank**—data on control animals and related to hematology, clinical chemistry, pathology, environment and husbandry, and growth and development.

Online searches for any of NLM's data bases are available through online terminals at over thirteen hundred academic, commercial, and government organizations in the United States. To find the name of the NLM Online Center nearest you, write to the Office of Inquiries and Publications Management, National Library of Medicine, 8600 Rockville Pike, Bethesda, MD 20209.

1139. National Library of Medicine. **Online Services Reference Manual.** NTIS, 1980. (PB80-114531.) OCLC 1372186. **HE20.3608:On1/980.**

This comprehensive manual for searching the various National Library of Medicine online data bases provides specifics for accessing these data bases, commands, search techniques, and instructions for individual data bases.

Periodicals and Serials

Bibliographies

1140. National Center for Health Statistics. **Bibliography on Health Indexes.** Hyattsville, MD: IA, 1979- . Quarterly. OCLC 2134072. **HE20.6216/2-2:date.**
Annotations are given for the Clearinghouse on Health Indexes recent publications and for documents in the Clearinghouse collection. Upcoming conferences, addresses of sponsors, contributors, and bibliographic listings of published literature are also listed. Most of the material is in English.

1141. National Library of Medicine. **Bibliography of Medical Reviews: Cumulations.** GPO, 1957- . Quinquennial. 1976-80 ed. S/N 017-052-00223-6. $34. **HE20.3610/2:date.**
These are cumulations of citations to review articles indexed in *Index Medicus.*

1142. National Library of Medicine. **Biomedical Serials, 1950-1960: A Selective List of Serials in the National Library of Medicine.** Comp. by Lela M. Spanier. GPO, 1962. 503 pp. (PHS publication no. 910.) LC 62-61276. **FS2.209:B52.**
Nearly nine thousand serials in the National Library of Medicine collection are listed, including annuals, review journals, and other periodicals. Proceedings of societies and organizations are excluded. Entries include publisher, place of publication, starting date, and frequency and extent of NLM holdings.

1143. National Library of Medicine. **Health Sciences Serials.** GPO, 1979- . Quarterly. OCLC 04094060. S/N 017-025-80009-4 (microfiche). $15/yr. **HE20.3614/3: date.**
Citations representing the NLM SERLINE (Serials-on-line) data base are listed. This source is available in microfiche only. Each issue supersedes the previous issue.

1144. National Library of Medicine. **International Bibliography of Medicolegal Serials, 1736-1967.** Comp. by Jaroslav Nemec. GPO, 1969. 110 pp. **FS2.209: M46/736-967.**
Journals either wholly concerned with medicolegal subjects or those which have regular features are included. Serials in twenty-two languages are listed alphabetically by current title. Entries include publisher, place of publication, beginning date (and closing date if applicable), frequency, data on indexes, editors, and title changes. There are six indexes: title, editor, publisher, subject, geographic, and chronological.

1145. National Library of Medicine. **List of Journals Indexed in Index Medicus.** GPO, 1960- . Annual. LC 73-642296. Z6660.U66a. 016.61. OCLC 02760305. 1984 ed. S/N 017-052-00245-7. $7. **HE20.3612/4:yr.**
The 2,695 journals being indexed for *Index Medicus* are listed by abbreviated title, by subject, by title, and by country of origin. Also included is a list of journals being indexed in cooperation with other institutions. A list of journal titles is also included in the January issue of *Index Medicus* and in *Cumulated Index Medicus.*

1146. National Library of Medicine. **List of Serials and Monographs Indexed for Online Users**. NTIS, 1980- . Annual. (PB80-131204.) OCLC 5883801. **HE20.3602:Se6/yr.**

This new NLM publication is designed to provide complete bibliographic citations for serials and proceedings of congresses cited in MEDLINE, Health Planning and Administration, and POPLINE (each is a MEDLARS subfile). Citations from these data files are published in several NLM recurring bibliographies and special subject indexes.

Indexes and Abstracts

1147. Department of the Army. Medical Department. **Index-Catalogue of the Library of the Surgeon General's Office, 1st-4th Series**. 58 vols. GPO, 1880-1955. **W44.7/1-4:vols.; M102.8:vols.; D8.9:vols.**

For annotation, *see* entry 1154.

1148. National Aeronautics and Space Administration. **Aerospace Medicine and Biology**. NTIS, 1964- . Monthly with annual cumulative index. (NASA SP-7011.) LC 65-062677. Z6664.3.A36. OCLC 01832161. **NAS1.21:7011(nos.).**

This is an annotated index to unclassified reports and journal articles on bioscience and biotechnology added to NASA's scientific and technical information system and announced in *Scientific and Technical Aerospace Reports* (STAR) and *International Aerospace Abstracts*.

1149. National Institute of Arthritis, Metabolism, and Digestive Diseases. **Endocrinology Index**. GPO, 1968-79. OCLC 1567880. **HE20.3309:vol./nos.**

This title was a current awareness bibliography produced from the National Library of Medicine's MEDLARS data base. It was aimed at scientists working in the field of endocrinology, to aid in integration of research and clinical effort in endocrinology.

1150. National Institute of Arthritis, Metabolism, and Digestive Diseases. **Index of Dermatology**. GPO, 1972-79. OCLC 1641567. **HE20.3315:vol./nos.**

This index, which ceased in 1979, identified relevant literature in the field of dermatology. The institute discontinued it when it determined that other resources were available for identifying citations and abstracts in the field, and that the bibliographic void that prompted the index's publication no longer existed.

1151. National Library of Medicine. **Abridged Index Medicus**. GPO, 1970- . Monthly. OCLC 01752727. S/N 017-052-80001-9. $43/yr. **HE20.3612/2:date.**

The abridged index covers 117 English-language biomedical journals each month, with the mission of serving the needs of individual practitioners and small hospital and clinical libraries. An annual cumulation is sold separately.

1152. National Library of Medicine. **Centenary of Index Medicus, 1879-1979**. Ed. by John B. Blake. GPO, 1980. 123 pp. OCLC 5744101. S/N 017-052-00212-1. $8. **HE20.3602:C33/879-979.**

A history of *Index Medicus* to 1979, this is a collection of scholarly papers written by librarians, historians, and physicians on bibliography, librarianship, and publishing as related to medicine and *Index Medicus*.

1153. National Library of Medicine. **Cumulated Abridged Index Medicus**. GPO, 1970- . Annual. LC 77-610781. 1983 ed. (vol. 14.) S/N 017-052-00244-9. $35. **HE20.3612/2-2:vol.**

1154. National Library of Medicine. **Index-Catalogue of the Library of the Surgeon General's Office, 5th Series**. 3 vols. GPO, 1959-61. **FS2.210:vols.**

This monumental work is a detailed bibliography and index of books, pamphlets, periodical articles, theses and dissertations, and even chapters of books. The fifth series lists only pre-1950 imprints by authors, titles, and subjects. Series 1-4 (entry 1147) are author and subject lists, in dictionary arrangement (series 4, 1936-55, covers the letters A through Mn only). It is continued by *Index Medicus, New Series,* and the *National Library of Medicine Catalog.*

1155. National Library of Medicine. **Index Medicus.** GPO, 1960- . Monthly. LC 61-060337. Z6660.I42. 016.61. OCLC 01752728. S/N 017-052-80004-3. $135/yr. **HE20.3612:vol./nos.**
Previous series were:

> **Index Medicus: A Classified Index of the Current Medical Literature of the World.** Washington, DC: Carnegie Institution, 1879-99 (1st series); 1903-20 (2d series). 39 vols. Monthly.

> **Index Medicus: A Quarterly Classified Record of the Current Medical Literature of the World.** Washington, DC: Carnegie Institution, 1921-27 (3d series). 6 vols.

> **Quarterly Cumulative Index to Current Medical Literature.** Chicago: American Medical Association, 1917-27. 12 vols.

> Army Medical Library. **Current List of Medical Literature.** GPO, 1941-49. 18 vols. Weekly. **D104.7:vol./nos.**

> **Quarterly Cumulative Index Medicus.** Chicago: American Medical Association, 1927-56. 60 vols.

> Armed Forces Medical Library. **Current List of Medical Literature.** GPO, 1950-59. Vols. 19-36. Monthly. **D8.8:vol./nos.** and **FS2.208:vol./nos.**

> Volumes 1-3, no.1 (1960- .) were called "new series."

Index Medicus is a bibliography of current journal and selected monographic literature of biomedicine worldwide. Each issue contains a subject listing and a name listing (which includes names of biographees). In addition, each issue contains a section entitled "Monthly Bibliography of Medical Reviews," which was absorbed in 1967. This section, which appears in both *Index Medicus* and the *Cumulated Index Medicus,* is designed to provide quick reference to latest reviews in periodical literature in the field of biomedicine, and contains an author and name section. The January issue also contains a complete list of journals indexed. Subsequent monthly issues list only those added or discontinued. Journals are listed by full title and by abbreviation used in *Index Medicus.*

The subscription to *Index Medicus* includes a separate part of each January issue entitled *Medical Subject Headings* (also available separately). Cross references are provided in this list, not in the index itself. Therefore, a search in *Index Medicus* on a particular topic is facilitated if this list is consulted first.

Annual cumulations were published by the American Medical Association from 1960 to 1964. Since 1965 they have been published by GPO but are not included in subscriptions to the monthly *Index Medicus.* Entitled *Cumulated Index Medicus,* these annual multi-volume sets are sold separately. Companion resources are MEDLARS and MEDLINE, both computerized literature retrieval services of NLM; *Medical Subject Headings* (MeSH); and *List of Journals Indexed in Index Medicus.*

1156. National Library of Medicine. **Index of NLM Serial Titles.** GPO, 1972- . Annual. LC 79-643036. Z6660.U66C. 016.61. OCLC 74199164. 1984 ed. S/N 017-052-00248-1. **HE20.3618:yr.**
This is a keyword-out-of-context index to over thirty-five thousand serials and numbered congresses on order, in process, or received by the National Library of

Medicine, and many ceased titles. Entries give information needed for interlibrary loan from NLM: title, ISSN, NLM call number, and NLM control number.

1157. Office on Smoking and Health. **Bibliography on Smoking and Health**. GPO, 1967- . Annual. (Public Health Service bibliography series, no. 45.) LC 68-60300. 1982 ed. S/N 017-001-00445-6. $7.50. **HE20.11:45/nos**.
Abstracts of current literature on smoking that have been published in the bimonthly *Smoking and Health Bulletin* are cumulated annually in this title. Related publications are the biennial *Directory of Ongoing Research in Smoking and Health*, the annual *Health Consequences of Smoking* report, and *State Legislation on Smoking and Health*. All items cited in the bibliography are in the collections of the Office on Smoking and Health, Technical Information Center, Park Building, Room 116, 5600 Fishers Lane, Rockville, MD 20857. The center has a free computer literature search service.

1158. President's Council on Physical Fitness and Sports. **Physical Fitness/Sports Medicine**. GPO, 1978- . Quarterly. OCLC 03622655. S/N 017-003-80001-8. $10/yr. **HE20.111:date**.
Citations from over three thousand periodicals on exercise physiology, sports injuries, physical conditioning, and medical aspects of exercise have been retrieved from the MEDLARS data base of the National Library of Medicine.

Statistics

1159. Alcohol, Drug Abuse, and Mental Health Administration. **The Alcohol, Drug Abuse, and Mental Health National Data Book: A Reference Book of National Data on Incidence and Prevalence, Facilities, Services Utilization, Practitioners, Costs, and Financing**. By Thomas R. Vischi. GPO, 1980. OCLC 6219968. S/N 017-024-00983-1. $6.50. **HE20.8002:D26**.
This reference book was developed to improve access to the complex and interrelated body of data on alcohol, drug abuse, and mental health problems and services. It provides data on incidence, facilities, services use, practitioners, cost, and financing. Highlights sections give overviews of the data. These data provide simple, direct answers to basic questions about the national services system, while references to more detailed data and analyses may be identified using the footnotes and bibliography.

1160. Health Resources Administration. **Health of the Disadvantaged: Chart Book-II**. IA, 1980. 141 pp. OCLC 6871423. **HE20.6017:D63/bk.2**.
This source provides charts and tables, with accompanying highlight statements, depicting major published and previously unpublished data on the health of racial and ethnic minorities and the poor. The section on manpower updates data on racial, ethnic minority enrollment in medical schools covered in *Minorities and Women in the Health Field* (1979).

1161. Health Resources Administration. **Women in Health Careers: Status of Women in Health Careers in United States and Other Selected Countries; Chart Book for International Conference on Women in Health, Washington, D.C., June 16-18, 1975**. By Maryland Pennell and Shirlene Showell. GPO, 1975. 147 pp., illus. S/N 017-041-00104-1. $6.50. **HE20.6002:W89/chartbook**.

1162. National Center for Health Statistics. **Advance Data from Vital and Health Statistics of the National Center for Health Statistics**. Hyattsville, MD: IA, 1976- . Irregular. LC 79-643688. RA407.3.U57c. 362.1/6/0973. OCLC 02778178. **HE20.6209/3:nos**.

This series provides for early release of selected data from the health and demographic surveys of the National Center for Health Statistics. It supplements *Monthly Vital Statistics Report*.

1163. National Center for Health Statistics. **Catalog of Publications of the National Center for Health Statistics.** Hyattsville, MD: IA, 1980- . Annual. LC 81-643666. OCLC 07062972. **HE20.6216:C29/yr.**
This continues *Current Listing and Topical Index to the Vital and Health Statistics Series, 1962-1978.* It covers NCHS reports published during the previous five years, including those in the *Vital and Health Statistics* series and the *Advance Data from Vital and Health Statistics* series.

1164. National Center for Health Statistics. **Current Listing and Topical Index to the Vital and Health Statistics Series, 1962-1978.** Hyattsville, MD: IA, 1979. OCLC 5096389. **HE20.6209/2:962-78.**
This is an index to health topics covered in the *Vital and Health Statistics* series and *Advance Data from Vital and Health Statistics* series. Indexing is by demographic and socioeconomic variables related to the health status of people and characteristics of health facilities and personnel. The index is not exhaustive, but covers frequently requested topics and variables. This 1979 edition, covering publications released between 1962 and 1978, was the last to contain the complete cumulative listing of the *Vital and Health Statistics* series from 1962. Editions of the *Catalog of Publications of the National Center for Health Statistics* will cover the previous five years and will include the *Current Listing and Topical Index* after 1980.

1165. National Center for Health Statistics. **Dietary Intake Source Data, United States 1971-74.** By Sidney Abraham et al. GPO, 1979. 421 pp., illus. LC 79-015082. TX360.U6U58 1979. 362.5. OCLC 5101694. **HE20.6202: D56/971-74.**

1166. National Center for Health Statistics. **Dietary Intake Source Data: United States, 1976-80.** GPO, 1983. 483 pp. (Vital and health statistics, series 11, no. 231.) S/N 017-022-00817-3. $11. **HE20.6209:11/231.**
Tables of data from the Health and Nutrition Examination Survey to assess the nutritional intake of U.S. citizens between ages one and seventy-four show dietary intake of calories and selected nutrients by age, sex, race, and income based on interviews of a sample population.

1167. National Center for Health Statistics. **Facts at Your Fingertips.** Hyattsville, MD: IA, 1978- . Irregular. OCLC 05094639. **HE20.6208:F11/yr.**
This guide to sources of statistical information on major health topics, while not definitive, attempts to identify major topics of interest and describe the types of data available from the National Center for Health Statistics, other Department of Health and Human Services sources, federal agencies, and private organizations. Some references to nonstatistical publications are included to provide general information on selected topics.

1168. National Center for Health Statistics. **Health Resources Statistics.** GPO, 1966- . Annual. Maps. LC 66-062528. RA407.3.A28. 362.1/0973. OCLC 1604947. **HE20.6212:yr.**
A series of periodic reports published since 1965, this is the most comprehensive collection of current statistics available on health manpower, health facilities, and health services in the United States. When possible, statistics are presented by state. For each occupation, information and supportive statistics are given on the number of personnel, availability of professional training, kinds of specialization, licensing requirements, and

registration and certification availability. The statistics are derived from public and private sources identified as the best information available. This title is a source of comprehensive statistics on recruitment, education, and training of professional, technical, and auxiliary health workers, and on health facilities such as hospitals and nursing homes.

1169. National Center for Health Statistics. **Health, United States.** 1975- . Annual. RA407.3.U57a. 362.1/0973. OCLC 03151554. **HE20.6223:yr.**
This statistical handbook on recent trends in the health care sector, with detailed discussion of selected current health issues, focuses on trends and comparisons over time. The detailed statistical tables are organized around four subject categories: health status and determinants, use of health resources, health care resources, and health care expenditures. Since 1980 every third year includes a section titled "Prevention Profile."

1170. National Center for Health Statistics. **Monthly Vital Statistics Report: Provisional Statistics from the National Center for Health Statistics.** GPO, 1952- . Monthly with annual summary. LC 66-051898. HA203.A43. 312/.0973. OCLC 01685363. **HE20.6217:vol./nos.**
Monthly and cumulative provisional data are given on births, natural increase, marriages, divorces, deaths, and infants' deaths for states and the United States with brief analyses for these vital statistics. The report also presents death rates by cause, age, color, and sex, estimated from a sample of death certificates filed in states.

Yearbooks

1171. National Institutes of Health. **National Institutes of Health Almanac.** Bethesda, MD: IA, 1965- . Annual. LC 66-62557. **HE20.3016:yr.**
This source is intended to "offer in one volume all important historical data and other reference material" pertinent to the National Institutes of Health, the nation's principal biomedical research agency. The information provided includes NIH's eleven research institutes and four divisions, the National Library of Medicine, the Clinical Center, and the John E. Fogarty International Center for Advanced Study in the Health Sciences.

1172. National Institutes of Health. **National Institutes of Health Scientific Directory and Annual Bibliography.** GPO, 1956- . Annual. LC 57-62015. OCLC 08066977. **HE20.3017:yr.**
Intended for researchers in the biomedical sciences, the directory lists NIH organization and structure, professional staff, and their publications.

DENTISTRY

1173. Bureau of Health Manpower. **Sources of Data Related to Dentistry: A Catalog.** IA, 1980. 119 pp. OCLC 6263516. **HE20.6602:D43/18.**
The catalog lists publications and data files related to dental health planning. All data sources are at the national level. Summaries include title, developer, year of collection, geographic area, format, variables, and target units of measurement. A complementary publication, *Annotated List of National Center for Health Statistics Reports Containing Dental Information*, contains documentation of selected data bases.

See also SB 22.

DISEASES AND HANDICAPS

General Works

1174. Architectural and Transportation Barriers Compliance Board. **Resource Guide to Literature on Barrier-Free Environments, with Selected Annotations**. GPO, 1980. 279 pp. OCLC 6946703. S/N 017-090-00049-6. $8.50. **Y3.B27:9R31/980**.
This is an annotated listing of print and nonprint, research and popular materials on creating barrier-free environments for the elderly and handicapped. The editors describe this guide as probably the most comprehensive published on architectural and transportation barriers. Materials included were published between 1960 and 1978.

1175. Department of Education. Office of Special Education and Rehabilitation Services. **Directory of National Information Sources on Handicapping Conditions and Related Services**. GPO, 1982. 3d ed. 270 pp. OCLC 04344577. S/N 065-000-00142-0. $8. **ED1.202:H19/2**.
The directory of national-level organizations provides information and direct services for specific handicapping conditions. It gives address, telephone number, and description of information services, including data bases.

1176. Office of Human Development Services. Office for Handicapped Individuals. **Digest of Data on Persons with Disabilities**. GPO, 1980. 141 pp., illus. OCLC 5962885. S/N 017-090-00050-0. $6.50. **HE23.2:D63**.
Tables and charts of aggregate data give an overview of the size and characteristics of the handicapped and disabled population. The report also discusses definitions and labels applied to this population, summarizes key facts, and discusses additional sources of information.

1177. President's Committee on Employment of the Handicapped. **Clothing for Handicapped People: An Annotated Bibliography and Resource List**. Comp. by Naomi Reich et al. IA, 1979. 84 pp. OCLC 5858783. **PrEx1.10/9:C62**.
This annotated bibliography of publications, nonprint resources, and products related to clothing for people with special needs includes listings under clothing categories, physical conditions, serials, unpublished literature, educational materials, and self-help devices.

See also SB 37.

Arthritis

1178. National Institute of Arthritis and Metabolic Diseases. **Arthritis and Rheumatic Diseases Abstracts**. GPO, 1964-70. Monthly. LC 66-4061. **HE20.3312:vol./nos.**
This journal is in classified arrangement with an author and subject index. Annual cumulative indexes were also published. It ceased with the completion of volume 6 in 1970.

Blood Diseases

1179. National Heart, Lung, and Blood Institute. **Hemostatis and Thrombosis: A Bibliography**. GPO, 1975-78. Monthly. LC 77-641741. OCLC 1924593. **HE20.3209/2:vol./nos.**
This title continued *Fibrinolysis, Thrombolysis, and Blood Clotting Bibliography*.

Cancer

1180. National Cancer Institute. **Carcinogensis Abstracts**. GPO, 1963-79. Monthly. OCLC 1553342. **HE20.3159:vol./nos.**
This title provided abstracts of significant articles on cancer from the world biomedical literature. It ceased in 1979, when it became too expensive to produce at government expense.

1181. National Cancer Institute. **A Compilation of Journal Instructions to Authors**. GPO, 1979. 440 pp. OCLC 5206153. **HE20.3152:J82/979.**
This is a compilation of instructions to authors given in journals to which National Cancer Institute researchers often submit manuscripts. It is designed to aid researchers writing papers for publication and secretaries typing them.

1182. National Cancer Institute. **Coping with Cancer: An Annotated Bibliography of Public, Patient, and Professional Information and Education Materials**. GPO, 1980. 113 pp. OCLC 6338994. **HE20.3165:C79.**
This annotated bibliography listing materials designed for use by the public, cancer patients, and professionals includes materials on cancer in adults, in children, breast cancer, head and neck cancer, leukemia, lung cancer, and colorectal cancer. Personal narratives, audiovisual materials, and bibliographies on cancer and on death and dying are included. Abstracts and availability information are given.

1183. National Cancer Institute. **Directory of Cancer Research Information Resources**. NTIS, 1977- . Biennial. LC 81-602157. 616.99/4/0072. OCLC 07406287. **HE20.3152:C16/17/yr.**
Developed to provide cancer researchers with a one-volume reference that lists "most of the available cancer information sources around the world," the directory includes descriptions of data bases; publications; research projects; information sources; organizations; U.S. government agencies, products, and services; cancer registries; dial-access services; libraries; classification schemes; special collections; and audiovisual information sources.

1184. National Cancer Institute. **ICRDB Cancergram (series)**. NTIS, 1977- . Monthly. ZQZ206.C24P. OCLC 04580826. **HE20.3173/2:ltrs.-nos.**
The International Cancer Research Data Bank (ICRDB) provides an abstracting service for researchers on various aspects of cancer. The Cancergrams are issued in three subseries: CB—Cancer Biology; CK—Chemical, Environmental, and Radiation Carcinogensis; and CT—Diagnosis and Therapy.

1185. National Cancer Institute. **Psychological Aspects of Breast Cancer**. GPO, 1978. 618 pp. OCLC 3978339. **HE20.3165:B74.**
Many factors make the diagnosis of breast cancer threatening and stressful for many women and their loved ones. This annotated bibliography focuses on materials about the problems and needs of breast cancer patients and their families, and those that provide direction for solving problems and meeting needs. It covers psychological factors in the etiology, management, and rehabilitation of the patient once diagnosis is made.

1186. National Cancer Institute. **U.S. Cancer Mortality by County, 1950-69**. By Thomas J. Mason and Frank W. McKay. GPO, 1974. 729 pp. **HE20.3152: C16/6/950-69.**

1187. National Library of Medicine. **CANCERLIT (Cancer Literature)**.
This online machine readable data file sponsored by the National Cancer Institute (NCI) contains more than 250,000 references dealing with various aspects of cancer. All references have English abstracts. Over 3,000 U.S. and foreign journals, as well as selected monographs, meeting papers, reports, and dissertations, are abstracted for inclusion in CANCERLIT, formerly called CANCERLINE.

NLM's online search services are coordinated by eleven regional medical libraries, each responsible for a geographic area of the United States. For information on the Online Center nearest to you, write to the Office of Inquiries and Publications Management, National Library of Medicine, 8600 Rockville Pike, Bethesda, MD 20209. In addition, this file may be searched from computer terminals at institutions with access to NLM's MEDLINE.

Diabetes

1188. National Institute of Arthritis, Metabolism, and Digestive Diseases. **Diabetes Literature Index**. GPO, 1966-79. Monthly. OCLC 1566565. **HE20.3310: vol./nos.**
This title, no longer published, indexed current scientific papers worldwide relevant to laboratory and clinical research into the nature, causes, and therapy for diabetes. It was prepared from the National Library of Medicine's MEDLARS data base and superseded *Diabetes-Related Literature Index.*

Epilepsy

1189. National Institute of Neurological and Communicative Disorders and Stroke. **Epilepsy Abstracts**. GPO, 1968- . Monthly. **HE20.3509:vol./nos.**
Abstracts of projects and developments related to epilepsy that have been reported in the medical literature are covered. An index for each volume is published at the end of the year. A two-volume compilation of the abstracts and indexes for 1947-67 was published in 1969 (entry 1190).

1190. National Institutes of Health. **Epilepsy Abstracts: A Review of Published Literature, 1947-1967**. Ed. by J. F. Mirandolle and L. M. Vencken. 2 vols. GPO, 1969. LC 70-604019. **FS2.22/59-2:947-67/v.1,2.**
This bibliography is concerned primarily with the clinical and therapeutic aspects of epilepsies, including research in physiology, biochemistry and psychological, sociological, and epidemiological aspects. Volume 1 contains the abstracts and gives authors' names, titles of articles, journal titles, volumes, page numbers, and years of publication. Volume 2 contains author and subject indexes.

1191. National Library of Medicine. **EPILEPSYLINE**.
This online machine readable data file sponsored by the National Institute of Neurological and Communicative Disorders and Stroke contains about thirty-seven thousand references and abstracts to articles on epilepsy that have been abstracted from *Excerpta Medica*.

NLM's online search services are coordinated by eleven regional medical libraries, each responsible for a geographic area of the United States. For information on the Online Center closest to you, write to the Office of Inquiries and Publications Management, National Library of Medicine, 8600 Rockville Pike, Bethesda, MD 20209. In addition, this file may be searched from computer terminals at institutions with access to NLM's MEDLINE.

Hypertension

1192.   National Heart, Lung, and Blood Institute. **Audiovisual Aids for High Blood Pressure Education**. GPO, 1980. 195 pp. OCLC 6159304. **HE20.3202:Au2**.
This is a nonevaluative listing of audiovisual aids dealing with high blood pressure. Titles listed would be useful for public, patient, and professional education. Entries give title, date, content, format, recommended audience, cost, availability, and ordering information.

Intestinal Diseases

1193.   National Institute of Arthritis, Metabolism, and Digestive Diseases. **Gastroenterology Abstracts and Citations**. GPO, 1966-78. Monthly. OCLC 1570458. **HE20.3313:vol./nos.**
Until it ceased in 1978, this source indexed and abstracted worldwide literature relevant to the nature, causes, and therapy of diseases of the gastrointestinal tract.

Kidney Diseases

1194.   National Institute of Arthritis, Metabolism, and Digestive Diseases. **Kidney Disease and Nephrology Index**. GPO, 1975-79. LC 77-646734. Z6664.K5K5. 016.6166/1. OCLC 2769292. **HE20.3318:vol./nos.**
This was a bimonthly index to publications on basic and clinical research in nephrology, clinical urology, and end-stage kidney disease, and included the *Artificial Kidney Bibliography*.

Mental Retardation

1195.   Department of Health and Human Services. Developmental Disabilities Office. **Developmental Disabilities Abstracts**. GPO, 1977-78. Quarterly. OCLC 3045409. **HE1.49:date**.
This title continued *Mental Retardation and Development Disabilities Abstracts*.

1196.   President's Committee on Mental Retardation. **International Directory of Mental Retardation Resources**. Ed. by Rosemary F. Dybwad. GPO, 1978. 2d ed. 360 pp. LC 79-601222. HV3004.D97 1978. 362.3/025. OCLC 5262980. **HE23.102:D62**.
Individual country listings include government agencies with primary responsibility related to mental retardation, voluntary organizations, research organizations, publications, and descriptive notes of program areas. Also listed are activities of international organizations.

Parkinson's Disease

1197.   National Institute of Neurological and Communicative Disorders and Stroke. **Parkinson's Disease and Related Disorders: Citations from the Literature**. NTIS, 1970- . Monthly. OCLC 01761917. **HE20.3511:vol./nos.**
Citations listed are pulled from the MEDLARS data base of the National Library of Medicine.

1198.   National Institute of Neurological and Communicative Disorders and Stroke. **Parkinson's Disease and Related Disorders: Cumulative Bibliography, 1800-1970**. 3 vols. GPO, 1971. LC 79-610736. **HE20.3511/3:800-970/v.1-3**.
Volume 1 contains citations. Volumes 2 and 3 are author and subject indexes, respectively.

1199.   National Institute of Neurological and Communicative Disorders and Stroke. **Parkinson's Disease and Related Disorders: International Directory of Scientists**. GPO, 1970- . Annual. **HE20.3511/2:yr.**
Arranged by countries, names, and institutions, entries give name, specialty, subject interests, and location of people engaged in research on Parkinson's disease and related neurological disorders.

Sudden Infant Death Syndrome

1200.   Bureau of Community Health Services. **Sudden Infant Death Syndrome Research and Grief Counseling: A Selected Bibliography**. GPO, 1981. 101 pp. LC 81-607992. RJ59.883. 618.72. OCLC 07555502. **HE20.5110:In3**.
This is a bibliography of nearly two hundred documents related to sudden infant death syndrome and state-of-the-art research. Abstracts are usually author-provided. Some retrospective studies are included.

Venereal Disease

1201.   Centers for Disease Control. **Directory of STD* Clinics. (*Sexually Transmitted Disease)**. Atlanta, GA: IA, 1981. 396 pp. LC 81-602580. OCLC 07455903. **HE20.7002:Se9**.
This state-by-state directory of clinics for sexually transmitted disease includes all counties in the United States. It gives the facility name, address, phone number, hours open, need for appointments, cost (if any), and diseases which the facility diagnoses or treats. Telephone hotlines are also listed.

1202.   Centers for Disease Control. **Sexually Transmitted Diseases: Abstracts and Bibliography**. Atlanta, GA: IA, 1979- . Irregular. LC 79-644375. Z6664.V45U52. 616.951. OCLC 05093205. **HE20.7311:date**.
Abstracts of journal articles selected from MEDLINE and related to sexually transmitted diseases are included. This was formerly titled *Abstracts for Current Literature on Venereal Disease*.

NURSING

1203.   Bureau of Health Manpower. **Community Health Nursing Models: A Selected Bibliography**. GPO, 1979. 103 pp. (Nurse planning information series, no. 11.) OCLC 5660131. **HE20.6613:11**.
This is an annotated bibliography of literature on health care services outside traditional institutions, in community settings such as neighborhood health centers and homes. It includes availability information.

1204. Bureau of Health Manpower. **Computer Technology in Nursing: A Comprehensive Bibliography**. By Dorothy B. Pocklington and Linda Guttman. NTIS, 1980. (Nurse planning information series, no. 16.) OCLC 06930836. **HE20.6613:16**.
This annotated bibliography of publications about computer technology and nursing gives information on how to obtain the cited documents.

1205. Bureau of Health Manpower. **Continuing Education in Nursing: A Selected Bibliography**. NTIS, 1980. 196 pp. (Nurse planning information series no. 13.) OCLC 6312123. **HE20.6613:13**.
Abstracts cover over three hundred publications on the state of continuing education in nursing, written by experts in the field.

1206. Bureau of Health Manpower. **Quality Assurance in Nursing: A Selected Bibliography**. By Norma M. Lang. NTIS, 1980. 259 pp. (Nurse planning information series, no. 12.) OCLC 6383280. **HE20.6613:12**.
Literature on the quality of nursing care, including some nonnursing references, is listed with annotations. Availability information, author index, and a subject matrix are included.

PHARMACOLOGY

General Bibliographies

1207. National Clearinghouse for Mental Health. **Bibliography of Drug Dependence and Abuse, 1928-1966**. GPO, 1969. 158 pp. LC 70-600726. **FS2.22/13: D84/928-66**.
This bibliography was compiled for the use of specialists and research workers and includes three thousand citations to books, monographs, articles, legal documents, and reports of congressional hearings. Material is arranged in eight groups: general reviews, incidence, sociological factors, treatment, attitudes and education, pharmacology and chemistry, psychological factors, and production, control, and legal factors. Citations give full bibliographic details but no annotations.

1208. National Institute on Drug Abuse. **Annotated Bibliography of Papers from the Addiction Research Center, 1935-75**. GPO, 1978. 234 pp. OCLC 4242485. S/N 017-024-00762-5. $5. **HE20.8211:Ad2/935-75**.
The Addiction Research Center began studies of narcotic addiction in 1933. Since then the center has been the major intramural program of the National Institute of Mental Health and the National Institute on Drug Abuse focusing on narcotic addition. This annotated bibliography gives a chronological record of the research generated through the center.

1209. National Library of Medicine. **Drug Interactions: An Annotated Bibliography with Selected Excerpts, 1967-1971**. GPO, 1975. 842 pp. S/N 017-052-00165-5. $24. **HE20.3614:D84/967-71/v.3**.

Drug Codes

1210. Food and Drug Administration. **National Drug Code Directory**. GPO, 1969- . Biennial. OCLC 01759180. S/N 017-012-81002-1. $90. (Subscription includes basic manual plus quarterly supplements for an indeterminate period.) **HE20.4012:yr**.

This directory is a "standardized, drug product identification system for the computer processing of drug information in the United States." It is essentially a computer-produced listing of over twelve thousand prescription and over-the-counter drugs. This listing of prescription drug products and their marketers is published every two years. Volume 1 is an alphabetic index by product name. Volume 2 consists of (1) a numerical index of products by drug class, (2) a numerical index of products by National Drug Code, and (3) an alphabetic index by the firm's short name.

1211. National Library of Medicine. **Russian Drug Index**. By Stanley Jablonski. GPO, 1967. 2d ed. 384 pp. **FS2.202:R92/2/967**.

This index was to aid persons using Russian medical literature by identifying the drug names found therein.

Directories

1212. National Institute on Drug Abuse. **National Directory of Drug Abuse Treatment Programs**. GPO, 1979. 350 pp. OCLC 5787992. **HE20.8202:T71/979**.

The directory lists approximately thirty-eight hundred federal, state, local, and private agencies responsible for drug abuse treatment services throughout the United States and its territories. For each state and city, it gives program name, address, telephone number, director's name, and program description. Most entries also give information on the services available and the environment in which they are provided.

Indexes and Abstracts

1213. National Institute on Drug Abuse. **Guide to the Drug Research Literature**. By Gregory A. Austin, Mary A. Macari, and Dan J. Lettieri. GPO, 1980. 397 pp. (Research issues 27.) OCLC 63311151. S/N 017-024-00980-6. $9.50. **HE20.8214:27**.

This cumulative index to all publications in the NIDA *Research Issues* series also serves as a guide to important literature in the drug research field. Entries include subject descriptors, sample group and size, location, and methodology. The guide also contains references to the data collection instruments covered in the *Drug Abuse Instrument Handbook*. References are given to the series volume in which abstracts appear. When the guide is used independently of the series, abstracts are not available.

1214. National Institute on Drug Abuse. **Research Issues Update, 1978**. Ed. by Gregory A. Austin, Mary A. Macari, and Dan J. Lettieri. GPO, 1979. 308 pp. (Research issues 22.) OCLC 4889134. S/N 017-024-00876-1. $8.50. **HE20.8214:22**.

Detailed summaries of selected research and theoretical expositions dealing with the psychological aspects of drug use are presented. This volume contains references on topics previously covered in numbers 1-7, 15, and 17-20 of the *Research Issues* series.

Psychopharmacology

1215. National Institute of Mental Health. **Psychopharmacology Abstracts.** 1961-82. Quarterly. LC 63-001143. RC475.P66. 616.89. OCLC 01763067. **HE20.8109/2: vol./nos.**
Abstracts cover new developments and research into the nature and causes of mental disorders and methods of treatment and prevention. A companion data base is the National Clearinghouse for Mental Health Information data base.

1216. National Institute of Mental Health. **Psychotropic Drugs and Related Compounds.** By Earl Usdin and Daniel H. Efron. GPO, 1972. 2d ed. 791 pp. **HE20.2402:P95/8.**
This is an exhaustive compendium of compounds with psychoactive properties, with information on their chemical structure, pharmacologic activity, and classification. It lists manufacturers and distributors and their addresses. References and formulas are given in appendixes.

PSYCHIATRY AND MENTAL HEALTH

Bibliographies

1217. National Institute of Mental Health. **Abstracts of the Collected Works of C. G. Jung.** Ed. by Carrie Lee Rothgeb and Siegfried M. Clemens. GPO, 1978. 237 pp. OCLC 4300577. S/N 017-024-00781-1. $7.50. **HE20.8113:J95.**
This comprehensive compilation of abstracts of Jung's work, keyed to his papers and essays, gives full bibliographic citations, abstracts, and a KWOC subject index.

1218. National Institute of Mental Health. **Bibliography on Suicide and Suicide Prevention, 1897-1957, 1958-1970.** By Norman L. Farberon et al. GPO, 1972. 285 pp. LC 72-602910. **HE20.2417:Su3.**
A bibliography of scholarly research culled from scientific indexes, this title lists journal articles alphabetically by author, with no annotations. It is in two parts, with part 1 covering 1897-1957 and part 2 covering 1958-1970.

1219. National Institute of Mental Health. **Changing Directions in the Treatment of Women: A Mental Health Bibliography.** GPO, 1979. 494 pp. **HE20.8113: W34/2.**
This comprehensive, annotated bibliography on psychotherapy for women between 1960 and 1977 covers theoretical literature on the psychology and biology of women, criticism of the treatment of women, research responses to criticism, modifications of therapy and new approaches, treatment of specific problems or groups, and alternative approaches.

1220. National Institute of Mental Health. **Community Mental Health Centers: Perspectives of the Seventies; An Annotated Bibliography.** Comp. by Frances H. Premo and Louise G. Wiseman. GPO, 1981. OCLC 07728470. **HE20.8113: C73/2.**
This is an annotated bibliography of scholarly publications on all aspects of mental health care.

1221.   National Institute of Mental Health. **Coping and Adaptation: An Annotated Bibliography and Study Guide**. Ed. by George V. Coelho and Richard I. Irving. GPO, 1981. 480 pp. OCLC 7163635. **HE20.8113:C79**.
This multidisciplinary bibliography focuses on mental health literature concerned with human responses to catastrophic events, life-threatening injuries and illnesses, and crises of developmental transitions.

1222.   Public Health Service. **Studies on Electroconvulsive Therapy, 1939-1963; A Selected Annotated Bibliography**. GPO, 1966. 413 pp. (Public health bibliography series, no. 64.) **FS2.21:64**.
This is a bibliography of the results of research on aspects of electroconvulsive therapy used as psychiatric treatment. It includes author and subject indexes.

See also SB 167.

Directories

1223.   National Institute of Mental Health. **The Consumer's Guide to Mental Health and Related Federal Programs**. Ed. by John J. Cohrssen and Louis E. Kopolow. GPO, 1979. 204 pp. OCLC 5927698. S/N 017-024-00953-9. $6. **HE20.8108:C76**.
The guide covers federal mental health services and federal programs and benefits related to employment, housing, social security, welfare, food, and transportation. Entries give program description, eligibility requirements, and application procedures. It is much more concise and easier to use than the *Catalog of Domestic Assistance Programs*, from which the listing was compiled. An appendix gives addresses and telephone numbers of agencies and regional offices.

1224.   National Institute of Mental Health. **Directory: Federally Funded Community Health Centers, 1981**. GPO, 1981. 110 pp. S/N 017-024-01103-7. $5. **HE20.8102:C73/981**.
This state-by-state listing gives name, address, telephone number, name of director and board chairperson, and information about federal support.

1225.   National Institute of Mental Health. **Mental Health Directory**. GPO, 1964- . Irregular. LC 65-60647. RA790.7.U5A55. OCLC 1714912. **HE20.8123:yr**.
This is a guide to mental health programs and services in the United States with information on programs, personnel, and facilities.

Machine Readable Data

1226.   National Institute of Mental Health. **National Clearinghouse for Mental Health Information Data Base**. 1965- .
This machine readable data base provides references to mental health literature worldwide and related topics such as chemistry and chemical engineering, life sciences, medicine, psychology, and social sciences. A companion source in print form is *Psychopharmacology Abstracts*. This data base is searchable through BRS.

PUBLIC HEALTH

1227. Bureau of Health Manpower. **Home Health Care Programs: A Selected Bibliography**. GPO, 1979. 97 pp. (Nurse planning information series, no. 10.) OCLC 5666535. **HE20.6613:10**.
Literature related to planning, managing, and evaluating health care for the ill and disabled in home settings is listed, with annotations and availability information.

1228. Bureau of Health Planning. **Health Planning Reports ... Index**. IA, 1981, LC 81-602746. OCLC 07445853. **HE20.6110/2:nos**.
The indexes are a bibliography of holdings in the National Health Planning Information Center's collection of literature and government reports. There are four index volumes: subject, personal author, corporate author, and title.

1229. Bureau of Health Planning and Resources Development. **Guidelines for Planning Health Services: An Annotated Bibliography**. IA, 1978. 250 pp. (Health planning bibliography series, no. 9.) OCLC 4580835. **HE20.6112/2:9**.
This is an annotated bibliography of materials that discuss guidelines for providing health services in specialized areas of health planning. References are organized to correspond with the standards discussed in the *National Guidelines for Health Planning* and supplement the bibliography in that publication. References cover thirteen specialities, including cardiac care, burn care, mental health services, and maternal and child care.

1230. Centers for Disease Control. **Health Information for International Travel**. GPO, 1976- . Annual. LC 77-649068. RA783.5.C45a. 614.4/2/02491. OCLC 2905736. **HE20.7009:vol./supp**.
Published as an annual supplement to the *Morbidity and Mortality Weekly Report*, this handbook for health departments, doctors, travel agents, and others advising international travelers lists the vaccinations required by various countries and gives information on measures travelers may take to protect their health and facilitate their travel. The weekly "Blue Sheet" (Countries with Areas Infected with Quarantinable Diseases) supplements this title by listing countries with outbreaks of cholera, plague, smallpox, or yellow fever.

1231. Centers for Disease Control. **Morbidity and Mortality Weekly Report**. GPO, 1976- . Weekly with annual supplement. OCLC 03454113. S/N 017-023-80003-5. $70/yr. **HE20.7009:vol./nos**.

1232. Public Health Service. **Public Health Engineering Abstracts**. 47 vols. GPO, 1928-67. LC 70-600422. **FS2.13:vol./nos**.
More than eight hundred domestic and foreign journals of science and engineering, reports of states and the federal government, and reports and proceedings of scientific research groups were reviewed. "Articles abstracted are selected for their relationship and importance to environmental health." Entries are arranged alphabetically by author under broad subjects. Two indexes were published annually: author and subject.

See also SB 122.

TOXICOLOGY

1233. Food and Drug Administration. **Handbook of Common Poisonings in Children.** GPO, 1977. 105 pp. OCLC 2858021. **HE20.4008:P75/3.**
This "pocket poison information center" gives information on seventy-three of the most common poisoners of children, including a brief description, toxicity data, clinical signs and symptoms, treatment, and bibliographic references.

1234. Food and Drug Administration. Office of Drugs. **Directory of United States Poison Control Centers.** GPO, 1983- . Annual. OCLC 09228773. **HE20.4003/2-2:yr.**
The directory is arranged alphabetically by state and lists facilities that provide information for the medical profession on the prevention and treatment of accidents involving ingestion of poisons. Centers are listed by city within each state with name and address, telephone number, and names of directors for each center. Only centers that have services available twenty-four hours a day are listed.

1235. National Institute for Occupational Safety and Health. **Registry of Toxic Effects of Chemical Substances.** GPO, 1975- . Quarterly. LC 75-649213. RA1215.N37a. 615.9/02/0212. OCLC 2246107. S/N 017-033-80001-4 (microfiche). $34/yr. **HE20.7112/3:date.**
Basic information is given on the toxic and biological effects of known toxic chemical substances. Reading the section titled "Detailed File Description" is a must for the first-time user. Entries give substance prime name, update, Chemical Abstracts Service registry number, molecular weight, molecular formula, synonyms, mutation data, skin and eye irritation, toxicity, cited reference, aquatic toxicity rating, reviews, standards and regulations, criteria documents, and status. A nonspecialist might have some difficulty using it, but the foreword says this publication is meant for anyone concerned with safe handling of chemicals, as well as physicians, industrial hygienists, toxicologists, and researchers.

1236. National Library of Medicine. **RTECS: Registry of Toxic Effects of Chemical Substances.**
This machine readable online data file is an annual compilation prepared by the National Institute for Occupational Safety and Health. It contains acute toxicity data for approximately forty-one thousand substances. For some compounds there are also threshold limit values, recommended standards in air, and aquatic toxicity data.

Eleven regional medical libraries, each responsible for a geographic area, coordinate NLM's online search services in the United States. For information on the Online Center nearest to you write to the Office of Inquiries and Publications Management, National Library of Medicine, 8600 Rockville Pike, Bethesda, MD 20209. In addition, RTECS may be searched from computer terminals at institutions with access to NLM's MEDLINE.

1237. National Library of Medicine. **TDB: Toxicology Data Bank.**
This is a machine readable file with chemical, pharmacological, and toxicological information and data on several thousand substances. Data have been taken from over a hundred major handbooks and textbooks. Over sixty data elements are provided, including synonyms, chemical and physical properties, molecular formulas, and Chemical Abstracts Service (CAS) registry numbers.

1238. National Library of Medicine. **Toxicity Bibliography.** GPO, 1968-77. Quarterly. OCLC 1607266. **HE20.3613:vol./nos.**

This highly specialized medical bibliography included the "entire range of chemical and biological interactions," drawn selectively from current citations in the MEDLARS files. It covered reports on toxicity studies, adverse drug reactions, and poisoning in man and animals. It was designed to provide "health professionals working in toxicology and related disciplines access to the world's relevant and significant journal literature in this field." Section I, "Drugs and Chemicals," is by entry number with its own author and subject index. Section II, "Adverse Reactions to Drugs and Chemicals," is subdivided into many categories and has no index.

VETERINARY MEDICINE

1239.	Agricultural Research Service. **Index-Catalogue of Medical and Veterinary Zoology**. 18 vols. GPO, 1939-52. **A77.219/2:vol.**

_____. **Supplements**. GPO, 1953- . Irregular. LC 79-3760. OCLC 1525723. First published in 1892, this is the standard, internationally known reference for researchers in parasitology. An index to the world's literature on parasitology in both animals and man, it has been issued in multivolume, numbered supplements since 1952. The supplements are issued biennially and each has seven parts.

Part 1. **Authors: A-Z**.

Part 2. **Protozoa**.

Part 3. **Trematoda and Cestoda**.

Part 4. **Nematoda and Acanthocephala**.

Part 5. **Arthropoda and Miscellaneous Phyla**.

Part 6. **Subject Headings and Treatment**.

Part 7. **Hosts**.

Entries are made in the various parts of the *Index-Catalogue* alphabetically by author, parasite, host, subject heading (immunity, monoclonal antibodies, pheromones, etc.), and drug treatment. Information recorded includes: parasites and hosts reported, body location on or in the host, geographic distribution, parasite synonymy, taxonomic changes, classification, keys, drug treatment, and brief phrases describing subject matter content. Basic bibliographic information is included on each entry. Recently discontinued by the federal government, the index is now published by Oryx Press.

1240.	Animal and Plant Health Inspection Service. **Animal Disease: Thesaurus**. GPO, 1979. 317 pp. OCLC 4824105. **A101.2:D63/3**.
This source was developed to fill the need for a method of indexing and coding veterinary literature for retrieval of information on animal diseases exotic to the United States. It may also be used for coding other diseases as well. It contains about forty-five hundred coded terms in alphabetic hierarchical arrangement.

1241.	Animal and Plant Health Inspection Service. **Directory of Animal Disease Diagnostic Laboratories**. IA, 1977. SF769.D57. 636.089/6/0072073. OCLC 2878566. **A101.2:D63/2/977**.
Laboratories performing diagnostic tests for diseases of domestic and wild animals are listed, with information on the types of tests performed at each and a list of national diagnostic reference centers.

1242.	Bureau of Animal Industry. **Index-Catalogue of Medical and Veterinary Zoology — Authors**. 5 vols. GPO, 1902-12. (Bulletin 39.) **A4.18:39**.

Physics

BIBLIOGRAPHIES

1243. National Bureau of Standards. **Atomic Energy Levels as Derived from Analysis of Optical Spectra**. 3 vols. GPO, 1949-58 (repr. 1971). (National standard reference data series, no. 35.) LC 75-609945. **C13.48:325/v.1-3**.

    Vol. 1. 309 pp. S/N 003-003-00949-1. $15.

    Vol. 2. 227 pp. S/N 003-003-00935-1. $14.

    Vol. 3. 245 pp. S/N 003-003-00950-4. $14.

1244. National Bureau of Standards. **Bibliography on the Analyses of Optical Atomic Spectra**. By C. E. Moore. 4 vols. GPO, 1968. (NBS special publication 306.) **C13.10:306-nos**.
The earlier work (entry 1243) contains for each optical spectrum a bibliography used in the compilation of the data. The newer work continues this, covering the literature published from 1949 to 1968. The selection of references is limited to those needed for the preparation of revised tables of atomic energy levels.

1245. National Bureau of Standards. **Bibliography of Flame Spectroscopy: Analytical Applications, 1880-1966**. GPO, 1967. 185 pp. (NBS special publication 281.) **C13.10:281**.
This major bibliography cites 5,113 works in flame spectroscopy selected with emphasis on analytical measurements. It covers the period 1880 to 1966. Subject indexes precede most sections.

1246. National Technical Information Service. **A Directory of Computer Software Applications: Physics, 1970-May 1978**. NTIS, 1978. 331 pp. (PB-281 642.) OCLC 4370512. **C51.ll/5:P56**.
Physics reports that list computer programs and/or their documentation are cited. Software listed pertains to topics such as acoustics, electricity and magnetism, fluid mechanics, masers and lasers, optics, nuclear physics, plasma physics, solid state physics, and thermodynamics. Solid mechanics studies are excluded. Bibliographic data and abstracts and subject and corporate author indexes are provided. The computer programs and documentation listed may be purchased from NTIS in hard copy or microfiche.

DICTIONARIES

1247. National Bureau of Standards. **Color: Universal Language and Dictionary of Names.** By Kenneth L. Kelley and Deane B. Judd. GPO, 1976. 189 pp. (NBS special publication 440.) LC 76-600071. OCLC 2935667. **C13.10:440.**

This is a combined issue of the classic *Color Names Dictionary* and its supplement, *The Universal Color Language*. The dictionary, a classic text in the field of color since its initial publication in 1956, describes the selection of the Inter-Society Color Council-National Bureau of Standards hue names and modifiers descriptive of the lightness and saturation of color. *The Universal Color Language* relates color-order systems and methods of designating color in six levels of fineness.

RESEARCH

1248. National Bureau of Standards. **Hydraulic Research in the United States.** GPO, 1933-70. Biennial. (NBS special publication series.) LC 34-3323. TC158.U5. 627.072. OCLC 1589234. **C13.10:nos. vary.**

Research projects and reports in hydraulics and hydrodynamics were described and research laboratories listed, with detailed subject indexes in each issue.

1249. National Bureau of Standards. **Hydraulic Research in the United States and Canada.** GPO, 1972- . (NBS special publication series.) LC 74-643168. TC158.U5. 627.07/2073. OCLC 1793242. **C13.10:nos. vary.**

This continues *Hydraulic Research in the United States.*

TABLES

1250. National Bureau of Standards. **Units of Weight and Measure: International (Metric) and U.S. Customary Definitions and Tables of Equivalents.** GPO, 1967. 251 pp. (NBS special publication 286.) **C13.10:286.**

The primary purpose of this publication is to make available the most often needed weights and measures conversion tables, that is, conversion between the U.S. customary system and the international (metric) system. A secondary purpose is to present a brief history of the international (metric) system from its origin through its progress in the United States.

1251. Smithsonian Institution. **Smithsonian Physical Tables.** GPO, 1954. 9th rev. ed. 827 pp. (Smithsonian miscellaneous collections, vol. 120.) LC 54-60067. **SI1.7:120.**

This volume consists of 901 tables giving "data of general interest to scientists and engineeers and of particular interest to those concerned with physics in its broader sense" (Preface). The very detailed index is necessary for access to the tables.

Transportation

GENERAL WORKS

1252. Bureau of the Census. **Census Bureau Guide to Transportation Statistics.** By Donald G. Wright and Evelyn S. Davis. GPO, 1976. 88 pp. LC 76-608059. HE18.B87 1976. 380.5/0973. OCLC 2075303. **C3.6/2:T68.**
The guide describes the 1972 Census of Transportation and its three components: the National Travel Survey, the Truck Inventory and Use Survey, and the Commodity Transportation Survey. Survey method and design, published and unpublished data, and public use tapes are described.

1253. Department of Transportation. **Symbol Signs: Development of Passenger/Pedestrian Oriented Symbols for Use in Transportation Related Facilities.** IA, 1974. 230 pp., illus. **TD1.2:Sy6.**

_____. **Symbol Signs 2.** GPO, 1979. 148 pp., illus. OCLC 5370725. S/N 050-000-00150-4. $7. **TD1.2:Sy6/979.**
This report and its supplement illustrate and describe the use of transportation-related, passenger- and pedestrian oriented symbol signs, which communicate their message without words.

1254. National Technical Information Service. **A Directory of Computer Software Applications: Transportation, 1970-April 1978.** NTIS, 1978. 83 pp. (PB-279 570.) OCLC 4179649. **C51.11/5:T68.**
Reports related to transportation that include lists of computer programs and/or their documentation are cited. Software listed is related to topics such as motor vehicle safety, aviation safety, air traffic control, rail freight handling, motor vehicle traffic control, marine transportation scheduling, global navigation systems, and noise exposure. Complete bibliographic data and abstracts are given, as well as subject and corporate author indexes. The computer programs and documentation listed may be purchased from NTIS in hard copy or microfiche.

1255. Transportation Research Board. **Transportation Research Information Services (TRIS).** 1968- .
This is an online machine readable data file of transportation research on air, highway, rail, and maritime transport; mass transit; and other transportation modes. In addition

to summaries of ongoing and recently completed research projects, TRIS includes abstracts of journal articles, technical papers in conference proceedings, and research reports. It is available on Lockheed DIALOG, or write to HRIS Manager, Transportation Research Board, 2101 Constitution Ave., N.W., Washington, DC 20418.

1256.   Urban Mass Transportation Administration. **Annotated Bibliography of Analytical Aids**. NTIS, 1979. 104 pp. OCLC 4979869. **TD7.11:IT-06-9020-79-1**.
In this descriptive listing of simplified, manual aids for transportation analysis, entries give source of the aid, description, and often cite a reference that describes the technique and its application. Emphasis is on simple aids to improve transportation decisions without computers or extensive data collection.

AVIATION

1257.   Civil Aeronautics Board. **Supplement to the Handbook of Airline Statistics**. NTIS, biennial. OCLC 4151991. **C31.249:yrs./supp**.
Current and some historical statistics on traffic, financial, and other data for each U.S. certified air carrier are provided. Other sections include chronologies of significant events affecting aviation, growth of the airline industry, miscellaneous air transport data, comparisons of air with other models of transportation, and carrier group data. Information involving classes of air carriers other than the certificated air carriers is also given.

1258.   Federal Aviation Administration. **Census of U.S. Civil Aircraft**. GPO, 1966- . Annual. LC 76-641161. HE9803.A1A27. 387.7/33/40973. OCLC 1136794. **TD4.18:yr**.
The annual FAA count of all registered civil aircraft in the United States is presented. Information is categorized by manufacturer and listed state by state, with the type and number of engines and size of each aircraft. Also listed are the numbers of U.S. registered aircraft kept in foreign countries.

1259.   Federal Aviation Administration. **FAA Aviation Forecasts**. IA, 1978/79- . Annual. OCLC 4341789. **TD4.2:Av5/yrs**.
The official FAA forecasts for domestic air activity for ten-year periods include activity at airports, air route traffic control centers, and services of flight service stations.

1260.   Federal Aviation Administration. **FAA Directory**. IA, 1978- . Irregular. LC 79-642912. HE9803.AlF43f. 353.008/77/025. OCLC 4554535. **TD4.52:date**.
Names, addresses, telephone numbers, and other directory information are provided for FAA offices in Washington and for regional and field offices. Additional information includes a directory of organizations concerned with aviation and a glossary describing various facilities.

1261.   Federal Aviation Administration. **FAA Statistical Handbook of Aviation**. GPO, 1959- . Annual. OCLC 02707503. **TD4.20:yr**.
This source of historical data helpful in evaluating progress, identifying trends, and estimating future activity includes charts, graphs, maps, and narrative descriptions of aspects of U.S. aviation activity.

1262.   Library of Congress. **Wilbur and Orville Wright: Pictorial Materials, a Documentary Guide**. By Arthur G. Renstrom. GPO, 1982. 221 pp. LC 82-600194. TL540.W525R46 1982. 016.62913/0092/2. OCLC 08495548. S/N 030-001-00100-8. $6. **LC1.6/4:W93**.

1263. Library of Congress. Science and Technology Division. **Wilbur and Orville Wright: A Bibliography Commemorating the 100th Anniversary of the Birth of Wilbur Wright, April 16, 1867.** Comp. by Arthur G. Renstrom. GPO, 1968. 187 pp. LC 68-60013. Z8986.33.R4. Free from the Science and Technology Division, Library of Congress, Washington, DC 20540. **LC33.2:W93.**

Issued as a "bibliographic service to scholars and others interested in aeronautical history ... and also as a tribute to Wilbur and Orville Wright by the Library of Congress," this bibliography is an expansion of the *Papers of the Wright Brothers* published in 1953 by McGraw-Hill. It is arranged first by broad subject headings (i.e., interviews, aeroplanes and flights, juvenile publications) and then, in most sections, chronologically. Entries are annotated and indexed by authors, persons, and institutions.

1264. Library of Congress. Science and Technology Division. **Wilbur and Orville Wright: A Chronology Commemorating the Hundredth Anniversary of the Birth of Orville Wright, August 19, 1871.** By Arthur Renstrom. GPO, 1975. 234 pp. LC 74-11244. TL540.W7R46. S/N 030-018-00014-1. $6. **LC33.2:W93/2.**

See also SB 12 and SB 13.

HIGHWAYS

1265. Federal Highway Administration. **Handbook of Highway Safety Design and Operating Practices.** GPO, 1978. 120 pp., illus. OCLC 4875445. S/N 050-003-00340-9. $6.50. **TD2.8:H53/978.**

This concise, well-illustrated handbook of general principles of highway safety design is not a standards list or a detailed design manual, but an educational tool and reference guide at the introductory level. It is useful for selecting solutions for hazardous situations, or for operational problems.

1266. Federal Highway Administration. **Highway Statistics.** GPO, 1945- . Annual. OCLC 01221546. **TD2.23:yr.**

This is a compilation of analyzed general interest statistics on motor fuel, vehicles, driver licensing, highway user taxes, state highway finance, mileage, and federal aid.

1267. Federal Highway Administration. **Highway Statistics: Summary to [year].** GPO, 1945- . Decennial. 1975 ed. S/N 050-001-00129-2. $5.50. **TD2.23/2:yr.**

This series summarizes the important statistical series in *Highway Statistics* and includes earlier data than the annual volumes.

1268. National Highway Safety Bureau. **NHSB Thesaurus of Traffic and Motor Vehicle Safety Terms.** GPO, 1970. 2d ed. 129 pp. **TD8.10/4:T34.**

This is a supplement to *Highway Safety Literature* and will aid researchers using this bibliography in finding the correct subject headings and related headings for specific areas of research.

1269. National Highway Traffic Safety Administration. **Driver Licensing: A Subject Bibliography from Highway Safety Literature.** Comp. by Lois Flynn et al. NTIS, 1979. 316 pp. (Subject bibliography, SB-36.) OCLC 5733440. **TD8.13/3:36.**

The bibliography has abstracts and sources of availability.

1270. National Highway Traffic Safety Administration. **Highway Safety Literature.** IA, 1974- . Monthly. OCLC 04795222. **TD8.10:nos.**

Abstracts are provided for documents acquired by the Technical Reference Division of the National Highway Traffic Safety Administration. The publication is divided into the following sections: abstract citations, index to abstracts, a keyword-out-of-context list of words in titles; author index; corporate author index; contract number index; and report number index. It continues *Announcement of Highway Safety Literature* and is also available in machine readable format, the Highway Safety Literature data base.

1271.   National Highway Traffic Safety Administration. **Passive Restraints: A Subject Bibliography from Highway Safety Literature**. Comp. by Lois Flynn. NTIS, 1979. 190 pp. (Subject bibliography, SB-37.) OCLC 5768221. **TD8.13/3:37**.
Literature on the development and use of passive restraints in motor vehicles is listed and annotated, with availability of sources noted.

1272.   National Research Council. Transportation Research Board. **HRIS Abstracts**. IA, 1967- . Quarterly. LC 75-642521. 338.1'08. **TD1.N469a**.
Compiled from the computer records of the Highway Research Information Service (HRIS), this publication provides abstracts of journal articles, research reports, and technical papers and announcements of bibliographies related to highway research worldwide. All abstracts are in English.

See also SB 3.

RAILROADS

1273.   Federal Railroad Administration. **The Railroad Situation: A Perspective on the Present, Past and Future of the U.S. Railroad Industry**. By C. E. Urba et al. GPO, 1978. 487 pp., illus. (FRA-OPPD-79-7.) S/N 050-005-00030-5. $11. **TD3.15/5:79-7**.
This overview of the U.S. railroad industry describes its current and historical aspects with emphasis on the period 1929-76. It forecasts the future of the industry through 1986.

See also SB 218.

Part Four

Humanities

Architecture

1274. ACTION. Peace Corps. **Handbook for Building Homes of Earth**. By Lyle A. Wolfskill, Wayne A. Dunlap, and Bob M. Gallaway. NTIS, 1980. 159 columns. Illus. (ACTION pamphlet 4200.36.) OCLC 6109407. **AA1.11:4200.36**.
This basic introduction to earth dwellings describes new developments in soil mechanics in simple terms, including kinds of soils found across the world, ways to use these soil types for buildings, types of earth construction, building sites, methods, and effects of various climates and conditions. It is illustrated with photographs and drawings. This title was written for Peace Corps volunteers, but is simple enough to be used by anyone, anywhere.

1275. Commission of Fine Arts. **Massachusetts Avenue Architecture**. By J. L. Sibley Jennings et al. 2 vols. GPO, 1973-75. **FA1.2:M38/v.1,2**.
This is a detailed survey of beaux-arts buildings on Massachusetts Avenue in northwest Washington, DC, which typify the avenue's rich, varied heritage. Illustrations, technical descriptions, permits, deeds, biographies of occupants, and physical and social histories are included.

1276. Commission of Fine Arts. **Sixteenth Street Architecture**. By Sue A. Kohler and Jeffrey R. Carson. GPO, 1978. Illus. LC 79-603275. NA735.W3K644. 975.3. OCLC 5847373. **FA1.2:Si9**.
The large, sometimes elaborate, residences of the 16th Street area of northwest Washington DC, are described. Their architects and owners were often nationally prominent.

1277. Commission of Fine Arts. **Washington Architecture, 1791-1861: Problems in Development**. By Daniel D. Reiff. GPO, 1972. 161 pp., illus. LC 72-602603. **FA1.2:W27/4/791-861**.

1278. Department of Housing and Urban Development. **The First Passive Solar Home Awards**. GPO, 1980. 226 pp., illus. OCLC 4995218. S/N 023-000-00517-4. $7.50. **HH1.2:P26/4**.
Examples of the best passive architecture available from HUD grant recipients are described. Designs are for homes needing few conventional energy sources. Design approaches, mistakes to avoid, construction, and energy calculations are covered, with many illustrations. A design for a solar doghouse is included.

1279.　National Park Service. **Historic Engineering Record Catalog**. Comp. by Donald
　　　　E. Sackheim. GPO, 1976. 193 pp., illus. T21.H53 1976. 609. OCLC 2332363.
　　　　I29.84/2:C28/976.
Because engineering and industrial sites are rapidly disappearing, the National Park
Service established the Historic American Engineering Record (HAER) in 1969 to
provide archival documentation on important historical structures. This catalog lists the
documentation available in the HAER collection housed in the Library of Congress. It
is arranged by states and cities, with a subject index.

1280.　National Park Service. **Shaker Built: Catalog of Shaker Architectural Records
　　　　from Historic American Buildings Survey**. Ed. by John Poppeliers. IA, 1974. 87
　　　　pp., illus. **I29.74:Sh1**.
The Historic Buildings Survey has one of the largest archival collections of Shaker
architecture and includes drawings, photographs, and documentation of buildings. For
many of these structures which are no longer standing, these are the only known
records. The catalog lists structures in six states, giving historic names, later names,
Shaker community "families," site, and a brief description. Photographs and illustrations are included.

See also SB 215.

Fine Arts

1281. Congress. House. **Art in the United States Capitol**. Prep. by the Architect of the Capitol under the direction of the Joint Committee on the Library. GPO, 1978. 453 pp., illus. (House document 94-660.) S/N 052-071-00546-3. $20. **X94-2:H.doc.660**.
This edition is the cumulation of various publications issued during the past seventy years and is the first with color photographs. It includes photographs and descriptions of portraits, paintings, busts, statues, reliefs, frescoes and murals, exterior sculpture, and miscellaneous art that make up the collection of art on display in the U.S. Capitol building.

1282. Freer Gallery of Art. **Chinese Art of the Warring States Period: Change and Continuity, 480-222 B.C.** By Thomas Lawton. GPO, 1982. 202 pp., illus. LC 82-600184. NK1068.L35 1983. 730/.0931/0740153. OCLC 08476720. S/N 047-001-00150-8. **SI1.2:C44**.
This catalog of an exhibition describes artifacts from the Chinese warring states period, including bronze vessels, fittings, weapons, bronze mirrors, bronze garment hooks, jades, and lacquer ware. Information on historical context is given, plus an index of Japanese and Chinese names and terms.

1283. Library of Congress. **A.L.A. Portrait Index: An Index to Portraits Contained in Printed Books and Periodicals**. Ed. by William Coolidge Lane and Nina E. Browne. GPO, 1906. 1,600 pp. LC 6-35019. N7626.A2. (Repr.: Burt Franklin, 3 vols., $73.) **LC1.2:P83**.
Over 6,200 volumes were analyzed in the compilation of this standard reference source. Approximately 40,000 persons and 120,000 portraits are listed. Excluded are references to original portraits, as such, engravings separately published, collections of engravings, and genealogical works. The brief entries give names, dates of birth and death, sources of portraits, and information concerning the artists or engravers. The index lists 1,181 titles (which contain 6,216 volumes) of works cited.

1284. Library of Congress. Prints and Photographs Division. **Catalog of the National Exhibition of Prints Held at the Library of Congress**. GPO, 1943-76. Annual. NE508.A3. The 21st (1969) through 25th (1976) are free from the Central Services Division, Library of Congress, Washington, DC 20540. **LC25.8:yr**.

Prints by artists residing in the United States and accepted by a panel of judges for showing in the annual National Exhibition of Prints are listed. Arrangement is alphabetic by artists with addresses, titles of prints, media, and costs. Selected prints from the exhibition are reproduced in the catalog.

1285.   Library of Congress. Prints and Photographs Division. **Graphic Sampler**. By Renata V. Shaw. GPO, 1979. 368 pp., illus. LC 79-12124. S/N 030-000-00092-7. $12. **LC25.2:G76**.

This is a selection of images, with explication, from the Prints and Photographs Division. The selection was determined by rediscovery of a group of drawings or prints, or by the newness or interest of recent acquisitions. It includes pictures created between the 15th century and 1800; prints and drawings from the 19th century; and prints, drawings, and paintings from 1900 to the 1960s.

1286.   National Collection of Fine Arts. **Academy: The Academic Tradition in American Art**. By Lois Marie Fink and Joshua C. Taylor. GPO, 1975. 272 pp., illus. LC 75-619121. **SI6.2:Ac1**.

This title represents an exhibition organized for the 150th anniversary of the National Academy of Design. The works included are by members or associates of the academy born before 1900, and were compiled to explore the Academy's past and the nature of the academic tradition in American art. Focus is on less well studied aspects and artists.

1287.   National Collection of Fine Arts. **America as Art**. By Joshua C. Taylor. GPO, 1976. 320 pp., illus. LC 76-004482. N6505.T37. 709/.73. OCLC 2048232. **SI6.2:Am3/4**.

This was not intended to be a comprehensive study of art in America, but an analysis of eight movements "in which art and the identity of America came close." The works included represent aspects of American art that are among the lesser known.

1288.   National Collection of Fine Arts. **American Art in the Barbizon Mood**. By Peter Bermingham. GPO, 1975. 191 pp., illus. LC 74-2664. **SI6.2:B23**.

This illustrated catalog of art from the mid-nineteenth century Barbizon School includes an historical overview, reproductions of paintings, biographies of artists, and a bibliography.

1289.   National Portrait Gallery. **Facing the Light: Historic American Portrait Daguerreotypes**. By Harold Francis Pfister. GPO, 1978. 378 pp., illus. TR680.P47. 779/.2/097 307 40153. OCLC 3868080. **SI11.2:L62**.

The daguerreotype dominated America's first fifty years of photography, and most examples were portraits. This catalog of a major exhibition of American portrait daguerreotypes features portraits of nationally prominent people, with essays on them and their portrait experiences.

1290.   Smithsonian Institution. **Finder's Guide to Prints and Drawings in the Smithsonian Institution**. IA, 1981. 210 pp., illus. LC 81-607070. N855.8.A56. 760.074/0153/2/19. OCLC 7597167.

This guide to works of art on paper is designed to be used by researchers. Included are scientific works, manuscripts, and archival collections as well as drawings, oils, and water colors. Each specific collection is described in essay form and the services available to researchers are noted. Bibliographies, a general index, and an index to works by artists' names are provided. This is the first volume in the *Finder's Guide to Works in the Smithsonian Institution* (series).

See also SB 107.

Literature

GENERAL WORKS

Bibliographies

1291. Library of Congress. Latin American, Portuguese, and Spanish Division. **Archive of Hispanic Literature on Tape: Descriptive Guide**. Comp. by Francisco Aguilera and ed. by Georgette Magassy Dorn. GPO, 1974. 516 pp., illus. LC 73-19812. Z1609.L7U54 1974. Free from the Central Services Division, Library of Congress, Washington, DC 20540. **LC24.2:H62/2**.

The archive contains recorded prose and poetry from Latin America and the Iberian peninsula. Recordings, made since 1943, are of writers reading their own work in Spanish, Portuguese, French, Catalan, and the Indian languages of Zapotec, Nahuatl, and Quechua. Poems, selections from novels, essays, and other commentaries are included. Each entry gives a biographical sketch of the author, discussion of his work, listing of holdings for him, and a bibliography of his important publications.

1292. Library of Congress. Manuscript Division. **Literary Recordings: A Checklist of the Archive of Recorded Poetry and Literature in the Library of Congress**. Comp. by Jennifer Whittington. GPO, 1981. 299 pp. PS306.5.Z9V53 1979. 016.811/5. OCLC 75727688. S/N 030-001-00084-2. $8.50. **LC4.2:L71/2**.

This is an inventory list of the Library of Congress collection of literary recordings of poets reading their own work, as of May 1975. Poem titles and first line of untitled poems are listed, along with the poet's name and the place and date of the reading. Copies of many of the recordings may be purchased.

See also SB 142.

Individual Authors

Louisa May Alcott

1293. Library of Congress. General Reference and Bibliography Division. **Louisa May Alcott: A Centennial for Little Women; an Annotated Selected Bibliography.** Comp. by Judith C. Ullom. GPO, 1969. LC 76-600591. Z8024.8.U5. Free from the Central Services Division, Library of Congress, Washington, DC 20540. **LC2.2:Al1/2.**

This illustrated bibliography serves as a catalog of the Library of Congress centennial exhibition of *Little Women* (1868) by Louisa May Alcott. Contents are: "Early Writings," "Novels," "Little Women Series," "Multi-Volume Collections," "Single-Volume Collections," "Separate Editions of Stories," "Collections," "Modern Anthologies," "Bio-Critical Studies," and a title index. This is a selective bibliography and contains only first editions and some later editions that are significant for the illustrations.

Samuel Langhorne Clemens

1294. Library of Congress. **Samuel Langhorne Clemens: A Centennial for Tom Sawyer; an Annotated, Selected Bibliography.** By Virginia Haviland and Margaret N. Coughlan. GPO, 1977. 86 pp., illus. LC 76-608129. Z8176.H38. S/N 030-001-00070-2. $4.75. **LC1.12/2:C59.**

Walt Whitman

1295. Library of Congress. **Walt Whitman: A Catalog Based upon the Collections of the Library of Congress.** By Charles E. Feinberg. GPO, 1955. 147 pp. LC 55-60006. Z8971.5.U62. (Repr.: Canner, $7.50; Folcroft, $17.50.) **LC29.2:W59.**

Works are listed by type: manuscript collections, separate works, collections, biography, bibliographies. Most are not annotated. An index of names and titles is included.

CHILDREN'S LITERATURE

1296. Library of Congress. **The Best of Children's Books, 1964-1978.** By Virginia Haviland. GPO, 1980. 90 pp., illus. LC 80-607070. Z1037.1.H38. 010. OCLC 6223085. S/N 030-001-00093-1. $5.50. **LC1.12/2:C43/5/964-78.**

The best from fifteen years of Library of Congress annual lists of books for children from preschool through junior high school are listed. Entries give bibliographic information, annotation, and a guide to grade level.

1297. Library of Congress. **Children's Books: A List of Books for Preschool through Junior High School Age.** GPO, 1964- . Annual. LC 65-60015. **LC2.11:yr.**

These short lists, published yearly since 1964, have been compiled by specialists in the Children's Literature Center of the Library of Congress. New books are described in terms of content, design, and grade level, with publisher, price, LC card number, and ISBN given. Picture books, fiction, folklore, poetry, biography, history, and nonfiction are covered.

1298. Library of Congress. **Children's Literature: A Guide to Reference Sources.** Comp. by Virginia Haviland. GPO, 1966. 341 pp., illus. LC 66-62734. S/N 030-001-00014-1. $12. **LC2.8:C43.**

> 1st Supplement. GPO, 1972. 316 pp., illus. S/N 030-001-00044-3. $12.

> 2d Supplement. GPO, 1977. 413 pp., illus. S/N 030-001-00075-3. $13.

> 3d Supplement. GPO, 1982. 279 pp., illus. S/N 030-001-00096-6. $11.

This indispensable bibliography covers all aspects of children's literature in the United States and worldwide. Books and articles about children's literature are described and critically evaluated. Material for children up to age fourteen or the eighth grade is covered. Critical appraisals of specific authors and illustrators, catalogs of collections, and exhibitions are discussed and evaluated. A teacher or librarian can use the guide to find information on storytelling, surveys and evaluations of library programs, and promoting reading. The third supplement directs the reader to recent studies in children's literature. Indexes to authors, titles, and subjects are included, along with illustrations from historical and contemporary children's books.

1299. Library of Congress. **Children and Poetry: A Selective, Annotated Bibliography.** Comp. by Virginia Haviland and William Jay Smith. GPO, 1978. 2d ed. 84 pp., illus.d LC 78-57071. Z1037.H36 1978. 028.52. OCLC 3915400. **LC1.12/2:P75/979.**

This selective, annotated bibliography of rhymes and more serious poetry, old and new, in English and translated from other languages will be useful for teachers, librarians, and parents in selecting poetry that will be pleasing and rewarding for children. This is a revision of the 1969 edition to include new poetry and fresh editions of the classics.

FABLES AND FOLKLORE

1300. Library of Congress. General Reference and Bibliography Division. **Folklore from Africa to the United States: An Annotated Bibliography.** Comp. by Margaret N. Coughlan. GPO, 1976. 161 pp., illus. LC 75-043905. Z5984.A35C68. 016.3982. OCLC 1976036. S/N 030-001-00066-4. $10. **LC2.2:F71.**

This bibliography was designed to reveal original sources of African tales and trace their relationship to stories carried to the West Indies and the American South. It is selective and annotated and describes collections held in the Library of Congress for children and adults which shed light on the cultures from which they arose.

POETRY

1301. Library of Congress. General Reference and Bibliography Division. **Sixty American Poets, 1896-1944.** By Allen Tate. GPO, 1954. Rev. ed. 155 pp. LC 54-60023. Z1231.P7U55 1954. (Repr.: Gale, $15.)

In this useful bibliography poets are listed alphabetically with critical notes, lists of publications, bibliographies, manuscript collections, and related information. Library locations of many items are noted.

Music

GENERAL WORKS

1302. Copyright Office. **Catalog of Copyright Entries, 3rd Series: Part 5, Music.** GPO, 1947-77. Semiannual. LC 6-35347. Z1219.U58C. **LC3.6/5:nos.**
Musical compositions listed in part 5 are in two sections; the first lists current and renewal registrations, and the second is an index to composers, lyricists, editors, and arrangers. From 1906 to 1946 music copyrights were listed in the *Catalog of Copyright Entries (New Series)* in part 3.

1303. Library of Congress. Processing Department. **Library of Congress Catalog: Music and Phonorecords; a Cumulative List of Works Represented by Library of Congress Printed Cards.** GPO, 1953-72. Semiannual. LC 53-60012. Z881.A1C328. **LC30.8/6:yr.**
Musical compositions and sound recordings cataloged by the Library of Congress were listed. Annual and quinquennial cumulations were also published. This is continued by *Music, Books on Music, and Sound Recordings.*

1304. Library of Congress. Processing Department. **Music, Books on Music, and Sound Recordings.** GPO, 1973- . Semiannual with annual and quinquennial cumulations. LC 74-64051. Z881.A1C328. 016.78. OCLC 01588934.

> Cumulation for 1973-77. 8 vols. (Repr.: Rowman & Littlefield, $89.97.)
>
> Cumulation for 1978. 2 vols. (LC, $55.)
>
> Cumulation for 1979. 2 vols. (LC, $60.)
>
> Cumulation for 1980. 2 vols. (LC, $70.)
>
> Cumulation for 1981. 653 pp. (LC, $80.)
>
> Cumulation for 1982. (LC, $90.)

For those available, write to the Cataloging Distribution Service, Library of Congress, Washington, DC 20541.

See also SB 221.

BIBLIOGRAPHIES

1305. Library of Congress. Music Division. **African Music: A Briefly Annotated Bibliography**. Comp. by Darius L. Thieme. GPO, 1964. 55 pp. LC 64-60046. ML120.A35U5. Free from the Central Services Division, Library of Congress, Washington, DC 20540. **LC12.2:Af8.**
Periodical and serial articles and books concerned with the music of Sub-Saharan Africa are listed. Entries include U.S. library locations and brief annotations and are indexed by authors, tribal names, and linguistic areas.

1306. Library of Congress. Music Division. **A Bibliography of Early Secular American Music, 18th Century**. By Oscar G. T. Sonneck. Rev. and enl. ed. by William Treat Upton. GPO, 1945. 616 pp. LC 45-35717. ML120.U5S6 1945. (Repr.: Da Capo, $45.)
This bibliography lists American secular music published in the eighteenth century. Entries are by title and include a complete citation and the first line of each work.

BRAILLE

1307. National Library Service for the Blind and Physically Handicapped. **Dictionary of Braille Music Signs**. By Bettye Krolick. IA, 1979. 199 pp. LC 78-021301. MT38.K76. 781/.24. OCLC 4494734. **LC19.2:B73/10.**
Braille music signs used since 1888 are defined, and explanations are given of the variety of formats used by publishers over time. Because this is a dictionary of braille signs rather than a dictionary of music, musical terms are not defined. It is available in both print and braille.

1308. National Library Service for the Blind and Physically Handicapped. **Music and Musicians (series)**. Available in braille or large print. Free from the National Library for the Blind and Physically Handicapped, Library of Congress, Washington, DC 20540. **LC19.2:M97/vol.**
   Braille Scores Catalog: Organ. 1978. 62 pp. Out of print.
   Braille Scores Catalog: Voice. 1979. 170 pp.
   Braille Scores Catalog: Piano. 1979. 209 pp.
   Braille Scores Catalog: Choral. 1979. 110 pp.
   Braille Scores Catalog: Instrumental. 1980.
   Large Print Scores and Books Catalog. 1980. 56 pp. Large print only.
   Instructional Disc Recordings Catalog. 1980. 26 pp. Available in large print and phonodisc.
   Instructional Cassette Recordings Catalog. 1978. 40 pp. Out of print.
Each of these titles lists materials in the collections of the National Library Service for the Blind and Physically Handicapped. Items listed may be borrowed from the collection.

CATALOGS

1309. Library of Congress. Music Division. **Catalogue of Early Books on Music (before 1800).** By Julia Gregory. GPO, 1913. 312 pp. LC 12-35008. MC136.U5C3. **LC12.2:M97/1.**

⎯⎯⎯⎯. **Supplement (Books Acquired by the Library, 1913-1942).** By Hazel Bartlett. GPO, 143 pp. LC 12-35008. ML136.U5C3 suppl. (Repr.: Da Capo, $32.50.)
Approximately fifteen hundred works in the Library of Congress are listed, with about five hundred more in the supplement. Entries are arranged alphabetically by author with an index of anonymous works. The supplement contains a list of books on music in Chinese and Japanese.

1310. Library of Congress. Music Division. **Catalogue of Opera Librettos Printed before 1800.** By Oscar G. T. Sonneck. 2 vols. GPO, 1914. LC 13-35009. ML136.U55C45. (Repr.: Burt Franklin, $92.50; Johnson, $115.50.)
Volume 1 lists works by title. Volume 2 contains author, composer, and aria indexes. Included with full bibliographic citations are historical notes that give dates of first performance, variant titles, and other pertinent data.

1311. Library of Congress. Music Division. **Dramatic Music: Catalogue of Full Scores.** Comp. by Oscar G. T. Sonneck. GPO, 1908. 170 pp. LC 8-35001. ML136.U55D7. (Repr.: Da Capo, $25.) **LC12.2:D79.**
Full scores of operas acquired by the Library of Congress from 1902 to 1907 are listed, arranged alphabetically by composers.

1312. Library of Congress. Music Division. **Orchestral Music Catalogue: Scores.** GPO, 1912. 663 pp. LC 11-35001. (Repr.: Da Capo, $55.) **LC12.2:Or1.**
Works published from 1830 to 1911 are included. The main entry is by composers with scores listed by opus numbers or, when these do not exist, in numerical order or alphabetical by title. A class index and a title index are included.

DISCOGRAPHIES

1313. Library of Congress. Music Division. **Check-List of Recorded Songs in English-Language Archive of American Folk Song to July 1940.** 3 vols. GPO, 1942. LC 42-15513. ML156.4.F6U5. (Repr.: 3 vols. in 1, AMS, $72.50.)
Volumes 1 and 2 are alphabetic lists by titles with names of singers and the dates and places the recordings were made. Volume 3 is a geographic index listing titles under states and countries.

1314. Library of Congress. Music Division. **Sousa Band: A Discography.** Comp. by James R. Smart. GPO, 1970. 123 pp. LC 70-604228. ML156.4.B3S6. Free from the Music Division, Library of Congress, Washington, DC 20540. **LC12.2:So8.**
The purpose of this work is to "present in one source the recording history of the Sousa Band." It also includes recordings made by the U.S. Marine Corps band during the last three years of Sousa's leadership (1890-92) and the Philadelphia Rapid Transit Company band, which recorded two compositions under Sousa's direction. Recordings by the Sousa band are listed first under one of two headings, cylinder records and disk records, and second alphabetically by title under record manufacturer. Foreign releases

of Sousa band records are not included. The lack of a title index makes it necessary for one to peruse the list of records of each individual company (as well as lists for the other two bands) in order to locate a specific title. The appendix contains a chronological list of Victor recording sessions. The list is indexed by soloists, composers, and conductors by companies.

Performing Arts

1315. Copyright Office. **Catalog of Copyright Entries, Cumulative Series (Motion Pictures)**. GPO, 1912- . LC 53-60032. PN 1998.U615. **LC3.8:M85/date**.

Cumulation for 1912-39. 1,256 pp. S/N 030-002-00123-3. $23.

Cumulation for 1940-49. 599 pp. S/N 030-002-00124-1. $18.

Cumulation for 1950-59. 494 pp. S/N 030-002-00125-0. $17.

Cumulation for 1960-69. 744 pp. S/N 030-002-00120-9. $21.

This is a comprehensive catalog of motion pictures registered with the Copyright Office. Citations give title, production company, physical description, author statement, copyright date, and copyright registration number. There is title and name access.

1316. Copyright Office. **Catalog of Copyright Entries, 3rd Series: Parts 12-13, Motion Pictures and Filmstrips**. GPO, 1947-77. Semiannual. LC 6-35347. Z1219.U5BC. **LC3.6/5:vol./nos./pts.12-13**.

1317. Copyright Office. **Catalog of Copyright Entries, 4th Series: Part 4, Motion Pictures and Filmstrips**. GPO, 1978- . Semiannual. LC 79-640902. S/N 030-002-80022-5 (microfiche). $7/yr. **LC3.6/6:vol./nos./pt.4**.

1318. Copyright Office. **Dramatic Compositions Copyrighted in the United States, 1870-1916**. 2 vols. GPO, 1918. 3,547 pp. LC 18-26789. (Repr.: Johnson, $146.50.) **LC3.2:D79/v.1,2**.

This catalog lists dramatic works copyrighted from 1870 to 1916. Later works are listed in the *Catalog of Copyright Entries*. Approximately sixty thousand plays are listed alphabetically by title with full bibliographic information and the number of acts in the play. Cross references from alternative titles are provided. A very detailed index facilitates use of this work by providing access through authors, editors, translators, and pseudonyms. Published and unpublished plays are included.

1319. Copyright Office. **Motion Pictures, 1894-1912, Identified from the Records of the United States Copyright Office**. By Howard L. Walls. GPO, 1953. 92 pp. LC 53-60033. PN1998.W25. OCLC 3872809. **LC3.8:M85/894-912**.

Over eighty-five hundred works copyrighted between 1894 and 1912 are listed. For later motion pictures see the *Catalog of Copyright Entries*.

1320. Library of Congress. Motion Picture, Broadcasting, and Recorded Sound Division. **The George Kleine Collection of Early Motion Pictures in the Library of Congress: A Catalog.** GPO, 1980. LC 79-607073. PN1998.A1U57. S/N 030-001-00088-5. **$15. LC40.2:K67.**

Part of the National Film Collection of the Library of Congress, the films and papers that comprise the collection were purchased in 1947 from the Kleine estate. The collection included films produced between 1898 and 1926 (later copies on 16-mm acetate film) produced by Thomas A. Edison, Gaumont and Pathe of France, Cines and Ambrosio of Italy, and others as well as scripts, stills, pressbooks, posters, correspondence, and other materials. This catalog lists and describes materials in the collection.

1321. Library of Congress. Motion Picture, Broadcasting and Recorded Sound Division. **Radio Broadcasts in the Library of Congress, 1924-1941: A Catalog of Recordings.** Comp. by James R. Smart. 149 pp. LC 81-607136. PN1991.9.L5 1981. 011/.38/19. S/N 030-000-00139-7. **$10. LC40.2:R11/924-41.**

This is a chronological listing of 5,100 live radio broadcasts held in the Library of Congress. Information includes broadcast date, program title, length, performer(s), and station call letters. It is significant because recordings from this period are rare; this list includes a wide range of topics and performers from Adolf Hitler to Major Bowes.

Philosophy and
Religion

1322. Library of Congress. **Checklist of Manuscripts in St. Catherine's Monastery, Mount Sinai: Microfilmed for the Library of Congress, 1950**. Prep. under the direction of Kenneth W. Clark. GPO, 1952. 53 pp. LC 52-60045. Z6621.S45G72. **LC1.2:M31**.
This is a checklist of the contents of 1,700 rolls of microfilm and 1,284 photographs made for the Library of Congress at St. Catherine's Monastery on Mount Sinai.

1323. Library of Congress. **Checklist of Manuscripts in the Libraries of the Greek and Armenian Patriarchates in Jerusalem: Microfilmed for the Library of Congress, 1949-1950**. Prep. under the direction of Kenneth W. Clark. GPO, 1953. 44 pp. LC 52-60045. Z6621.J55C54.
The contents of microfilm and photographs made for the Library of Congress in Jerusalem are detailed.

1324. Library of Congress. **A Descriptive Checklist of Selected Manuscripts in the Monasteries of Mount Athos**. GPO, 1957. 36 pp. LC 57-60041. Z6623.U6. **LC1.2:M31/2**.
The contents of photoreproductions of manuscripts belonging to the various monasteries on Mount Athos, Greece, are detailed.

Index